the
ART
of
PROBLEM
SOLVING

Volume 2:
and BEYOND

Richard Rusczyk

Sandor Lehoczky

ISBN #: 978-0-9773045-8-5

Published by: AoPS Incorporated
                P.O. Box 2185
                Alpine, CA 91903-2185
                (619) 659-1612
                books@artofproblemsolving.com

Visit the Art of Problem Solving website at http://www.artofproblemsolving.com

Printed in the United States of America.
Seventh Edition; printed in 2008.

Editor: David Patrick

Cover image designed by Vanessa Rusczyk using KaleidoTile software.

Cover Image: "Niagara Falls" by Vanessa Rusczyk.

This book was produced using the LaTeX document processing system.

www.artofproblemsolving.com

The Art of Problem Solving (AoPS) is:

▷ Books

For over 14 years, *the Art of Problem Solving* books have been used by students as a resource for the American Mathematics Competitions and other national and local math events.

> *Every school should have this in their math library.*
> – Paul Zeitz, past coach of the U.S. International Mathematical Olympiad team

▷ Classes

The Art of Problem Solving offers online classes on topics such as number theory, counting, geometry, algebra, and more at beginning, intermediate, and Olympiad levels.

> *All the children were very engaged. It's the best use of technology I have ever seen.*
> – Mary Fay-Zenk, coach of National Champion California MATHCOUNTS teams

▷ Forum

As of February 2008, the Art of Problem Solving Forum has over 38,000 members who have posted over 1,000,000 messages on our discussion board. Members can also join any of our free "Math Jams".

> *I'd just like to thank the coordinators of this site for taking the time to set it up. . . I think this is a great site, and I bet just about anyone else here would say the same. . .*
> – AoPS Community Member

▷ Resources

We have links to summer programs, book resources, problem sources, national and local competitions, and a LaTeX tutorial.

> *I'd like to commend you on your wonderful site. It's informative, welcoming, and supportive of the math community. I wish it had been around when I was growing up.*
> – AoPS Community Member

▷ . . . and more!

Membership is **FREE**! Come join the Art of Problem Solving community today!

www.artofproblemsolving.com

Yalli: I know that somewhere deep down you believe in me, and that makes this worthwhile. I flower dogs.
—SL

Vanessa, thank you for your dedication, support, and patience. Without you, these books would still just be an idea. Thank you for making all my dreams real.
—RR

Thanks

A large number of individuals and organizations have helped make *the ART of PROBLEM SOLVING* possible. All of the following people and groups made very significant contributions, and we offer our deepest gratitude to them all.

Samuel Vandervelde. Sam collaborated with us in creating the Mandelbrot Competition; he continues producing the contest to this day. His work in developing innovative and challenging problems astounds us. In addition to writing these tests, Sam has also contributed problems to the U.S.A. Mathematical Olympiad and created the Stanford Math Circle. Sam is a 1993 graduate of Swarthmore College and earned his Ph.D. in mathematics from the University of Chicago. He was a member of the 1989 U.S. International Mathematics Olympiad team, and was a grader for three years at the Math Olympiad Program, a seminar that determines and prepares that team. Many times when trying to find a proof for some theorem, we'd call on Sam and he'd give us three or four. We owe Sam many thanks for his contributions as a mathematician, our partner, and our friend.

MATHCOUNTS is the premier extracurricular middle school mathematics program in the United States. MATHCOUNTS produces educational problem solving materials and conducts a nationwide contest consisting of school, chapter, state, and national levels. Over 30,000 students participate in the contest each year and hundreds of thousands learn from MATHCOUNTS materials. MATHCOUNTS was the starting point in mathematics for one of the authors, and is a great entry into mathematics for seventh and eighth graders. To Barbara Xhajanka we offer an extra thank you for her help. For more information, visit www.mathcounts.org.

The Mandelbrot Competition was started in 1990 by Sam Vandervelde and the authors. It is a four round high school competition designed to teach students not only the common subjects of geometry and algebra, but also subjects that don't appear in high school classes, like number theory and proof techniques. Each round of the Competition consists of an Individual Test and a Team Test. The Individual Test is a short answer test while the Team Test is a series of proofs designed to enhance participants' knowledge of a particular subject area. There are two divisions of the competition, one for beginners and one for more advanced problem solvers. For more information regarding the Mandelbrot Competition, visit www.mandelbrot.org.

Dr. George Berzsenyi. We could go on for pages about Dr. Berzsenyi's many contributions to mathematics education through his involvement in competitions and summer programs. He has been involved in writing the AHSME, AIME, and USAMO as well as other independent competitions. He also created the *U.S.A. Mathematical Talent Search* and its international counterpart; participating students in each round are given a month to prepare full solutions to five problems. These solutions are graded by mathematicians and comments on the papers are returned to the students. The USAMTS is an excellent way for students to learn how to write proofs. The USAMTS is now administered by the Art of Problem Solving Foundation (`www.artofproblemsolving.org`), and is funded primarily by the National Security Agency. For more information on the USAMTS, visit `www.usamts.org`.

Dr. Berzsenyi was also an editor and contributor to the **Mathematics and Informatics Quarterly** (M&IQ). In addition to many practice problems, M&IQ contains articles written (in English) by people all over the world on various subjects of interest to the high school mathematician. While entirely within the reach of the average student, the articles are fascinating and have shown the authors many new approaches to various fields of mathematics.

American Mathematics Competitions. The AMC produces the series of tests that determine the United States mathematics team. The tests are currently called the AMC 10, the AMC 12, the *American Invitational Mathematics Exam* (AIME), and the *U.S.A. Mathematical Olympiad* (USAMO). The AMC 12 used to be called the *American High School Mathematics Exam* (AHSME). Top performers in the contests are invited to the Math Olympiad Summer Program (MOP). For more information on the contests and the MOP, visit `www.unl.edu/amc`. There are a handful of problems in this book that appeared on tests at the MOP. These were kindly provided by Professor Cecil Rousseau, who instructed both of the authors of this text at the Math Olympiad Program in 1989.

The **American Regions Mathematics League** (ARML) is an annual competition in which 15-member teams representing schools, cities, and states compete in short answer, proof, and relay contests. The contest is held concurrently at Pennsylvania State University, the University of Iowa, and the University of Nevada Las Vegas. The authors of this text were teammates on the Alabama team at ARML in 1988 and 1989. We highly recommend this experience to students, as they will learn not only about mathematics but also about teamwork. ARML's primary question writers for the tests from which we have drawn are Gilbert Kessler and Lawrence Zimmerman. For more information on ARML, visit `www.arml.com`.

David Patrick, Amanda Jones, and Naoki Sato. The orignial *the ART of PROBLEM SOLVING* texts were written in 1993 and 1994 on old Macintosh PCs that have less computing power than most watches now have. To produce the current edition, Amanda Jones recovered these ancient files from our old Macs. Unfortunately, recovering the files was not enough. David Patrick reformatted and edited the book, using his LATEX expertise to convert our decade-old code to modern LATEX standards. Finally, nearly all of the diagrams of the book were re-created by Richard Rusczyk, Naoki Sato, and Amanda Jones.

This text also contains questions from the Mu Alpha Theta (MAΘ) National Convention. Mu Alpha Theta is a national high school math honor society. For more information, visit their website at `www.mualphatheta.org`.

We gathered some problems from a few international sources in order to offer a wealth of challenging problems on some advanced topics. We collected problems from the national olympiads of **Bulgaria** (provided by Borislav Lazarov) and **Canada** (provided by Graham Wright). Both of these sources provide excellent practice for problem solvers. We also include problems that were either used in or proposed for the **International Mathematical Olympiad** (IMO). Each year many of the countries in the world send a six person team to the IMO to participate in the Olympiad. The problems in this text come from the 1989 Olympiad in Germany (provided by Paul Jainta), and the 1986 and 1985 Olympiads in Poland and Finland respectively (provided by Dr. George Berzsenyi).

Key Curriculum Press produces **The Geometer's Sketchpad**, which was used to generate most of the diagrams in the first edition of this text. The Sketchpad is an amazing program that forces students to learn geometry while producing fascinating visual output. The Sketchpad can be used to do everything from teaching simple geometric principles in an interactive way to generating complex fractals. For more information on the Geometer's Sketchpad, visit www.keypress.com.

Special thanks to Vanessa Rusczyk and Vladmir Vukicevic for their help in proofreading this book and to Kai Huang, Joon Pahk, Lauren Williams, and many members of the online Art of Problem Solving Community at www.artofproblemsolving.com, and particularly Hussain Zahid Sheikh, for their corrections for this seventh edition.

To Students

Unless you have been much more fortunate than we were, this book is unlike anything you have used before (except Volume 1!).

The information in this book cannot be learned by osmosis. What the book teaches is not *facts*, but *approaches*. To learn from a section, you have to read, and comprehend, the text. You will not gain from just looking for the key formulas.

Important ideas may be in seemingly out-of-the-way places, where someone skimming might miss them, since things are ordered by topic, not by importance. Don't expect to find a uniform difficulty level. Read slowly, spending minutes on a single line or equation when you need to. Fly when you can. There will be times for both, so don't get impatient.

Some very important concepts are introduced only in examples and exercises. Even when they are simply meant to increase your comfort with the idea at hand, the examples and exercises are the key to understanding the material. Read the examples with even more attention than you pay to the rest of the text, and, no matter what kind of hurry you are in, take the time to do the exercises thoroughly.

This book is about methods. If you find yourself memorizing formulas, you are missing the point. The formulas should become obvious to you as you read, without need of memorization. This is another function of the examples and exercises: to make the methods part of the way you think, not just some process you can remember.

The subjects in this volume cover a much broader range of difficulty than those in Volume 1; therefore, you may wish to do a lot of skipping around. If you hit a subject you simply don't understand, move on and return later when you've had more practice problem solving. Don't give up; learning takes time.

to great lengths to compile the end-of-chapter problems and other problems in the book. Do them, as many as you possibly can. Don't overload on a single subject, though, or you'll forget everything in a week. Return to each subject every now and then, to keep your understanding current, and to see how much you've grown since you last thought about that subject.

If you have trouble with the problems, don't get neurotic, GET HELP! Consult other students, consult your teachers and, as a last resort, consult the Solution Manual. Don't give up too quickly and begin using the Solution Manual like a text. It should be referred to only after you've made a serious effort on your own. Don't get discouraged. Just as importantly, if these last sentences don't apply to you, you should be the one other students can come to for help.

The book thus comes with one warning: you will not learn if you don't do the problems. Cultivate a creative understanding of the thought processes which go into solving the problems, and before too long you will find you can do them. At that same instant you'll discover that you enjoy them!

To Teachers

the ART of PROBLEM SOLVING is our conception of what a motivated student's instruction in high school non-calculus mathematics should be.

We strongly feel that a student should learn all subjects simultaneously. There are two reasons for this. First, it is better to convey the interconnectedness of it all; how geometry naturally leads to coordinates and how those coordinates make it easy to define conic sections and the complex plane; how counting leads to probability, the Binomial Theorem, and number theoretical ideas. Second, it all sinks in better. Overloading on a single subject can cause students to acquire a surface understanding which doesn't connect to any deeper comprehension, and is thus rapidly lost.

There are many subjects in this text which your students have likely not seen before. We feel it is very unfortunate that students aren't introduced to such subjects as collinearity, inequalities, and number theory. Again in this volume we put an emphasis on geometry, which we feel is the most neglected subject in many curricula: students take a year of geometry, then don't ever see it again.

We also warn the teacher that the difficulty level of the subjects in this book vary much more greatly than in the first volume. Some of the text may be too advanced for your beginners, while other portions are likely too elementary for your advanced students. Thus, take care in the chapters or sections you assign your students.

Our notation sometimes diverges from the accepted notation. In these cases, however, our decisions have been made with full deliberation. We strive to use symbols which evoke their meanings, as in the use of the less-popular ⌊ ⌋ to denote the greatest integer function instead of the usual [ ].

Each chapter of the text is meant to feel like the discussion of a subject with a friend. In one aspect of such a discussion, the text must fail: the answering of questions. This weakness must be repaired by teachers or strong students who are able to assume a leadership role. Teachers are crucial to the process of the book, whether teaching the material directly or simply being available for explanation.

We urge teachers using *the ART of PROBLEM SOLVING* in a classroom or club setting to encourage students who understand certain areas to explain the subjects to the rest of the class, or perhaps rotate such responsibility among a large group of willing students. This will not only give the other students a different view, perhaps closer to their own thought process, but it also greatly enhances the teaching student's understanding of the subject. Furthermore, the instructing student will have a chance to see the rewards that come from teaching.

We also suggest that after covering each subject, students attempt to write problems using the principles they have learned. In writing a problem, one does much more math than in solving one. This further inspires the creative drive which is so essential to problem solving in math and beyond, and if students are asked to take a crack at each others' creations, the competitive urge will also be tickled.

In closing, this book is about methods, not memory. The formulas we prove are important ones, but we intend for our explanations to be such that memorization is not necessary. If a student truly understands why a formula is true, then the formula can be internalized without memorization. However you choose to use this book, we hope that the focus remains that students understand *why* formulas work. Only in this way can they understand the full range of the formulas' applications and the full beauty of the mathematics they are learning.

Justify Your Love

Throughout high school and even middle school, the authors of this text participated in of math contests. After high school we then produced our own contest, The Mandelbrot Competition, along with Sam Vandervelde. One question has persisted from the skeptics: why bother? They argue that the math involved in competitions is largely useless for the rest of participants' lives. While correct (It won't be often that your boss says, "Tell me $\phi(45)$ or you're fired!"), this argument is misguided, because math is by far not the most important aspect of the contests.

Through math competitions and projects, students learn how to attack problems. Unlike specific techniques, this skill is crucial to virtually any area of life. Successful problemists go on to be successful not only in mathematics, but also in every other field (not just technical ones!) that you can think of. The authors' math training didn't just make us able to write this text, but it taught us the rewards of hard work, gave us confidence, and—most importantly—developed our ability to solve problems.

Good problemists are very creative people. Knowing all the tools at your disposal will not always guarantee finding a solution; the key to solving problems is cleverly choosing the right method of attack. A great way to 'train' for problem solving is to do various brainstorming and other creative ideas. Not only will these help you open your eyes to new ideas, but they can often be a lot of fun.

This is not to say that the mathematics itself is useless. Hopefully through this text and other work, you'll develop the same interest in mathematics we have. While some people might think we're nuts, we view an elegant mathematical concept or a neat proof with the same admiration as others view a Rembrandt painting or a Beethoven symphony. This is the reason for our choices of the covers of our texts. The beauty of nature is dictated by a mathematics which we humans are still struggling to understand.

The last and, for many, most important aspect of math contests is the people. The authors of this text met each other and Sam, as well as many other friends, through math. When your days in contests are over, you'll cherish the memories far more than you will the contests themselves.

The eye will be found looking at especially important areas of the text. When you see it, pay extra attention.

 The threaded needle indicates particularly difficult problems or concepts. If your hands are too shaky, you may need help from someone else.

 The bomb signals a warning. If you see it, tread lightly through the material it marks, making sure you won't make the mistakes we warn against.

Contents

Chapter 0

Prove It!

Unfortunately, proofs in the standard school curriculum are either overlooked or confined to geometry classes. Proofs are absolutely essential to mathematical understanding, because if you don't know why a tool works, you can't use it to its full capacity. Don't ignore the proofs in this text! While they don't occur in most classes of competitions, they do occur in the most challenging contests.

In Volume 1 we dedicated an entire chapter to proof techniques and the language of proofs. We'll review certain methods here because they are the most common and have the widest variety of uses. The many other less common techniques are scattered throughout the text, included among the subjects where they are most commonly used.

- **Contradiction**. Suppose we wish to prove some statement A. We can use contradiction by showing that if A were false, then some impossible statement would have to be true.

- **Mathematical Induction**. Induction is generally used to prove statements which are true for all positive or all nonnegative integers. Suppose we wish to show that some statement B is true for all integers n. We show that B is true for $n = 1$, then we show that *if B is true for $n = k$* (commonly called the **inductive hypothesis**) *then* it is also true for $n = k + 1$. Hence, since B is true for $n = 1$, it is true for $n = 1 + 1 = 2$. Therefore it is true for $2 + 1 = 3$, then 4, and so on.

- **Pigeonhole Principle**. The Pigeonhole Principle states that given $kn + 1$ objects which are placed in n boxes, there must be some box with $k + 1$ objects. The principle is clearly most useful in problems where there is something that can be divided into categories.

EXAMPLE 0-1 Prove that there are infinitely many prime numbers.

Proof: Suppose there aren't infinitely many primes and look for a contradiction. Let there be k prime numbers, namely $p_1, p_2, \ldots, p_k$. Consider the number

$$Z = p_1 p_2 p_3 \cdots p_{k-1} p_k + 1.$$

Clearly Z isn't divisible by any of our k prime numbers, so it must divisible by some other prime. This contradicts our assumption that there are only k prime numbers, so there cannot be a finite number of primes.

EXAMPLE 0-2 Let $F_n = F_{n-1} + F_{n-2}$ and $F_0 = F_1 = 1$. Prove that for all n,

$$F_0 + F_1 + F_2 + \cdots + F_n = F_{n+2} - 1.$$

Proof: The recursion in the problem generates the **Fibonacci numbers**. There are many identities like the one in this problem which are true for Fibonacci numbers. Most of these can be proven with mathematical induction. For this one, we prove the statement first for $n = 0$, for which we have $F_0 = F_2 - 1$, which is obviously true. Now we assume the statement is true for $n = k$:

$$F_0 + F_1 + F_2 + \cdots + F_k = F_{k+2} - 1.$$

This is our inductive hypothesis. We then wish to show the identity holds for $n = k + 1$, or

$$F_0 + F_1 + F_2 + \cdots + F_k + F_{k+1} = F_{k+3} - 1.$$

From our inductive hypothesis, the sum $F_0 + F_1 + \cdots + F_k$ equals $F_{k+2} - 1$. Hence we have

$$\begin{aligned} F_0 + F_1 + F_2 + \cdots + F_k + F_{k+1} &= F_{k+2} - 1 + F_{k+1} \\ &= F_{k+3} - 1, \end{aligned}$$

as desired.

EXAMPLE 0-3 Prove that if we select 5 points within the boundaries of a unit square, then some pair of them are no more than $\sqrt{2}/2$ apart.

Proof: We can apply the Pigeonhole Principle by dividing the square into four squares with side length $1/2$. By the Pigeonhole Principle at least two of the points must fall in the same square. The farthest apart two points can be in a $1/2$ inch square is $\sqrt{2}/2$, where the points are on opposite ends of a diagonal. Since there must be two points in one of the little squares, there must somewhere be a pair of the five points at most $\sqrt{2}/2$ apart.

Chapter 1

Logarithms

As we mentioned in *the BIG PICTURE* in Volume 1, logarithms were originally devised to turn multiplication and division problems into addition and subtraction ones. Let's take a closer look at how this works.

Suppose we are asked to find (1234)(5678). Normal multiplication would be quite tedious. Instead, we note that for some x and y, we can write

$$10^x = 1234 \text{ and } 10^y = 5678,$$

so that

$$\log 1234 = x \text{ and } \log 5678 = y.$$

Hence, $(1234)(5678) = 10^x 10^y = 10^{x+y}$. Taking logarithms of this last relation (remember that a logarithm with no base indicated is assumed to be base 10), we have

$$\log(10^x 10^y) = \log(10^{x+y}) = x + y = \log 10^x + \log 10^y.$$

In other words, $\log(1234)(5678) = \log 1234 + \log 5678$. Neat! The logarithm of a product of two numbers is the sum of the logarithms of the two numbers.

Think about why this must be so. Recall that the value of a logarithm is an exponent. We *add* exponents when we *multiply* two numbers with the same base. As logarithms are these exponents (x and y above), their sum must be the exponent of the product ($\log(1234)(5678) = x + y$ above).

Now to find the product, we merely look up $\log 1234$ and $\log 5678$ in logarithm tables, find the sum of the two values, then find the number z from the tables such that $\log z = \log 1234 + \log 5678$. If you try this, you may find that your logarithm table only goes from 1 to 10. How can you find $\log 1234$? Use scientific notation, so that

$$\log 1234 = \log(1.234)(10^3) = \log(1.234) + \log(10^3) = 3 + \log 1.234.$$

This relationship between multiplication and addition is not the only useful property of logarithms. Using the same logic as above, division becomes subtraction:

$$\log \frac{1234}{5678} = \log 1234 - \log 5678,$$

and exponentiation becomes multiplication:

$$\log 1234^{5678} = 5678 \log 1234.$$

These are by no means proofs, nor are these manipulations confined to base 10 logarithms. In the following pages, we'll formalize these rules and introduce a few more, as well as show you how to prove them.

Properties of Logarithms

1. $\log_a b^n = n \log_a b$

2. $\log_a b + \log_a c = \log_a bc$

3. $\log_a b - \log_a c = \log_a b/c$

4. $\left(\log_a b\right)\left(\log_c d\right) = \left(\log_a d\right)\left(\log_c b\right)$

5. $\dfrac{\log_a b}{\log_a c} = \log_c b$

6. $\log_{a^n} b^n = \log_a b$

WARNING: Note that in Properties 2, 3, and 5, the bases of the logarithms added, subtracted, or divided are the same. This is very important to understand; we can't simplify $\log_2 x^2 + \log_3 y^3$ with Property 2 for the same reason we can't add exponents to evaluate the product $2^2 3^3$, as we would for $2^2 2^3$.

You should try to prove these properties on your own, as the proofs are fairly simple. Some are proven on page 5, and the proofs of the others are left as exercises.

EXAMPLE 1-1 Evaluate each of the following in terms of x and y given $x = \log_2 3$ and $y = \log_2 5$.

    i. $\log_2 15$
Solution: Since $15 = 3(5)$ we think of Property 2:

$$\log_2 15 = \log_2 3(5) = \log_2 3 + \log_2 5 = x + y.$$

    ii. $\log_2(7.5)$
Solution: Since we already know $\log_2 15$, we note that $7.5 = 15/2$ and think of Property 3. This is a bit tricky, but remember that in addition to $\log_2 3$ and $\log_2 5$, we also know $\log_2 2 = 1$:

$$\log_2(7.5) = \log_2(15/2) = \log_2 15 - \log_2 2 = x + y - 1.$$

    iii. $\log_3 2$
Solution: Since we have a different base in this than in the given quantities x and y, we look for a property which allows us to change the base. Thus, we use Property 5:

$$\log_3 2 = \frac{\log_2 2}{\log_2 3} = \frac{1}{x}.$$

In general, it is always true that $\log_w z = 1/\log_z w$. (Can you prove it?) Remember this; you'll probably see it again.

iv. $\log_3 15$

Solution: First, $15 = 3(5)$, and we know $\log_3 3$, so we use Property 2 to get $\log_3 15 = \log_3 3 + \log_3 5 = 1 + \log_3 5$. Now we must find a logarithm with base 3, but we only know base 2 logarithms. This leads us to Property 5:

$$\log_3 15 = 1 + \log_3 5 = 1 + \frac{\log_2 5}{\log_2 3} = 1 + \frac{y}{x}.$$

v. $\log_4 9$

Solution: Our base is the square of the base we are given in our information, so we look to Property 6. When working problems, always try to manipulate the bases so they are the same, or as close as possible, throughout the problem. When working with various powers of the same number, like 2 and 4, use Property 6 like this:

$$\log_4 9 = \log_{2^2} 3^2 = \log_2 3 = x.$$

vi. $\log_5 6$

Solution: Seeing a different base that is not a power of 2, we look to Property 5. Noting that $6=2(3)$, we also apply Property 2:

$$\log_5 6 = \frac{\log_2 6}{\log_2 5} = \frac{\log_2 3 + \log_2 2}{y} = \frac{x+1}{y}.$$

We'll now prove three of the six properties; the proofs of the other three are left as exercises. The first step for the proofs, since we can't do anything with the expressions as they are written, is to write the logarithms in exponential notation. Thus, we let

$$x = \log_a b, \quad y = \log_a c, \quad \text{and} \quad z = \log_b c,$$

from which we have

$$a^x = b, \quad a^y = c, \quad \text{and} \quad b^z = c.$$

These relationships will be used in the first two proofs below.

EXAMPLE 1-2 Prove Properties 1, 2, and 4.

i. Property 1: $\log_a b^n = n \log_a b$.

Proof: Let $w = \log_a b^n$. We want to show that $w = n\log_a b = nx$. Make sure you understand why this will complete the proof. Putting our expression for w in exponential notation, we have $a^w = b^n$. Since $a^x = b$, we find $a^w = b^n = (a^x)^n = a^{xn}$, so $xn = w$. Thus, $n\log_a b = \log_a b^n$.

ii. Property 2: $\log_a b + \log_a c = \log_a bc$.

Proof: We wish to show that $\log_a bc = x + y$. Since $a^x = b$ and $a^y = c$, we can get the quantity $x + y$ by multiplying a^x and a^y: $a^x a^y = a^{x+y} = bc$. Putting this last equality in logarithmic notation gives us $\log_a bc = x + y = \log_a b + \log_a c$. (Notice how this proof is similar to our discussion of evaluating $\log(1234)(5678)$.)

iii. Property 4: $(\log_a b)(\log_c d) = (\log_a d)(\log_c b)$.

Proof: We let

$$x = \log_a b, \quad y = \log_c d, \quad w = \log_a d, \quad \text{and} \quad z = \log_c b.$$

We wish to show that $xy = wz$. As before, we write the above logarithmic equations exponentially. We find

$$b = a^x = c^z \quad d = a^w = c^y,$$

$$a = c^{(z/x)} \quad a = c^{(y/w)},$$

$$c^{(z/x)} = c^{(y/w)}.$$

Thus we have

$$\frac{z}{x} = \frac{y}{w},$$

from which we have the desired $xy = wz$.

 Using this relation we can show that $\left(\log_a b\right)\left(\log_b c\right) = \log_a c$, a frequently occurring identity sometimes called the **chain rule** for logarithms.

It is important that you realize that these proofs are not just pulled out of thin air. They involve methods that you should learn, namely, the practice of changing logarithmic notation to exponential notation and manipulating the exponential expressions. Make sure you understand this method before proceeding to the exercises. After writing logarithmic expressions in exponential notation, ask yourself what you wish to prove in terms of the exponents (x, y, etc. above). Then, manipulate the exponential equations to complete the proof.

EXERCISE 1-1 Prove Properties 3, 5, and 6 without using Properties 1, 2, and 4.

EXERCISE 1-2 Prove the chain rule for logarithms using Property 4.

WARNING: Don't overlook the fact that the base and the argument of all logarithms must be positive, for sometimes devious, or careless, test writers will create problems in which some seemingly correct solutions violate one of these rules.

EXAMPLE 1-3 Find all x such that $\log_6 (x + 2) + \log_6 (x + 3) = 1$.

Solution: Seeing the sum of two logarithms with the same base, we think of Property 2, which yields

$$\log_6 (x + 2) + \log_6 (x + 3) = \log_6 (x^2 + 5x + 6) = 1.$$

Putting this equation in exponential notation gives $x^2 + 5x + 6 = 6$, or $x^2 + 5x = 0$, so our solutions are $x = -5$ and $x = 0$. You may be tempted to stop here and claim that these are both valid solutions, but your last step in all problems involving logarithms must be checking that each solution makes the argument and the base of all logarithms positive. In the given problem the arguments of the initial logarithms are negative when $x = -5$, so this is not a valid solution. The only valid solution is $x = \mathbf{0}$.

EXAMPLE 1-4 Find the sum

$$\log \frac{1}{2} + \log \frac{2}{3} + \log \frac{3}{4} + \cdots + \log \frac{99}{100}.$$

Solution: Seeing the sum of logarithms we think of $\log x + \log y = \log xy$. Calling our given sum S, this identity gives

$$S = \log\left(\frac{1}{2}\cdot\frac{2}{3}\cdot\frac{3}{4}\cdot\cdots\cdot\frac{97}{98}\cdot\frac{98}{99}\cdot\frac{99}{100}\right) = \log\frac{1}{100} = \log 10^{-2} = -2.$$

Notice that in the product every number from 2 to 99 appears once in the numerator and once in the denominator, so they all cancel.

EXERCISE 1-3 Find $\log_3 10$ and $\log_3 1.2$ in terms of $x = \log_3 4$ and $y = \log_5 3$.

EXERCISE 1-4 I want to use my calculator to evaluate $\log_2 3$, but my calculator only does logarithms in base 10. Should I go find a better calculator, or should I be able to find a way to make my calculator tell me $\log_2 3$?

EXERCISE 1-5 Show that $x^{\log_x y} = y$.

Problems to Solve for Chapter 1

1. Evaluate the product $(\log_2 3)(\log_3 4)(\log_4 5)(\log_5 6)(\log_6 7)(\log_7 8)$.

2. If $\log 36 = a$ and $\log 125 = b$, express $\log(1/12)$ in terms of a and b. (MAΘ 1992)

3. In how many points do the graphs of $y = 2\log x$ and $y = \log 2x$ intersect? (AHSME 1961)

4. Find all the solutions of

$$x^{\log x} = \frac{x^3}{100}.$$

(AHSME 1962)

5. If $a > 1$, $b > 1$, and $p = \dfrac{\log_b(\log_b a)}{\log_b a}$, then find a^p in simplest form. (AHSME 1982)

6. If one uses only the information $10^3 = 1000$, $10^4 = 10000$, $2^{10} = 1024$, $2^{11} = 2048$, $2^{12} = 4096$, $2^{13} = 8192$, what are the largest a and smallest b such that one can prove $a < \log_{10} 2 < b$? (AHSME 1967)

7. For all positive numbers $x \neq 1$, simplify

$$\frac{1}{\log_3 x} + \frac{1}{\log_4 x} + \frac{1}{\log_5 x}.$$

(AHSME 1978)

8. Given that $\log_{10} 2 = 0.3010$, how many digits are in 5^{44}? (MAΘ 1991)

9. If $\log_8 3 = P$ and $\log_3 5 = Q$, express $\log_{10} 5$ in terms of P and Q. (MAΘ 1990)

10. Suppose that p and q are positive numbers for which

$$\log_9 p = \log_{12} q = \log_{16}(p + q).$$

What is the value of q/p? (AHSME 1988)

 11. Given that $\log_{4n} 40\sqrt{3} = \log_{3n} 45$, find n^3. (MAΘ 1991)

12. Suppose a and b are positive numbers for which

$$\log_9 a = \log_{15} b = \log_{25}(a + 2b).$$

What is the value of b/a? (MAΘ 1992)

13. If $60^a = 3$ and $60^b = 5$, then find $12^{[(1-a-b)/2(1-b)]}$. (AHSME 1983)

the BIG PICTURE

One area in which logarithms play a surprisingly large role is music. Musical sound is created by something vibrating—a string on a violin, a column of air in a flute. The rate of vibration translates to a **pitch**; the faster the vibration, the higher the pitch. For instance, top C on a flute is 2048 Hz (Hz, or **Hertz**, means "cycles per second," so this is 2048 vibrations per second), a violin's low G is 192 Hz, and bottom A on a piano is 27.5 Hz.

Notes played together either "sound good" or they don't. This sounding good corresponds to the frequency of one tone being a nice multiple of another. Two tones an octave apart have frequencies differing by a factor of two, like middle C (256 Hz) and the next C up (512 Hz); two tones a major fifth apart have frequencies in the ratio 3/2, as C (256) and the next G up (384). On the other hand, tones with nasty frequency ratios (say 31/17) sound displeasing, in part because the ear hears not only the two frequencies, but an artificial **beat frequency** resulting from the times when the two vibrations are in sync.

Scales were originally formed on the basis of frequency ratios described, but such scales were found to be lacking. A scale in which every note was the right frequency multiple of C would no longer work when A♯ was the central note. The resolution of this problem came with the discovery of **even tempering** in the early 1700's, in which the octave was divided up into 12 pieces such that each frequency was the right multiple of the last. To see how this works, let the octave go from frequency F to $2F$. For some multiplier m, the scale would be F, Fm, Fm^2, Fm^3, $\cdots$, $Fm^{12} = 2F$. Solving this last equation, we find that the multiplier is $2^{1/12}$. Why is this scale special? Suppose we wanted to start four notes up, at Fm^3; the scale would then be Fm^3, Fm^4, Fm^5, $\ldots$, all notes in the original scale. The scale works in any **key**.

We can find out about what note a tone at $1.5F$ is by solving $1.5F = 2^{k/12}F$ for k as $k = 12\log_2 1.5 \approx 7$. Thus our note is seven notes up, so it's a G.

Even with an even-tempered scale, we'd still like to get, as closely as possible, nice frequency ratios; otherwise our mathematically perfect scale will contain no worthwhile harmonies. But it does. For example, we found above that the tone $1.5F = 3F/2$ is almost exactly seven notes up the scale. Check for yourself where other notes which harmonize well with F, like $4F/3$ or $5F/4$, end up in the new scale; it turns out the new scale does very well musically as well as mathematically. J. S. Bach proved this explicitly in his *Well-Tempered Clavier*, which contained pieces in every major and minor key.

Chapter 2

Not Just For Right Triangles

2.1 Trigonometric Functions

In Volume 1 we introduced sine, cosine, and other trigonometric quantities as ratios of sides of a right triangle. In fact, these quantities are used for much more than just right triangle geometry. To be able to use them as widely as possible we must first understand what the values of sine and cosine are for non-acute angles.

Consider the unit circle; that is, the circle with radius 1 centered at the origin. Any point on the circle can be described by the polar coordinates $(r, \theta) = (1, \theta)$. For example, the point $(0, 1)$ in rectangular coordinates can be described by $(1, 90°)$ in polar coordinates. It could also, however, be described by $(1, 450°)$, since we could go around the circle once before continuing 90° more to our final point, for a total of $360° + 90° = 450°$. Conversely, given the coordinates $(1, 450°)$, we could convert to the more manageable $(1, 90°)$. By adding multiples of 360° (or 2π), we can find an equivalent angle between 0° and 360° for any angle, even negative angles (which mean going around the circle clockwise rather than counterclockwise).

EXAMPLE 2-1 Find angles between 0° and 360° which are the same as $-\pi/2$, 1180°, and $9\pi/4$.

Solution: The first is negative, so we add 2π: $-\pi/2 + 2\pi = \mathbf{3\pi/2}$. The last are both over 360°, so we subtract, sometimes repeatedly:

$$1180° = 1180° - 360° = 820° = 460° = \mathbf{100°}$$

$$9\pi/4 = 9\pi/4 - 2\pi = \mathbf{\pi/4}.$$

Why are we fussing with the unit circle when we are supposed to be discussing sines and cosines? First consider an acute angle θ as shown in the diagram. The point described by $(1, \theta)$ is in the first quadrant. If we draw an altitude from A to B on the x axis and see that $\angle AOB = \theta$, we can find the (x, y) coordinates of point A from trigonometric relations applied to $\triangle AOB$. For example, since $\cos \theta = OB/AO = OB$ (since $OA = 1$), we have $x = OB = \cos \theta$. Similarly, $y = AB = \sin \theta$. Thus the rectangular coordinates of the polar point $A = (1, \theta)$ are $(\cos \theta, \sin \theta)$.

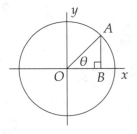

Impressed by this success, we could naïvely try to apply it to $(1, \theta)$ for an *obtuse* angle θ. But we don't know what $\cos \theta$ and $\sin \theta$ are for obtuse θ! To solve this problem, we simply *define* $\cos \theta$ and $\sin \theta$ to be the Cartesian coordinates of the polar point $(1, \theta)$.

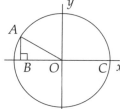

Now matters are a little trickier. We'll consider $\theta = 150°$. Once again, we draw an altitude from A to point B on the x axis. Since $\angle AOC = 150°$, we have $\angle AOB = 30°$. Thus we find $x = -OB = -\cos 30°$, where we have a negative sign since B is clearly on the negative x axis. Hence, $\cos 150° = -\cos 30° = -\sqrt{3}/2$. Similarly, we see that $\sin 150° = AB = \sin 30° = 1/2$, where we have a positive result since A is above the x axis.

This gives a general method to find the sine and cosine of *any* angle, whether acute, obtuse, or worse. First we determine which quadrant the angle is in, then we draw the picture and make a right triangle by drawing an altitude to the x axis. We use basic trigonometry to get the rectangular coordinates (x, y) of the point $(1, \theta)$, remembering that points to the left of the y axis have a negative x and those below the x axis have a negative y. We then set $\cos \theta = x$ and $\sin \theta = y$.

EXAMPLE 2-2 Find $\tan 7\pi/4$.

Solution: First we determine the quadrant of $7\pi/4$. Since $7\pi/4$ is greater than $3\pi/2$ and less than 2π, the angle is in the fourth quadrant, as shown. We draw our altitude and find $\angle BOA$. Since the arc from C to A counterclockwise has measure $7\pi/4$ radians and an entire circle has 2π radians, the remaining arc $\widehat{AC}$ has $2\pi - 7\pi/4 = \pi/4$ radians. Thus $OB = \cos \pi/4 = \sqrt{2}/2$ and $AB = \sin \pi/4 = \sqrt{2}/2$. Since A is in the fourth quadrant, x is positive and y is negative, so $\cos 7\pi/4 = OB = \sqrt{2}/2$ and $\sin 7\pi/4 = -AB = -\sqrt{2}/2$. Hence we have

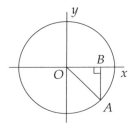

$$\tan 7\pi/4 = \frac{\sin 7\pi/4}{\cos 7\pi/4} = -\mathbf{1}.$$

(Notice that we found the sine and cosine of the angle and then used these to determine the tangent; this is how we will almost always determine trigonometric functions.)

Do not be too intimidated by this example; finding sines and cosines is very easy once you've had practice. Eventually you'll be able to do all this reasoning in your head quite quickly.

EXERCISE 2-1 In what quadrants are $30°$, $700°$, $5\pi/3$, and $-3\pi/5$?

EXERCISE 2-2 How would we find $\sin \theta$ and $\cos \theta$ if the point $(1, \theta)$ is on the x axis? the y axis? For what angles θ does this occur?

EXERCISE 2-3 Evaluate $\sin 300°$, $\cos 225°$, $\csc 150°$, $\cot 5\pi/3$, $\tan \pi$, and $\sec 5\pi/6$.

EXERCISE 2-4 Evaluate more trig (shorthand for trigonometric or trigonometry) functions using angles which are multiples of $30°$ or $45°$. Then use a calculator to check your work.

EXERCISE 2-5 Always make sure your sign (positive or negative) is correct when evaluating trig functions. How can we tell what the signs of $\cos \theta$ and $\sin \theta$ are given an angle θ?

It's awfully easy to mix up the cosine and sine values for multiples of $30°$. If you're ever confused, draw the angle on the unit circle; using the resulting geometry you should be able to reason which is which.

EXAMPLE 2-3 Use our geometric approach to show that for any obtuse angle θ, $\sin\theta = \sin(\pi - \theta)$.

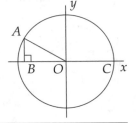

   Solution: In our figure we have $AB = \sin\angle AOB$ from right triangle AOB (with $AO = 1$). Since A is in the second quadrant, we have $AB = \sin\angle AOC = \sin\theta$. Equating these expressions for AB, we find

$$\sin\theta = \sin\angle AOB = \sin(\pi - \theta)$$

as desired.

EXERCISE 2-6 Use the same reasoning as above to show that $\cos\theta = -\cos(\pi - \theta)$.

2.2 Graphing Trigonometric Functions

Knowing what a function looks like is often quite useful in understanding problems involving the function. In this section we'll discuss the graphs of the basic trigonometric functions $\sin x$, $\cos x$, and $\tan x$.

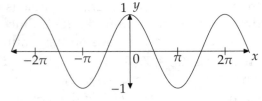

   For cosine, we know that $\cos 0 = 1$, $\cos\pi/2 = \cos 3\pi/2 = 0$, and $\cos\pi = -1$. We also know that outside the range $0 \le x < 2\pi$, the values of cosine repeat those inside the range (since the angles outside the range $[0, 2\pi)$ are equivalent to those inside). Thus, we sketch $\cos x$ for the range $0 \le x < 2\pi$ and continue this pattern indefinitely in both directions as above. This graphical form is called a **sinusoid**.

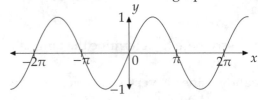

Using the same analysis as for cosine we can generate the graph of $\sin x$, shown at left. Make sure you see how this graph describes sine. Look for particular points you know, like $\sin\pi/2 = 1$, and look for where you know sine is positive. Graphing $\tan x$ is a little trickier, and we do so by noting that $\tan x = \sin x/\cos x$. Since $\sin 0 = 0$ and $\cos 0 = 1$, the graph of $\tan x$ must pass through the origin. Since sine and cosine are both positive in the first quadrant, $\tan x$ is positive for $0 < x < \pi/2$. Finally, since $\cos x$ gets closer and closer to zero as we approach $x = \pi/2$, $\tan x$ gets larger and larger. Try dividing 1 by 0.1, 0.01, and 0.001 to see what happens to $\tan x$ as we approach $x = \pi/2$.

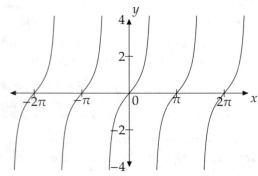

   On the other side of the origin, where the angle is in quadrant IV for $-\pi/2 < x < 0$ (make sure you see why), sine is negative and cosine is positive, so $\tan x$ is negative. As before, as we approach $x = -\pi/2$, cosine approaches 0, so the magnitude of $\tan x$ grows and grows, producing the graph on the right. (It continues past $y = 4$ upward and $y = -4$ downward.) Unlike the graphs of $\sin x$ and $\cos x$, the graph of $\tan x$ repeats after evey interval of length π rather than 2π. (Why?) Use your knowledge of $\sec x$, $\csc x$, and $\cot x$ to graph these functions.

EXERCISE 2-7 Before proceeding, make sure you are satisfied that the above graphs do indeed represent sine, cosine and tangent.

Now that we understand the trigonometric functions, let's try applying the functional transformations we discussed in Volume 1 to trig functions.

We'll start by letting $f(x) = \sin x$. The values of this function range from -1 to 1. It follows that the function $2f(x)$ (a vertical stretch of $f(x)$) varies from -2 to 2. This length of this range can be used to help describe trigonometric functions. The **amplitude** of a graph is half the difference between its largest and smallest values. Thus, for $f(x) = \sin x$, the amplitude is 1 and that of $2f(x) = 2\sin x$ is 2. A simple extension of this reveals that for any trigonometric function, the amplitude is dictated by the coefficient of the function. (Remember, amplitude measures a distance so it is never negative.)

Let's look at $f(2x) = \sin 2x$. At right are the graphs of $f(x)$ (solid line) and $f(2x)$ (dashed line). The transformation $f(2x)$ is a horizontal *shrink* by a factor of 2. Thus, while $f(x)$ goes from 0 to 1 as x goes from 0 to $\pi/2$, $f(2x)$ goes from 0 to 1 in half this interval.

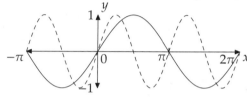

We now are ready to define the **period** as the amount of the graph (in terms of x) we can draw before we must start repeating. For example, to graph $f(2x)$ we draw the graph from $x = 0$ to $x = \pi$ then repeat this range indefinitely. Thus, the period of $f(2x) = \sin 2x$ is π. Similarly, the period of $\sin x$ is 2π. Clearly, the coefficient of x in our trig functions determines the period, since this coefficient is responsible for the horizontal shrinking or stretching of the graph. From this analysis of period, we see that the period of $f(kx) = \sin kx$ is $2\pi/k$ for all k since $f(x)$ is shrunk by a factor of k by the transformation $f(kx)$.

Related to the period of a function is the **frequency**, or how often the graph of the function repeats. For example, the graph of $\sin x$ repeats every 2π, so the frequency is one per 2π, or $1/(2\pi)$. Since a graph of a function repeats every period of the graph, the frequency is always 1/(period).

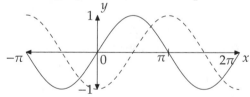

Having looked at a horizontal shrink, we move on to the horizontal slide $f(x - \pi/2) = \sin(x - \pi/2)$. The graphs of $f(x)$ (solid line) and $f(x - \pi/2)$ (dashed line) are shown at left. As discussed in Volume 1, the transformation $f(x - \pi/2)$ results in a $\pi/2$ slide to the right of $f(x)$. We define the **phase shift** of a function $f(x - k)$ as the amount the graph is shifted from the 'parent' function $f(x)$. If a direction is not given for the phase shift, a positive phase shift is to the right and a negative to the left.

WARNING: What about the phase shift of $\sin(2x - \pi/2)$? Referring to our above discussion of phase shift, the 'parent' function is $g(x) = \sin 2x$, since $\sin(2x - \pi/2)$ is a shift of $\sin 2x$, not a shift of $\sin x$. (Graph them and see!) The desired function $\sin(2x - \pi/2)$ is $g(x - \pi/4)$ (make sure you see this), so the phase shift is $\pi/4$ to the right, not $\pi/2$.

EXAMPLE 2-4 Determine the period, amplitude, phase shift, and frequency of $f(x) = 3\sin(4x + \pi) + 7$.

Solution: Since the period of $\sin x$ is 2π, the period of $f(x)$ is $2\pi/4 = \boldsymbol{\pi/2}$. Since $3\sin(4x + \pi)$ ranges from 3 to -3, $f(x)$ ranges from $3 + 7 = 10$ to $-3 + 7 = 4$, so the amplitude is $(10 - 4)/2 = \boldsymbol{3}$. Notice that the amplitude is still the coefficient of the trigonometric function despite the '+7'.

For the phase shift, we see that the parent function is $g(x) = \sin 4x + 7$ and $f(x) = g(x + \pi/4)$. Hence the phase shift is $x = -\pi/4$ (or $\pi/4$ to the left). Finally, the frequency is just the reciprocal of the period, or **$2/\pi$**.

EXERCISE 2-8 Prove that the phase shift of $f(x) = \sin(ax + b)$ is $-b/a$.

EXAMPLE 2-5 Find the frequency, period, and amplitude of the function at right.

Solution: The important thing here is that trigonometric functions are not the only **periodic** functions; there are many, many functions which repeat over and over. Draw some yourself! Since the given graph repeats every 3 units, its period is **3** and its frequency is **1/3**. Since it varies from −2 to 5, its amplitude is $[5 - (-2)]/2 = $ **3.5**.

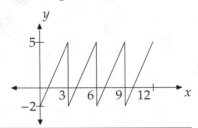

 EXERCISE 2-9 What is the period of $\tan 2x$? (*Not* π!)

2.3   Going Backwards

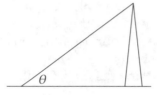 Suppose we are 1000 feet away from a 500 foot tall tower and we wish to aim a laser at a mirror mounted on top of the tower. At what angle θ should we aim the laser? Although we don't have the angle immediately, we do have enough information to figure it out. The tangent of the desired angle is $500/1000 = 1/2$. Looking back at our graph of $\tan x$, we see there is only one acute angle θ for which $\tan \theta = 1/2$. This is our desired angle, and we write it as $\theta = \tan^{-1}(1/2)$. This is also often written as $\theta = \arctan(1/2)$. WARNING: The expression $\tan^{-1} y$ does *not* mean $1/(\tan y)$, and the same is true of the other trigonometric functions. To write the reciprocal of $\sin x$, we must write $(\sin x)^{-1}$. (Unlike $\sin^2 x$, which does mean $(\sin x)^2$. Sorry for this discrepancy, but we didn't make the rules!)

 Even a casual glance at the graph of $\tan x$ will show that there are actually many values of x at which $\tan x = 1/2$. How do we know which one is intended by the expression $\tan^{-1}(1/2)$? We don't. There are infinitely many values of $\tan^{-1}(1/2)$. To show that we want the acute angle as in the diagram above (rather than one of the other values), we write $\theta = \text{Tan}^{-1} 1/2$, where the capital T shows that we are interested only in the **principal value**, or the value that lies in the first period of $\tan x$. Since this period ranges from $-\pi/2$ to $\pi/2$, we will always have $-\pi/2 < \text{Tan}^{-1} x < \pi/2$. Similarly, Arctan x implies the principal value as well.

If we apply this concept to $\text{Sin}^{-1} 1/2$, we will note that there are still two values of x in the first period of $\sin x$ for which $\sin x = 1/2$. Thus we need to restrict ourselves to the first half-period in which $\sin x$ ranges from −1 to 1. So, we have $-\pi/2 \leq \text{Sin}^{-1} y \leq \pi/2$. (Note that $\text{Sin}^{-1} y$ can equal $\pi/2$ or $-\pi/2$, while $\text{Tan}^{-1} y$ cannot.)

After seeing that the principal values of inverse sine and inverse tangent are both between $-\pi/2$ and $\pi/2$, we may suspect that the principal values of inverse cosine are also in that range. So what is $\text{Cos}^{-1}(-1/2)$? For all x in the range from $-\pi/2$ to $\pi/2$, $\cos x$ is positive. This is clearly not the right range. We should use $0 \leq \text{Arccos } x \leq \pi$ instead. Convince yourself by looking at the graph of $\cos x$ that this is a sufficient range.

EXAMPLE 2-6 Find $\sin^{-1} 0$ and Arcsec 2.

Solution: Since $\sin x = 0$ at all x which are integral multiples of π, we can write $\sin^{-1} 0 = n\pi$, for $n = \ldots, -2, -1, 0, 1, 2, \ldots$.

Since $\sec x = 1/\cos x$, for Arcsec 2 we seek the angle in the range $[0, \pi)$ such that $\cos x = 1/2$. Thus, $x = \pi/3$. Is it clear why the principal values of inverse secant are in the same range as those of inverse cosine?

EXERCISE 2-10 What is wrong with the statement $\sin^{-1} 1 - \operatorname{Sin}^{-1} 1 = 0$?

EXERCISE 2-11 Evaluate $\operatorname{arccsc} -1$, $\operatorname{Cos}^{-1} \sqrt{2}/2$, and $\operatorname{Arctan}(-\sqrt{3}/3)$.

2.4 Tying It All Together

Since the graphs of $\sin x$ and $\cos x$ are very similar, you may suspect that they can be easily related. You're right. First, since $\sin x$ is the same as $\cos x$ shifted to the right by $\pi/2$, we can say $\sin x = \cos(x - \pi/2)$. (Look at the graphs and see!)

In the graph at right, we have plotted $\sin x$ and $\sin(x - \pi)$ on the same graph. We see that $\sin(x - \pi)$ is the reflection of $\sin x$ in the x axis! Thus, $\sin(x - \pi)$ is everywhere the negative of $\sin x$, or $\sin(x - \pi) = -\sin x$. Try finding the relationship between $\cos x$ and $\cos(x - \pi)$.

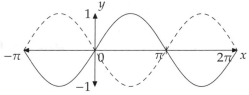

Now consider reflections in the y axis. Just as $-f(x)$ is the reflection of $f(x)$ in the x axis, $f(-x)$ is the reflection of $f(x)$ in the y axis. Choose a few functions $f(x)$ and plot the functions and the respective $f(-x)$ to see their relationships to each other. Applying this principle to $\cos x$, we see that the reflection of $\cos x$ in the y axis gives the same graph back. Thus, $\cos(-x) = \cos x$, so we find that $\cos x$ is an **even** function.

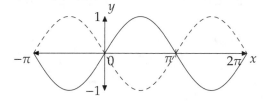

The reflection of $\sin x$ in the y axis is another matter. As with $\sin(x - \pi)$, $\sin(-x)$ is everywhere the negative of $\sin x$, so $\sin x = -\sin(-x)$ and $\sin x$ is an **odd** function.

When working with expressions involving negatives and multiples of 90° as we have above, it is often useful to look at the graphs of the resulting functions to determine their connections to $\sin x$, $\cos x$, or $\tan x$. While we will later examine faster methods to do this, it is very important to learn how the trigonometric functions are related and to understand their graphical representations.

EXAMPLE 2-7 Use graphical analysis as above to show $\sin x = \cos(90° - x)$, which we showed in Volume 1 using the geometry of right triangles.

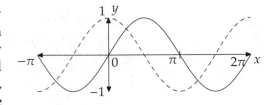

Solution: We'll draw $\cos(\pi/2-x)$ in steps. First we draw $\cos(-x)$ by reflecting $\cos x$ in the y axis (the dashed lines in the graph). Then we draw $\cos(\pi/2 - x) = \cos(-x + \pi/2)$ by shifting the graph of $\cos(-x)$ to the right by $\pi/2$ (the solid lines). Make sure you see that why this is a shift to the right, not the left. The resulting graph of $\cos(-x + \pi/2)$ is the same as $\sin x$, as you can verify.

EXERCISE 2-12 Which of the following functions are odd and which are even: $\sin x$, $\cos x$, $\tan x$, $\csc x$, $\sec x$, and $\cot x$?

EXERCISE 2-13 Find each of the following as trigonometric functions of x: $\sec(270° + x)$, $\cos(\pi + x)$, $\tan(450° + x)$, and $\sin(3\pi - x)$.

We've figured out how to handle trigonometric functions of sums and differences of angles where one of the angles is a multiple of $90°$. How about other angles? To answer this, we will use a method proposed by Masakazu Nihei of Japan in *Mathematics & Informatics Quarterly* (Vol. 3, No. 2).

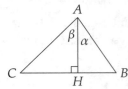

Consider the triangle ABC at left. We'll find the area of this triangle in two ways, both as $\frac{1}{2}(AB)(AC)(\sin \angle BAC)$ and also as $[ABH] + [ACH]$. We let $AH = 1$ and express the sides of right triangles ACH and ABH in terms of α and β. (For example, $\cos \alpha = AH/AB = 1/AB$ so $AB = 1/\cos \alpha$.) Hence, we have

$$
\begin{aligned}
[ABC] &= [ABH] + [ACH] \\
\tfrac{1}{2}(AC)(AB)(\sin \angle BAC) &= \tfrac{1}{2}(AH)(BH) + \tfrac{1}{2}(AH)(CH) \\
\tfrac{1}{2}(1/\cos \beta)(1/\cos \alpha)(\sin \angle BAC) &= \tfrac{1}{2}(1)(\tan \alpha) + \tfrac{1}{2}(1)(\tan \beta) \\
\frac{\sin(\alpha + \beta)}{\cos \alpha \cos \beta} &= \frac{\sin \alpha}{\cos \alpha} + \frac{\sin \beta}{\cos \beta} \\
\sin(\alpha + \beta) &= \sin \alpha \cos \beta + \sin \beta \cos \alpha,
\end{aligned}
$$

where we get the last equation by multiplying both sides by $\cos \alpha \cos \beta$. This equation and the similar equations which are introduced below can be used to find trigonometric functions of sums and differences of angles.

 Note that you will find no eyeballs staring at the problems below. This is because they are all, *every single one*, very important, and it would be silly to have eight or nine eyeballs.

EXAMPLE 2-8 Find $\sin 105°$.

Solution: Let's write $105°$ as the sum of angles whose sine and cosine we can easily evaluate. Since multiples of $30°$ and $45°$ are manageable, we have

$$
\begin{aligned}
\sin 105° &= \sin(60° + 45°) \\
&= \sin 60° \cos 45° + \sin 45° \cos 60° \\
&= (\sqrt{6} + \sqrt{2})/4.
\end{aligned}
$$

This gives us a slick method to handle angles which are multiples of $15°$ but not multiples of $30°$.

EXERCISE 2-14 Use the figure at right to show that

$$\sin(\alpha - \beta) = \sin \alpha \cos \beta - \sin \beta \cos \alpha.$$

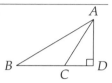

EXERCISE 2-15 How could we use our expression for $\sin(\alpha + \beta)$ to derive an expression for $\sin(\alpha - \beta)$ without using geometry?

EXAMPLE 2-9 Use $\sin(90° - \alpha) = \cos \alpha$ to find an expression for $\cos(\alpha + \beta)$ similar to those above.

Solution: Since $\cos(\alpha + \beta) = \sin(90° - \alpha - \beta)$, we have

$$\begin{aligned} \cos(\alpha + \beta) &= \sin([90° - \alpha] - \beta) \\ &= \sin(90 - \alpha) \cos \beta - \sin \beta \cos(90 - \alpha) \\ &= \cos \alpha \cos \beta - \sin \alpha \sin \beta. \end{aligned}$$

EXERCISE 2-16 Find an expression for $\cos(\alpha - \beta)$.

EXAMPLE 2-10 Find $\tan(\alpha + \beta)$ in terms of $\tan \alpha$ and $\tan \beta$.

Solution: First we'll write the tangent in terms of sine and cosine:

$$\begin{aligned} \tan(\alpha + \beta) &= \frac{\sin(\alpha + \beta)}{\cos(\alpha + \beta)} \\ &= \frac{\sin \alpha \cos \beta + \sin \beta \cos \alpha}{\cos \alpha \cos \beta - \sin \alpha \sin \beta}. \end{aligned}$$

We can divide the top and bottom of this fraction by $\cos \alpha \cos \beta$, yielding

$$\tan(\alpha + \beta) = \frac{\tan \alpha + \tan \beta}{1 - \tan \alpha \tan \beta}.$$

EXERCISE 2-17 Find $\cot(\alpha - \beta)$ in terms of $\cot \alpha$ and $\cot \beta$.

EXERCISE 2-18 (Finally some numbers!) Evaluate $\sin 15°$, $\sec 5\pi/12$, and $\cos(-345°)$.

Once again, it is not necessary to memorize all of these formulas; once you have used them a couple times though, it is hard not to. It is perhaps best to know just $\sin(\alpha + \beta)$ by heart; it's easy to derive the rest quickly from that one, as we have seen.

An important application of the sum and difference formulas is in handling expressions like $\sin 2x$. Writing $\sin 2x = \sin(x + x)$ and using the sum formula, we generate one of the **double angle formulas**,

$$\sin 2x = 2 \sin x \cos x.$$

Similarly, we find that

$$\cos 2x = \cos^2 x - \sin^2 x$$

and

$$\tan 2x = \frac{2 \tan x}{1 - \tan^2 x}.$$

Use the sum formulas for cosine and tangent to prove these. Using $\sin^2 x + \cos^2 x = 1$, which we proved in the first volume, we can write $\cos 2x$ in a couple other, equally useful, ways:

$$\begin{aligned} \cos 2x &= 2\cos^2 x - 1 \\ &= 1 - 2\sin^2 x. \end{aligned}$$

These two are often used to evaluate integrals involving cosines and sines, so when you learn integral calculus, you'll be seeing them again.

Related to $\sin^2 x + \cos^2 x = 1$ are the identites $1 + \tan^2 x = \sec^2 x$ and $1 + \cot^2 x = \csc^2 x$, which were also discussed in the first volume. (And which you should be able to prove quickly.) These three identities are clearly most useful when working with squares of trigonometric functions.

 EXAMPLE 2-11   Use the above formula for $\cos 2x$ to create formulas for $\sin x/2$ and $\cos x/2$.

Solution: Applying our double angle formulas to $\cos x$, we have

$$\cos x = \cos^2 \frac{x}{2} - \sin^2 \frac{x}{2} = 2\cos^2 \frac{x}{2} - 1 = 1 - 2\sin^2 \frac{x}{2}.$$

The first of the three expressions for $\cos x$ isn't terribly useful, but the second and third are, as we can solve for the desired expressions in terms of $\cos x$:

$$\cos \frac{x}{2} = \pm\sqrt{\frac{1 + \cos x}{2}}$$

$$\sin \frac{x}{2} = \pm\sqrt{\frac{1 - \cos x}{2}}.$$

The $\pm$ signs are a result of taking square roots. How do we know which to use? We use our knowledge of the signs of sine and cosine. If $x/2$ is in the first quadrant, we use $+$ for both, and so on.

EXERCISE 2-19   Use the above formula for $\sin x/2$ to determine $\sin 15°$.

EXERCISE 2-20   When I use $\sin(60° - 45°)$ to evaluate $\sin 15°$, I get $(\sqrt{6} - \sqrt{2})/4$, but when I use $\sin(30°/2)$, I get $\left(\sqrt{2 - \sqrt{3}}\right)/2$. Have I done something wrong? Which method is easier?

EXERCISE 2-21   Find two expressions which contain no square roots for $\tan x/2$ in terms of $\sin x$ and $\cos x$.

EXAMPLE 2-12   Find the amplitude of $f(x) = 3\sin x + \cos x$.

Solution: We might be tempted to say the answer is $(3 + 1) = 4$, but this is not right. (Can you find an x for which this function equals 4?) If we can express this sum as a single sine or cosine, we can find the amplitude easily.

Recall our formula for $\sin(x + y)$,

$$\sin(x + y) = \sin x \cos y + \sin y \cos x.$$

Comparing this to $f(x)$, we can write the function as a single sine if we find an angle y for which $\cos y = 3$ and $\sin y = 1$. However, $\cos y = 3$ is ridiculous for real numbers y. A little better is

$f(x)/4 = (3/4) \sin x + (1/4) \cos x$. Now we need an angle for which $\cos y = 3/4$ and $\sin y = 1/4$. Still no such angle exists, because these values violate $\sin^2 y + \cos^2 y = 1$. We're not lost yet, though. Let's try a generic scaling A, so we can write

$$A f(x) = 3A \sin x + A \cos x,$$

where $\cos y = 3A$ and $\sin y = A$. We thus have $\sin^2 y + \cos^2 y = 10A^2 = 1$, or $A = 1/\sqrt{10}$. We then have

$$\frac{f(x)}{\sqrt{10}} = \cos y \sin x + \cos x \sin y = \sin(x + y).$$

Thus $f(x) = \sqrt{10} \sin(x + y)$. Remembering that y is a constant angle, the amplitude of $f(x)$ is $\sqrt{10}$.

EXERCISE 2-22 Notice that the answer to the previous problem is $\sqrt{3^2 + 1^2}$, where the 3 and the 1 are the coefficients of sine and cosine. Is this true in general, i.e. is the amplitude of $a \sin x + b \cos x$ always $\sqrt{a^2 + b^2}$?

EXAMPLE 2-13 Find the period of $f(x) = \sin 2x + \cos 3x$.

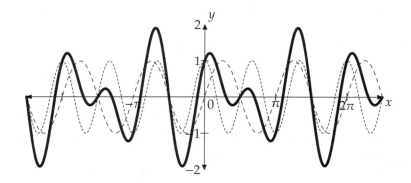

Solution: The period of $\sin 2x$ (light dashed line) is π and that of $\cos 3x$ (light dotted line) is $2\pi/3$. In one full period of length T of $f(x)$, both $\sin 2x$ and $\cos 3x$ must go through an integral number of periods. (Why?) Hence, for some positive integers m and n, we have $T = m\pi = 2n\pi/3$. Writing this as $n = 3m/2$, the smallest possible solutions are $(m, n) = (2, 3)$. (Why do we want the smallest solutions?) The period of $f(x)$ is then $T = 2\pi$.

EXERCISE 2-23 Extend the above argument to find the period of $\sin(ax/b) + \cos(cx/d)$, where a, b, c, and d are integers and a/b and c/d are in lowest terms.

To derive a final set of trig identities, notice what happens when we add $\cos(x + y)$ and $\cos(x - y)$. The products of sines cancel and we are left with $2 \cos x \cos y$! Thus

$$\cos(x + y) + \cos(x - y) = 2 \cos x \cos y.$$

Letting $\alpha = x + y$ and $\beta = x - y$, we can write this as

$$\cos \alpha + \cos \beta = 2 \cos \left(\frac{\alpha + \beta}{2} \right) \cos \left(\frac{\alpha - \beta}{2} \right).$$

Similarly, we can find the following expressions:

$$\cos\alpha - \cos\beta = -2\sin\left(\frac{\alpha+\beta}{2}\right)\sin\left(\frac{\alpha-\beta}{2}\right)$$

$$\sin\alpha + \sin\beta = 2\sin\left(\frac{\alpha+\beta}{2}\right)\cos\left(\frac{\alpha-\beta}{2}\right)$$

$$\sin\alpha - \sin\beta = 2\cos\left(\frac{\alpha+\beta}{2}\right)\sin\left(\frac{\alpha-\beta}{2}\right).$$

2.5 Solving Problems Using Trigonometric Identities

Look closely at each of the following examples; each one exhibits a common technique in attacking problems using the trig identites of the previous sections. Some methods of solving these trig identity problems are discussed below, but the best tool is experience, so take the time to work through all the problems yourself.

▷ Look for angles whose sum or difference is a multiple of 90°. If these exist, we can often use our relations like $\sin(180° - x) = \sin x$ and $\sin(90° - x) = \cos x$.

▷ When you see squares of trigonometric relations, try using $\sin^2 x + \cos^2 x = 1$ or the related identites.

▷ Look for pairs of angles whose ratio is a power of 2. For example,

$$\frac{\sin 20°}{\cos 10°} = \frac{2\sin 10° \cos 10°}{\cos 10°} = 2\sin 10°.$$

Using the double angle formulas as above will often simplify such expressions.

▷ When working with the trigonometric functions besides sine and cosine, it is often helpful to write the problem in terms of just sine and cosine.

▷ Don't work with inverse trig functions. Apply trigonometric functions to equations involving inverse trig functions to get rid of them.

EXAMPLE 2-14 Evaluate
$$\tan 10° \tan 20° \tan 30° \cdots \tan 80°.$$

   Solution: Writing this in terms of sines and cosines, we have

$$\frac{\sin 10° \sin 20° \sin 30° \cdots \sin 80°}{\cos 10° \cos 20° \cos 30° \cdots \cos 80°}.$$

Applying $\sin x = \cos(90° - x)$ to each term in the numerator, we get

$$\frac{\cos 80° \cos 70° \cos 60° \cdots \cos 10°}{\cos 10° \cos 20° \cos 30° \cdots \cos 80°} = \mathbf{1}.$$

EXAMPLE 2-15 Write

$$(\sin 13° + \sin 167° + \cos 13° + \cos 167°)(\sin 13° - \sin 167° + \cos 13° - \cos 167°)$$

in the form $a\sin x°$.

Solution: Instead of multiplying out the product, we note that $13° + 167° = 180°$ and use the relations $\sin x = \sin(180° - x)$ and $\cos x = -\cos(180° - x)$. Thus $\sin 13° = \sin 167°$ and $\cos 13° = -\cos 167°$, and our product is

$$(2\sin 13°)(2\cos 13°) = 4\sin 13° \cos 13° = 2\sin 26°.$$

EXAMPLE 2-16 Find x if $\text{Tan}^{-1} x = \text{Tan}^{-1} 4 + \text{Tan}^{-1} 6$.

Solution: Working with inverse functions is pretty difficult, so how do we get rid of them? Simply use $\tan(\text{Tan}^{-1} y) = y$. Taking tangents of both sides of the given equation, we have

$$
\begin{aligned}
x &= \tan(\text{Tan}^{-1} 4 + \text{Tan}^{-1} 6) \\
&= \frac{\tan(\text{Tan}^{-1} 4) + \tan(\text{Tan}^{-1} 6)}{1 - \tan(\text{Tan}^{-1} 4)\tan(\text{Tan}^{-1} 6)} \\
&= (4 + 6)/(1 - 4 \cdot 6) = \mathbf{-10/23}.
\end{aligned}
$$

EXAMPLE 2-17 Find $\sec x$ in terms of y if $x = \text{Tan}^{-1} y$.

Solution: Taking tangents of the given equation, we have $\tan x = y$. Using $1 + \tan^2 x = \sec^2 x$, we get $\sec^2 x = 1 + y^2$, or $\sec x = \pm\sqrt{1 + y^2}$.

EXERCISE 2-24 Simplify $\sqrt{\dfrac{2\sin x - \cos x \, \sin 2x}{\sin 2x \, \sec x}}$. (MAΘ 1992)

===

You will have many more opportunities to try your hand at using trigonometric identities in the problems below. You will also be asked to solve equations given in terms of trigonometric functions. Two important guidlines for solving these are:

▷ Write the equation as $f(x) = 0$ and use all the identies you know to factor $f(x)$ as much as possible. (Double angle formulas and $\cos^2 x + \sin^2 x = 1$ are very useful here.) Setting each factor equal to 0 should then give you all the answers. It is often useful to write the equation in terms of a single trigonometric function.

▷ Given a value for $\sin x + \cos x$ or $\sin x - \cos x$, we can find $\sin 2x$, and hence x, by squaring the given relation. Try it and see!

Problems to Solve for Chapter 2

14. Find the value of $\sin^2 10° + \sin^2 20° + \sin^2 30° + \cdots + \sin^2 90°$. (MAΘ 1992)

15. Evaluate $\csc\left(\text{Arcsin } \frac{1}{2} - \text{Arccos } \frac{1}{2}\right)$. (MAΘ 1991)

16. Given that $\text{Arcsin } x = y$, find $\tan y$ in terms of x.

17. Given a positive integer n and a number c, $-1 < c < 1$, for how many values of q in $[0, 2\pi)$ is $\sin nq = c$? (MAΘ 1992)

18. Given the triangle ABC with side a opposite $\angle A$, side b opposite $\angle B$, and side c opposite $\angle C$, find $\sin A + \sin 2B + \sin 3C$ if $a = 3$, $b = 4$, and $c = 5$. (MAΘ 1991)

19. Solve for x: Arctan $\frac{x}{2}$ + Arctan $\frac{2x}{3}$ = $\frac{\pi}{4}$. (MAΘ 1991)

20. Find the period of $2\sin(4\pi x + \pi/2) + 3\cos(5\pi x)$. (MAΘ 1992)

21. Write $\sin^4 x$ in terms of $\cos 2x$ and $\cos 4x$. (MAΘ 1991)

22. Which of the following equals $\cot 10 + \tan 5$: $\csc 5$, $\csc 10$, $\sec 5$, $\sec 10$, or $\sin 15$? (AHSME 1989)

23. If $\sin x = \cos 2x$ and $0 \le x \le \pi/2$, then find x. (MAΘ 1992)

24. Prove the following equalities. (M&IQ 1992)

    i. $\sin 10° \sin 20° \sin 30° = \sin 10° \sin 10° \sin 100°$;

    ii. $\sin 20° \sin 20° \sin 30° = \sin 10° \sin 20° \sin 80°$;

    iii. $\sin 20° \sin 30° \sin 30° = \sin 10° \sin 40° \sin 50°$.

25. Compute the number of degrees in the smallest positive angle x such that $8\sin x \cos^5 x - 8\sin^5 x \cos x = 1$. (ARML 1988)

26. If $\sin x + \cos x = -1/5$ and $3\pi/4 \le x \le \pi$, find the value of $\cos 2x$. (MAΘ 1992)

27. If $0° < x < 180°$ and $\cos x + \sin x = 1/2$, then find (p, q) such that $\tan x = -\frac{p + \sqrt{q}}{3}$. (ARML 1988)

28. Quadrilateral $ABCD$ is inscribed in a circle with diameter $AD = 4$. If sides AB and BC each have length 1, then find CD. (AHSME 1971)

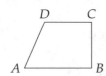

29. Find $\tan x$ if

$$\frac{\sin^2 x}{3} + \frac{\cos^2 x}{7} = \frac{-\sin(2x) + 1}{10}.$$

(MAΘ 1991)

30. If $A = 20°$ and $B = 25°$, then find the value of $(1 + \tan A)(1 + \tan B)$. (AHSME 1985)

31. If θ is acute and $\sin \frac{1}{2}\theta = \sqrt{\dfrac{x-1}{2x}}$, then find $\tan \theta$ in terms of x. (AHSME 1973)

32. If $ABCD$ is a trapezoid with DC parallel to AB, $\angle DCB$ is a right angle, $DC = 6$, $BC = 4$, $AB = y$, and $\angle ADB = x$, find y in terms of x. (MAΘ 1990)

33. Evaluate $\cos 36° - \cos 72°$. (AHSME 1975)

34. Using the area of a regular pentagon, prove that $4\sin \frac{2\pi}{5} + \tan \frac{2\pi}{5} = 5\cot \frac{\pi}{5}$. (M&IQ 1993)

35. Use a $36°$-$72°$-$72°$ triangle to prove that $\sin 18° = (\sqrt{5} - 1)/4$ and $\cos 36° = (\sqrt{5} + 1)/4$.

the BIG PICTURE

In the 1700's, Daniel Bernoulli, one of a large family of brilliant mathematicians and physicists, was studying the vibration of guitar strings. Supposing the string is of length 1, the fundamental vibration of the string can be represented as $\sin \pi x$. With this function, the two ends are fixed at zero, while the middle vibrates freely. (Plot the function for $0 \leq x \leq 1$ and see.)

Bernoulli knew that when a string is plucked, you hear more than just the fundamental vibration, however; you hear a series of **overtones** with vibrational speed two times higher, three times higher, and so on. Extending the argument used to justify $\sin \pi x$, Bernoulli argued that the overtones could be represented as $\sin 2\pi x$, $\sin 3\pi x$, and so on. (In fact, if you vibrate the ends of, say, a phone cord, you can see these vibrational modes yourself.) Bernoulli asserted that the general vibration would be some combination of the fundamental tones and overtones,

$$a_1 \sin(\pi x) + a_2 \sin 2(\pi x) + a_3 \sin(3\pi x) + \cdots$$

Other mathematicians of the time also used such series, including Leonhard Euler, who came up with a method to find the coefficients a_i.

In 1822 the French engineer Joseph Fourier published a treatise on heat transfer, looking at situations like, what would be the temperature anywhere on a rectangular plate if one side was held at a temperature of 100 degrees and the other three sides at $0°$. Fourier used infinite series of sines and cosines in his solutions, and tried to prove the controversial assertion that any periodic function $f(x)$ could be written as a sum

$$f(x) = \sum_{n=0}^{\infty} [a_n \cos(2n\pi x/T) + b_n \sin(2n\pi x/T)],$$

where T is the period. (Do you see why the sum of all these sines and cosines have period T?)

This surprising fact was proven in 1829 by Dirichlet, but such series continued to be called **Fourier series**. Fourier series are now crucially important in most branches of mathematics and physics, as they break complicated functions down into manageable sines and cosines.

Chapter 3

More Triangles!

3.1 Triangle Laws

 How many non-congruent triangles ABC are there such that $AC = 4$, $BC = 3$, and $\angle ACB = 30°$? Recall that by SAS congruency all triangles which satisfy the above criteria are congruent; thus, AB can only have one length. (Try drawing 2 non-congruent triangles which satisfy the above specifications!) At left is the described triangle. Since there is only one possible value of AB, we should be able to find it, but how?

Draw a circle with center A and AC as the radius. Let F be the point where side BC (extended if necessary) meets the circle. Since $\triangle CFD$ is right (why?), $CF = CD \cos 30° = 4\sqrt{3}$, so point B must be on segment CF (since $CB < CF$) and hence is inside the circle. We continue the sides of the triangle to meet the circle at the points shown. Applying the Power of a Point Theorem to point B, we have $(BG)(BE) = (BF)(BC)$.

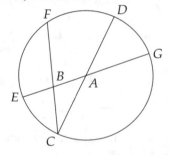

Now we relate these lengths to sides and angles of our original $\triangle ABC$. First we have $AG = AC = AE = b$ as radii of the circle, so $BE = AE - AB = AC - AB = b - c$. Furthermore, we find $BG = BA + AG = BA + AC = c + b$ and $BF = CF - BC = CD \cos C - a = 2b \cos C - a$, where we have used right triangle FCD to determine $CF = CD \cos C = 2b \cos C$. Putting these expressions into our Power of a Point equation, we get

$$
\begin{aligned}
(BG)(BE) &= (BF)(BC) \\
(b + c)(b - c) &= (2b \cos C - a)(a) \\
b^2 - c^2 &= -a^2 + 2ab \cos C,
\end{aligned}
$$

or the more common

$$c^2 = a^2 + b^2 - 2ab \cos C$$

This is called the **law of cosines** and can always be used to determine the third side of a triangle when given two sides (a and b) and the angle included between them ($\angle C$).

EXAMPLE 3-1 Use the law of cosines to find the answer to our introductory example.

Solution: Applying the law directly, we have

$$AB^2 = 3^2 + 4^2 - 2(3)(4)(\cos 30°),$$

so $AB = \sqrt{25 - 12\sqrt{3}}$.

EXAMPLE 3-2 Use the law of cosines to find $\angle B$ if $a = 5$, $b = \sqrt{21}$, and $c = 4$ in $\triangle ABC$.

Solution: Using the law of cosines, we have

$$\cos B = \frac{b^2 - a^2 - c^2}{-2ac} = \frac{1}{2}.$$

Thus, $\angle B = \mathbf{60°}$. Hence, we can find any angle of a triangle if given the three sides of the triangle.

EXERCISE 3-1 In our proof of the law of cosines, point B was inside the circle centered at A with radius AC. Complete the proof of the law of cosines by addressing the cases in which B is on the circle and outside the circle.

In any field involving geometry, such as land surveying or architecture, the law of cosines is a necessity in determining lengths and angles. However, the law of cosines is sometimes not enough. For example, suppose we are given two *angles* $\angle A$ and $\angle B$ and the *side c* included between them. The law of cosines alone fails here, because we don't have two sides and an included angle.

To attack this new problem we draw the circumcircle of our triangle and add diameter AE as shown. Since $\angle AEB$ and $\angle C$ are inscribed angles which subtend the same arc, they are equal. Hence, we have

$$\sin C = \sin \angle AEB = \frac{AB}{AE} = \frac{c}{2R},$$

where R is the circumradius of $\triangle ABC$. This can be rewritten as $2R = c/\sin C$. This relationship must also hold for the other two sides of the triangle as well, since there is nothing special about side AB. (Note this use of symmetry; it is a useful simplification technique.) Writing this expression for each side we get the **law of sines**:

$$\frac{a}{\sin A} = \frac{b}{\sin B} = \frac{c}{\sin C} = 2R.$$

Given two angles and one side of any triangle, we can determine the remaining sides using the law of sines.

EXAMPLE 3-3 Find AB and BC if $\angle C = 45°$, $\angle B = 30°$, and $AC = 6$.

Solution: From the law of sines,

$$\frac{AC}{\sin B} = \frac{AB}{\sin C} = \frac{BC}{\sin A}.$$

From the given information, the first fraction equals 12. Hence, $AB = 12\sin C = \mathbf{6\sqrt{2}}$, $\angle A = 180° - 45° - 30° = 105°$, and

$$BC = 12\sin A = 12\sin 105° = 12\sin(60° + 45°) = \mathbf{3\sqrt{6} + 3\sqrt{2}}.$$

EXERCISE 3-2 What is the circumradius of the triangle in the prior example?

EXERCISE 3-3 Complete the proof of the law of sines by showing that $a/\sin A = 2R$ when $\angle A$ is obtuse and when $\angle A$ is right.

EXAMPLE 3-4 Given $\angle A = 75°$, $AB = 4$, and $AC = 2\sqrt{6}$, find $\angle B$, $\angle C$, and BC.

Solution: First we use the law of cosines to find

$$\begin{aligned} BC^2 &= AB^2 + AC^2 - 2(AB)(AC)\cos A \\ &= 16 + 24 - 2(4)(2\sqrt{6})[(\sqrt{6} - \sqrt{2})/4] = 16 + 8\sqrt{3}, \end{aligned}$$

so $BC = \sqrt{16 + 8\sqrt{3}} = 2\sqrt{4 + 2\sqrt{3}} = 2(1 + \sqrt{3}) = \mathbf{2 + 2\sqrt{3}}$. We can use either the law of sines or the law of cosines to find the remaining angles. The law of sines is much easier to use, so we write $BC/\sin A = AB/\sin C$, and

$$\sin C = \frac{AB\sin A}{BC} = \frac{4}{2 + 2\sqrt{3}} \cdot \frac{\sqrt{6} + \sqrt{2}}{4} = \frac{\sqrt{6} + \sqrt{2}}{2 + 2\sqrt{3}} = \frac{\sqrt{2}}{2}.$$

Hence $\angle C = \mathbf{45°}$ (why not 135°?), and $\angle B = 180° - 75° - 45° = \mathbf{60°}$.

These examples should have given you a grasp of how and why the law of sines and the law of cosines are used in basic problems and in many fields. In problem solving, the law of cosines is used in problems involving squares of sides (for obvious reasons). These problems are usually pretty easy to spot, as expressions such as $(c^2 - a^2 - b^2)/(-2ab)$ are hard to miss. Make sure you recognize this expression as $\cos C$! The use of the law of cosines in a problem can often get very algebraic. Try not to resort to the law of cosines immediately in problems besides those already discussed; chances are there is a more elegant approach.

The law of sines is much less complicated algebraically than the law of cosines and hence can be used creatively in a broader range of problems. Problems involving sines of angles and the circumradius of a triangle are often ripe for the use of the law of sines. The presence of the circumradius or $a/\sin A$ terms is often a giveaway that the law of sines will be useful. The law of sines is also useful when circles are present; equal inscribed angles allow us to make clever manipulations like those in the proof of the law of sines.

EXAMPLE 3-5 Prove the **law of tangents**, which states that in triangle ABC with $a = BC$ and $b = AC$,

$$\frac{a - b}{a + b} = \frac{\tan\frac{A-B}{2}}{\tan\frac{A+B}{2}}.$$

Proof: First we write the latter fraction in terms of sines and cosines:

$$\frac{\tan\frac{A-B}{2}}{\tan\frac{A+B}{2}} = \frac{\sin\left(\frac{A-B}{2}\right)\cos\left(\frac{A+B}{2}\right)}{\sin\left(\frac{A+B}{2}\right)\cos\left(\frac{A-B}{2}\right)}.$$

Recalling our expressions for the sum and difference of sines from page 20, we recognize the numerator as $(\sin A - \sin B)/2$ and the denominator as $(\sin A + \sin B)/2$, so

$$\frac{\tan\frac{A-B}{2}}{\tan\frac{A+B}{2}} = \frac{\sin A - \sin B}{\sin A + \sin B}.$$

We're clearly very close now. We need a way to relate the sines to the sides a and b; looks like a good place for the law sines. Since $\sin A = a/2R$ and $\sin B = b/2R$, we have

$$\frac{\tan \frac{A-B}{2}}{\tan \frac{A+B}{2}} = \frac{a/2R - b/2R}{a/2R + b/2R} = \frac{a - b}{a + b}.$$

EXERCISE 3-4 Use the law of sines to show that in $\triangle ABC$, $\angle A > \angle B$ if and only if $BC > AC$.

EXAMPLE 3-6 Use the law of cosines to justify the statement that if a, b, and c are the sides of triangle $\triangle ABC$ and $a \le b \le c$, then $\triangle ABC$ is acute if $a^2 + b^2 > c^2$ and obtuse if $a^2 + b^2 < c^2$.

Solution: From the law of cosines,

$$\cos C = \frac{c^2 - a^2 - b^2}{-2ab}.$$

If $c^2 < a^2 + b^2$, then the numerator of the right side is negative, so $\cos C$ is positive and $\angle C$ is acute. Similarly, if $c^2 > a^2 + b^2$, $\cos C$ is negative and $\angle C$ is obtuse.

EXERCISE 3-5 In $\triangle ABC$, let D be a point on BC such that AD bisects $\angle A$. If $AD = 6$, $BD = 4$, and $DC = 3$, then find AB. (MAΘ 1991)

3.2 Areas, Areas, Areas

In the first volume we investigated three methods of finding the area of $\triangle ABC$, namely

$$[ABC] = \frac{ah_a}{2} = \frac{ab}{2} \sin C = rs,$$

where r is the inradius, s the semiperimeter, and h_a the altitude to side BC. There are far more formulas for the area of a triangle than are useful to remember; in this section we will explore a few more useful methods.

If we are told the three side lengths of a triangle, we can draw the triangle in only one way. By this we mean that all triangles we draw with these three side lengths will be exactly alike (by SSS congruence). Hence, we should be able to find the area of a triangle from just its three sides, but how? Our three formulas all involve either angles or other lengths. Hence, we look for a way to modify one formula to be in terms of only the sides of a triangle.

Since we know how to relate the angles of a triangle to the sides, we'll use $[ABC] = \frac{1}{2}ab \sin C$. The law of sines isn't directly useful because it introduces the circumradius, a length we don't know. The law of cosines has only the triangle side lengths, so we'll try that by writing $\sin C = \sqrt{1 - \cos^2 C}$. From the law of cosines and lots of algebra (mostly recognizing perfect squares and factoring differences of squares), we have

$$\begin{aligned}
[ABC] &= \frac{ab}{2} \sqrt{1 - \cos^2 C} \\
&= \frac{ab}{2} \sqrt{1 - \frac{(c^2 - a^2 - b^2)^2}{4a^2b^2}}
\end{aligned}$$

$$
\begin{aligned}
&= \sqrt{\left(4a^2b^2 - (c^2 - a^2 - b^2)^2\right)/16} \\
&= \sqrt{(2ab - c^2 + a^2 + b^2)(2ab + c^2 - a^2 - b^2)/16} \\
&= \sqrt{[(a+b)^2 - c^2][c^2 - (a-b)^2]/16} \\
&= \sqrt{(a+b-c)(a+b+c)(a-b+c)(-a+b+c)/16} \\
&= \sqrt{s(s-a)(s-b)(s-c)},
\end{aligned}
$$

where s is the semiperimeter of the triangle. The last step can be seen by noting that $(a + b - c)/2 = (a + b + c - 2c)/2 = s - c$. This formula for the area of a triangle is commonly called **Heron's formula**.

EXAMPLE 3-7 Find the area of the incircle of a triangle with side lengths 13, 14, and 15.

Solution: The only relation we know so far involving the inradius of $\triangle ABC$ is $[ABC] = rs$. We do know $s = (13 + 14 + 15)/2 = 21$, so if we find $[ABC]$, we can find r. Since we also know $[ABC] = \sqrt{s(s-a)(s-b)(s-c)}$, we can find r from $rs = \sqrt{s(s-a)(s-b)(s-c)}$, or

$$
r = \sqrt{\frac{(s-a)(s-b)(s-c)}{s}}.
$$

We thus find $r = 4$, and the desired area is **16π**.

What if we used the law of sines to evaluate the area? Writing $\sin C = c/2R$, we find

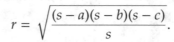

$$
[ABC] = \frac{ab}{2} \sin C = \frac{abc}{4R},
$$

which is another very important relation.

As we saw in the previous example, the importance of these area formulas is not only in finding the area of a triangle, but they also can be used to relate various important triangle lengths and angles. In the following examples, you will have some practice with such formulas and manipulations. Among these problems and those at the end of the chapter you will see many more formulas for the area of a triangle and for various lengths and angles. Don't memorize them all; learn how they are derived.

EXAMPLE 3-8 Find the circumradius of a triangle whose sides are 13, 14, and 15.

Solution: In the previous example we saw that the inradius of such a triangle is 4. Since $rs = [ABC] = abc/4R$, we have

$$
R = abc/4rs = \mathbf{65/8}.
$$

EXAMPLE 3-9 Given two angles and side a of a triangle, how would you find the area of the triangle without determining any more side lengths?

Solution: Notice that it doesn't matter which two angles we know, as we can determine the third from the two given. Starting from the formula $[ABC] = (ab/2) \sin C$, we can express b in terms of a from the law of sines, or $b = (a \sin B)/\sin A$, so

$$
[ABC] = \frac{a^2 \sin B \sin C}{2 \sin A}.
$$

After finding the third angle from the two given we can use this expression to find the area.

EXERCISE 3-6 Show that $[ABC] = 2R^2 \sin A \sin B \sin C$.

Once again, these formulas aren't always most important for the determination of areas. You will see them again in our discussion of geometric inequalities (page 165) and you will often use them as intermediate steps to solutions. The information given in a problem usually indicates which methods are useful: if we are given the sides of a triangle, Heron's formula is appropriate; given two sides and the angle between them, we use $(ab/2) \sin C$; for problems involving altitudes, inradii, or circumradii, we use the corresponding methods. Finally, problems involving perimeter often call for $[ABC] = rs$, and keep an eye out for the product abc and remember that it equals $4R[ABC]$.

3.3 More Important Lines

A segment drawn from a vertex of a triangle to the opposite side is called a **cevian**. In the first volume we discussed a few important cevians, namely angle bisectors, medians, and altitudes. In this section we will discuss methods of finding the lengths of these cevians.

Altitudes are the easiest, because we can use the area of a triangle to find the altitude from $[ABC] = ah_a/2$. Since we have many ways to find the area, we have many ways to find the altitude.

EXERCISE 3-7 Find the length of the shortest altitude of a triangle with side lengths 13, 14, and 15.

Angle bisectors and medians are significantly more difficult than altitudes; we will first reiterate a method we mentioned in the first volume.

EXERCISE 3-8 Use the law of cosines to show that the sum of the squares of the diagonals of a parallelogram equals the sum of the squares of the sides.

EXAMPLE 3-10 Use the previous exercise to find the length of median AD of $\triangle ABC$ if $AB = 5$, $BC = 7$, and $AC = 8$.

Solution: Extend median AD beyond D to E such that $AD = DE$. Since D is the midpoint of both AE and BC, the diagonals of $ABEC$ bisect each other. Thus, $ABEC$ is a parallelogram, so we can apply the previous exercise:

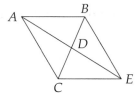

$$AE^2 + BC^2 = AB^2 + BE^2 + EC^2 + AC^2.$$

Since $AC = BE$, $AE = 2(AD)$, and $AB = EC$, we have

$$4AD^2 + BC^2 = 2(AB^2 + AC^2),$$

so $AD = \sqrt{2(25 + 64) - 49}/2 = \sqrt{129}/2$.

EXERCISE 3-9 Use the previous example to find a general formula for the length of median AD of $\triangle ABC$.

We've now figured out medians. Before addressing angle bisectors, we will introduce and prove **Stewart's Theorem**.

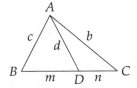

In the figure, cevian AD with length d cuts BC (length a) into segments of length m and n as shown. Since $\cos \angle ADB = -\cos \angle ADC$ (because the angles are supplementary), we can relate all the given lengths using the law of cosines:

$$\cos \angle ADB = \frac{c^2 - d^2 - m^2}{-2dm} = -\frac{b^2 - d^2 - n^2}{-2dn} = -\cos \angle ADC,$$

or after multiplying by $-2mnd$,

$$c^2 n - d^2 n - nm^2 = -b^2 m + d^2 m + n^2 m.$$

Rearranging this, we have $c^2 n + b^2 m = d^2(m + n) + mn(m + n)$, or (since $m + n = BC = a$) the easier to remember

$$cnc + bmb = dad + man.$$

You will usually only use Stewart's Theorem to find the lengths of angle bisectors and medians.

To find the length of an angle bisector, we recall the Angle Bisector Theorem, which gives $n/m = b/c$. We can use this relation and Stewart's Theorem (and a bit of algebra) to find

$$d^2 = bc \left(1 - \frac{a^2}{(b + c)^2} \right).$$

If you don't see how to get this, solve Stewart's Theorem for d and use the Angle Bisector Theorem in the form $m/(m + n) = c/(b + c)$.

EXERCISE 3-10 Don't take our word for it; work through the algebra to obtain the above formula.

EXAMPLE 3-11 Show that if AD is an angle bisector of $\triangle ABC$, then

$$AD^2 + (BD)(CD) = (AB)(AC).$$

Solution: Dividing both sides of Stewart's Theorem by a, with $d = AD$, $m = BD$, and $n = CD$, we have

$$d^2 + mn = \frac{bmb + cnc}{a}.$$

From the Angle Bisector Theorem, $bm = cn$, so

$$d^2 + mn = \frac{cnb + bmc}{a} = \frac{bc(m + n)}{a} = bc,$$

which is the desired result.

EXERCISE 3-11 Use Stewart's Theorem to find an expression for the length of median AD in terms of the sides of $\triangle ABC$. Does your formula agree with your earlier result for median AD?

EXAMPLE 3-12 Segment CX divides AB such that $AX = 2BX = 4$. If $AC = 7$ and $BC = 5$, find CX.

Solution: Applying Stewart's Theorem, we have

$$2(6)(4) + 6\,CX^2 = 5(4)(5) + 7(2)(7),$$

so $CX = \mathbf{5}$.

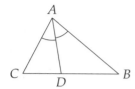

The most important lesson to learn from Stewart's Theorem is the method of using the law of cosines on two equal angles or two supplementary angles. For example, if AD is an angle bisector in $\triangle ABC$, we could use the law of cosines to determine $\cos \angle BAD$ and $\cos \angle CAD$ and set these equal. This will achieve the same result as $\cos \angle ADC = -\cos \angle ADB$ (Stewart's Theorem).

Problems to Solve for Chapter 3

36. Is a triangle whose side lengths are in the ratio $6:8:9$ acute, right, or obtuse? (AHSME 1952)

37. Find the length of the altitude to the 14 inch side of a triangle whose two other sides have lengths of 13 inches and 15 inches. (MAΘ 1990)

38. In $\triangle ADC$, angle bisector DB is drawn. If $AB = 3$, $AD = 6$, and $CD = 8$, find BD. (MAΘ 1987)

39. If the sides of a triangle are in the ratio $4:6:8$, then find the cosine of the smallest angle. (MAΘ 1991)

40. Triangle ABC is such that $AB = 4$ and $AC = 8$. If M is the midpoint of BC and $AM = 3$, what is the length of BC? (AHSME 1975)

41. Use the law of sines to prove the Angle Bisector Theorem.

42. Find $\tan C$, where C is the angle opposite side c of a triangle whose side lengths a, b, and c satisfy

$$\frac{a^3 + b^3 + c^3}{a + b + c} = c^2.$$

(MAΘ 1991)

43. Point O is the center of the circle circumscribed about isosceles $\triangle ABC$. If $AB = AC = 7$ and $BC = 2$, find AO. (Mandelbrot #3)

44. Prove that if the sides of trapezoid $ABCD$ ($AB \parallel CD$) satisfy the condition $AC^2 + BD^2 = (AB + CD)^2$, then $ABCD$ is orthodiagonal. (M&IQ 1991)

45. In $\triangle ABC$, $a \geq b \geq c$. If $\dfrac{a^3 + b^3 + c^3}{\sin^3 A + \sin^3 B + \sin^3 C} = 7$, compute the maximum value of a. (ARML 1984)

46. Show that in $\triangle ABC$,

$$\sin \frac{A}{2} = \sqrt{\frac{(s-b)(s-c)}{bc}}.$$

47. Use the last problem to find a similar expression for $\cos(A/2)$ without using the law of cosines.

48. Show that

$$[ABC] = r^2 \cot \frac{A}{2} \cot \frac{B}{2} \cot \frac{C}{2}.$$

49. Points A, B, C, and D are on a circle of diameter 1, and X is on diameter AD. If $BX = CX$ and $3\angle BAC = \angle BXC = 36°$, then find AX in terms of trigonometric functions of acute angles. (AHSME 1993)

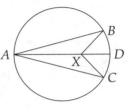

50. Show that if AD is a median of triangle ABC, then

$$4AD^2 = AB^2 + AC^2 + 2(AB)(AC)\cos\angle BAC.$$

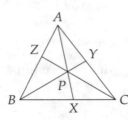

51. The magnitudes of the sides of $\triangle ABC$ are $a = BC$, $b = AC$, and $c = AB$, with $c \le b \le a$. Through interior point P and the vertices A, B, C, lines are drawn meeting the opposite sides at X, Y, and Z, respectively. Prove that $AX + BY + CZ < 2a + b$. (AHSME 1964)

52. In $\triangle ABC$ we have $\angle A = 60°$, $\angle B = 40°$, and $\angle C = 80°$. If O is the center of the circumcircle of $\triangle ABC$ and the radius of the circle O is 1, find the radius of the circumcircle of $\triangle BOC$. (Mandelbrot #1)

53. Let ABC be a triangle with sides of lengths a, b, and c. Let the bisector of the angle C cut AB at D. Prove that the length of CD is

$$\frac{2ab\cos\frac{C}{2}}{a+b}.$$

(Canada 1969)

54. In triangle ABC, CD is the bisector of angle C, with D on AB. If $\cos(C/2) = 1/3$ and $CD = 6$, compute $\dfrac{1}{a} + \dfrac{1}{b}$. (ARML 1986)

55. In $\triangle ABC$ in the adjoining figure, AD and AE trisect $\angle BAC$. The lengths of BD, DE, and EC are 2, 3, and 6, respectively. Find the length of the shortest side of $\triangle ABC$. (AHSME 1981)

56. Triangle ABC is reflected in its median AM as shown. If $AE = 6$, $EC = 12$, $BD = 10$, and $AB = k\sqrt{3}$, compute k. (ARML 1987)

57. Prove that if $\alpha, \beta, \gamma > 0$ and $\alpha + \beta + \gamma = \pi$, then $\sin 2\alpha + \sin 2\beta + \sin 2\gamma = 4\sin\alpha\sin\beta\sin\gamma$. (M&IQ 2)

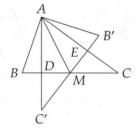

Chapter 4

Cyclic Quadrilaterals

4.1   Properties of Cyclic Quadrilaterals

Unlike triangles, not all quadrilaterals can be inscribed in a circle. Those which can be are called **cyclic quadrilaterals**. Such quadrilaterals have the following two special properties.

▷ The sum of the opposite angles in a cyclic quadrilateral is always 180°. Thus,

$$\angle A + \angle C = \angle B + \angle D = 180°$$

To prove this, we note that angles A and C are inscribed angles, so

$$\angle A + \angle C = \frac{\widehat{BCD}}{2} + \frac{\widehat{BAD}}{2} = \frac{\widehat{BCD} + \widehat{BAD}}{2} = \frac{360°}{2} = 180°.$$

▷ When we draw the diagonals of a cyclic quadrilateral, we form four pairs of equal angles like the pair shown below.

These angles are equal because they are inscribed angles which subtend the same arc. We have such a pair of equal angles for each side of the quadrilateral:

$$\angle ABD = \angle ACD \qquad \angle ACB = \angle ADB$$

$$\angle BAC = \angle BDC \qquad \angle CBD = \angle CAD$$

4.2   Finding Cyclic Quadrilaterals

Knowing these two useful properties of cyclic quadrilaterals does you no good if you don't know how to recognize a cyclic quadrilateral. The two methods of spotting cyclic quadrilaterals are the converses of the two properties discussed in the previous section.

If the sum of a pair of opposite angles of a quadrilateral is 180°, then the quadrilateral is cyclic. (If one pair of opposite angles has sum 180°, then the other pair must also because the sum of all four angles is 360°.)

Using the sum of opposite angles is the most common and easiest method to prove that a quadrilateral is cyclic. Given quadrilateral $ABCD$, to prove that $\angle B + \angle D = 180°$ implies the quadrilateral is cyclic, we draw the circumcircle of $\triangle ABC$ and show that if $\angle B + \angle D = 180°$, the circle must pass through D as well. We do this by proving that D cannot be inside or outside the circle of ABC, so D must be on the circumference.

In both of the diagrams below, we let

$$\widehat{EF} = \theta, \quad \widehat{AEC} = \alpha, \quad \text{and} \quad \widehat{ABC} = \beta.$$

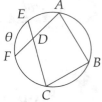

Since $\widehat{AEC}$ and $\widehat{ABC}$ make up the whole circle, their sum is $360°$.

For the case where D is inside the circle,

$$\angle B + \angle D = \frac{\alpha}{2} + \frac{\beta + \theta}{2} = \frac{\beta + \alpha}{2} + \frac{\theta}{2} = 180° + \frac{\theta}{2}.$$

Thus the sum is greater than $180°$ if D is inside the circle, violating the given fact that $\angle B + \angle D = 180°$.

For the case of D being outside the circle, we do the same thing:

$$\angle B + \angle D = \frac{\alpha}{2} + \frac{\beta - \theta}{2} = \frac{\alpha + \beta}{2} - \frac{\theta}{2} = 180° - \frac{\theta}{2}.$$

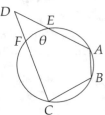

If D is outside the circle, $\angle B + \angle D$ is less than $180°$, which is again a contradiction.

Since D cannot be outside or inside the circumcircle of $\triangle ABC$ when $\angle B + \angle D = 180°$, it must be on the circle.

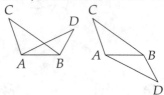

The other method for proving that four points are **concyclic**, meaning they all lie on the same circle, is as follows. If points C and D lie on the same side of segment AB such that $\angle ACB = \angle ADB$, then the four points $A, B, C,$ and D are concyclic. By 'the same side' we mean the points are as in the diagram on the left and not the right. We can prove this just like we proved the prior method for showing a quadrilateral is cyclic. We draw the circumcircle of $\triangle ABC$ and show that if D is inside this circle, then $\angle ADB > \angle ACB$, a contradiction to the two being equal. Similarly, if D is outside this circle, $\angle ADB < \angle ACB$, a contradiction. Thus, point D is on the circumcircle of $\triangle ABC$. Since this proof is almost exactly like the one we did above, we'll let you do it yourself.

Now that we know how to find cyclic quadrilaterals and how we can use them once we find them, we must discuss when to look for them and how they are useful. Cyclic quadrilaterals are most useful for proving that angles are supplementary or equal. In fact, usually problems involving cyclic quadrilaterals involve first showing that a quadrilateral is cyclic, then using the equal angles formed by the diagonals and sides to show that a pair of angles are equal.

Although cyclic quadrilaterals can be used to show that angles are supplementary, this is more commonly the way we show that a quadrilateral is cyclic. We then use the cyclic quadrilateral to show that angles are equal. We can use cyclic quadrilaterals to show that angles are equal when the angles are situated as in the top diagram at right. Angles A and B have sides which intersect at C and D, so we can show that $\angle A = \angle B$ by proving that $ABCD$ is a cyclic quadrilateral. Note that we cannot use cyclic quadrilaterals in the bottom figure to show $\angle A = \angle B$ because A and B are on opposite sides of CD.

In more difficult problems, using cyclic quadrilaterals is one of the most frequent methods of proving two angles are equal. This is because it is easy to 'hide' a cyclic quadrilateral in a problem. Of course, don't go into every problem looking for cyclic quadrilaterals; usually you should look for similar and congruent triangles first. But there are certain types of problems where cyclic quadrilaterals stick out. In problems involving right angles, cyclic quadrilaterals are often very obvious because any quadrilateral with a pair of opposite right angles is cyclic.

EXAMPLE 4-1 Let H be the orthocenter of $\triangle ABC$ and D and E be the feet of the altitudes from A and B, respectively. Show that $\angle DCH = \angle DEH$.

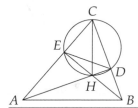

Proof: Since $\angle ADC + \angle BEC = 90° + 90° = 180°$, quadrilateral $HECD$ is cyclic. (We've drawn the circle to show this explicitly.) Since $\angle DCH$ and $\angle DEH$ are inscribed and these two angles subtend the same arc, they are equal.

EXAMPLE 4-2 Consider cyclic quarilateral $ABCD$ with $AB = 6$, $BC = 7$, $CD = 8$, and $AD = 9$. Find $(AC)^2$. (MAΘ 1991)

Solution: Since $ABCD$ is cyclic, $\angle B = 180° - \angle D$, so $\cos B = -\cos D$. Letting $x = AC$ and applying the law of cosines to both $\triangle ABC$ and $\triangle ADC$, we have

$$\cos B = \frac{x^2 - 36 - 49}{-2(6)(7)} = -\frac{x^2 - 64 - 81}{-2(8)(9)} = -\cos D.$$

Solving for x^2, we find $AC^2 = \mathbf{2035/19}$. Remember that the law of cosines can be used in this manner since the opposite angles of cyclic quadrilaterals are supplementary.

EXERCISE 4-1 In quadrilateral $ABCD$, we have $AB = 20$, $BC = 15$, $CD = 7$, $DA = 24$, and $AC = 25$. Let $\angle ACB = \alpha$ and $\angle ABD = \beta$. What is $\tan(\alpha + \beta)$? (Mandelbrot #2)

EXERCISE 4-2 Prove that if the diagonals of $ABCD$ intersect at O and $(AO)(CO) = (BO)(DO)$, then $ABCD$ is cyclic. This is the converse of part of the Power of a Point Theorem, and is occasionally used to show that a quadrilateral is cyclic.

4.3 Ptolemy's Theorem

Because of the many equal angles formed by the sides and diagonals of a cyclic quadrilateral, we are able to find and investigate many similar triangles.

For example, since $\angle ADB = \angle ACB$ in the diagram at right, we can pick a point E on BD such that $\angle DAE = \angle CAB$ to get $\triangle DAE \sim \triangle CAB$. Since

$$\angle BAE = \angle BAD - \angle DAE = \angle BAD - \angle CAB = \angle DAC$$

and $\angle ABE = \angle ACD$, we further have $\triangle ABE \sim \triangle ACD$. From these two triangle similarities we have

$$\frac{BC}{AC} = \frac{ED}{AD} \quad \text{and} \quad \frac{AB}{BE} = \frac{AC}{CD}.$$

Rearranging these, we have the equations

$$(BC)(AD) = (AC)(ED)$$
$$(AB)(CD) = (AC)(BE).$$

We then add these to get

$$(AB)(CD) + (BC)(AD) = (AC)(ED + BE) = (AC)(BD).$$

This, finally, is **Ptolemy's Theorem**, which states that in cyclic quadrilateral $ABCD$, with $a = AB$, $b = BC$, $c = CD$, $d = DA$, and diagonals e and f, we have

$$ac + bd = ef.$$

The use of Ptolemy is generally quite straightforward once we have shown that a quadrilateral is cyclic.

EXAMPLE 4-3   Find the diagonal length of an isosceles trapezoid with bases of lengths 8 and 20 and legs of length 10.

   Solution: Since the opposite angles of an isosceles trapezoid are supplementary, the trapezoid is cyclic. Since the trapezoid is isosceles, its diagonals are equal. Letting these diagonals have length x, we apply Ptolemy's Theorem and find

$$x^2 = (8)(20) + (10)(10) = 260,$$

so $x = 2\sqrt{65}$.

Problems to Solve for Chapter 4

58. Prove that a trapezoid is cyclic if and only if it is isosceles.

59. In cyclic quadrilateral $ABCD$ with diagonals intersecting at E, we have $AB = 5$, $BC = 10$, $BE = 7$, and $CD = 6$. Find CE.

60. In the diagram, let $\angle ADM = \angle ACD$ and $\angle ABM = \angle ACB$. Prove that $AB = AD$. (Mandelbrot #2)

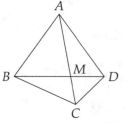

61. Quadrilateral $ABCD$ with consecutive sides of 8, 15, and 12 is inscribed in a circle with circumference 17π. Given that AC is a diameter of the circle, what is the length of the other diagonal of the quadrilateral? (MAΘ 1987)

62. Inscribed in a circle is a quadrilateral having sides of lengths 25, 39, 52, and 60 taken consecutively. What is the diameter of this circle? (AHSME 1972)

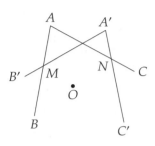

63. Suppose an angle BAC is rotated about point O to a new angle $B'A'C'$ such that AB and $A'B'$ intersect at M and AC and $A'C'$ intersect at N, as shown. Prove that A, A', M, N, and O all lie on a circle. (Mandelbrot #3)

64. A parallelogram $ABCD$ with an acute angle BAD is given. The bisector of $\angle BAD$ intersects CD at point L, and the line BC at point K. Let O be the circumcenter of $\triangle LCK$. Prove that the quadrilateral $DBCO$ is inscribed in a circle. (Bulgaria 1993)

65. Side AB of the square $ABCD$ is also the hypotenuse of right triangle ABP (ABP lies outside $ABCD$). Prove that the angle bisector of $\angle APB$ bisects the area of $ABCD$. (M&IQ 1992)

66. Prove that the midpoints of the sides of a quadrilateral lie on a circle if and only if the quadrilateral is orthodiagonal. (M&IQ 1991)

67. In the figure, $ABCD$ is a quadrilateral with right angles at A and C. Points E and F are on AC, and DE and BF are perpendicular to AC. If $AE = 3$, $DE = 5$, and $CE = 7$, then find BF. (AHSME 1990)

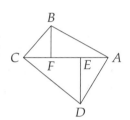

68. In quadrilateral $ABCD$ with diagonals AC and BD intersecting at O, $BO = 4$, $OD = 6$, $AO = 8$, $OC = 3$, and $AB = 6$. Find AD. (AHSME 1967)

69. Prove that if in $ABCD$ we let $a = AB$, $b = BC$, $c = CD$, and $d = DA$, we have

$$[ABCD]^2 = (s - a)(s - b)(s - c)(s - d) - abcd \cos^2\left(\frac{B + D}{2}\right),$$

where s is the semiperimeter of the quadrilateral. What does this expression, called **Brahmagupta's formula**, yield for a cyclic quadrilateral?

Chapter 5

Conics and Polar Coordinates

In Volume 1 we examined methods of graphing lines and circles. In this chapter we develop methods of describing and graphing other curves as well as using polar coordinates to describe curves. Be forewarned that while there are seemingly many formulas to be memorized in this chapter, if you take the time to understand the forms of the conics and the derivations thereof, you will need *no* memorization, only logic, to determine the formulas. Take the time to understand the proofs and the lessons and intuition they offer.

5.1 Parabolas

We already know how to solve quadratic expressions like $x^2 + 2x + 4 = 0$, but how do we graph the quadratic $y = x^2 + 2x + 4$? The answer to this question is the **parabola**. Given a line l and a point P, a parabola is the set of points S such that the length SP equals the distance from S to l. The point P is called the **focus** and the line is called the **directrix**.

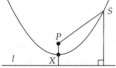

Using this definition of a parabola, we can make the rough sketch shown, where l is a horizontal line. The minimum point on the curve is called the **vertex**, and we label it $X = (h, k)$. If we let the distance from X to P be a, we have $P = (h, k + a)$. Similarly, l is a below X (since X is equidistant from P and l) and thus can be described by $y = k - a$. (Remember, l is a horizontal line.) If we choose any point $S = (x, y)$ on the parabola, we have $SP = \sqrt{(x - h)^2 + (y - k - a)^2}$ and the distance from S to l is merely $y - (k - a) = y - k + a$. Hence, from our definition of a parabola we have

$$\sqrt{(x - h)^2 + (y - k - a)^2} = y - k + a.$$

Squaring both sides and rearranging, we have

$$
\begin{aligned}
(x - h)^2 + (y - k - a)^2 &= (y - k + a)^2 \\
(x - h)^2 &= (y - k + a)^2 - (y - k - a)^2 \\
(x - h)^2 &= [y - k + a - y + k + a][y - k + a + y - k - a] \\
(x - h)^2 &= [2a][2(y - k)].
\end{aligned}
$$

Dividing by $4a$ we have the general form of a parabola with a horizontal directrix:

$$y - k = \frac{1}{4a}(x - h)^2.$$

Such parabolas always open either upward or downward (the one in this example opens upward). Similarly, if the directrix is vertical, the equation

$$x - h = \frac{1}{4a}(y - k)^2$$

describes the parabola (which then points either to the right or the left). In this case, the vertex is still (h, k), but now the focus is $+a$ to the right of the vertex, or $(h + a, k)$, and the directrix is a vertical line $-a$ from the vertex, or $x = h - a$.

EXERCISE 5-1 In the two general equations for the parabola above, what effect does the $1/4a$ term have on the graph of the parabola? What does negative a mean? Large a?

EXERCISE 5-2 The **axis of symmetry** is the line through the focus and the vertex of a parabola. The axis thus divides the parabola precisely in half. Find the equation of the axis of a parabola which opens upward and that of a parabola which opens to the right.

EXAMPLE 5-1 Graph and find the vertex, focus, and directrix of the parabola

$$x = -2y^2 + 12y - 15.$$

Solution: First we complete the square to get the parabola in one of our general forms:

$$
\begin{aligned}
x &= -2(y^2 - 6y) - 15 \\
x + (-2)(9) &= -2(y^2 - 6y + 9) - 15.
\end{aligned}
$$

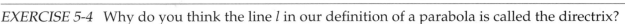

Hence our parabola is described by $x - 3 = -2(y - 3)^2$. Our vertex then is $(h, k) = (3, 3)$. To determine the focus and directrix, we find a by noting $1/4a = -2$, so $a = -1/8$. Hence, the directrix is $x = 3 - (-1/8) = 25/8$ (remember, the y term is squared, so the directrix is vertical) and the focus is $(3 - 1/8, 3) = (23/8, 3)$. To plot the parabola, we first plot the vertex, then find a few more points on the parabola by selecting values for y and finding the corresponding x values. We then plot the parabola as shown.

EXERCISE 5-3 Draw a line through the focus parallel to the directrix. Suppose this line intersects the parabola at A and B. The **latus rectum** is the segment AB. Prove for our above described parabolas that $AB = |4a|$. How can this fact be used to sketch parabolas easily?

EXERCISE 5-4 Why do you think the line l in our definition of a parabola is called the directrix?

EXERCISE 5-5 Find the focus, the vertex, the directrix, and the length of the latus rectum of the parabola

$$y = x^2/2 + 3x + 4.$$

Now that we can find all the significant points and lines of a parabola, we should be able to find the equation of a parabola given some of these points or lines. We do so by first determining the direction of the parabola (right, left, up, or down), then using the given information to determine h, k, and a.

EXAMPLE 5-2   Find the equation of a parabola with focus $(3, 2)$ and vertex $(3, 4)$.

    Solution: Since the vertex and focus lie on a vertical line $(x = 3)$ and the vertex is above the focus, the parabola points downward. Hence, we are dealing with the form $y - k = (1/4a)(x - h)^2$. From the vertex we know that $h = 3$ and $k = 4$ and we expect a to be negative (since the parabola opens downward). We know the focus is always a away from the vertex. In this case, the focus is 2 units below the vertex, so $a = -2$. Hence, our parabola is $y - 4 = -(1/8)(x - 3)^2$.

EXERCISE 5-6   Find the equation of a parabola with directrix $x = 3/2$ and focus $(5/2, 4)$.

EXAMPLE 5-3   A box with two dimensions of 10 feet and 4 feet is to be slid through a parabolic arch which is 5 feet tall at the center and 6 feet wide at the base. If the side facing the ground is 4 feet by 10 feet, what is the largest the other dimension can be and still slide through the arch?

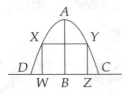

    Solution: Draw the segment AB from the top of the arch to the midpoint of the base as shown. If we let B be the origin, we can determine $A = (0, 5)$, $C = (3, 0)$, and $D = (-3, 0)$, since the arch is 5 feet high and 6 feet wide. Hence, the vertex of our parabola is $(0, 5)$ and it passes through $(3, 0)$. Since the parabola points downward, we have $y - 5 = (1/4a)x^2$ as its equation. Using the point $(3, 0)$, we have $-5 = 9/4a$, or $1/4a = -5/9$. Hence, the equation of the parabola is

$$y - 5 = -\frac{5}{9}x^2.$$

Now we draw the box $WXYZ$ in the arch as shown. Since $WZ = 4$, point Z has coordinates $(2, 0)$. Point Y then has coordinates $(2, z)$, where z is the desired third dimension. Since Y is on the parabola, we have $z - 5 = (-5/9)(2^2)$. Hence $z = 25/9$ and our largest possible third dimension is **25/9** feet. Make sure you understand this problem. Variations of it using elliptical and hyperbolic arches (figures which are discussed in the next few sections) are very common. Don't let them trip you up!

5.2   Ellipses

The general equation for a circle is

$$(x - h)^2 + (y - k)^2 = R^2.$$

Dividing by R^2, we can write this as

$$\frac{(x - h)^2}{R^2} + \frac{(y - k)^2}{R^2} = 1.$$

    In our discussion of distortion in Volume 1, we noted that we can stretch a circle to form an **ellipse**. Namely, we could stretch the radius in the x direction so that it differs from that in the y direction. The resulting curve is at right. We could then associate two radii, a and b, with our curve and write it as

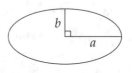

$$\frac{(x - h)^2}{a^2} + \frac{(y - k)^2}{b^2} = 1.$$

From our diagram, we see that we have two different 'diameters' in the x and y direction. These have length $2a$ and $2b$, respectively. These are called the **major axis** and the **minor axis** of the ellipse, where the major axis is the longer of the two.

EXERCISE 5-7　What if $a = b$ above? Do you see why circles are ellipses?

Taking two points F_1 and F_2, we can define an ellipse as the set of points Z such that $ZF_1 + ZF_2$ has some constant value. We call F_1 and F_2 the **foci** of the ellipse. To see that this new definition of an ellipse satisfies our equation form, we apply the distance formula. First we draw the axes of the ellipse and note that $CD = 2b$ and $AB = 2a$. Now we can find the constant sum $ZF_1 + ZF_2$. Letting Z be A we have

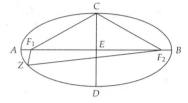

$$ZF_1 + ZF_2 = AF_1 + AF_2 = BF_2 + AF_2 = AB = 2a,$$

where we note that $AF_1 = BF_2$. (Why?) Hence our constant sum is $2a$, or the length of the major axis. Since $F_1C = CF_2$ and $F_1C + CF_2 = 2a$, from right triangle CEF_1 we have

$$2a = 2CF_1 = 2\sqrt{CE^2 + EF_1^2} = 2\sqrt{b^2 + EF_1^2}.$$

If we let $c = EF_1$ be the distance from each focus to the center, we square $a = \sqrt{b^2 + EF_1^2}$ to find $c^2 = a^2 - b^2$. (Why are the foci equidistant from the center?) Now we are ready to apply our constant sum principle to find the equation of an ellipse. We let the center of the ellipse be the origin, so that $F_1 = (-c, 0)$ and $F_2 = (c, 0)$. Taking a general point $Z = (x, y)$ on the ellipse, we have

$$2a = ZF_1 + ZF_2 = \sqrt{(x+c)^2 + y^2} + \sqrt{(x-c)^2 + y^2}.$$

We move one radical to the other side of the equation and square, so

$$\left(2a - \sqrt{(x+c)^2 + y^2}\right)^2 = \left(\sqrt{(x-c)^2 + y^2}\right)^2$$
$$4a^2 - 4a\sqrt{(x+c)^2 + y^2} + (x+c)^2 + y^2 = (x-c)^2 + y^2$$
$$4a^2 - 4a\sqrt{(x+c)^2 + y^2} + x^2 + 2xc + c^2 + y^2 = x^2 - 2xc + c^2 + y^2.$$

Again we rearrange the equation to isolate the square root. Then we divide by 4 and square both sides of the resulting equation, yielding

$$\left(-a\sqrt{(x+c)^2 + y^2}\right)^2 = (-a^2 - xc)^2$$
$$a^2[(x+c)^2 + y^2] = a^4 + 2a^2xc + x^2c^2$$
$$a^2x^2 + 2a^2xc + a^2c^2 + a^2y^2 = a^4 + 2a^2xc + x^2c^2.$$

Simplifying where possible and applying the relation $c^2 = a^2 - b^2$, we have

$$a^2x^2 + a^2c^2 + a^2y^2 = a^4 + x^2c^2$$
$$a^2x^2 + a^2(a^2 - b^2) + a^2y^2 = a^4 + x^2(a^2 - b^2).$$

Putting all terms involving x and y on the left and the constants on the right we find

$$b^2x^2 + a^2y^2 = a^2b^2$$

or

$$\frac{x^2}{a^2} + \frac{y^2}{b^2} = 1.$$

The simple translation from (x, y) to $(x - h, y - k)$ gives us the equation for an ellipse with center (h, k) rather than $(0, 0)$, or

$$\frac{(x - h)^2}{a^2} + \frac{(y - k)^2}{b^2} = 1.$$

For this ellipse, the foci are $(h \pm c, k)$ since they are c to the right and c to the left of the center.

We measure the amount an ellipse is stretched away from a circle by its **eccentricity**, which is c/a. Finally, the area enclosed in an ellipse is $ab\pi$, which is proven on page 242.

EXAMPLE 5-4 What happens to our ellipse equation if the major axis is parallel to the y axis rather than the x axis as above?

Solution: Again we let the major axis have length $2a$ and the minor axis length $2b$, so that through the same discussion as above, the equation of the ellipse is

$$\frac{(x - h)^2}{b^2} + \frac{(y - k)^2}{a^2} = 1.$$

The foci are now c above and c below the center (at $(h, k \pm c)$) and c still equals $\sqrt{a^2 - b^2}$.

EXERCISE 5-8 Why is the quantity c/a called the eccentricity?

Now we have a way to describe all important points and lengths of an ellipse whose axes are parallel to the coordinate axes. WARNING: In describing an ellipse, we associate the letter a with the larger of the 'radii' in the x and y directions. Always make sure your value of a is greater than that of b; otherwise, your value of $c = \sqrt{a^2 - b^2}$ will be nonsense. Furthermore, make sure you know which direction the major axis points. This will help you determine where the foci are.

EXAMPLE 5-5 Graph and find the center, foci, area, and lengths of the axes of the ellipse given by $9x^2 - 36x + 4y^2 - 24y + 36 = 0$.

Solution: We attack this just as we did parabolas that weren't written in the nice general form; we complete the square:

$$9(x^2 - 4x) + 4(y^2 - 6y) = -36.$$

To make perfect squares, we add $(-4/2)^2 = 4$ inside the x parentheses and $(-6/2)^2 = 9$ inside the y parentheses. Hence, we have

$$9(x^2 - 4x + 4) + 4(y^2 - 6y + 9) = -36 + 9(4) + 4(9)$$
$$9(x - 2)^2 + 4(y - 3)^2 = 36.$$

Dividing by 36, we get our form for the ellipse,

$$\frac{(x-2)^2}{4} + \frac{(y-3)^2}{9} = 1.$$

Hence the center is $(2, 3)$. Since the number under the y is greater than that under the x, the major axis is parallel to the y axis. From our equation we have $a = \sqrt{9} = 3$ and $b = \sqrt{4} = 2$. Thus, the major and minor axes have lengths **6** and **4**, respectively.

From a and b we find that the area is **6π** and $c = \sqrt{9-4} = \sqrt{5}$. Since the major axis is parallel to the y axis, the foci are then found by adding and subtracting c from the y coordinate of the center, or $(2, 3 \pm \sqrt{5})$. To graph the ellipse, we locate the endpoints of the axes. The major axis endpoints are 3 above and below the center (since the major axis has length 6) and thus are $(2, 6)$ and $(2, 0)$. Similarly the endpoints of the minor axis are $(0, 3)$ and $(4, 3)$. Plotting these points, we can draw the ellipse as shown.

EXAMPLE 5-6 What are a and b for the ellipse

$$\frac{4(x-1)^2}{9} + \frac{(y-2)^2}{8} = 1?$$

Solution: Neither a nor b is $\sqrt{9} = 3$! Notice the 4 before the $(x-1)^2$. We put this in the denominator as

$$\frac{(x-1)^2}{9/4} + \frac{(y-2)^2}{8} = 1.$$

Our a and b values are then $\sqrt{8} = \mathbf{2\sqrt{2}}$ and $\sqrt{9/4} = \mathbf{3/2}$, respectively.

EXERCISE 5-9 Find the center, foci, and length of the axes of the ellipse

$$3x^2 + 4y^2 - 6x + 8y + 3 = 0.$$

EXERCISE 5-10 What if I complete the square for a problem like the the previous exercise and find

$$\frac{(x-2)^2}{4} + \frac{(y+1)^2}{3} = 0$$

as my equation of the ellipse? (Notice there is a 0 on the right, not a 1.) How many solutions (x, y) are there to this equation? What if I get a negative number on the right? These are cases of **degenerate ellipses**, or ellipse equations with either no solution or only one solution.

EXERCISE 5-11 As with the parabola, we can define the latus recti of an ellipse as the segments through the foci parallel to the minor axis with endpoints on the ellipse. Find the length of each of these segments in terms of a and b.

Just as with parabolas, we are often asked to find the equation of an ellipse given certain information about the ellipse. Again the first step is to determine which direction the ellipse points (i.e. the direction of the major axis). We then use the given information to determine the center as well as a and b.

EXAMPLE 5-7   Find the ellipse with major axis length 8, center $(2, 1)$, and one focus at $(2, 3)$.

     Solution: Since the given focus is directly above the center, the major axis is parallel to the y axis. From the information we can also deduce $h = 2$, $k = 1$, and $a = 8/2 = 4$. Since the given focus is 2 away from the center, we have $c = 2$. Thus, from $c^2 = a^2 - b^2$, we find $b^2 = a^2 - c^2 = 12$ and our ellipse is

$$\frac{(x-h)^2}{b^2} + \frac{(y-k)^2}{a^2} = \frac{(x-2)^2}{12} + \frac{(y-1)^2}{16} = 1.$$

Make sure you see why the 12 is under $(x - 2)^2$ rather than $(y - 1)^2$.

EXERCISE 5-12   Find the equation of the ellipse with foci at $(3, 1)$ and $(-5, 1)$ and minor axis with length 4.

     With the ability to find the equation of an ellipse given some information about it, we move on to less obvious applications of ellipses.

EXAMPLE 5-8   To give my dog some space to run, I drive two stakes in my lawn 10 feet apart. I tie the ends of a 30 foot rope to the stakes (one end to each stake) and loop my dog's collar loosely around the rope, so she is free to move along the rope. Over how many square feet is my dog free to roam?

     Solution: If my dog walks until the rope pulls taut, she will get to the boundary of her roaming area. This boundary is an ellipse since the sum of the distances from any point on the boundary to the stakes is the length of the rope, 30 feet. The stakes correspond to the foci and the rope to the constant sum of distances. Hence, the major axis has length 30. If we let the stakes lie on the x axis and the midpoint of the line connecting the stakes be the origin, the equation of the ellipse is (since $a = 30/2 = 15$):

$$\frac{x^2}{225} + \frac{y^2}{b^2} = 1.$$

We then find b by noting that the distance from a focus to the center is $c = 5$ since the stakes are 10 feet apart, so $b = \sqrt{a^2 - c^2} = 10\sqrt{2}$. The area of the roaming region is the area of the ellipse, or $ab\pi = \mathbf{150\pi\sqrt{2}}$ square feet.

     Keep an eye out for these slick applications of the constant sum of distances property of an ellipse to problems.

5.3   Hyperbolas

Suppose we change the + in the general ellipse equation to a −, resulting in

$$\frac{(x-h)^2}{a^2} - \frac{(y-k)^2}{b^2} = 1.$$

The graph of this equation is called a **hyperbola**. As you may have guessed, with each hyperbola we can associate a pair of foci F_1 and F_2 so that the hyperbola is the set of all points S where $|F_1S - F_2S|$

has some constant value. We can slug through the same exact algebra as we did with the ellipse to show the equivalence of the constant difference condition to the above equation. If you don't trust us, try it yourself. Find this common difference of distances and use the fact that $c^2 = a^2 + b^2$ (where c is the distance from the focus to the center).

If you find a bunch of points on the hyperbola, you will eventually find a curve like the bold curve shown below. The center O has coordinates (h, k), just like the ellipse. Points I and J are the foci and have coordinates $(h \pm c, k)$ since they are c to the right and left of the center. The points C and G are the vertices. They have the same y coordinate as the center, so letting $y = k$ in the equation for a hyperbola, we have $(x - h)^2/a^2 = 1$, so $x = h \pm a$ and the vertices are $(h \pm a, k)$.

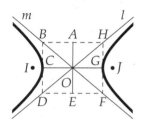

The segment CG is called the **transverse axis**, and like the major axis of an ellipse it has length $2a$. Similar to the minor axis we define the **conjugate axis** as the segment with endpoints $(h, k \pm b)$.

Suppose we sketch the rectangle, as we have in dashed lines, with center O and sides equal in length to our two axes. The lines l and m which are the extensions of the diagonals of this rectangle are called the **asymptotes** of the hyperbola. These are lines which the curve approaches but never actually meets. We can find the equation of line l by noting that it passes through the center $O = (h, k)$ and has slope $HG/OG = b/a$. Hence, the equation of line l is $y - k = (b/a)(x - h)$. Similarly, the equation for line m is $y - k = (-b/a)(x - h)$. As the following example will show you, using the asymptotes helps graph the hyperbola.

Please do not memorize all of these formulas; understand them instead.

EXERCISE 5-13 Why are the lines $y - k = \pm\frac{b}{a}(x - h)$ asymptotes of the above hyperbola? What happens in our hyperbola equation if we let $y - k = \pm\frac{b}{a}(x - h)$?

EXAMPLE 5-9 Find the asymptotes, vertices, center, foci, and lengths of the axes of $9x^2 - 4y^2 + 18x + 16y - 43 = 0$ and graph the hyperbola.

Solution: Grouping our x and y terms we have $9(x^2 + 2x) - 4(y^2 - 4y) = 43$. Completing the square then dividing by 36 we get

$$\frac{(x + 1)^2}{4} - \frac{(y - 2)^2}{9} = 1.$$

(Always make sure you have positive 1 on the right.) The center is $(-1, 2)$, and we have $a = 2$ and $b = 3$. Hence, the transverse axis has length $2(2) = 4$, the conjugate axis has length 6, and the vertices are $(-3, 2)$ and $(1, 2)$. Since $c = \sqrt{a^2 + b^2} = \sqrt{13}$, the foci of the hyperbola are $(-1 \pm \sqrt{13}, 2)$. Finally, the asymptotes are $y - 2 = \pm\frac{3}{2}(x + 1)$.

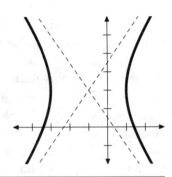

To graph the hyperbola, we plot its center and vertices. We then draw our asymptotes, which we can do most easily by sketching the rectangle with center $(-1, 2)$ and sides of length $2a$ and $2b$ as in our introduction. The lines through the opposite corners of the rectangle are the shown asymptotes. Now we can draw the curve through the vertices approaching the lines asymptotically as shown.

EXERCISE 5-14   Find the center, vertices, foci, asymptotes, and the lengths of the axes of the hyperbola

$$\frac{(y-k)^2}{a^2} - \frac{(x-h)^2}{b^2} = 1.$$

Note that with a hyperbola we always associate a with the positive term rather than the one with the larger denominator.

EXERCISE 5-15   We can define the latus recti of a hyperbola as the segments through the foci parallel to the conjugate axis with endpoints on the hyperbola. We can also define the eccentricity as we did for the ellipse, c/a. Find the length of the latus recti of a hyperbola.

EXAMPLE 5-10   What if completing the square for the hyperbola results in $(x-1)^2/4 - (y+2)^2/9 = 0$, rather than equalling 1 like usual?

Solution: This is a **degenerate hyperbola**. We can write the equation as $(x-1)^2/4 = (y+2)^2/9$. Taking the square root of both sides, we find

$$(x-1)/2 = \pm(y+2)/3,$$

so the degenerate hyperbola is just a pair of lines.

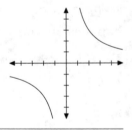

Consider the graph of the curve $xy = 6$. Graphing several of the points on the graph we find the curve shown. This looks very much like a hyperbola, and it is! The coordinate axes are the asymptotes and the origin is the center. We can find the vertices of the hyperbola by noting that $x = y$ at the vertex. (Why?) Hence the vertices are $(\sqrt{6}, \sqrt{6})$ and $(-\sqrt{6}, -\sqrt{6})$. Similar to this example, any curve of the form $xy = c$ is a hyperbola.

EXERCISE 5-16   Why are the coordinate axes asymptotes of the hyperbola $xy = 6$?

Once again, we can determine the equation of a hyperbola given various information about the hyperbola.

EXERCISE 5-17   Find the equation of a hyperbola with vertices $(-2, -1 \pm 2\sqrt{2})$ and conjugate axis of length 4.

Now that we've finished introducing parabolas, ellipses, and hyperbolas, we can discuss why we call them conic sections. Take a pair of congruent cones and hold them tip to tip so they have the same vertex and same axis but open in opposite directions. Consider the various cross-sections that occur when you cut the resulting solid with a plane. Cutting completely through one cone forms an ellipse. Cutting with a plane parallel to the axis will form a hyperbola, and a plane intersecting one cone but not the other (but not passing all the way through the first cone) forms a parabola.

5.4 Polar Coordinates Revisited

As we saw in the first volume, we can identify any point P in the plane by its distance from the origin (OP) and the angle θ which OP forms with the positive x axis. Calling the distance from the point to the origin r, we relate the polar point $P = (r, \theta)$ to the rectangular coordinate point (x, y) by $x = r \cos \theta$ and $y = r \sin \theta$. Hence, we have

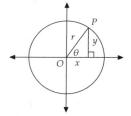

$$x^2 + y^2 = r^2 \cos^2 \theta + r^2 \sin^2 \theta = r^2,$$

and we relate the angle θ to x and y by

$$\frac{y}{x} = \frac{\sin \theta}{\cos \theta},$$

or $\theta = \tan^{-1} \frac{y}{x}$. WARNING: Make sure when determining θ that it properly corresponds to the quadrant in which (x, y) lies.

EXAMPLE 5-11 Convert the rectangular point $(3, -3)$ to polar coordinates and the polar point $(6, 30°)$ to rectangular coordinates.

Solution: For the point $(3, -3)$, we have $r = \sqrt{x^2 + y^2} = \sqrt{18} = 3\sqrt{2}$. We find the angle as $\theta = \tan^{-1}(-1)$. Since $(3, -3)$ is in the fourth quadrant, $\theta = 315°$. The point $(3, -3)$ in polar coordinates is then $(3\sqrt{2}, 315°)$. Notice that we could use $315° + n(360°)$ for any n as the angle to determine the point in polar coordinates as well.

For the polar point $(6, 30°)$, we have $x = 6 \cos 30° = 3\sqrt{3}$ and $y = 6 \sin 30° = 3$. Our point thus is $(3\sqrt{3}, 3)$.

EXERCISE 5-18 Express $(6, -6\sqrt{3})$ in polar coordinates and $(-2, 405°)$ in rectangular coordinates.

Polar coordinates are often useful in describing curves. For example, the equation $r = 3$ represents a circle with center $(0, 0)$ and radius 3. Using the expressions $x = r \cos \theta$ and $y = r \sin \theta$, we can easily turn any curve in rectangular coordinates into a polar equation.

EXAMPLE 5-12 Express the equation $x^2 - y^2 = 9$ in polar coordinates.

Solution: Using $x = r \cos \theta$ and $y = r \sin \theta$, we have $x^2 - y^2 = r^2(\cos^2 \theta - \sin^2 \theta) = r^2 \cos 2\theta$. Hence, our polar form is $r^2 \cos 2\theta = 9$.

EXERCISE 5-19 Express $6xy = 8$ in polar coordinates.

Going from polar coordinates to rectangular is generally a little bit tougher. To do so, we replace any r^2 with $x^2 + y^2$, $r \cos \theta$ with x, and $r \sin \theta$ with y. Sometimes we have to manipulate the equation a bit first, as you will see.

EXAMPLE 5-13 Write $r = \dfrac{5}{3 - \cos \theta}$ in rectangular coordinates.

Solution: First we multiply by $3 - \cos \theta$, yielding

$$3r - r \cos \theta = 5.$$

Since $r \cos \theta = x$, we have $3r - x = 5$. Isolating the r we find $3r = 5 + x$. Squaring this (to get r^2 on the left) yields $9r^2 = 25 + 10x + x^2$. Since $r^2 = x^2 + y^2$, we have $9(x^2 + y^2) = 25 + 10x + x^2$, or

$$8x^2 + 9y^2 - 10x = 25.$$

You should now be able to recognize this as an ellipse.

EXAMPLE 5-14 Identify the curve $r = 3 \cos \theta$.

Solution: To identify a curve in polar coordinates, it is often best to convert the equation to rectangular coordinates and name the resulting curve. For this equation, we multiply by r to force an r^2 on one side and $r \cos \theta$ on the other, namely $r^2 = 3r \cos \theta$. Hence, $x^2 + y^2 = 3x$ and our curve is a circle.

EXERCISE 5-20 Express $r = 4 \sec \theta$ and $r = 3 \sin \theta$ in polar coordinates.

EXERCISE 5-21 How would you express vertical or horizontal lines in polar coordinates? How about a line through the origin?

EXERCISE 5-22 Describe as specifically as possible the class of curves described by $r = a \sin \theta + b \cos \theta$.

Finally, for you trivia buffs, there are a few more families of curves which have simple polar forms.

A **limaçon** has the one of the forms:

$$r = a + b \sin \theta \qquad r = a + b \cos \theta$$
$$r = a - b \sin \theta \qquad r = a - b \cos \theta.$$

Try choosing some pairs (a, b) (where $a, b > 0$) and sketching the resulting graphs by choosing different values for θ, then computing r.

If a limaçon has $a/b < 1$, it will have a loop. If $a/b = 1$, the curve, which is shown at left, is called a **cardioid**. If $1 < a/b < 2$, the limaçon is 'dimpled,' and otherwise, it is 'convex.'

Curves of the form $r^2 = \pm a^2 \cos 2\theta$ or $r^2 = \pm a^2 \sin 2\theta$ are called **lemniscates**, which look like infinity symbols.

The curve $r = a\theta$, where the radius increases with the angle, is called the **spiral of Archimedes**. Graph it and see why.

Finally, $r = a\sin n\theta$ and $r = a\cos n\theta$ represent **roses**. Shown is a graph with $n = 5$, which has 5 'petals.' Try choosing other values of n and plotting the results. Can you develop a rule for the number of petals in a rose?

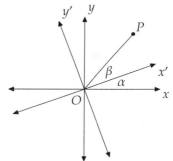

As we initially stated, these curves aren't terribly useful for problem solving outside of trivial pursuits, however through using computer graphics you may be able to generate quite artistic results based on these simple polar forms.

5.5 That Pesky xy Term

A general conic has the form $Ax^2 + Bxy + Cy^2 + Dx + Ey + F = 0$. In previous sections, the only time we have seen an xy term is when we discussed hyperbolas of the form $xy = c$ for some constant c. Otherwise, we have avoided xy as much as possible because conics without xy terms are easy to analyze. Those with an xy term have axes which are no longer parallel to the coordinate axes and these are much more difficult to resolve. We call these conics **oblique**.

Now that we've mastered polar coordinates we can analyze oblique conics by rotating them so that their axes are parallel to the coordinate axes. But how do we perform the rotation?

Rather than rotate the conic, we rotate the coordinate axes to be parallel to the axes of the conic. In the diagram is the rotation of the coordinate axes through an angle α counterclockwise about the origin. Point P, which originally has coordinates (x, y) before rotation is at (x', y') with respect to our new axes x' and y'. Letting the angle OP forms with the positive x' axis be β, we can relate the two pairs of rectangular coordinates of P to α and β through polar coordinates (where $r = OP$) as

$$x = r\cos(\alpha + \beta) \quad \text{and} \quad y = r\sin(\alpha + \beta),$$

and

$$x' = r\cos\beta \quad \text{and} \quad y' = r\sin\beta.$$

(Make sure you understand these.) Expanding our expressions for x and y and using the ones for x' and y' we find

$$\begin{aligned} x &= r\cos\alpha\cos\beta - r\sin\alpha\sin\beta = x'\cos\alpha - y'\sin\alpha \\ y &= r\sin\alpha\cos\beta + r\cos\alpha\sin\beta = x'\sin\alpha + y'\cos\alpha, \end{aligned}$$

where we have used our expressions for x' and y' to express (x, y) in terms of (x', y') and the angle of rotation.

EXERCISE 5-23 In our above rotation, find x' and y' in terms of x, y, and α.

Now we return to our conic $Ax^2 + Bxy + Cy^2 + Dx + Ey + F = 0$, where $B \neq 0$. Our problem now is to rotate the axes through some angle α such that the resulting conic has no $x'y'$ term in (x', y') coordinates. Using the above equations for x and y in terms of x', y', and α, we have

$$A(x'\cos\alpha - y'\sin\alpha)^2 + B(x'\cos\alpha - y'\sin\alpha)(x'\sin\alpha + y'\cos\alpha) + C(x'\sin\alpha + y'\cos\alpha)^2$$

$$+D(x'\cos\alpha - y'\sin\alpha) + E(x'\sin\alpha + y'\cos\alpha) + F = 0.$$

Since we want to get rid of the $x'y'$ term, we only consider those terms which produce $x'y'$ terms. Combining these terms and setting their sum equal to 0, we have

$$-2Ax'y'\cos\alpha\sin\alpha + Bx'y'(\cos^2\alpha - \sin^2\alpha) + 2Cx'y'\cos\alpha\sin\alpha = 0$$
$$x'y'(C-A)(2\cos\alpha\sin\alpha) + Bx'y'(\cos^2\alpha - \sin^2\alpha) = 0$$
$$x'y'(C-A)(\sin 2\alpha) + Bx'y'(\cos 2\alpha) = 0.$$

Dividing by $x'y'$ and rearranging a bit, we find $B\cos 2\alpha = (A-C)\sin 2\alpha$, so $\cot 2\alpha = (A-C)/B$. Hence, α as given by $\cot 2\alpha = (A-C)/B$ is the angle through which we must rotate the axes to eliminate the xy term of $Ax^2 + Bxy + Cy^2 + Dx + Ey + F = 0$.

EXAMPLE 5-15 Through what acute angle(s) can the conic $3x^2 + 4xy - 4y^2 - 6 = 0$ be rotated in order to remove the xy term?

Solution: From the above discussion, we have $\cot 2\alpha = 7/4$ for the angle α through which we must rotate the *axes* counterclockwise; hence, we must rotate the *conic* clockwise α to get rid of the xy term. Thus, one such angle is $\alpha = (1/2)\,\mathrm{Cot}^{-1}(7/4)$ clockwise. We can also rotate the conic through an angle $90° - \alpha$ counterclockwise to get rid of the xy term. The axis which becomes parallel to the x axis under a rotation of α clockwise will be parallel to the y axis upon a rotation of $90° - \alpha$ counterclockwise. Make sure you see why!

How can we tell if the general conic $Ax^2 + Bxy + Cy^2 + Dx + Ey + F = 0$ is an ellipse, parabola, or a hyperbola? We already know how if $B = 0$. The conic is a parabola if A or C is 0; it's an ellipse if AC is positive, and it's a hyperbola if AC is negative. (Why?) If $B \neq 0$, we rotate the conic so that there is no xy term, just as above. For those of you with a yen for algebra, use our rotation method above to prove that if we rotate

$$Ax^2 + Bxy + Cy^2 + Dx + Ey + F = 0$$

to

$$A'x'^2 + B'x'y' + C'y'^2 + D'x' + E'y' + F' = 0,$$

then $B'^2 - 4A'C' = B^2 - 4AC$, no matter what the angle of rotation is. This value, $B^2 - 4AC$, is called the **discriminant** of the conic. Suppose the rotated conic is such that $B' = 0$. Hence, $B^2 - 4AC = B'^2 - 4A'C' = -4A'C'$. Since our new conic has no xy term, it is an ellipse if $A'C' > 0$, a parabola if $A'C' = 0$, or a hyperbola if $A'C' < 0$. Thus, if $B^2 - 4AC = -4A'C' = 0$, the original conic is a parabola, if the discriminant is negative (so that $A'C' > 0$), the conic is an ellipse, and if the discriminant is positive, the conic is a hyperbola.

EXERCISE 5-24 Can every circle be described without an xy term?

Problems to Solve for Chapter 5

70. Find the equation of a hyperbola with asymptotes $y - 1 = \pm\frac{3}{2}(x - 4)$ and one vertex at $(6, 1)$.

71. A parabola $y = ax^2 + bx + c$ has vertex $(4, 2)$. If $(2, 0)$ is on the parabola, then find abc. (AHSME 1986)

72. Find the radius of the smallest circle whose interior and boundary completely contain the two circles with centers $(0, 0)$ and $(24, 7)$ and radii 3, 4, respectively. (Mandelbrot #2)

73. A tiny bug starts at a point (x, y) on the graph of $x^2/9 + y^2/4 = 1$. It walks in a straight line to the point $(-\sqrt{5}, 0)$, then in a straight line to $(\sqrt{5}, 0)$, and then in a straight line to its initial point. How far has the bug walked? (MAΘ 1990)

74. If each of two intersecting lines intersects a hyperbola and neither line is tangent to the hyperbola, then what are the possible numbers of places where the lines can intersect the hyperbola? (AHSME 1956)

75. Points A and B are selected on the graph of $y = -x^2/2$ so that triangle ABO is equilateral, where O is the origin. Find the length of one of the sides of $\triangle ABO$. (MATHCOUNTS 1991)

76. A parabolic arch has a span of 24 feet. Its height is 18 feet at a point 8 feet from the center of the span. What is the height, in feet, of the arch? (MAΘ 1992)

77. If the line $y = mx + 1$ intersects the ellipse $x^2 + 4y^2 = 1$ exactly once, then find m^2. (AHSME 1971)

78. Find the equation in rectangular coordinates of the curve whose polar equation is $r = 2\sec\theta + \cos\theta$. (MAΘ 1987)

79. A circle has the same center as an ellipse and passes through the foci F_1 and F_2 of the ellipse. The two curves intersect in four points. Let P be any point of intersection. If the major axis of the ellipse has length 15 and the area of triangle PF_1F_2 is 26, compute the distance between the foci. (ARML 1984)

80. A point P lies in the same plane as a given square of side 1. Let the vertices of the square, taken counterclockwise, be A, B, C, and D. Also, let the distances from P to A, B, and C, respectively, be u, v, and w. What is the greatest distance that P can be from D if $u^2 + v^2 = w^2$? (AHSME 1983)

81. An ellipse is drawn with major and minor axes of lengths 10 and 8 respectively. Using one focus as the center, a circle is drawn that is tangent to the ellipse, with no part of the circle being outside the ellipse. Compute the radius of the circle. (ARML 1986)

82. The points of intersection of $xy = 12$ and $x^2 + y^2 = 25$ are joined in succession. What is the resulting figure? (AHSME 1956)

83. A circle rests in the interior of the parabola with equation $y = x^2$ so that it is tangent to the parabola at two points. How much higher is the center of the circle than the points of tangency? (Mandelbrot #2)

Chapter 6

Polynomials

6.1   What is a Polynomial?

In Volume 1, the equations of one variable we saw were usually no more complicated than quadratic equations. What happens when we introduce terms with higher powers than 2? This brings us to the general subject of polynomials. A **polynomial** is a function of the form

$$f(x) = a_n x^n + a_{n-1} x^{n-1} + \cdots + a_0,$$

where the a_i are called **coefficients** (any of these except a_n can be 0) and n, the highest power of x in the polynomial, is the **degree**, written $\deg f$. As the form suggests, n is always a nonnegative integer. Examples of polynomials in x are:

$$x^3 + 2x + 5 \qquad x^4 - 2x^3 + 5.6x^2 - \sqrt{2}\,x + 4 \qquad x^2 - 5.$$

The expressions below are not polynomials in x:

$$\frac{x-1}{x^2+4} \qquad \sqrt{x} - 7 \qquad 4x - \frac{1}{x} \qquad \log_2 x + \sin x.$$

Throughout this chapter, unless we specifically state otherwise, we are considering only polynomials with all rational coefficients.

6.2   Multiplying and Dividing Polynomials

In working with polynomials we sometimes encounter expressions like

$$(x^2 + 3x + 1)(x^2 - 3x + 4) \quad \text{and} \quad \frac{x^3 + 3x^2 + 4x + 4}{x^2 + 2x + 1}.$$

We can expand this first expression, the product of polynomials, using the distributive property. Usually it is easiest to set up the multiplication just like when we multiply large numbers. An example of this is shown below.

$$
\begin{array}{rrrr}
x^2 + & 3x + & 1 \\
x^2 - & 3x + & 4 \\
\hline
4x^2 + & 12x + & 4 & (1) \\
- 3x^3 - 9x^2 - & 3x & & (2) \\
x^4 + 3x^3 + & x^2 & & (3) \\
\hline
x^4 + 0x^3 - 4x^2 + & 9x + & 4 &
\end{array}
$$

Here we have multiplied $x^2 + 3x + 1$ and $x^2 - 3x + 4$ by multiplying $(x^2 + 3x + 1)$ first by 4 (line (1)), then by $-3x$ (line (2)), then finally by x^2 (line (3)). Last, we add the results as shown; grouping the common terms in columns makes this easy. Multiplying the two given quadratics yields $x^4 - 4x^2 + 9x + 4$. (There is no need to keep the $0x^3$ term).

One pretty obvious result of polynomial multiplication is that for all polynomials f and g,

$$\deg(fg) = \deg f + \deg g.$$

The proof of this is straightforward. If the degree of f is n and that of g is m, then the product will contain only one x^{m+n} term and no terms of higher degree. Can you show that if $\deg f \geq \deg g$, then $\deg(f + g) \leq \deg f$?

Just like multiplication of polynomials, division of polynomials can be done very much like long division. The best way to describe this is by example.

$$
\begin{array}{r}
x + 1 \qquad (1) \\
x^2 + 2x + 1 \overline{\smash{\big)}\ x^3 + 3x^2 + 4x + 4} \\
\underline{- x^3 - 2x^2 - x} \qquad\quad (2) \\
x^2 + 3x + 4 \\
\underline{- x^2 - 2x - 1} \quad (3) \\
x + 3 \quad (4)
\end{array}
$$

Let $g(x) = x^2 + 2x + 1$ and $f(x) = x^3 + 3x^2 + 4x + 4$. We divide the first term, x^2, of $g(x)$ into the first term of $f(x)$, x^3, yielding the x on line (1). We then multiply $g(x)$ by x and subtract this product from $f(x)$ as shown on line (2). Again we divide the first term of $g(x)$ into the first term of the result of the subtraction, yielding 1. Finally, we multiply this quotient, 1, by $g(x)$ and subtract the result as in line (3). The result is line (4). Since we can't evenly divide the leading term of $g(x)$ into that of line (4), we are done. The quotient is $x + 1$ and the **remainder**, line (4), is $x + 3$. Compare this process to long division of large numbers—it's exactly the same. Don't memorize the steps; understand the process of division.

If we let the remainder be $r(x)$ and the quotient be $q(x)$, we can write the above division as

$$\frac{f(x)}{g(x)} = q(x) + \frac{r(x)}{g(x)}, \quad \text{or} \quad f(x) = q(x)g(x) + r(x).$$

It is very important to note that the quotient and the remainder above are unique. That is, given $g(x)$ and $f(x)$, there is only one pair of polynomials $(q(x), r(x))$ such that $\deg r < \deg g$ and

$$f(x) = q(x)g(x) + r(x).$$

EXERCISE 6-1   Prove that the quotient and remainder ($q(x)$ and $r(x)$) are unique for each pair $(f(x), g(x))$.

There is a special shorthand method called **synthetic division** for dividing polynomials by expressions of the form $(x - a)$. To introduce synthetic division, we'll take you step by step through a problem which will be solved with both long division and synthetic division. Pay close attention not only to how to perform synthetic division, but also why it works.

$$
\begin{array}{r r}
x^2 + 3x + 2 & (1) \\
x - 1 \,\big|\; \overline{x^3 + 2x^2 - x + 3} & (2) \\
-\,x^3 + 1x^2 & (3) \\
\hline
3x^2 - x + 3 & (4) \\
-\,3x^2 + 3x & (5) \\
\hline
2x + 3 & (6) \\
-\,2x + 2 & (7) \\
\hline
5 & (8)
\end{array}
$$

Above we did the long division of $x - 1$ into $f(x) = x^3 + 2x^2 - x + 3$. For synthetic division (shown below), we don't write any x's. The 1 from the constant term of $x - 1$ goes to the left of the vertical line on line (9). The coefficients of $f(x)$ are then copied into the remainder of that line. Line (11) represents the coefficients of the quotient. Clearly the first such coefficient is the first coefficient of $f(x)$ (since the leading coefficient in $(x - 1)$ is 1). Hence, we copy the first coefficient of $f(x)$ in line (9) into line (11). Now we have to figure out how to get the rest of line (11).

$$
\begin{array}{r l}
1\,\big|\;\;\; 1 \;\; 2 \; -1 \;\; 3 & (9) \\
\mathbf{1} \;\;\; \mathbf{3} \;\; \mathbf{2} & (10) \\
\hline
1 \;\; 3 \;\;\; 2 \;\; 5 & (11)
\end{array}
$$

Line (10) represents the subtractions at lines (3), (5), and (7) in the long division. In the long division, we get these by subtracting the product of the quotient and $x - 1$. Since the first term in the long divisions on these three lines always cancel, we are only interested in the second terms (the boldface coefficients). These results are from multiplying $-(-1)$ by the quotient (line (1)). (The first negative comes from the fact that we are *subtracting* the products of the quotient and $x - 1$ on lines (3), (5), and (7).) The coefficients of the quotient are on line (11), so we get line (10) from multiplying line (11) and the 1 at the left of our vertical line.

Finally, how do we determine line (11), the quotient? Since the leading coefficient of $(x - 1)$ is one, the coefficients of the quotient are the coefficients of the leading terms resulting from the combinations of lines (2) and (3), lines (4) and (5), and lines (6) and (7). Note that these are just the sums of the boldface numbers and the coefficients of the original $f(x)$! Hence, we get line (11) from just adding lines (9) and (10).

Here's how synthetic division works in action. We'll divide $x - 2$ into $x^3 - 3x^2 + 7x + 4$. First we copy the 2 from the constant term of $x - 2$ and the coefficients of $x^3 - 3x^2 + 7x + 4$ into our table. Then, we copy the first coefficient into line (3):

$$
\begin{array}{r l}
2\,\big|\;\;\; 1 \; -3 \;\; 7 \;\; 4 & (1) \\
 & (2) \\
\hline
1 & (3)
\end{array}
$$

We now get the first number in line (2) by multiplying the 2 to the left of the vertical line and the 1 in line (3). After this, we add the number in line (2) to the number above it to get the next coefficient of the quotient in line (3):

$$
\begin{array}{r|rrrrl}
2 & 1 & -3 & 7 & 4 & (1) \\
& & 2 & & & (2) \\
\hline
& 1 & -1 & & & (3)
\end{array}
$$

We continue by multiplying our 2 and the next term in line (3), −1, to get the next term in line (2):

$$
\begin{array}{r|rrrrl}
2 & 1 & -3 & 7 & 4 & (1) \\
& & 2 & -2 & & (2) \\
\hline
& 1 & -1 & 5 & & (3)
\end{array}
$$

Now we can finish off the problem by getting our last terms in lines (2) and (3):

$$
\begin{array}{r|rrrrl}
2 & 1 & -3 & 7 & 4 & (1) \\
& & 2 & -2 & 10 & (2) \\
\hline
& 1 & -1 & 5 & 14 & (3)
\end{array}
$$

So what's the answer? The last line gives us the coefficients of $x^2 - x + 5$, but what's the 14 for? Compare synthetic division to long division and you'll find that 14 is the remainder, so the above synthetic division tells us that

$$
\frac{x^3 - 3x^2 + 7x + 4}{x - 2} = x^2 - x + 5 + \frac{14}{x - 2}.
$$

There are a couple of important points to remember when doing synthetic division. First, it only works when we are dividing by a linear polynomial $(x - a)$. Second, the leading coefficient of this linear term must be 1. (Look at our development of synthetic division to see why we can't use synthetic division with a linear coefficient other than 1.) Finally, in synthetic division the term to the left of the vertical line is the negative of the constant term of the linear divisor. For example, in the above problem where we divided $x - 2$ into $x^3 - 3x^2 + 7x + 4$, we put 2, not −2, at the left of the vertical line.

EXAMPLE 6-1 Use synthetic division to determine $(8x^4 - 12x^3 + 2x + 1)/(2x + 1)$.

Solution: First, we must make the coefficient of x in the divisor 1. Hence, we divide the numerator and denominator by 2 to get

$$
\frac{4x^4 - 6x^3 + x + 1/2}{x + 1/2}.
$$

Now we do our synthetic division:

$$
\begin{array}{r|rrrrr}
-1/2 & 4 & -6 & 0 & 1 & 1/2 \\
& & -2 & 4 & -2 & 1/2 \\
\hline
& 4 & -8 & 4 & -1 & 1
\end{array}
$$

(Why is there a 0 in the first line above?) Thus, we find

$$\frac{4x^4 - 6x^3 + x + 1/2}{x + 1/2} = 4x^3 - 8x^2 + 4x - 1 + \frac{1}{x + 1/2},$$

so

$$\frac{8x^4 - 12x^3 + 2x + 1}{2x + 1} = 4x^3 - 8x^2 + 4x - 1 + \frac{2}{2x + 1}.$$

EXERCISE 6-2   Use synthetic division to divide $x + 3$ into $x^5 + 3x^4 + 2x^3 - x^2 + x - 7$.

6.3   Finding Roots of Polynomials

Suppose we are given the polynomial $f(x)$ and asked to find the solutions to $f(x) = 0$. We call these solutions **roots** of the polynomial. Unfortunately, no quick and easy method like the quadratic formula exists to solve general polynomials. Instead we must go searching for the roots. Does this mean that we just have to keep guessing values for x until we find one for which $f(x) = 0$? And how will we know if we've found all such x? Fortunately, we are not completely consigned to guessing. We do have some helpful hints to guide our way.

First, if a is a root, then $(x - a)$ divides $f(x)$ evenly; that is, there is no remainder when we perform the division. To see this we write

$$f(x) = (x - a)q(x) + r(x).$$

Since $\deg r(x) < \deg(x - a) = 1$, $\deg r(x) = 0$, and $r(x)$ is some constant c. Letting $x = a$ gives

$$f(a) = (a - a)h(a) + c = c.$$

If $f(a) = 0$, we have $c = 0$, and thus there is no remainder when we divide $f(x)$ by $(x - a)$.

 EXAMPLE 6-2   Prove that the remainder upon dividing $f(x)$ by $x - a$ is $f(a)$.

    Solution: As above, we write

$$f(x) = (x - a)h(x) + r(x).$$

Since $\deg r(x) < \deg(x - a)$, $r(x)$ is a constant r. Letting $x = a$ gives $f(a) = r$, so the remainder upon dividing $f(x)$ by $x - a$ is $f(a)$. Therefore, we can use synthetic division to determine $f(a)$ by finding the remainder when $f(x)$ is divided by $(x - a)$.

EXAMPLE 6-3 $P(x)$ is a polynomial with real coefficients. When $P(x)$ is divided by $x - 1$, the remainder is 3. When $P(x)$ is divided by $x - 2$, the remainder is 5. Find the remainder when $P(x)$ is divided by $x^2 - 3x + 2$. (MAΘ 1990)

    Solution: We write

$$P(x) = (x^2 - 3x + 2)q(x) + r(x),$$

where $r(x)$ is the desired remainder. Since $\deg r(x) < \deg(x^2 - 3x + 2)$, we can write $r(x) = ax + b$ for some constants a and b. From the given information, we know $P(1) = 3$ and $P(2) = 5$. Since $x^2 - 3x + 2 = 0$ for $x = 2$ and $x = 1$, we put these values in our equation for $P(x)$, yielding

$$(0)q(1) + r(1) = a + b = P(1) = 3$$

$$(0)q(2) + r(2) = 2a + b = P(2) = 5.$$

Solving this system, we find $(a, b) = (2, 1)$, so the remainder is **$2x+1$**. Remember this method of cleverly choosing values for x in polynomial equations; it can be very useful!

The **Fundamental Theorem of Algebra** states that every polynomial has at least one root. Thus, there is at least one value a such that $f(a) = 0$. This a may be real, imaginary, rational, or irrational, but the Fundamental Theorem of Algebra assures us that at least one such root exists. Unfortunately the proof is a bit too complex for this text, but we shall put the theorem to good use by showing that any degree n polynomial has exactly n roots. This means we can write any polynomial $f(x)$ as

$$f(x) = a_n x^n + a_{n-1} x^{n-1} + \cdots + a_1 x + a_0 = a_n(x - r_1)(x - r_2) \cdots (x - r_n).$$

The r_i are the roots of the polynomial and they are not necessarily real or rational. It should be clear why $f(r_i) = 0$.

To show that all polynomials can be written in such a fashion we invoke the Fundamental Theorem of Algebra. By this theorem, we know that for some number r_1 we can write

$$f(x) = (x - r_1)q_1(x).$$

Since $\deg f = n = \deg[(x - r_1)q_1(x)] = \deg(x - r_1) + \deg q_1$, we find $\deg q_1 = n - 1$. Now we apply the Fundamental Theorem to $q_1(x)$ to get

$$f(x) = (x - r_1)(x - r_2)q_2(x),$$

where $\deg q_2 = n - 2$. Thus, we can continue applying the Fundamental Theorem until finally we have the desired factorization

$$f(x) = a_n(x - r_1)(x - r_2) \cdots (x - r_n).$$

Showing the roots exist is one thing; finding them is another thing altogether. Rather than provide a recipe-like formula, the best we can do is give a batch of methods to guide us to the roots.

For the *rational* roots of a polynomial, there is a method we can use to narrow the search. Although there are infinitely many rational numbers we could guess as roots of $f(x)$, the only ones which have a chance of being roots are given by the **Rational Root Theorem**. For any polynomial

$$f(x) = a_n x^n + a_{n-1} x^{n-1} + \cdots + a_0$$

with integer coefficients, all rational roots are of the form p/q, where $|p|$ and $|q|$ are relatively prime integers, p divides a_0 evenly, and q divides a_n evenly. The Rational Root Theorem will be proven as an example on page 58.

EXAMPLE 6-4 Find all the roots of $x^3 - 6x^2 + 11x - 6$.

Solution: From the Rational Root Theorem, we know that all possible roots are of the form p/q, where p divides -6 and q divides 1. Thus the possible roots are $\{\pm 1, \pm 2, \pm 3, \pm 6\}$. If we substitute these in the polynomial, we find that $\{1, 2, 3\}$ all satisfy $f(x) = 0$, so these are the three roots of the polynomial. (How do we know there aren't any more?)

EXAMPLE 6-5 Find all the roots of $2x^3 - 5x^2 + 4x - 1$.

Solution: Once again we apply the Rational Root Theorem and determine that the possible roots are $\{\pm 1/2, \pm 1\}$. Trying these, we find that both 1 and $1/2$ are roots of the polynomial. We know that there must be one more (why?), but we also know that no other rationals could possibly be roots. We might think that the third root is irrational or perhaps imaginary, but as we will see, no polynomial with rational coefficients can have just one irrational or one imaginary root. Thus, we come to the conclusion that this polynomial must have a double root, just like quadratic expressions which are perfect squares, such as $x^2 + 2x + 1$. Indeed, in this problem, we can use synthetic division to find $(2x^3 - 5x^2 + 4x - 1)/(x - 1) = 2x^2 - 3x + 1$. Factoring this quadratic, we find

$$2x^3 - 5x^2 + 4x - 1 = (x - 1)^2(2x - 1),$$

so that the root $x = 1$ is a **double root**, meaning the factor $(x - 1)$ occurs twice.

We have already come across two shortcomings of using the Rational Root Theorem alone. One is that we will miss multiple roots. Another is that it could still end up taking a very long time, as there are many numbers for polynomials like $12x^4 - x - 60$ which satisfy the Rational Root Theorem criteria.

To avoid missing multiple roots and to shorten our search for the roots, when we find a root r_1 of the polynomial, we divide $(x - r_1)$ into $f(x)$, as

$$f(x) = (x - r_1)q(x).$$

Then, we continue our search for roots with $q(x)$, because all roots of $q(x)$ are also roots of $f(x)$. As we saw in the previous section, synthetic division provides a swift method for performing the division.

EXAMPLE 6-6 Prove the Rational Root Theorem.

Proof: Let p/q be a rational root of the polynomial $f(x)$, where p and q are relatively prime positive integers. The case where the root is $-p/q$ is virtually the same. Since p/q is a root, we have

$$f\left(p/q\right) = a_n \left(\frac{p}{q}\right)^n + a_{n-1} \left(\frac{p}{q}\right)^{n-1} + \cdots + a_0 = 0.$$

Multiplying by q^n gives

$$a_n p^n + a_{n-1} p^{n-1} q + \cdots + a_1 p q^{n-1} + a_0 q^n = 0.$$

Now look at this equation modulo p. The first n terms on the left will become 0 since they are multiples of p, so we have

$$a_n p^n + a_{n-1} p^{n-1} q + \cdots + a_1 p q^{n-1} + a_0 q^n \equiv 0 + \cdots + 0 + a_0 q^n \ (\text{mod } p) \equiv 0 \ (\text{mod } p)$$

Thus, $a_0 q^n \equiv 0 \pmod{p}$, so $p | a_0 q^n$. Since p and q are relatively prime, it follows that $p | a_0$.

By the same argument, we can evaluate the sum mod q to show that $q | a_n p^n$. Thus $q | a_n$ and the proof is complete.

There are a few more guides to tell us where to look for roots. The first is **Descartes' Rule of Signs**, which gives us a method to count how many positive and how many negative roots there are. We do this by counting sign changes. The number of sign changes in the coefficients of $f(x)$ (meaning we list the coefficients from first to last and count how many times they change from positive to negative) tells us the maximum number of positive roots the polynomial has, and the number of sign changes in the coefficients of $f(-x)$ gives us the maximum number of negative roots the polynomial has. Hence, for

$$f(x) = 3x^5 + 2x^4 - 3x^2 + 2x - 1,$$

there are at most 3 positive roots and at most 2 negative roots (since $f(-x) = -3x^5 + 2x^4 - 3x^2 - 2x - 1$). Furthermore, the actual number of positive or negative roots will always differ by an even number from the aforementioned maximum, so our above $f(x)$ has 1 or 3 positive roots and 0 or 2 negative roots.

Another root location method is finding upper and lower bounds. Suppose we use synthetic division to find $f(x)/(x - c)$ where $f(x)$ has a positive leading coefficient and $c \geq 0$ as below:

$$\begin{array}{r|rrrr} 3 & 1 & -1 & 2 & 6 \\ & & 3 & 6 & 24 \\ \hline & 1 & 2 & 8 & 30 \end{array}$$

If all the resulting coefficients in the quotient are positive (including the remainder), as in the example above, then no roots are greater than c. (Why?) This c is called an **upper bound** on the solutions since no roots can be higher. Similarly, if $c < 0$ and the coefficients of the quotient and remainder alternate in sign, then there is no root smaller than c (which we then call a **lower bound** for the roots). Locating upper and lower bounds will often help you shorten your search for roots.

Lastly, recall from our discussion of quadratic equations in Volume 1 that complex roots and roots of the form $a + b\sqrt{c}$ come in pairs if the coefficients of the quadratic are rational. This is also true of any polynomial with rational coefficients. For example, if the complex number $z = a + bi$ is a root of $f(x)$, we have

$$f(z) = a_n z^n + a_{n-1} z^{n-1} + \cdots + a_1 z + a_0 = 0.$$

Now we use some of our useful properties of complex numbers, such as $\overline{w + z} = \overline{w} + \overline{z}$, $\overline{z^k} = (\overline{z})^k$, and $w = z$ implies $\overline{w} = \overline{z}$. Applying these principles to $f(z)$, we have

$$\overline{a_n z^n + a_{n-1} z^{n-1} + \cdots + a_1 z + a_0} = \overline{0}$$
$$\overline{a_n z^n} + \overline{a_{n-1} z^{n-1}} + \cdots + \overline{a_1 z} + \overline{a_0} = 0$$
$$a_n \overline{z}^n + a_{n-1} \overline{z}^{n-1} + \cdots + a_1 \overline{z} + a_0 = 0.$$

Hence, if $f(z) = 0$, then $f(\overline{z}) = 0$, so $\overline{z}$ is also a root. This proof, with slight modifications, can be used to show that if $z = a + b\sqrt{c}$ is a root, then $z = a - b\sqrt{c}$ is also a root.

EXAMPLE 6-7 Find all of the solutions to the equation

$$x^4 - 10x^3 + 35x^2 - 50x + 24 = 0.$$

Solution: Since the signs of the coefficients of $f(-x)$ are all positive, none of the roots are negative. This cuts our search in half. Now we use the Rational Root Theorem to deduce that the roots are all factors of 24. (Why?) We'll start with 1 (usually the best place to start). Synthetic division yields

$$\begin{array}{r|rrrrr} 1 & 1 & -10 & 35 & -50 & 24 \\ & & 1 & -9 & 26 & -24 \\ \hline & 1 & -9 & 26 & -24 & 0 \end{array}$$

Since there is no remainder, $x - 1$ is a factor. Now we continue our search, not with $x^4 - 10x^3 + 35x^2 - 50x + 24$, but with the quotient above, since

$$x^4 - 10x^3 + 35x^2 - 50x + 24 = (x - 1)(x^3 - 9x^2 + 26x - 24).$$

Continuing in this manner we find that $x = 2$ is also a root and we have

$$x^4 - 10x^3 + 35x^2 - 50x + 24 = (x - 1)(x - 2)(x^2 - 7x + 12).$$

Factoring the quadratic yields $(x - 1)(x - 2)(x - 3)(x - 4) = 0$ and our solutions are **1, 2, 3**, and **4**.

 EXAMPLE 6-8 I'm trying to find the roots of $f(x) = 2x^4 - 15x^3 + 15x^2 + 20x - 12$. I start with $x = 1$. After finding $f(1) = 10$, what should I try next?

Solution: Since $f(0) = -12$ and $f(1) = 10$, there must be some number c between 0 and 1 such that $f(c) = 0$, because $f(0)$ and $f(1)$ have opposite signs. (Graph $y = f(x)$, noting that the points $(0, -12)$ and $(1, 10)$ are on the graph, to see why there's a root between $x = 0$ and $x = 1$.) From the Rational Root Theorem, the only possible rational root between 0 and 1 is $1/2$. Using synthetic division we find that this indeed works.

Using this 'location principle' we can zero in on roots. Namely, if $f(a)$ and $f(b)$ have opposite signs, then there is a root between a and b.

EXERCISE 6-3 Find the roots of $x^4 + x^3 + 2x^2 + 17x - 21$.

EXERCISE 6-4 Given a quartic polynomial with rational coefficients and roots $3 - i$ and $4 + \sqrt{2}$, find the other two roots.

6.4   Coefficients and Roots

Suppose we are asked to find the sum of the roots of a polynomial. We could just find the roots and add them all, but that may not be easy to do and could take a long time. Of course, there is a better way. For example, remember from Volume 1 that the coefficients of a quadratic are directly related to the sum and product of the roots.

The coefficients of a polynomial tell us much more than just the sum of the roots. To see this, let the roots of $f(x) = x^3 + a_2x^2 + a_1x + a_0$ be r_1, r_2, and r_3, so we can factor $f(x)$ as

$$f(x) = (x - r_1)(x - r_2)(x - r_3).$$

If we multiply this out we get (check and see)

$$f(x) = x^3 - (r_1 + r_2 + r_3)x^2 + (r_1r_2 + r_2r_3 + r_1r_3)x - r_1r_2r_3.$$

By comparing this with $f(x) = x^3 + a_2x^2 + a_1x + a_0$, we see that the coefficients not only give us the sum of the roots $(-a_2)$, but the product of the roots $(-a_0)$ and the sum of the products of the roots taken two at a time $(a_1 = r_1r_2 + r_2r_3 + r_1r_3)$.

Now, what if the leading coefficient of the cubic is something besides 1? Like we did with quadratics, we change the problem to one involving a **monic** polynomial, i.e. a polynomial with leading coefficient 1. The roots of

$$f(x) = a_3x^3 + a_2x^2 + a_1x + a_0 = 0$$

are the same as those of

$$g(x) = \frac{f(x)}{a_3} = x^3 + \frac{a_2}{a_3}x^2 + \frac{a_1}{a_3}x + \frac{a_0}{a_3} = 0,$$

since if $f(x) = 0$, then $g(x) = f(x)/a_3 = 0$. Thus, the sum of the roots of $g(x)$, and therefore $f(x)$, is $-a_2/a_3$, the product of the roots is $-a_0/a_3$, and so on.

Now a quick definition and we will be ready to use these results on any polynomial, not just cubics. Suppose our polynomial has n roots. We define the sum of all products of the roots taken k at a time, or the kth symmetric sum, as the sum of all products formed by multiplying k of the n roots. Thus, if we have 4 roots which are 1, 1, 2, and 3, the second symmetric sum is

$$1 \cdot 1 + 1 \cdot 2 + 1 \cdot 3 + 1 \cdot 2 + 1 \cdot 3 + 2 \cdot 3 = 17.$$

For the general polynomial $f(x) = a_nx^n + \cdots + a_0$, the kth symmetric sum of the roots is $(-1)^k a_{n-k}/a_n$. We can prove this through algebra much like our $n = 3$ case above. The proof is made rigorous through induction.

EXERCISE 6-5 Use induction to prove the assertion that the kth symmetric sum is $(-1)^k a_{n-k}/a_n$.

EXAMPLE 6-9 Find the constant term of a quartic polynomial with rational coefficients that has two roots equal to $2 - i$ and $2 + \sqrt{3}$.

Solution: The other two roots are $2 + i$ and $2 - \sqrt{3}$, so the product of the roots is $(2 + i)(2 - i)(2 + \sqrt{3})(2 - \sqrt{3}) = (5)(1) = 5$. The constant term of a quartic is equal to $(-1)^4 = 1$ times the product of the roots, so the constant term is **5**.

EXAMPLE 6-10 If three roots of $x^4 + Ax^2 + Bx + C = 0$ are $-1, 2$, and 3, then what is the value of $2C - AB$? (MAΘ 1992)

Solution: Since the coefficient of x^3 is 0, the sum of the roots is 0. Thus the fourth root is −4. Hence

$$\begin{aligned}
A &= (-1)(2) + (-1)(3) + (-1)(-4) + (2)(3) + (2)(-4) + (3)(-4) = -15 \\
B &= -[(-1)(2)(3) + (-1)(2)(-4) + (-1)(3)(-4) + (2)(3)(-4)] = 10 \\
C &= (-1)(2)(3)(-4) = 24,
\end{aligned}$$

so $2C - AB = \mathbf{198}$.

EXERCISE 6-6 Find the largest solution of $x^3 - 27x^2 + 242x - 720 = 0$ given that one root equals the average of the other two roots. (MAΘ 1990)

6.5 Transforming Polynomials

Through the following examples, we will examine how to transform polynomials in various ways.

EXAMPLE 6-11 Find the polynomial whose roots are the reciprocals of the roots of $x^4 - 3x^2 + x - 9$.

Solution: Once again, let the given polynomial be $f(x)$ and the roots be r_1, r_2, r_3, and r_4. One equation whose solutions are the reciprocals of these is just $f(1/x) = 0$ because

$$f\left(\frac{1}{1/r_i}\right) = f(r_i) = 0.$$

Thus, the solutions of $f(1/x) = 0$ are the reciprocals of the roots of $f(x)$, as claimed. Unfortunately, $f(1/x)$ is not a polynomial. On the other hand, the function given by $g(x) = x^4 f(1/x)$, which also has roots $1/r_i$, is a polynomial:

$$g(x) = x^4 \left(\frac{1}{x^4} - \frac{3}{x^2} + \frac{1}{x} - 9\right) = -9x^4 + x^3 - 3x^2 + 1.$$

This $g(x)$ is our desired polynomial. Now compare $g(x)$ to $f(x)$. Look closely and you'll see that the coefficients of $g(x)$ are the same as those of $f(x)$ *in reverse order!* We can prove that this is true in general in the same way. Let the general polynomial $f(x)$ be $f(x) = a_n x^n + a_{n-1} x^{n-1} + \cdots + a_0$ with roots $r_1, \ldots, r_n$. The solutions to $f(1/x) = 0$ are $x = 1/r_1, 1/r_2, \ldots, 1/r_n$, because again we have

$$f\left(\frac{1}{1/r_i}\right) = f(r_i) = 0.$$

Thus, the solutions of $f(1/x) = 0$ are the reciprocals of the roots of $f(x)$. The desired polynomial is then

$$g(x) = x^n f(1/x) = x^n \left(\frac{a_n}{x^n} + \frac{a_{n-1}}{x^{n-1}} + \cdots + \frac{a_1}{x} + a_0\right) = a_0 x^n + a_1 x^{n-1} + \cdots + a_n,$$

or the original polynomial with the coefficients reversed.

EXAMPLE 6-12 Find a polynomial whose roots are twice those of $f(x) = x^4 - 3x^2 + x - 9$.

Solution: If we are given a polynomial $f(x) = a_n x^n + a_{n-1} x^{n-1} + \cdots + a_0$, a polynomial with roots which are k times the roots of $f(x)$ is $f(x/k)$. (Let the roots of $f(x)$ be $r_1, r_2, \ldots, r_n$; then for $x = kr_1, kr_2, \ldots, kr_n$, we have $f(x/k) = f(r_i) = 0$.) Hence, the desired polynomial is

$$f(x/k) = \frac{a_n x^n}{k^n} + \frac{a_{n-1} x^{n-1}}{k^{n-1}} + \cdots + \frac{a_1}{k} + a_0.$$

Multiplying both sides by k^n to simplify the expression (i.e. to get rid of the fractions), we have

$$g(x) = k^n f(x/k) = a_n x^n + k a_{n-1} x^{n-1} + \cdots + k^{n-1} a_1 x + k^n a_0$$

as a polynomial with roots kr_i. We form $g(x)$ by multiplying the coefficients of $f(x)$ in turn by 1, k, $k^2, \ldots, k^n$. Hence, one answer to our problem is

$$g(x) = x^4 - (2^2)(3)x^2 + (2^3)x - (2^4)(9) = x^4 - 12x^2 + 8x - 144.$$

EXAMPLE 6-13 Find the polynomial whose roots are half the reciprocals of the roots of $5x^4 + 12x^3 + 8x^2 - 6x - 1$.

Solution: Let the roots of this polynomial be a, b, c, and d. We seek the polynomial whose roots are $1/2a$, $1/2b$, $1/2c$, and $1/2d$.

The polynomial whose roots are $2a$, $2b$, $2c$, and $2d$ is

$$g(x) = 5x^4 + 12(2)x^3 + 8(2^2)x^2 - 6(2^3)x - 1(2^4) = 5x^4 + 24x^3 + 32x^2 - 48x - 16.$$

The polynomial we desire is the one whose roots are reciprocals of the roots of $g(x)$, or

$$h(x) = -16x^4 - 48x^3 + 32x^2 + 24x + 5.$$

EXAMPLE 6-14 Find an equation whose roots are 3 greater than those of $x^4 - 3x^3 - 3x^2 + 4x - 6$.

Solution: Let the given polynomial be $f(x)$ and the roots be r_1, r_2, r_3, and r_4. In the spirit of the examples involving reciprocals and multiples of roots, consider the polynomial $g(x) = f(x - 3)$. We have

$$g(r_i + 3) = f(r_i + 3 - 3) = f(r_i) = 0,$$

so the roots of $g(x)$ are 3 greater than those of $f(x)$. Hence, $g(x)$ is the desired polynomial and our answer is

$$g(x) = f(x - 3) = (x - 3)^4 - 3(x - 3)^3 - 3(x - 3)^2 + 4(x - 3) - 6.$$

Similarly, we can show that the polynomial whose roots are k greater than those of a general polynomial $h(x)$ is $h(x - k)$. However, the above expression for $g(x)$ will take quite a bit of time to evaluate, so it is useful to find a swifter method if possible.

We will determine $f(x - 3)$ term by term. First we find the constant term, which is just the polynomial evaluated at $x = 0$, or $f(-3)$. (Why?) Now we must find the coefficient of x. This is tricky. If we subtract the constant term from a polynomial and divide the result by x, the constant term of the new polynomial is the coefficient of x in the original. This is shown for $f(x)$ below:

$$[f(x) - f(0)]/x = \left[x^4 - 3x^3 - 3x^2 + 4x - 6 - (-6)\right]/x = x^3 - 3x^2 - 3x + 4.$$

Now we need a swift way to find $\left(f(x-3) - f(-3)\right)/x$ in order to get the coefficient of x in $f(x-3)$. Remember that we can write $f(x)$ as

$$f(x) = (x+3)q_1(x) + f(-3)$$

for some polynomial $q_1(x)$. This leads us to our short cut:

$$f(x-3) = (x-3+3)q_1(x-3) + f(-3) = xq_1(x-3) + f(-3),$$

or

$$\frac{f(x-3) - f(-3)}{x} = q_1(x-3).$$

Since we want the constant term of $q_1(x-3)$, we want $q_1(-3)$ (since setting $x = 0$ eliminates all terms except the constant term). Now our problem is determining $q_1(x)$. Synthetic division of $f(x)$ by $(x+3)$ gives us this polynomial, and synthetic division of $q_1(x)$ by $(x+3)$ gives us the desired remainder $q_1(-3)$. By the same argument as above, to find the coefficient of x^2 we divide $q_1(x-3) - q_1(-3)$ by x and find the constant term of the resulting polynomial. Once again, synthetic division of $q_1(x)$ by $x+3$ can be used to find this polynomial and constant term. Since after each synthetic division, the resulting quotient is used for the next synthetic division, we can just 'stack' our divisions as below:

$$
\begin{array}{r|rrrrr}
-3 & 1 & -3 & -3 & 4 & -6 \\
   &   & -3 & 18 & -45 & 123 \\
\hline
-3 & 1 & -6 & 15 & -41 & \mathbf{117} \\
   &   & -3 & 27 & -126 & \\
\hline
-3 & 1 & -9 & 42 & \mathbf{-167} & \\
   &   & -3 & 36 & & \\
\hline
-3 & 1 & -12 & \mathbf{78} & & \\
   &   & -3 & & & \\
\hline
-3 & 1 & \mathbf{-15} & & & \\
\hline
   & 1 & & & &
\end{array}
$$

Our desired coefficients, then, are the boldface remainders above, so the polynomial $f(x-3)$ is

$$x^4 - 15x^3 + 78x^2 - 167x + 117.$$

What we have done here to describe this method is not a complete proof, but we hope it gives you a clear idea why this 'trick' works. While this method is somewhat quicker and more reliable for higher degree polynomials, it is also easy to forget. It is most important to remember that the polynomial whose roots are k more than those of polynomial $f(x)$ is always given by $f(x-k)$.

EXERCISE 6-7 The roots of $f(x) = 3x^3 - 14x^2 + x + 62 = 0$ are a, b, and c. Find the value of

$$\frac{1}{a+3} + \frac{1}{b+3} + \frac{1}{c+3}.$$

(MAΘ 1991)

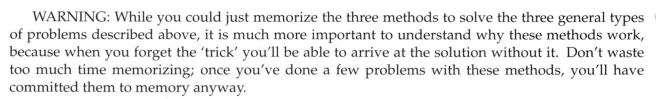

WARNING: While you could just memorize the three methods to solve the three general types of problems described above, it is much more important to understand why these methods work, because when you forget the 'trick' you'll be able to arrive at the solution without it. Don't waste too much time memorizing; once you've done a few problems with these methods, you'll have committed them to memory anyway.

6.6 Newton's Sums

Given $x+y$ and xy, how would we find x^2+y^2? As we saw in Volume 1, we write $x^2+y^2 = (x+y)^2-2xy$. Let's try a tougher one. Write $x^3 + y^3$ in terms of $x^2 + y^2$, $x + y$, and xy without squaring or cubing any of these expressions. We can only get $x^3 + y^3$ from the product $(x + y)(x^2 + y^2) = x^3 + y^3 + xy^2 + x^2y$. Hence, we have

$$x^3 + y^3 = (x + y)(x^2 + y^2) - xy^2 - x^2y = (x + y)(x^2 + y^2) - xy(x + y).$$

Now let x and y be the roots of the quadratic $a_2z^2 + a_1z + a_0 = 0$ and $s_k = x^k + y^k$. Our above expression can then be written as

$$s_3 = -\frac{a_1}{a_2}s_2 - \frac{a_0}{a_2}s_1$$

since $x + y = -a_1/a_2$ and $xy = a_0/a_2$. Rearranging this, we can write

$$a_2s_3 + a_1s_2 + a_0s_1 = 0.$$

This nice form suggests that other similar relationships may be true as well.

EXAMPLE 6-15 Show that if s_k is the sum of the kth powers of the roots of $a_3x^3 + a_2x^2 + a_1x + a_0$, then $a_3s_2 + a_2s_1 + 2a_1 = 0$.

Proof: Let $S = a_3(s_2 + a_2s_1/a_3 + 2a_1/a_3)$. We wish to show that $S = 0$. Using our relationships between the roots of the polynomial, which we call r, s, and t, and its coefficients, we have

$$
\begin{aligned}
S &= a_3\left(\left(r^2 + s^2 + t^2\right) + \left(-(r + s + t)(r + s + t)\right) + 2(rs + rt + st)\right) \\
&= a_3\left(\left(r^2 + s^2 + t^2\right) - (r^2 + s^2 + t^2 + 2rs + 2rt + 2st) + (2rs + 2rt + 2st)\right) \\
&= 0.
\end{aligned}
$$

Perhaps you see where we're going with this. The family of equations which relates the sum of the mth powers of the roots of a polynomial to the coefficients of the polynomial as we've done above is called **Newton's sums**. If we let s_m be the sum of the mth powers of the roots of $f(x) = a_nx^n + \cdots + a_0$, then the Newton's sums can be written as

$$a_ns_1 + a_{n-1} = 0$$

$$a_ns_2 + a_{n-1}s_1 + 2a_{n-2} = 0$$

$$a_ns_3 + a_{n-1}s_2 + a_{n-2}s_1 + 3a_{n-3} = 0$$

$$a_ns_4 + a_{n-1}s_3 + a_{n-2}s_2 + a_{n-3}s_1 + 4a_{n-4} = 0$$

and so on.

EXERCISE 6-8 What happens to the Newton's sum $a_n s_k + a_{n-1} s_{k-1} + \cdots + k a_{n-k} = 0$ when $n < k$?

EXAMPLE 6-16 Find the sum of the cubes of the solutions of $x^2 - 3x + 3 = 0$.

   Solution: We use Newton's sums:

$$s_1 + (-3) = 0, \text{ so } s_1 = 3;$$

$$s_2 + (-3)s_1 + 2(3) = 0, \text{ so } s_2 = 3.$$

Now, in the next Newton sum, we have a term $3a_{-1}$, but there is no a_{-1}, so this term is just 0. We find

$$s_3 + (-3)s_2 + 3s_1 = 0, \text{ so } s_3 = \mathbf{0}.$$

This is much easier than cubing the solutions to the quadratic.

EXERCISE 6-9 Find the sum of the cubes of the roots of $2x^4 + 3x^3 + x^2 - 4x - 4$.

   As we've seen, Newton's sums are just a result of algebraically manipulating expressions involving the roots of polynomials. The Newton's sums equations can be proven in general using the same algebraic techniques as above. Those of you very comfortable with summation notation and manipulation should try to do so. The leading term in every Newton's sum is $a_n s_k$. We present here a less algebraic proof for all Newton's sum equations in which $k \geq n$ because it involves a very important problem solving technique.

   Let the roots of the polynomial $f(x)$ be $r_1, r_2, \ldots, r_n$. Since these are solutions of the equation $f(x) = 0$, for each r_i we have

$$f(r_i) = a_n r_i^n + a_{n-1} r_i^{n-1} + \cdots + a_0 = 0.$$

Multiplying each of these equations by r_i^{k-n} yields

$$a_n r_1^k + a_{n-1} r_1^{(k-1)} + \cdots + a_0 r_1^{k-n} = 0$$

$$a_n r_2^k + a_{n-1} r_2^{(k-1)} + \cdots + a_0 r_2^{k-n} = 0$$

$$\vdots$$

$$a_n r_n^k + a_{n-1} r_n^{(k-1)} + \cdots + a_0 r_n^{k-n} = 0.$$

We can add all of these equations, which gives us

$$a_n \left(r_1^k + \cdots + r_n^k \right) + a_{n-1} \left(r_1^{k-1} + \cdots + r_n^{k-1} \right) + \cdots + a_0 \left(r_1^{k-n} + \cdots + r_n^{k-n} \right) = 0.$$

Thus, we find

$$a_n s_k + a_{n-1} s_{k-1} + \cdots + a_0 s_{k-n} = 0.$$

In the special case where $k = n$, we have

$$s_{k-n} = s_0 = r_1^0 + r_2^0 + \cdots + r_n^0 = 1 + 1 + \cdots + 1 = n,$$

so the Newton sum is

$$a_n s_n + a_{n-1} s_{n-1} + \cdots + n a_0 = 0.$$

EXAMPLE 6-17 If $r_1, r_2, \ldots, r_{1000}$ are the roots of $x^{1000} - 10x + 10 = 0$, find $r_1^{1000} + r_2^{1000} + \cdots + r_{1000}^{1000}$.

Solution: Since only a_{1000}, a_1, and a_0 are nonzero, we can write the 1000th Newton sum as

$$s_{1000} - 10s_1 + 1000(10) = 0.$$

Since the coefficient of x^{999} is 0, $s_1 = 0$ and $s_{1000} = \mathbf{-10000}$.

Problems to Solve for Chapter 6

84. Find the remainder when $x^{13} + 1$ is divided by $x - 1$. (AHSME 1950)

85. Find all the roots of $2y^4 - 9y^3 + 14y^2 + 6y - 63 = 0$.

86. Find all values of m which will make $x + 2$ a factor of $x^3 + 3m^2x^2 + mx + 4$. (MAΘ 1991)

87. Find the product of the nth roots of 1. (MAΘ 1991)

88. The equation $x^4 - 16x^3 + 94x^2 + px + q = 0$ has two double roots. Find $p + q$. (MAΘ 1991)

89. Let $f(x) = ax^7 + bx^3 + cx - 5$, where a, b, and c are constants. If $f(-7) = 7$, then find $f(7)$. (AHSME 1982)

90. For nonzero constants c and d, the equation $4x^3 - 12x^2 + cx + d = 0$ has two real roots which add to give 0. Find d/c. (MAΘ 1991)

91. The equation with roots $3+\sqrt{2}, 3-\sqrt{2}, -3+i\sqrt{2}$, and $-3-i\sqrt{2}$ is in the form $x^4+Ax^3+Bx^2+Cx+D = 0$. Find $A + B + C + D$. (MAΘ 1991)

92. Polynomial $P(x)$ contains only terms of odd degree. When $P(x)$ is divided by $x - 3$, the remainder is 6. What is the remainder when $P(x)$ is divided by $x^2 - 9$? (MAΘ 1991)

93. Let

$$p(x) = a_nx^n + a_{n-1}x^{n-1} + \cdots + a_1x + a_0,$$

where the coefficients a_i are integers. If $p(0)$ and $p(1)$ are both odd, show that $p(x)$ has no integral roots. (Canada 1971)

94. If $x^4 + 4x^3 + 6px^2 + 4qx + r$ is exactly divisible by $x^3 + 3x^2 + 9x + 3$, then find $(p + q)r$. (AHSME 1965)

95. Let r, s, and t be the roots of $x^3 - 6x^2 + 5x - 7 = 0$. Find

$$\frac{1}{r^2} + \frac{1}{s^2} + \frac{1}{t^2}.$$

(MAΘ 1991)

96. Suppose $x = a + bi$ is a solution of the polynomial equation

$$c_4z^4 + ic_3z^3 + c_2z^2 + ic_1z + c_0 = 0,$$

where c_0, c_1, c_2, c_3, c_4, a, and b are real constants and $i^2 = -1$. Show that $-a + bi$ is also a solution. (AHSME 1982)

97. If $q_1(x)$ and r_1 are the quotient and remainder, respectively, when the polynomial x^8 is divided by $x + \frac{1}{2}$, and if $q_2(x)$ and r_2 are the quotient and remainder, respectively, when $q_1(x)$ is divided by $x + \frac{1}{2}$, then find r_2. (AHSME 1979)

98. Solve the equation $(x + 1)(x + 2)(x + 3)(x + 4) = -1$. (M&IQ 3)

99. Let $(1 + x + x^2)^n = a_0 + a_1 x + a_2 x^2 + \cdots + a_{2n} x^{2n}$ be an identity in x. Find $a_0 + a_2 + a_4 + \cdots + a_{2n}$ in terms of n. (AHSME 1966)

100. Give the remainder when $x^{203} - 1$ is divided by $x^4 - 1$. (MAΘ 1991)

101. Given the equation

$$\left(x^2 - 3x - 2\right)^2 - 3(x^2 - 3x - 2) - 2 - x = 0,$$

prove that the roots of the equation $x^2 - 4x - 2 = 0$ are roots of the initial equation and find all real roots of the given equation. (Bulgaria 1993)

102. Let k be a positive integer. Find all polynomials with real coefficients which satisfy the equation

$$P(P(x)) = [P(x)]^k.$$

(Canada 1975)

103. If a, b, c, d are the solutions of the equation $x^4 - mx - 3 = 0$, then find the polynomial with leading coefficient 3 whose roots are

$$\frac{a + b + c}{d^2}, \quad \frac{a + b + d}{c^2}, \quad \frac{a + c + d}{b^2}, \quad \text{and} \quad \frac{b + c + d}{a^2}.$$

(AHSME 1981)

104. For $n > 1$ let $a_1, a_2, \ldots, a_n$ be n distinct integers. Prove that the polynomial $f(x) = (x - a_1)(x - a_2)\cdots(x - a_n) - 1$ cannot be written as $g(x)h(x)$ where g and h are nonconstant polynomials with integer coefficients. (MOP)

Chapter 7

Functions

7.1 The Inverse of a Function

A function is a machine. It takes one thing in, and outputs something else. But what if we ran this in reverse? If we cram something into the output slot, is the machine flexible enough to give us back the input which would create that output when run forwards?

The **inverse** function to a function $f(x)$ is a new function $g(x)$ which "undoes" f, so that $g(f(x)) = x$. In other words, if you put an input x into f, then put the output, $f(x)$, into g, you will get back x—the original input.

EXAMPLE 7-1 Prove that if g is the inverse of f, then f is the inverse of g.

Solution: Consider some x in the domain of f, so that $f(x) = y$ for some y. By the definition of the inverse, we have $g(y) = x$. Substituting this for x, we have $f(g(y)) = y$. Since the range of g is the domain of f, we don't have to worry about $g(y)$ not being in the domain of f; thus, since $f(g(y)) = y$ holds for all y in the domain of g, f is the inverse of g. *The inverse of the inverse is the original function.*

EXAMPLE 7-2 Let's find the inverse g of the function $f(x) = x/(1 + x)$. Since g is the inverse of f, we have from Example 7-1 that f is the inverse of g, so that

$$f(g(x)) = g(x)/[1 + g(x)] = x.$$

Solving the second equality for $g(x)$, we obtain $g(x) = x/(1 - x)$.

EXERCISE 7-1 Find the inverse function of $f(x) = \sqrt[3]{x}$.

The method of Example 7-2 can be used to find the inverse of many functions.

The inverse of a function $f(x)$ is denoted by $f^{-1}(x)$. To be really perverse, we can iterate the inverse function, as we iterated functions in Volume 1: $f^{-1}(f^{-1}(x)) = f^{-2}(x)$, and so on.

EXAMPLE 7-3 The "composition exponents" can be manipulated in some of the same ways as normal exponents. For example,

$$(f^3 \circ f^4)(x) = f(f(f(f(f(f(f(x))))))) = f^7(x);$$

that is, we can add the "exponents." As we warned in Volume 1, though, don't let these similarities confuse function composition with exponentiation.

EXERCISE 7-2 To what should $f^0(x)$ correspond? Is it equal to $[f(x)]^0$?

Does every function have an inverse function? The inverse, if it exists, must itself be a function. Consider the function $f(x) = x^2$. The inverse is found by setting $x = (g(x))^2$, so that $g(x) = \pm\sqrt{x}$. But this is not a function! Why? Consider the input $x = 4$; $g(4)$ could be either 2 or -2, but a function can have only one output.

Thus x^2 does not have an inverse function. In general, no function can have an inverse function if it assigns two different x values to the same y, because in the inverse function, that value y won't know which of the two x's to go to. A function which *has* an inverse function takes different x values to different y values, and is thus called **one to one function**, which is often written 1:1. One way to see if a function has an inverse function is to graph it. If any horizontal line crosses through the function at more than one point, then there is a y which can be generated by two different x's, and the function cannot be one to one.

EXERCISE 7-3 Which are 1:1?

   i. $f(x) = x^3$

   ii. $g(x) = |x|$

   iii. $h(x) = \lfloor x \rfloor$

   iv. $j(x) = x/2$

The most interesting thing about inverses comes last. What happens when we draw the graphs of a function and its inverse on the same axes? Because the one takes x to y, and the other takes y to x, the graph of the inverse is exactly the original graph with the axes reversed. In practice, this means that the graph is flipped over the line $x = y$ to form the graph of the inverse. Examine the picture at right to see this graphically, then try graphing some yourself to get a feel.

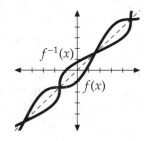

7.2   Functional Identities

An important thing to consider in some problems involving functions is the identities they might satisfy. For example, the logarithm $f(x) = \log x$ always satisfies

$$f(xy) = f(x) + f(y),$$

since $\log(xy) = \log x + \log y$ for any positive x and y.

In our study of trigonometry we have already encountered some other functional identities, though they were not identified as such. If we let $f(x) = \sin x$ and $g(x) = \cos x$, then two important trig identities can be expressed as

$$f(x + y) = f(x)g(y) + f(y)g(x)$$

and

$$[f(x)]^2 + [g(x)]^2 = 1.$$

EXERCISE 7-4   Verify these two trigonometric identities.

EXERCISE 7-5   Which of the following identities are satisfied by $f(x) = |x|$?

     i. $f(xy) = f(x)f(y)$

    ii. $f(x + y) = f(x) + f(y)$

   iii. $f(f(x)) = x$

EXERCISE 7-6   Does the floor function (greatest integer function) $f(x)$ satisfy $f(nx) = nf(x)$

     i. if both n and x are integers?

    ii. if n is an integer but x is any real?

   iii. if n and x are any reals?

EXERCISE 7-7   Find some identities which are satisfied by $f(x) = x$.

7.3   Solving Functional Identities

We have seen how some functions satisfy interesting identities, but the real trick is to go backwards—given only the identity, to find the functions which satisfy it. There are many general techniques for this.

7.3.1   Isolation

The method of **isolation** is exemplified in solving an identity like

$$yf(x) = xf(y).$$

In cases like this, we can bring all expressions involving x to one side and all those with y to the other, converting the given expression to

$$\frac{f(x)}{x} = \frac{f(y)}{y}.$$

We can now define a new function $g(t) = f(t)/t$; then we have

$$g(x) = g(y)$$

for any x and y. Clearly this can only happen for all pairs (x, y) if $g(x)$ is a constant, say c. Thus

$$\frac{f(x)}{x} = c,$$

so $f(x) = cx$, for any constant c, is the family of solutions.

    WARNING: Once we have shown that all solutions must be of the form $f(x) = cx$, we also need to test to show that *every* function of this form is a solution. To do this we go back to the defining identity $yf(x) = xf(y)$ and substitute in the functional form. Then $f(x)$ becomes cx and $f(y)$ becomes cy, making our relation $ycx = xcy$, which is always satisfied. Thus any function $f(x) = cx$ does the job.

7.3.2 Substituting in Values

A surprising amount of information can often be obtained by substituting in values for the variables. For example, consider the general functional identity

$$f(xy) = xf(y).$$

Substituting in the value $y = 1$ yields $f(x) = xf(1)$. Letting $f(1) = c$ since $f(1)$ is a constant, all the solutions to the identity are given by $f(x) = cx$.

EXERCISE 7-8 Are all functions $f(x) = cx$ solutions of $f(xy) = xf(y)$?

As another example of the power of substitution, consider the seemingly complicated

$$f(x + y) + f(x - y) = 2x^2 + 2y^2.$$

Substituting $y = 0$ immediately gives $2f(x) = 2x^2$, or $f(x) = x^2$ as the only candidate for a solution. Does this work? We have $f(x+y)+f(x-y) = (x+y)^2+(x-y)^2 = x^2+2xy+y^2+x^2-2xy+y^2 = 2x^2+2y^2$, as desired, so $f(x) = x^2$ is a solution. It is unique.

EXAMPLE 7-4 The previous example differs from earlier ones in that there is no loose constant; $f(x) = x^2$ is the *only* solution. In an earlier example where $f(x) = cx$, there was instead an infinite family of solutions: some examples include $f(x) = x$, $f(x) = 100x$, $f(x) = -\pi x$, and so on.

EXERCISE 7-9 Find all solutions to the equation

$$f(x + y) + f(x - y) = 2x^2 - 2y^2.$$

7.3.3 Using Cyclic Functions

A **cyclic function** is a function $g(x)$ such that

$$g(g(\cdots g(x)\cdots)) = x \tag{7.1}$$

for some number of nested g's. For example, $g(x) = 1/x$ is cyclic because $g(g(x)) = g(1/x) = 1/(1/x) = x$. The number of nested g's in (7.1) is called the **order** of g; for example, the order of $1/x$ is 2.

EXERCISE 7-10 Which of the following are cyclic? Of what order?

   i. $x + \dfrac{1}{x}$

   ii. $\dfrac{x}{x-1}$

   iii. $\dfrac{1}{1+x}$

   iv. $1 - x$

How do cyclic functions help with solving functional identities? Consider one like

$$f(x) + 2f(1/x) = x.$$

If we substitute $1/x$ for x, we get a new equation,

$$f(1/x) + 2f(x) = 1/x.$$

Subtracting the first equation from the twice the second to eliminate $f(1/x)$ yields $3f(x) = 2/x - x$, so the only possible solution is

$$f(x) = \frac{2}{3x} - \frac{x}{3}.$$

Substituing this into the original equation shows that this is in fact a solution. We have used the fact that $1/x$ is cyclic to help us find the solutions.

7.3.4   Arbitrary Functions

We have seen solutions to functional equations which were unique, and some which depended on an arbitrary constant. However, the solutions to some functional equations are much more general. Consider the functional equation

$$f\left(\frac{1+a}{2}\right) = f\left(\frac{1-a}{2}\right) + a.$$

If we notice that

$$a = \frac{1+a}{2} - \frac{1-a}{2},$$

the equation becomes

$$f\left(\frac{1+a}{2}\right) - \frac{1+a}{2} = f\left(\frac{1-a}{2}\right) - \frac{1-a}{2}.$$

Thus, if we create a new function $g(x) = f(x) - x$, we have the simpler equation

$$g\left(\frac{1+a}{2}\right) = g\left(\frac{1-a}{2}\right).$$

To simplify still further, we'll create a third function h, such that $g\left(x + \frac{1}{2}\right) = h(x)$. Then

$$g\left(\frac{1+a}{2}\right) = g\left(\frac{1}{2} + \frac{a}{2}\right) = h\left(\frac{a}{2}\right),$$

and similarly $g\left(\frac{1-a}{2}\right) = h\left(\frac{-a}{2}\right)$. Our equation for g thus becomes

$$h\left(\frac{a}{2}\right) = h\left(\frac{-a}{2}\right).$$

But this last equation is satisfied as long as h is even! (Recall that if h is even, then $h(-x) = h(x)$ for any x.) Thus for *any* even function $h(x)$, we can construct $g(x) = h\left(x - \frac{1}{2}\right)$ and $f(x) = g(x) + x = h\left(x - \frac{1}{2}\right) + x$, and we'll have a solution to our equation. Rather than just having an arbitrary constant, our solution has an arbitrary *function*, because h can be chosen any way we like (as long as it's even).

EXERCISE 7-11   We have claimed that the function $f(x) = h\left(x - \dfrac{1}{2}\right) + x$ will solve our functional equation for any even function h. For the particular even function $h(x) = x^2$, show that it does.

Problems to Solve for Chapter 7

105. If $f(2x) = \frac{2}{2+x}$ for all $x > 0$, then find $2f(x)$. (AHSME 1993)

106. If $f(x) = \frac{4}{x-1}$ and $g(x) = 2x$, then find all x such that $f(g(x)) = g(f(x))$. (MAΘ 1991)

107. Given that $f(ax) = af(x)$ for all real a, and $f(2) = 5$, find $f(17)$. (MAΘ 1992)

108. Find all solutions to the functional equation $f(x) + f(x + y) = y + 2$. (M&IQ 1991)

109. Find all solutions to the functional equation $f(x)/f(y) = y/x$. (M&IQ 1991)

110. Given $g(x) = 2x + 8$ and $f(x) = \frac{1}{x+2}$, find $g \circ f^{-1}(-2)$. (MAΘ 1990)

111. Let $f(t) = \frac{t}{1-t}$, $t \neq 1$. If $y = f(x)$, then x can be expressed as:

A. $f(1/y)$ B. $-f(y)$ C. $-f(-y)$ D. $f(-y)$ E. $f(y)$

(AHSME 1967)

112. How many of the following sets of functions have the property that, given any two elements $f(x)$ and $g(x)$ of the set, the composition $f(g(x))$ is in the set?

  1. functions of the form $ax + b$

  2. functions of the form $ax^2 + bx + c$

  3. polynomial functions

  4. polynomial functions with 12 as a root

(MAΘ 1992)

113. Given $f(ax) = \log_a x$, find $f(x)$. (MAΘ 1992)

114. Find all solutions to the functional equation $21f(x) - 7f\left(\dfrac{1}{x}\right) = 12x$. (M&IQ 1991)

115. If $g(x) = 1 - x^2$ and $f(g(x)) = \frac{1-x^2}{x^2}$ when $x \neq 0$, then find $f(1/2)$. (AHSME 1974)

116. If, for all x, $f(x) = f(2a)^x$ and $f(x + 2) = 27f(x)$, then find a. (MAΘ 1992)

117. Suppose $f(x)$ is defined for all real numbers x; $f(x) > 0$ for all x; and $f(a)f(b) = f(a + b)$ for all a and b. Which of the following statements are true? (AHSME 1975)

$$\text{I.} \qquad f(0) = 1$$
$$\text{II.} \qquad f(-a) = 1/f(a) \text{ for all } a$$
$$\text{III.} \qquad f(a) = \sqrt[3]{f(3a)} \text{ for all } a$$
$$\text{IV.} \qquad f(b) > f(a) \text{ if } b > a$$

118. If $f\left(\frac{x}{x-1}\right) = \frac{1}{x}$ for all $x \neq 0, 1$ and $0 < \theta < \frac{\pi}{2}$, then find $f(\sec^2 \theta)$. (AHSME 1991)

119. If $f(x) = x^2 + x - 1$ for $x \geq -2$ and $g(x) = x^2 - x$ for $x < 5$, then what is the domain of $g \circ f$? (MAΘ 1991)

120. Solve the functional equation $f(x + t) - f(x - t) = 4xt$. (M&IQ 1991)

121. Given $f(x)$ such that $f(1 - x) + (1 - x)f(x) = 5$, find $f(5)$. (MAΘ 1992)

122. Consider a family of functions $f_b(x)$ such that $f_b(0) = b$ and $f_b(x) = 2^a f_b(x-a)$. Find an expression for $f_c(2x)$ in terms of $f_b(x)$. (MAΘ 1992)

123. If $f(x) = \log\left(\frac{1+x}{1-x}\right)$ for $-1 < x < 1$, then find $f\left(\frac{3x+x^3}{1+3x^2}\right)$ in terms of $f(x)$.

124. Find an expression for $f(4x)$ in terms of $f(x)$ given that $f(x) = x/(x - 1)$. (MAΘ 1992)

125. Given a function $f(x)$ satisfying $f(x) + 2f(1/(1 - x)) = x$, find $f(2)$. (MAΘ 1992)

126. Solve the equation $f(x + t) = f(x) + f(t) + 2\sqrt{f(x)}\sqrt{f(t)}$ for $f(x)$. (M&IQ 1991)

127. Find all solutions to the functional equation $f(x + y) - f(y) = x/y(x + y)$. (M&IQ 1991)

128. If $f(n + 1) = (-1)^{n+1}n - 2f(n)$ for integral $n \geq 1$, and $f(1) = f(1986)$, compute $f(1) + f(2) + f(3) + \cdots + f(1985)$. (ARML 1985)

129. Find all solutions to the functional equation $f(1 - x) = f(x) + 1 - 2x$. (M&IQ 1991)

130. Let $g : \mathbb{C} \to \mathbb{C}$, $\omega \in \mathbb{C}$, $a \in \mathbb{C}$, $\omega^3 = 1$, and $\omega \neq 1$. Show that there is one and only one function $f : \mathbb{C} \to \mathbb{C}$ such that

$$f(z) + f(\omega z + a) = g(z), \ z \in \mathbb{C},$$

and find the function f. (IMO 1989)

Chapter 8

Taking it to the Limit

8.1 What is a Limit?

Consider the sequence

$$\left\{ \frac{n}{n+1} \right\} = \frac{1}{2}, \frac{2}{3}, \frac{3}{4}, \ldots$$

A particularly interesting question that one can ask about such a sequence is *to what value does it tend?* The value of the sequence for $n = 17$ is obviously 17/18, but as n goes to ∞, what is the limiting value?

To be rigorous about this concept is fairly difficult, so we will try to examine the limit in a commonsense way. In this case, as n gets larger and larger, the fraction gets closer and closer to 1.

EXERCISE 8-1 Does the last sentence make sense to you? If not, you should talk to someone before you go on. If you understand that one sentence, the rest of this chapter should be a breeze. Really.

To express the concept that the sequence $\frac{n}{n+1}$ approaches 1 as n gets larger, we say that **the sequence tends to 1**, or that **the limit of the sequence as n tends to ∞ is 1**. To express this concept in symbols, we write

$$\lim_{n \to \infty} \frac{n}{n+1} = 1.$$

EXAMPLE 8-1 One important example of a limit is

$$\lim_{n \to \infty} \frac{1}{n}.$$

As n increases, the sequence decreases:

$$\frac{1}{1}, \frac{1}{2}, \frac{1}{3}, \ldots$$

It is clear that the sequence tends to 0.

EXERCISE 8-2 What is $\lim_{n \to \infty} \frac{1}{n^2}$? $\lim_{n \to \infty} \frac{1}{n^3}$? Generalize.

The previous examples can be used to evaluate a great many limits. For example, they immediately solve the entire category of **rational functions**, functions like

$$\frac{3x^3 + 9x + 2}{5x^3 - 12x^2 + x + 1} \tag{8.1}$$

which are the ratio of one polynomial to another. What happens as x tends smoothly to ∞?

To analyze a rational function like (8.1), we divide the top and bottom by the highest power of x present. In this case, the power is x^3, so the result is

$$\frac{3 + \frac{9}{x^2} + \frac{2}{x^3}}{5 - \frac{12}{x} + \frac{1}{x^2} + \frac{1}{x^3}}.$$

When we take the limit $x \to \infty$, everything with x in the denominator goes to 0 and we are left with $3/5$, the final limit.

EXERCISE 8-3 Evaluate

  i. $\displaystyle\lim_{x\to\infty} \frac{2x^4 - 7x^2 + 1}{4x^4 - 4x^3 + 4x^2 - 6x + 17}$

  ii. $\displaystyle\lim_{x\to\infty} \frac{2x^3 - 7x^2 + 1}{4x^4 - 4x^3 + 4x^2 - 6x + 17}$

  iii. $\displaystyle\lim_{x\to\infty} \frac{2x^5 - 7x^2 + 1}{4x^4 - 4x^3 + 4x^2 - 6x + 17}$

8.2 Tricky

Though the limits we dealt with in the previous section were quite simple, limits can actually be a very tricky business. For many sequences, the limit may not even exist! The simple example of a function for which this is a sequence like $1, 2, 3, \ldots$, for which there is simply no limiting value. A similar case was the third part of Exercise 8-3; there, as x increased, the function increased without bound. A sequence or function for which there is no upper limit on the values is called **unbounded**; we write $\lim\limits_{x\to\infty} f(x) = \infty$. (WARNING: This "$\infty$" is just a symbolic shorthand for saying that the limit diverges in the positive direction. DO NOT treat it as a regular number.)

EXAMPLE 8-2 Let's construct a rigorous definition of our terms. A sequence $\{a_n\}$ or function $f(x)$ is unbounded if and only if it gets as big as we want at some point; that is, if

  for every number N, there is some choice of n or x such that $|a_n| > N$ or $|f(x)| > N$.

Note that by using the absolute value we have allowed for functions to be unbounded toward the negative as well, like $-1, -2, -3, \ldots$. We've also taken care of others that might try to evade the definition, like $1, -2, 3, -4, \ldots$ or similar miscreants.

EXERCISE 8-4 Rigorously define what it means for a sequence or function to be **bounded**, the opposite of unbounded.

EXERCISE 8-5 Is every sequence either bounded or unbounded?

This boundless increase (or decrease or alternation) is only the simplest way in which a sequence or function can fail to have a limit. We can come up with many other devious ways as well. For example, consider the sequence

$$0, 1, 0, 1, 0, 1, \ldots,$$

or alternatively the function $\sin x$. Although the sequence and the function are both bounded, there is again no limiting value. (Why?) So being bounded is not enough for a function to have a limit.

A function which has no limit, regardless of the particular way in which it fails, is called **divergent**.

EXERCISE 8-6 Think about how you might rigorously define a convergent sequence or function. Before you get too confident about this task, think about this: your definition should distinguish between a sequence like $0, 1, 0, 1, 0, 1, 0, 1, \ldots$, which has no limit, and one like $0, 1, 0, 1, 0, 1, 0, 0, 0, 0, 0, \ldots$, which has limit 0. Only the long term behavior should matter.

EXERCISE 8-7 Which rational functions are convergent? Which are convergent to nonzero values?

8.3   Working with Limits

In Section 8.1, we analyzed the limits of rational functions. But we implicitly assumed several things. For example, we assumed that the limit of a ratio is equal to the ratio of the individual limits; that is, that

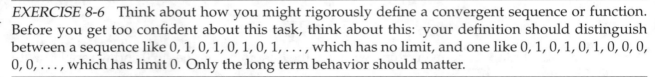

$$\lim_{n \to \infty} \frac{f(x)}{g(x)} = \frac{\lim_{x \to \infty} f(x)}{\lim_{x \to \infty} g(x)}.$$

Without this being true, we would have been unable to make the crucial last step, where we said that since the limit of the numerator of

$$\frac{3 + \frac{9}{x^2} + \frac{2}{x^3}}{5 - \frac{12}{x} + \frac{1}{x^2} + \frac{1}{x^3}}.$$

was 3 and that of the denominator 5, the final limit must be 3/5.

We made another assumption as well, that the limit of a sum equals the sum of the individual limits. This assumption is what allows us to say that the limit of the top,

$$\lim_{x \to \infty} \left(3 + \frac{9}{x^2} + \frac{2}{x^3} \right)$$

must equal

$$\lim_{x \to \infty} 3 + \lim_{x \to \infty} \frac{9}{x^2} + \lim_{x \to \infty} \frac{2}{x^3} = 3 + 0 + 0 = 3.$$

In fact, these two assumptions are generally true (and similar results hold for multiplication and exponentiation), as long as all the limits exist and no divisions by zero occur. A proof of this is a little too complicated to deal with here.

WARNING: When divisions by zero occur, interesting—and dangerous—things occur. Suppose we have two functions $f(x)$ and $g(x)$ and we wish to evaluate

$$\lim_{x \to \infty} \frac{f(x)}{g(x)}.$$

If $\lim\limits_{x\to\infty} g(x) \neq 0$, then everything is fine; we just write

$$\lim_{x\to\infty} \frac{f(x)}{g(x)} = \frac{\lim\limits_{x\to\infty} f(x)}{\lim\limits_{x\to\infty} g(x)}.$$

Even if $\lim\limits_{x\to\infty} g(x) = 0$, we can make an immediate conclusion if $\lim\limits_{x\to\infty} f(x) \neq 0$. We then have

$$\lim_{x\to\infty} \frac{f(x)}{g(x)} = \frac{\text{something other than } 0}{0} = \infty.$$

(Why?) But if both $\lim\limits_{x\to\infty} g(x) = 0$ and $\lim\limits_{x\to\infty} f(x) = 0$, interesting things can happen. The top could go to zero *much faster* than the bottom, resulting in a limit of 0 (for example, try $f(x) = x^2$, $g(x) = x$). The top could go to zero *much slower* than the bottom, resulting in a limit of ∞. (Can you find an example of this situation?) Or, in the most interesting case, the two can go to zero at comparable speeds, resulting in some finite, nonzero limit. A simple example of this last case is $f(x) = 3x$, $g(x) = 5x$, in which $\lim\limits_{x\to\infty} f(x)/g(x) = 3/5$. A more complicated example is $f(x) = \sin(1/x)$, $g(x) = (1/x)$.

EXERCISE 8-8 On a calculator, evaluate $\sin(1/1000)/(1/1000)$. (Make sure you are using radians for the angle measure!) Do you have a guess as to what $\lim\limits_{x\to\infty} \sin(1/x)/(1/x)$ is?

Be very careful that you don't see a limit in which the top and bottom both go to 0 and automatically assume that the limit is 1. As we have shown, a 0/0 limit can have any value whatsoever.

EXAMPLE 8-3 Certain simple transformations are possible when working with limits. For example, suppose we know that $\lim\limits_{x\to\infty} f(x) = L$ and we want to know $\lim\limits_{x\to\infty} f(5x)$. As x goes off to infinity, so does $5x$, so we can write

$$\lim_{x\to\infty} f(5x) = \lim_{5x\to\infty} f(5x) = \lim_{y\to\infty} f(y) = L,$$

where we have made the substitution $y = 5x$.

EXAMPLE 8-4 A more useful transformation can be used to convert a limit as x tends to infinity into a limit as x tends to 0, or vice versa. We simply define $y = 1/x$ and note that as x goes to infinity y goes to 0, and as x goes to 0, y goes to infinity. Thus

$$\lim_{x\to\infty} f(x) = \lim_{y\to 0} f(1/y) \quad \text{and} \quad \lim_{x\to 0} f(x) = \lim_{y\to\infty} f(1/y).$$

EXAMPLE 8-5 Find

$$\lim_{x\to 3} \frac{\sqrt{2x+10} - \sqrt{x+13}}{x-3}.$$

Solution: For $x = 3$, we find that our limit is 0/0. A general technique in dealing with limits involving square roots is multiplying top and bottom by a conjugate expression, or $\sqrt{2x+10} + \sqrt{x+13}$ in this case:

$$\lim_{x\to 3} \frac{\sqrt{2x+10} - \sqrt{x+13}}{x-3} = \lim_{x\to 3} \frac{(\sqrt{2x+10} - \sqrt{x+13})(\sqrt{2x+10} + \sqrt{x+13})}{(x-3)(\sqrt{2x+10} + \sqrt{x+13})}$$

$$= \lim_{x\to 3} \frac{x-3}{(x-3)(\sqrt{2x+10} + \sqrt{x+13})}$$

$$= \lim_{x\to 3} \frac{1}{\sqrt{2x+10} + \sqrt{x+13}} = \frac{1}{8}.$$

Remember this use of multiplication by the conjugate of a radical expression, it is often the key to simplifying limits.

8.4 Continuity

We have so far only considered the limit of a function as $x \to \infty$. This is because other limits usually aren't all that interesting! For example, $\lim_{x \to 2} x^2 + 2$ is just $2^2 + 2 = 6$.

In general, saying that the limit of a function $f(x)$ as x goes to some finite a is equal to $f(a)$ is the same as saying the function is **continuous** at the point a. In Volume 1, we defined a continuous function as being one which could be drawn without picking up the pen. However, we didn't make the distinction that a function is often continuous in most places with isolated discontinuities.

For example, consider a function $g(x)$, defined as

$$g(x) = \begin{cases} x, & \text{for } x \neq -2; \\ 3, & \text{for } x = -2. \end{cases}$$

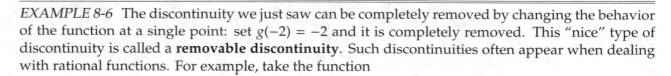

We have plotted $g(x)$ at right. Clearly $g(x)$ is continuous everywhere except at $x = -2$. But consider the behavior near that point. The limit $\lim_{x \to -2} g(x)$ is the value that is being approached as we get closer and closer to -2, *not* the value at -2. Thus $\lim_{x \to -2} g(x) = -2$, while of course, $g(-2) = 3$. The limit is not equal to the value! This means that the function is not continuous at $x = -2$. Everywhere else, the limit equals the value, so the function is continuous everywhere else.

WARNING: Always remember that the limit is the value which the function approaches as we get closer and closer to a point, not the value of the function at the point. The two are equal only for continuous functions.

EXAMPLE 8-6 The discontinuity we just saw can be completely removed by changing the behavior of the function at a single point: set $g(-2) = -2$ and it is completely removed. This "nice" type of discontinuity is called a **removable discontinuity**. Such discontinuities often appear when dealing with rational functions. For example, take the function

$$f(x) = \frac{x^2 - 4x + 3}{x^2 - 3x + 2}.$$

Since the top factors into $(x-1)(x-3)$ and the bottom into $(x-1)(x-2)$, the function is always equal to $(x-3)/(x-2)\ldots$ EXCEPT when $x-1$ equals zero. Then the function is not defined. Thus there is a "hole" in the function at $x = 1$, where it is not defined at all.

Why do we say this discontinuity is removable? Because we can set the value of the original function at $x = 1$ to its limit,

$$\lim_{x \to 1} \frac{x^2 - 4x + 3}{x^2 - 3x + 2} = \lim_{x \to 1} \frac{x - 3}{x - 2} = \frac{1 - 3}{1 - 2} = 2,$$

which will immediately remove the discontinuity.

Other types of discontinuities aren't so easy to remove. Consider the **step function**

$$f(x) = \begin{cases} 0, & \text{for } x \le 0 \\ 1, & \text{for } x > 0. \end{cases}$$

Here there is no way to remove the discontinuity at $x = 0$, since the limit of the function does not exist at $x = 0$! We can define separate limits from the left- and right-hand sides to see why this is so; the left-hand limit (limit approaching 0 from the negative side)

$$\lim_{x \to 0^-} f(x)$$

is 0, while the right-hand limit

$$\lim_{x \to 0^+} f(x)$$

is 1. Clearly, the limit of a function at a point only exists if the left and right limits are equal to one another at that point. Since there is no limit for the step function at 0, we certainly can't "fix" the discontinuity just by changing the value at one point. Thus this is an **essential** discontinuity.

EXERCISE 8-9   Evaluate

$$\lim_{x \to 0^-} \frac{x}{|x|} \quad \text{and} \quad \lim_{x \to 0^+} \frac{x}{|x|}.$$

Does

$$\lim_{x \to 0} \frac{x}{|x|}$$

exist?

8.5 Asymptotes

Limits are especially useful for functions, because the limits give vital information as to a function's structure. For example, let's try to plot

$$f(x) = \frac{3x^2 - 6x + 3}{5x^2 - 25x + 20}.$$

Plotting point-by-point would be very tedious for such a function, and important structural details might be missed altogether. In seeking a different way to plot the function, we note that

$$\lim_{x \to \infty} f(x) = \lim_{x \to -\infty} f(x) = \frac{3}{5}.$$

This immediately tells us something that we wouldn't find using the plug-in method of plotting: for very large and very small x, the function must get closer and closer to the horizontal line $y = 3/5$. This line, shown at right, is called an **asymptote**, and will be a useful guide; try to identify it now in the final graph of the function, shown below. (Can you see how to find the horizontal asymptotes of any rational function?)

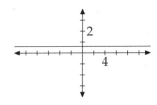

Factoring the top and bottom of the equation yields $f(x) = 3(x-1)^2/5(x-4)(x-1)$, which presents more guidelines. The function is not defined for $x = 4$ and $x = 1$, since the bottom of the fraction becomes 0 at those points. But the two points don't behave the same. The limit of $f(x)$ as x approaches 4 is undefined, since the top does not go to 0 and the bottom does. As x approaches 4 from the right, $f(x)$ will diverge to positive ∞; as x approaches 4 from the left, $f(x)$ will diverge to $-\infty$. (To see what the signs should be, imagine, but don't actually calculate, what would happen for $x = 4.1$ and $x = 3.9$.) As x gets closer and closer to 4, the graph gets closer and closer to the line $x = 4$, so this line is a **vertical asymptote**. Identify the line in the graph below, and figure out why it is also called an asymptote. (How can we find vertical asymptotes of a general rational function?)

On the other hand, the limit of the function as x approaches 1 can easily be evaluated:

$$\lim_{x\to 1} \frac{3(x-1)^2}{5(x-4)(x-1)} = \lim_{x\to 1} \frac{3(x-1)}{5(x-4)} = \lim_{x\to 1} \frac{0}{-15} = 0.$$

Unlike the unruly behavior near $x = 4$, the behavior near $x = 1$ is nice: the curve is smooth except for the removable discontinuity exactly at $x = 1$.

As a final clue to the shape of the graph, let's see where the function crosses the x axis. The numerator of the fraction must be 0, so $x = 1$ is the only point, but this point is the removable discontinuity shown with the open circle. Combining this with our knowledge of the function as it nears both the vertical and the horizontal asymptotes generates the graph at right.

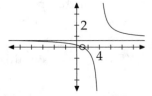

 EXAMPLE 8-7 Plot the function $\dfrac{2x^3 - 3x^2 + x - 6}{x^2 - 3x + 2}$.

Solution: Factoring the bottom yields $(x - 2)(x - 1)$, so we see if either $x - 2$ or $x - 1$ also divides the top. The first does, and the top factors into $(x - 2)(2x^2 + x + 3)$. Since the top and bottom share a factor $x - 2$, there is a removable discontinuity at $x = 2$, with value

$$\lim_{x\to 2} \frac{(x-2)(2x^2 + x + 3)}{(x-2)(x-1)} = \lim_{x\to 2} \frac{(2x^2 + x + 3)}{(x-1)} = 13.$$

On the other hand, $x - 1$ does not divide the top, so there is a vertical asymptote at $x = 1$. As x approaches 1 from the positive side the function soars to ∞, and as x comes in from the negative side the function dives to $-\infty$.

There is no horizontal asymptote since the numerator has greater degree than the denominator; thus you might think we have gleaned all the clues we can. On the contrary, getting rid of the $(x - 2)$ which is common to the numerator and denominator, we are left with $(2x^2 + x + 3)/(x-1)$, which upon polynomial division becomes

$$2x + 3 + \frac{6}{x - 1}.$$

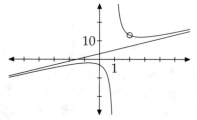

For $x \to \infty$ or $x \to -\infty$, the fraction tends to zero, so the function approaches the line $2x + 3$! This **slant asymptote** is an important graphing tool, as you can see. We now sketch the graph noticing its behavior at $x = 1$, and that it approaches the line $2x + 3$ as x gets large and as x gets small. The open circle on the curve represents the removable discontinuity.

8.6 Trig Limits

Many, if not most, limits require the machinery of calculus to be done with any efficiency. However, certain basic trigonometric limits can be done with simple geometry, and are nevertheless very important.

The simplest trigonometric limits one can think of might be things like $\lim_{x \to \infty} \sin x$ or $\lim_{x \to 0} \cos x$. These aren't too interesting—the first diverges, with $\sin x$ oscillating between 1 and −1; the second is equal to $\cos 0 = 1$ since cosine is continuous.

A more challenging limit is $\lim_{x \to 0} \sin x / x$. Here the limits of the top and bottom are both 0, so the usual methods don't apply.

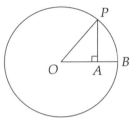

Consider the diagram at right to get an intuitive feeling for the limit in question. If the radius of the circle is 1 and $\angle POB = x$, where x is in radians, then elementary trig shows that $PA = \sin x$, where $\angle PAO$ is a right angle. Moreover, the arc $\overset{\frown}{PB}$ is equal to x, since by geometry the length of a cutoff arc is $r\theta$. Thus the ratio $\sin x / x$ is the ratio between the length of the vertical line and the arc. It seems likely that as the angle x gets smaller and smaller, the arc will differ less and less from the line, so the limit of their ratio appears to be 1.

We can get a quantitative look at the ratio by using a calculator. For a very small value of x, say $x = 0.01$, we find that $\sin x / x = 0.99998 \approx 1$. This confirms our geometric insight that the limit as $x \to 0$ seems to be 1.

EXERCISE 8-10 How does the calculation we just did compare to the calculation done in Exercise 8-8?

Assuming you're convinced that the limit is going to be 1, the only question is how to prove it. We will resort to the **squeeze principle**, which states that if the function $f(x)$ is always between the functions $f_1(x)$ and $f_2(x)$, so that $f_1(x) \le f(x) \le f_2(x)$, then

$$\lim f_1(x) \le \lim f(x) \le \lim f_2(x).$$

This is intuitively clear: if all the values of one function are between those of two others, its limits should be between the limits of the other functions.

We put the squeeze on the diagram above by drawing an additional circle, with center O and radius OA. Let C the point where the new circle intersects segment PO. We can then say that

$$\text{Area sector } OAC < \text{Area } \triangle OAP < \text{Area sector } OBP.$$

The length of OA is $\cos x$, by elementary trigonometry, so the area of sector OAC is $x \cos^2 x / 2$ using the formula for the area of a sector in Volume 1. Similarly, the area of sector OBP is $x/2$. We also know that the area of $\triangle OAP$ is $\cos x \sin x / 2$, since it is a right triangle with legs $OA = \cos x$ and $AP = \sin x$. Substituting this into the equation above, we have

$$\frac{x \cos^2 x}{2} < \frac{\cos x \sin x}{2} < \frac{x}{2},$$

or

$$\cos x < \frac{\sin x}{x} < \frac{1}{\cos x}.$$

Now $\lim_{x \to 0} \cos x = 1$, so $\lim_{x \to 0}(1/\cos x) = 1$. Taking limits, we thus have

$$1 \leq \lim_{x \to 0} \frac{\sin x}{x} \leq 1,$$

so that

$$\lim_{x \to 0} \frac{\sin x}{x} = 1,$$

as we had guessed.

A similar trigonometric limit is

$$\lim_{x \to 0} \frac{1 - \cos x}{x}. \tag{8.2}$$

Like $\lim_{x \to 0} \frac{\sin x}{x}$, this limit is of the form 0/0. But unlike that limit, (8.2) is 0, as can be shown with a similar squeezing argument.

EXAMPLE 8-8 Evaluate $\lim_{x \to 0} \tan 3x/4x$.

Solution: We have

$$\begin{aligned}
\lim_{x \to 0} \frac{\tan 3x}{4x} &= \lim_{x \to 0} \frac{3}{4}\left(\frac{\tan 3x}{3x}\right) \\
&= \frac{3}{4} \lim_{3x \to 0} \left(\frac{\sin 3x}{3x}\right)\left(\frac{1}{\cos 3x}\right) \\
&= \frac{3}{4} \lim_{y \to 0} \left(\frac{\sin y}{y}\right) \lim_{y \to 0} \left(\frac{1}{\cos y}\right) \\
&= \frac{3}{4} \cdot 1 \cdot 1 \\
&= \frac{3}{4}.
\end{aligned}$$

We have used the fact that a limit as $x \to 0$ is the same as a limit as $3x \to 0$ and then substituted $y = 3x$.

8.7 *e*

If I put a dollar in the bank at 100% interest per year, after one year I will have \$2. Suppose, however, that the interest is **compounded** once during the year. This means that after six months I receive the interest so far, 1/2 dollar, and for the second six months I receive interest on all the money I have, $1 + 1/2$ dollars. Hence my total at the end of the year is $(1 + 1/2) + 1/2(1 + 1/2) = (1 + 1/2)^2$. (Figure out how much this is.) I have more with the compound interest, because I am paid interest on the first six months' interest during the second six months.

My interest can be compounded more than once. If my interest is compounded twice, at the end of 1/3 year I have $1 + 1/3$, at the end of 2/3 year I have $(1 + 1/3) + 1/3(1 + 1/3) = (1 + 1/3)^2$, and at the end of the year I have $(1 + 1/3)^2 + 1/3(1 + 1/3)^2 = (1 + 1/3)^3$. Similarly, if my interest is compounded n times during the year, at the end of the year I have $(1 + 1/n)^n$ dollars.

EXERCISE 8-11 Evaluate the expression $(1 + 1/n)^n$ on your calculator for $n = 10$ and $n = 100$. As my interest is compounded more and more often, does my yield diverge or approach a fixed limit?

As you should have seen in Exercise 8-11, compounding interest more and more often does not lead to an infinite amount of money. Rather, it approaches the fixed limit $2.71\dots$. We define this limit to be the constant e:

$$\lim_{n\to\infty}\left(1 + \frac{1}{n}\right)^n = e.$$

The importance of the constant e really comes out in calculus, but it also has some importance in our discussion. For example, the so-called **natural logarithm** $\ln x$ denotes the logarithm base e, $\log_e x$. Moreover, the exponential function e^x appears in many contexts.

EXAMPLE 8-9 Evaluate $\lim_{x\to\infty}\left(1 + \frac{2}{x}\right)^{3x}$.

Solution: We first use the substitution $x = 2u$ to write the given limit as $\lim_{u\to\infty}\left(1 + \frac{1}{u}\right)^{6u}$. We then use the fact that $\lim y^k = (\lim y)^k$ to write

$$\lim_{u\to\infty}\left(1 + \frac{1}{u}\right)^{6u} = \left(\lim_{u\to\infty}\left(1 + \frac{1}{u}\right)^u\right)^6 = e^6.$$

Problems to Solve for Chapter 8

131. For what value of k is the following function continuous at $x = 2$? (MAΘ 1991)

$$f(x) = \begin{cases} \frac{\sqrt{2x+5} - \sqrt{x+7}}{x-2} & \text{for } x \neq 2 \\ k & \text{for } x = 2 \end{cases}$$

132. Evaluate the following limits.

i. $\lim_{x\to\infty} \frac{\sin 3x}{6x}$

ii. $\lim_{x\to-2} \frac{x^3 + 8}{x + 2}$

iii. $\lim_{x\to 16} \frac{\sqrt{x} - 4}{x - 16}$

133. The graph of $f(x) = (x^2 - x - 2)/(x + 2)$ has an oblique (slant) asymptote. Find the equation of this asymptote. (MAΘ 1990)

134. Evaluate $\lim\limits_{x \to \infty} (\sqrt{4x^2 + 5x} - \sqrt{4x^2 + x})$.

135. Evaluate $\lim\limits_{x \to 0} \sin^2 x/x$.

136. Evaluate $\lim\limits_{\theta \to 0} \theta \cot \theta$.

137. Use the identity $\dfrac{1 - \cos x}{x} = \dfrac{\sin^2 x}{x(1 + \cos x)}$ to prove that $\lim\limits_{x \to 0}(1 - \cos x)/x = 0$.

138. Find all asymptotes of the function $x^3/(x^2 - 1)$.

139. Evaluate $\lim\limits_{x \to \infty} 6x/\sqrt{9x^2 + 17x}$.

140. Evaluate $\lim\limits_{x \to \infty} \dfrac{\sqrt{3x^2 + 17x}}{x}$.

the BIG PICTURE

Centrally important in the field of computer science is the study of **algorithms**, repetitive procedures used to accomplish tasks on a computer. For example, suppose I was given a list $(a_1 \ a_2 \ a_3 \cdots a_n)$ of numbers and asked to find the largest element L. A simple algorithm would be as follows: first take $L = a_1$. Then go down the list, comparing each a_i to the current value of L; if $a_i > L$, then set L to be a_i. Thus if the list were (2 1 3 4 2), after each step, the current largest element would be 2, 2, 3, 4, 4.

An algorithm is only useful if it can be run in a reasonable length of time. For this reason, computer scientists have a way to classify algorithms based on their running time; this notation depends on several concepts of limits. An algorithm's running time is some function $f(N)$ of the size of the problem given. Our example above would take 3 steps if the list of numbers had length 3, 17 steps if the list were legth 17, and so on, so in this case $f(N) = N$. This is simple, but in general a complex algorithm might have a very complicated function $f(N)$, like $18N^2 \log N - 12N(\log N)^2 + 7$.

In practice, though, the complicated details of the function f aren't all that interesting. What really determines the running time is the term of f which is largest as $N \to \infty$. To classify an algorithm, then, computer scientists use only this first term. The algorithm with the complicated function above would thus be called "an $N^2 \log N$ algorithm." To denote this type of approximation, we use a capital O, as in $O(N^2 \log N)$.

The most important types of algorithms are, from fastest to slowest, $O(1)$, $O(\log N)$, $O(N)$, $O(N^2)$, and $O(2^N)$. The last is of particular importance, because an $O(2^N)$ algorithm is *very* slow for large N. This can be seen in the fact that if the problem size goes from N to $N + 1$, the running time goes from 2^N to 2^{N+1}—it doubles! For even moderately-sized problems, an $O(2^N)$ algorithm is impractical. On the other end of the spectrum, the running time of an $O(\log N)$ algorithm grows very slowly with the problem size N, and the running time of an $O(1)$ algorithm is a constant regardless of problem size. (For example, the problem of finding the 12th element of a list is an $O(1)$ algorithm.)

Chapter 9

Complex Numbers

9.1 Drawing the Complex Numbers

The standard picture of the real numbers is a line:

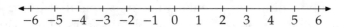

Each real number is associated with a point on the line, and each point with a real number.

Can we devise a similar representation for all complex numbers? Suppose we place the pure imaginaries on a line perpendicular to the reals. If we then put the two lines together, so that they overlap at their zero points (since $0i = 0$), then we can associate every point in the *plane* with a complex number, where the x-coordinate is the real part and the y-coordinate is the complex part. To see how this works, examine the figure at right. It should be fairly clear that we can represent any complex number by a point in this plane, and that every point in the plane represents a different complex number.

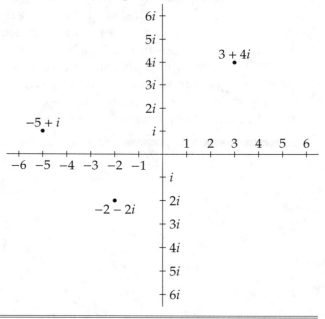

EXERCISE 9-1 Draw a complex plane with the points $\frac{1}{2} + \frac{3}{2}i$ and $-\frac{7}{3} + \sqrt{2}\,i$.

EXERCISE 9-2 Draw the set of points z in the complex plane such that:

    i. $\operatorname{Re}(z) = 1$.

    ii. $\operatorname{Im}(z) + \operatorname{Re}(z) = 1$.

    iii. $\operatorname{Im}(z) < 1$.

EXERCISE 9-3 For $z = 3 + 2i$, draw z, $\bar{z}$, z^2, and $z - 1$.

Once we understand the complex plane, we can use it to expand our understanding of complex numbers. For example, we have used rectangular coordinates to locate points in the complex plane. But these are not the only coordinates we could use. Let's apply polar coordinates instead. In our discussion of polar coordinates (page 47) we saw that the polar coordinates (r, θ) of a point (x, y) are such that

$$\begin{cases} x = r\cos\theta \\ y = r\sin\theta \end{cases} \quad \text{and} \quad \begin{cases} r = \sqrt{x^2 + y^2} \\ \theta = \arctan(y/x) \end{cases}$$

For a complex number z, we have chosen the rectangular coodinates to be $\big(\mathrm{Re}(z), \mathrm{Im}(z)\big)$. Thus the associated polar coordinates (r, θ) of z will be such that

$$\begin{aligned} \mathrm{Re}(z) &= r\cos\theta \\ \mathrm{Im}(z) &= r\sin\theta. \end{aligned} \tag{9.1}$$

But since $z = \mathrm{Re}(z) + i\,\mathrm{Im}(z)$, we then have

$$z = r\cos\theta + ir\sin\theta. \tag{9.2}$$

This is called the **trigonometric representation** of a complex number, and is sometimes written simply $z = \mathrm{cis}\,\theta$. Of course, just giving the polar coordinates (r, θ) is enough to determine z completely; this is called the **polar representation**.

EXAMPLE 9-1 Find the polar representation for i.

Solution: We use equations (9.1) to get $r\cos\theta = 0$ and $r\sin\theta = 1$. Clearly θ must be $\pi/2$ and r must be 1, so the polar representation is $(\mathbf{1}, \boldsymbol{\pi/2})$.

EXERCISE 9-4 Draw the points $r = 2, \theta = \pi/3$ and $r = 3, \theta = \pi$.

EXERCISE 9-5 Draw the curves $r = 1$ and $\theta = \pi/3$ in the complex plane.

As with regular polar coordinates, the numbers r and θ are the distance from the origin to z and the angle between z and the positive real axis, respectively. It is important to remember the ambiguity in the value of θ as well; for a given θ we could just as well use $\theta + 2\pi$, $\theta + 4\pi$, etc. See page 47 for a discussion of this ambiguity.

9.2   The Complex Absolute Value

The value of r is particularly important. Like the absolute value for real numbers, it is simply the distance to the origin of coordinates. We therefore call r the **absolute value**, or sometimes **magnitude**, of a complex number z and denote it by $|z|$. For a generic complex number $x + iy$, we have $|x + iy| = r = \sqrt{x^2 + y^2}$.

The complex absolute value has some interesting properties. Perhaps the most important is that

$|zw| = |z||w|$ for any z and w. To see this, we just write

$$
\begin{aligned}
|zw| &= |(z_1 + z_2 i)(w_1 + w_2 i)| \\
&= |(z_1 w_1 - z_2 w_2) + (z_1 w_2 + z_2 w_1)i| \\
&= \sqrt{(z_1 w_1 - z_2 w_2)^2 + (z_1 w_2 + z_2 w_1)^2} \\
(\text{cancelling terms}) \quad &= \sqrt{z_1^2 w_1^2 + z_2^2 w_2^2 + z_1^2 w_2^2 + z_2^2 w_1^2} \\
&= \sqrt{(z_1^2 + z_2^2)(w_1^2 + w_2^2)} \\
&= \sqrt{z_1^2 + z_2^2}\,\sqrt{w_1^2 + w_2^2} \\
&= |z||w|,
\end{aligned}
$$

and we're done. Similarly we can show that $|z/w| = |z|/|w|$.

EXERCISE 9-6 Find the absolute value of the complex number $(12 + 5i)(7 - 24i)$.

EXERCISE 9-7 Find a counterexample to the false claim $|w + z| = |w| + |z|$.

Let's examine the relationship between $|w + z|$ and $|w| + |z|$. Above you should have found that these two quantities are not always equal, but you should also have seen, or at least suspected, that $|w + z|$ is never larger than the sum $|w| + |z|$. To prove our suspicion, we write $|w| + |z| \geq |w + z|$ in terms of $w = w_1 + w_2 i$ and $z = z_1 + z_2 i$:

$$
\sqrt{z_1^2 + z_2^2} + \sqrt{w_1^2 + w_2^2} \geq \sqrt{(z_1 + w_1)^2 + (z_2 + w_2)^2}.
$$

Squaring both sides and cancelling common terms leaves

$$
2\sqrt{z_1^2 + z_2^2}\,\sqrt{w_1^2 + w_2^2} \geq 2z_1 w_1 + 2z_2 w_2.
$$

Cancelling the 2's and squaring again, we get

$$
z_1^2 w_1^2 + z_1^2 w_2^2 + z_2^2 w_1^2 + z_2^2 w_2^2 \geq z_1^2 w_1^2 + 2z_1 z_2 w_1 w_2 + z_2^2 w_2^2,
$$

or

$$
z_1^2 w_2^2 - 2z_1 z_2 w_1 w_2 + z_2^2 w_1^2 \geq 0.
$$

Recognizing the left as a perfect square, we write

$$
(z_1 w_2 - z_2 w_1)^2 \geq 0,
$$

which is clearly always true. Furthermore, we can find when $|w| + |z| = |w + z|$ by noting that these can only be equal when $(z_1 w_2 - z_2 w_1)^2 = 0$. (Why?) This occurs when $z_1 w_2 = z_2 w_1$, or $z_1/w_1 = z_2/w_2$. If we let this common ratio be c, we find that our equality condition is $z_1 = cw_1$ and $z_2 = cw_2$, so $z = cw$ and one number is just a real multiple of the other!

The inequality $|w| + |z| \geq |w + z|$ is called the **Triangle Inequality** for complex numbers. Given the name, you might think the inequality has something to do with geometry. You're right; using a geometric representation of complex numbers and complex addition, we can prove the Triangle Inequality quite easily. (This is done on page 103.)

EXERCISE 9-8 What is the equality condition of the Triangle Inequality when w and z are written in polar form?

EXERCISE 9-9 Prove that $|z| + |w| \geq |z - w|$.

9.3 Complex Multiplication and Coordinates

We now ask the question: what is the effect of complex multiplication in our new coordinate perspective? We can answer this immediately. Consider two complex numbers $z_1 = r_1(\cos\theta_1 + i\sin\theta_1)$ and $z_2 = r_2(\cos\theta_2 + i\sin\theta_2)$. Their product is

$$
\begin{aligned}
z_1 z_2 &= r_1 r_2 (\cos\theta_1 \cos\theta_2 + i\cos\theta_1 \sin\theta_2 + i\sin\theta_1 \cos\theta_2 - \sin\theta_1 \sin\theta_2) \\
&= r_1 r_2 \Big((\cos\theta_1 \cos\theta_2 - \sin\theta_1 \sin\theta_2) + i(\cos\theta_1 \sin\theta_2 + \sin\theta_1 \cos\theta_2) \Big) \\
&= r_1 r_2 \Big(\cos(\theta_1 + \theta_2) + i\sin(\theta_1 + \theta_2) \Big).
\end{aligned}
$$

The coordinates of the product of (r_1, θ_1) and (r_2, θ_2) are thus $(r_1 r_2, \theta_1 + \theta_2)$. When we multiply two complex numbers, *the magnitudes multiply and the angles add.*

EXAMPLE 9-2 Take the complex number $\frac{1}{2} + i\frac{\sqrt{3}}{2} = (\cos\frac{\pi}{3} + i\sin\frac{\pi}{3})$. When it is multiplied by any complex number $r(\cos\theta + i\sin\theta)$, the product is $r\big(\cos(\theta + \frac{\pi}{3}) + i\sin(\theta + \frac{\pi}{3})\big)$. Thus multiplication by $\frac{1}{2} + i\frac{\sqrt{3}}{2}$ is a rotation by the angle $\frac{\pi}{3}$.

EXERCISE 9-10 To what geometrical motion does multiplication by i correspond, in the sense of Example 9-2?

EXERCISE 9-11 On a complex plane, draw the points $2 + 3i$, $1 + 2i$, and $(2 + 3i)(1 + 2i)$ to convince yourself that the magnitudes multiply and the angles add to form the product.

While the polar method is a more satisfying way to look at complex multiplication, for routine calculation it is usually easier to fall back on the distributive law as used in Volume 1. However, for more complicated calculations and clever applications, the polar approach is often much more fruitful.

9.4 Complex Powers and Geometry

Once we have a representation for multiplication, we can tackle powers. Consider the generic complex number $z = r(\cos\theta + i\sin\theta)$. The power z^n (where n is a positive integer) is just a product $zzz\cdots z$ with n z's multiplied together. Thus the magnitude is the product of the individual magnitudes, or r^n, and the angle is the sum of the individual angles, or $n\theta$. For positive integers n, we immediately have

$$
\big[r(\cos\theta + i\sin\theta)\big]^n = r^n\Big(\cos(n\theta) + i\sin(n\theta)\Big),
$$

which can be written in the more memorable form

$$
(r, \theta)^n = (r^n, n\theta). \tag{9.3}
$$

EXERCISE 9-12   How could we express the powers of i in polar form?

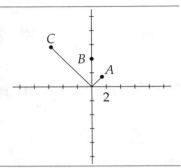

EXAMPLE 9-3   To see what exponentiation looks like, let's consider the powers of $\sqrt{2} + i\sqrt{2} = 2(\cos\frac{\pi}{4} + i\sin\frac{\pi}{4})$. The second power is $4(\cos\frac{\pi}{2} + i\sin\frac{\pi}{2}) = 4i$, the third power $8(\cos\frac{3\pi}{4} + i\sin\frac{3\pi}{4}) = -4\sqrt{2} + 4\sqrt{2}\,i$, the fourth power $16(\cos\pi + i\sin\pi) = -16$, etc. The first three powers are at points A, B, and C at right, where one tick mark equals 2 units. To go from one power to the next, we rotate $45°$ counterclockwise and double the distance from the origin.

EXAMPLE 9-4   We can easily extend the result of equation (9.3) to negative integers as well. Take $(r, \theta)^{-n}$, where n is a positive integer. We can set $(r, \theta)^{-n} = (s, \phi)$ and write $1 = (r, \theta)^{-n}(r, \theta)^n = (s, \phi)(r^n, n\theta)$, where the last equality comes from equation (9.3). Using the fact that magnitudes multiply and angles add, we then have $(sr^n, \phi + n\theta) = (1, 0)$, so $s = r^{-n}$ and $\phi = -n\theta$. Thus $(r, \theta)^{-n} = (r^{-n}, -n\theta)$, as desired.

EXERCISE 9-13   What is the geometrical relationship of $z = (1, \theta)$ and its reciprocal for any angle θ?

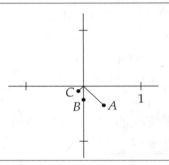

EXAMPLE 9-5   Let's extend Example 9-3 to some negative powers of $\sqrt{2} + i\sqrt{2} = 2(\cos\frac{\pi}{4} + i\sin\frac{\pi}{4})$. The -1st power is $\frac{1}{2}\left(\cos(-\frac{\pi}{4}) + i\sin(-\frac{\pi}{4})\right)$, the -2nd power $\frac{1}{4}\left(\cos(-\frac{1\pi}{2}) + i\sin(-\frac{1\pi}{2})\right)$, the -3rd power $\frac{1}{8}\left(\cos(-\frac{3\pi}{4}) + i\sin(-\frac{3\pi}{4})\right)$, etc. The 0th power is $1(\cos 0 + i\sin 0) = 1$, as we expect. The first three negative powers are at A, B, and C, where we get from each one to the next by rotating by $45°$ clockwise and halving the distance to the origin.

EXERCISE 9-14   Duplicate Example 9-3 and Example 9-5 for the numbers $\frac{\sqrt{2}}{2} + i\frac{\sqrt{2}}{2}$ and $\frac{1}{2} + i\frac{1}{2}$.

9.5 DeMoivre's Theorem

In equation (9.3) we found a very nice property of *integral* powers of a complex number. However, we can just as easily look at fractional powers. Consider a complex number which we have written in the polar form (r, θ). How can we find $(r, \theta)^{p/q}$, where p and q are integers?

To begin with, we get rid of the p. By equation (9.3), we immediately have

$$(r, \theta)^{p/q} = (r^p, p\theta)^{1/q}.$$

Thus our problem boils down to finding the qth roots of $(r^p, p\theta)$. This isn't so hard. We can by guesswork write down one qth root: $(r^{p/q}, p\theta/q)$. This is a qth root because its qth power is

$$(r^{p/q}, p\theta/q)^q = \left((r^{p/q})^q, q(p\theta/q)\right) = (r^p, p\theta),$$

using equation (9.3). So we have one qth root immediately. How do we find others? Remember that the complex number $(r^p, p\theta)$ is equal to $(r^p, p\theta + 2\pi k)$ for any integer k; adding a full circle to the angle doesn't change our location. From these equivalent numbers we can easily write down the qth roots

$$\left(r^{p/q}, \frac{p\theta}{q} + \frac{2\pi k}{q} \right). \qquad (9.4)$$

In fact, the numbers generated by equation (9.4), as k ranges over the integers, are *all* the p/q powers of (r, θ). This assertion, the simple proof of which is below, is called **DeMoivre's Theorem** (de MAUVE's theorem).

EXAMPLE 9-6 Find all cube roots of $4 + 4\sqrt{3}i$.

Solution: We can readily convert this number into the trigonometric form $8(\cos 60° + \sin 60°)$, which gives the polar form $(8, 60°)$. Then by DeMoivre, the cube roots (1/3 powers) are given by $(8^{1/3}, 20° + 360°k/3) = (2, 20° + 120°k)$. For $k = 0$, we have $(2, 20°)$. For $k = 1$, we have $(2, 20° + 120°) = (2, 140°)$. For $k = 2$, we have $(2, 260°)$. For $k = 3$, we have $(2, 380°)$, which is equal to $(2, 20°)$ again. Similarly, as k takes on other integral values, we will just get our three basic values over and over again. Thus our roots are $(\mathbf{2, 20°})$, $(\mathbf{2, 140°})$, and $(\mathbf{2, 260°})$.

EXERCISE 9-15 Find all values of $(-4\sqrt{2} + 4\sqrt{2}i)^{3/4}$.

Let's now prove DeMoivre's Theorem. Clearly every number of the form (9.4) with k an integer is a p/q power of (r, θ). We verify this by taking the expression to the qth power and observing that the result is a pth power of (r, θ) in agreement with equation (9.3). Since the expression (9.4) is a qth root of a pth power of (r, θ), it is a p/q power.

We now need only to prove that *every* p/q power of (r, θ) can be written in the form (9.4). Consider some general complex number (s, ϕ) such that $(r, \theta)^{p/q} = (s, \phi)$. We can write $(r, \theta)^p = (s, \phi)^q$, so (9.3) gives $(r^p, p\theta) = (s^q, q\phi)$. The only way these two sets of polar coordinates can be equal is if

$$r^p = s^q \qquad \text{and} \qquad p\theta + 2\pi k = q\phi,$$

which clearly forces (s, ϕ) to be of the form (9.4), so we're done.

EXAMPLE 9-7 In Example 9-6 above, we found that there are three cube roots of $4 + 4\sqrt{3}i$. This is no accident. In fact, DeMoivre guarantees that there will be exactly q qth roots of any nonzero complex number. Why? Because the allowed angles of $(r, \theta)^{1/q}$ are

$$\frac{\theta}{q} + \frac{2\pi k}{q} = \frac{\theta}{q}, \frac{\theta}{q} + \frac{2\pi}{q}, \frac{\theta}{q} + \frac{4\pi}{q}, \dots$$

All of these values will be different until we get to $k = q$, when we will have $\theta/q + 2\pi q/q = \theta/q + 2\pi$. This is the same as just θ/q, so we are back where we started: adding $2\pi/q$ just gives $\theta/q + 2\pi/q$ again, and so on. Similarly, negative values of k give the same roots as well.

9.6   Exponential Form

We have in De Moivre's Theorem a very powerful tool for examining the powers of a complex number. We can make this tool still sharper, however. Consider the powers of the complex number $\cos\theta + i\sin\theta$. De Moivre's Theorem tells us that

$$(\cos\theta + i\sin\theta)^n = \cos(n\theta) + i\sin(n\theta).$$

This is a very special property of the function $f(\theta) = \cos\theta + i\sin\theta$, namely that

$$[f(\theta)]^n = f(n\theta).$$

Which known functions behave like this? Only the exponentials, as in $(a^x)^n = a^{nx}$. This possible connection was closed by Euler, who showed that the usual exponential e^x, x real, could be extended to the imaginaries by taking, for any real number y,

$$e^{iy} = \cos y + i\sin y. \tag{9.5}$$

We should emphasize that this is neither pure coincidence nor arbitrary choosing. In fact, students familiar with calculus should be able to prove the necessity of this extension using Taylor series.

EXAMPLE 9-8 Evaluate the complex number $e^{3/2 + i\pi/4}$.

Solution: We split the given expression into the product $e^{3/2}e^{i\pi/4}$. The first part cannot be simplified, but the second part becomes $\frac{\sqrt{2}}{2} + \frac{\sqrt{2}}{2}i$ using (9.5). Thus our number is $e^{3/2}(\frac{\sqrt{2}}{2} + \frac{\sqrt{2}}{2}i)$.

The relation (9.5) is very useful for the understanding of complex numbers. We define the **exponential form** of a complex number to be $re^{i\theta}$, where r and θ are the same as for polar form. In fact, the exponential form turns out to be just a more powerful way to express polar form. For one thing, De Moivre's Theorem is *obvious* in exponential form, saying that

$$(re^{i\theta})^n = r^n e^{ni\theta}.$$

Just by writing exponential form, we get De Moivre's Theorem for free! However, always remember that if the exponent is not an integer, we must write

$$\left(re^{i(\theta + 2\pi k)}\right)^g = r^g e^{gi\theta + 2\pi ikg}$$

where all the gth powers are achieved by ranging k over the integers.

To write the exponential form of an arbitrary complex number we just find r and θ as for polar form.

EXAMPLE 9-9 Find i^i.

Solution: It's easy with exponential form. We just write $i = e^{i(\pi/2+2\pi k)}$, so $i^i = (e^{i(\pi/2+2\pi k)})^i = e^{-(\pi/2+2\pi k)}$. There are thus infinitely many such powers (!), all of which are real:

$$\ldots, e^{\frac{-5\pi}{2}}, e^{\frac{-\pi}{2}}, e^{\frac{3\pi}{2}}, e^{\frac{7\pi}{2}}, \ldots$$

This should not be *too* disturbing, given that even fractional powers give many answers. The reason this is so weird is that we are using the notion of "powers" very abstractly; we can no longer expect intuitive results.

We can use this method to take complex powers of any complex number which we can put into exponential form.

Note that in Example 9-9, we used De Moivre's Theorem for the *complex* power i, though the theorem was proven only for real powers. Fortunately, the theorem still holds for complex powers. (Can you prove it?)

EXAMPLE 9-10 Equation (9.5) tells us that $e^{ix} = \cos x + i \sin x$; substituting $-x$ for x, we similarly get $e^{-ix} = \cos(-x) + i \sin(-x) = \cos x - i \sin x$. Adding these two equations and dividing by 2, we get

$$\cos x = \frac{e^{ix} + e^{-ix}}{2},$$

while subtracting them and dividing by $2i$ yields

$$\sin x = \frac{e^{ix} - e^{-ix}}{2i}.$$

This is not some kind of trick; these expressions are perfectly valid ways to express sine and cosine, and are useful in many ways.

EXERCISE 9-16 Use the expressions of Example 9-10 to prove that $\sin^2 x + \cos^2 x = 1$ and $\sin 2x = 2 \sin x \cos x$.

EXAMPLE 9-11 Using the expressions of the previous example as a basis, we can define two new functions, the **hyperbolic sine and cosine** $\sinh x$ and $\cosh x$. The functions are defined as

$$\sinh x = \frac{e^x - e^{-x}}{2} \quad \text{and} \quad \cosh x = \frac{e^x + e^{-x}}{2}.$$

The similarity to the expressions given for sine and cosine in Example 9-10 is obvious.

The tie between hyperbolic and ordinary sine and cosine is made still clearer by the fact that the hyperbolics satisfy similar identities; for example, $\cosh^2 x - \sinh^2 x = 1$.

EXERCISE 9-17 Prove the validity of $\cosh^2 x - \sinh^2 x = 1$ and investigate formulas for $\sinh 2x$, $\cosh 2x$, etc.

The hyperbolic tangent, secant, etc. are defined in the familiar way; for example, $\tanh x = \sinh x / \cosh x = (e^x - e^{-x})/(e^x + e^{-x})$.

9.7   Two for One

When we are working with rational variables and functions, the equation $f(x) = g(x)$ is just that, one equation. Let's consider the complex variable equation $a + bi = c + di$. The points in the complex plane represented by $a + bi$ and $c + di$ can only be the same if $a = c$ and $b = d$, so $a + bi = c + di$ gives us two equations, not just one. Now let's look at how this can be useful.

EXAMPLE 9-12   Use DeMoivre's Theorem to get an expression for $\cos 3\theta$ in terms of $\cos\theta$.

Solution: If we write DeMoivre's Theorem for $(\cos\theta + i\sin\theta)^3$, we have

$$\begin{aligned}
\cos 3\theta + i\sin 3\theta &= (\cos\theta + i\sin\theta)^3 \\
&= \cos^3\theta + 3i\cos^2\theta\sin\theta - 3\cos\theta\sin^2\theta - i\sin^3\theta.
\end{aligned}$$

To get $\cos\theta$, we equate the real parts of the above equation, yielding

$$\begin{aligned}
\cos 3\theta &= \cos^3\theta - 3\cos\theta\sin^2\theta \\
&= \cos^3\theta - 3\cos\theta(1 - \cos^2\theta) \\
&= 4\cos^3\theta - 3\cos\theta.
\end{aligned}$$

EXERCISE 9-18   Find an expression for $\sin 3\theta$ in terms of $\sin\theta$.

EXERCISE 9-19   Show that

$$\operatorname{Im}\left(\sum_{n=1}^{j} k e^{in\theta}\right) = \sum_{n=1}^{j} k\sin n\theta.$$

When is this helpful?

Clearly our new technique is very useful for problems involving $\cos n\theta$ and $\sin n\theta$.

9.8   The Roots of Unity

DeMoivre's Theorem can easily be used to find the n nth roots of 1. Since $1 = e^{2\pi ki}$ for integers k, the nth roots are given by

$$1^{1/n} = e^{2\pi ki/n} = 1, \; \cos\frac{2\pi}{n} + i\sin\frac{2\pi}{n}, \; \cos\frac{4\pi}{n} + i\sin\frac{4\pi}{n}, \ldots$$

EXERCISE 9-20   Write the three 3rd roots and the four 4th roots of 1 in Cartesian form.

These nth roots are interesting in a number of ways. First, we consider plotting them all in the complex plane. Since all their amplitudes are 1, all the roots lie on the unit circle. Moreover, their angles are equally spaced from 0 to 2π, so they form a regular polygon! This is shown at right for $n = 7$. (In fact, the roots of any number form a regular polygon, but this fact is generally most often used for roots of unity.)

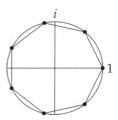

EXERCISE 9-21 For what n is -1 an nth root of 1? For what n does -1 lie on the polygon drawn above?

EXERCISE 9-22 How many 17th roots of 1 are there in the second quadrant?

Another property of the nth roots of 1 is that they all satisfy the equation

$$x^n - 1 = 0.$$

Since we know 1 is a root, $(x - 1)$ divides the polynomial on the left, which we can then factor as

$$(x - 1)(x^{n-1} + x^{n-2} + \cdots + 1) = 0.$$

For any root $\omega \neq 1$, we thus have

$$\omega^{n-1} + \omega^{n-2} + \cdots + 1 = 0,$$

a relation which is useful for many problems.

EXAMPLE 9-13 If ω is one of the imaginary roots of the equation $x^3 = 1$, then find the product $(1 - \omega + \omega^2)(1 + \omega - \omega^2)$. (AHSME 1971)

Solution: Writing the given equation as $x^3 - 1 = 0$, we factor and find $(x - 1)(x^2 + x + 1) = 0$. Since ω is imaginary, it is a root of $x^2 + x + 1$, so $\omega^2 + \omega + 1 = 0$. Hence we have $1 + \omega = -\omega^2$ and $1 + \omega^2 = -\omega$ and

$$(1 - \omega + \omega^2)(1 + \omega - \omega^2) = (-\omega - \omega)(-\omega^2 - \omega^2) = 4\omega^3 = \mathbf{4},$$

since $\omega^3 = 1$.

Problems to Solve for Chapter 9

141. Find $\left|\frac{7-24i}{4+3i}\right|$. (MAΘ 1991)

142. Find $(1 + i)^4(2 - 2i)^3$. (MAΘ 1987)

143. Find the product of the n nth roots of 1 in terms of n.

144. If $f(z) = \frac{z+1}{z-1}$, then find $f^{1991}(2 + i)$. (MAΘ 1991)

145. For how many positive real values of K will $(2 + Ki)^3$ be a real number? (MAΘ 1992)

146. Show the line through the complex points w and z plotted in the complex plane has slope $\text{Im}(z - w)/\text{Re}(z - w)$.

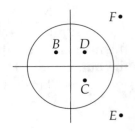

147. The diagram at right shows several numbers in the complex plane. The circle is the unit circle centered at the origin. Which of the shown points could possibly be the reciprocal of F? (AHSME 1983)

148. If the six solutions of $x^6 = -64$ are written in the form $a + bi$, where a and b are real, then find the product of those solutions with $a > 0$. (AHSME 1990)

149. What is the graph of $|z| = \operatorname{Im} z + 1$? (MAΘ 1991)

150. Write $\cos 5\theta$ as a function of $\cos \theta$. (MAΘ 1990)

151. Find $\operatorname{Im}(\cos 12° + i \sin 12° + \cos 48° + i \sin 48°)^6$.

152. If θ is a constant such that $0 < \theta < \pi$ and $x + \frac{1}{x} = 2\cos\theta$, then for each positive integer n, find $x^n + \frac{1}{x^n}$ in terms of n and θ. (AHSME 1981)

153. Evaluate

$$\sum_{n=0}^{\infty} \frac{\cos(n\theta)}{2^n},$$

where $\cos\theta = 1/5$. (MAΘ 1991)

154. Suppose that the coefficients of the equation $x^n + a_{n-1}x^{n-1} + \cdots + a_1 x + a_0 = 0$ are real and satisfy $0 < a_0 \le a_1 \le \cdots \le a_{n-1} \le 1$. Let z be a complex root of the equation with $|z| \ge 1$. Show that $z^{n+1} = 1$. (This problem originally appeared on a contest used to determine the Chinese national team.) (MOP)

——the BIG PICTURE——

Carl Friedrich Gauss was, among his many other achievements, one of the primary popularizers of complex numbers. One of the discoveries of which Gauss himself was proudest was the constructibility of the regular 17-gon.

The ancient Greeks were able to construct the equilateral triangle, and the regular pentagon, but no other regular polygons with a prime number of sides, but Gauss was at last able to extend this repertory. Given a segment of length 1, Gauss knew that any integer-length segment could be constructed. Moreover, the sum, difference and quotient of two segments can be constructed, and the square root of a segment can be constructed. Thus any segment whose length is an expression made up of sums, differences, quotients, and square roots of integers can be constructed.

As a simple example of such an expression, Gauss used the 17 seventeenth roots of unity to show that

$$\cos 360^\circ/17 = -\frac{1}{16} + \frac{1}{16}\sqrt{17} + \frac{1}{16}\sqrt{34 - 2\sqrt{17}}$$
$$+ \frac{1}{8}\sqrt{17 + 3\sqrt{17} - \sqrt{34 - 2\sqrt{17}} - 2\sqrt{34 + 2\sqrt{17}}}.$$

Once he could construct a segment of length $\cos 360^\circ/17$, Gauss could construct the point $(\cos 360^\circ/17, \sin 360^\circ/17)$, by laying off $\cos 360^\circ/17$ along the x axis and drawing a perpendicular to the x axis at that point. The intersection, P, of this line and the unit circle has polar angle $360^\circ/17$; copying the angle between the positive x axis and OP (O is the origin) seventeen times around the unit circle provides the seventeen vertices of a 17-gon.

Gauss's construction of the 17-gon is one of the most compelling examples of the geometry of complex numbers, and Gauss asked that his tombstone be made in the shape of this wonderful, constructible polygon.

Chapter 10

Vectors and Matrices

10.1 What is a Vector?

A vector is simply an arrow from one point to another. For example, at right we have drawn some vectors in two dimensions (2D). Vectors can also be in three or, abstractly, even more dimensions. A vector is typically given a variable-type name, like v, and is denoted by $\vec{v}$. Also, the base point of a vector is called the **tail** and the end of the arrow the **head**.

The length of the vector $\vec{v}$ (distance from tail to head) is denoted by $\|\vec{v}\|$. A vector is typically regarded as depending only on its *length* and *direction*; the location of the starting point of the arrow is immaterial. Since the starting point doesn't matter, we can "add" two vectors by moving the tail of one vector to the head of the other, as at left, where the boldface vector is the sum of the other two.

We can easily verify that vector addition defined in this way is commutative, so that $\vec{v} + \vec{w} = \vec{w} + \vec{v}$. Just draw the two additions and note that the two copies each of $\vec{v}$ and $\vec{w}$ are parallel, as at right.

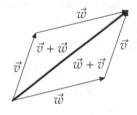

Using our definition of vector addition we can quickly expand to multipication by a positive real number: the vector $c\vec{v}$ for c a positive real is the vector in the same direction as $\vec{v}$ but with length $c\|\vec{v}\|$. (Convince yourself that this makes sense.) The vector $\vec{0}$ is defined to be the vector with length zero.

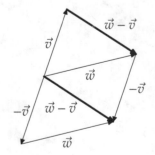

Similarly, the vector $-\vec{v}$ is just a vector with the same length as $\vec{v}$, but in the opposite direction. This way we get $\vec{v} + (-\vec{v}) = \vec{0}$, as we would normally expect. We can then define $\vec{w} - \vec{v} = \vec{w} + (-\vec{v})$, and we see from the diagram that $\vec{w} - \vec{v}$ is the vector that runs from the head of $\vec{v}$ to the head of $\vec{w}$. This should not be a surprise since $\vec{v} + (\vec{w} - \vec{v}) = \vec{w} + (\vec{v} - \vec{v}) = \vec{w}$.

10.2   The Dot Product

The length of the vector $\vec{w} - \vec{v}$ can be found using the law of cosines. Since $\vec{v}$, $\vec{w}$, and $\vec{w} - \vec{v}$ form a triangle whose sides have lengths $\|\vec{v}\|$, $\|\vec{w}\|$, and $\|\vec{w} - \vec{v}\|$, we have

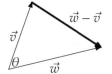

$$\|\vec{w} - \vec{v}\|^2 = \|\vec{v}\|^2 + \|\vec{w}\|^2 - 2\|\vec{v}\|\|\vec{w}\| \cos \theta, \qquad (10.1)$$

where θ is the angle between $\vec{v}$ and $\vec{w}$.

The expression $\|\vec{v}\|\|\vec{w}\| \cos \theta$ is called the **dot product** of $\vec{v}$ and $\vec{w}$; it is denoted by $\vec{v} \cdot \vec{w}$. We can then write (10.1) as

$$\|\vec{w} - \vec{v}\|^2 = \|\vec{v}\|^2 + \|\vec{w}\|^2 - 2\vec{v} \cdot \vec{w},$$

so that the dot product is given explicitly as

$$\vec{v} \cdot \vec{w} = \frac{\|\vec{v}\|^2 + \|\vec{w}\|^2 - \|\vec{w} - \vec{v}\|^2}{2}. \qquad (10.2)$$

We can establish certain nice properties of the dot product.

1. $\vec{v} \cdot \vec{w} = \vec{w} \cdot \vec{v}$. (The dot product is **commutative**.)

2. $\vec{v} \cdot \vec{w} = 0$ if and only if $\vec{v}$ and $\vec{w}$ are perpendicular.

3. $(c\vec{v}) \cdot \vec{w} = c(\vec{v} \cdot \vec{w})$ for any real number c.

4. $\vec{u} \cdot (\vec{v} + \vec{w}) = \vec{u} \cdot \vec{v} + \vec{u} \cdot \vec{w}$. (The dot product is **distributive**.)

EXAMPLE 10-1   Prove property 1 above.

Proof: Let $\theta_{\vec{w} \to \vec{v}}$ be the angle from $\vec{w}$ to $\vec{v}$, so that $\theta_{\vec{w} \to \vec{v}} = -\theta_{\vec{v} \to \vec{w}}$. Now we just write

$$\vec{w} \cdot \vec{v} = \|\vec{w}\|\|\vec{v}\| \cos \theta_{\vec{w} \to \vec{v}} = \|\vec{v}\|\|\vec{w}\| \cos(-\theta_{\vec{v} \to \vec{w}}) = \|\vec{v}\|\|\vec{w}\| \cos(\theta_{\vec{v} \to \vec{w}}) = \vec{v} \cdot \vec{w},$$

where we have used the fact that $\cos(-\theta) = \cos \theta$.

EXERCISE 10-1   Prove properties 2 and 3 above.

Property 4 is proved using coordinates in the next section (see Example 10-2).

Properties 3 and 4 mean that the dot product is **linear**.

The use of vectors as abstract "arrows" is most useful in vector geometry, which we do not treat until Chapter 12. In the next section we will begin to examine vectors in a particular coordinate system, which is more pertinent to elementary problems.

10.3   Coordinate Representation of Vectors

The standard way to represent vectors in a coordinate system is to define an origin and place the tails of our vectors there. We can then use regular rectangular coordinates with the given origin at the center, as at right. We associate a vector with the coordinates of its head; if the head coordinates are (x, y), the vector is represented as $\begin{pmatrix} x & y \end{pmatrix}$ or $\begin{pmatrix} x \\ y \end{pmatrix}$. The former representation is called a **row vector** and the latter a **column vector**. We'll generally use row vectors because they take up less space.

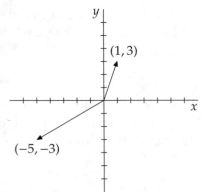

The power of the coordinate representation comes from the fact that we can use regular coordinate techniques. For example, the vector sum $\begin{pmatrix} x_1 & y_1 \end{pmatrix} + \begin{pmatrix} x_2 & y_2 \end{pmatrix}$ is just

$$\begin{pmatrix} (x_1 + x_2) & (y_1 + y_2) \end{pmatrix}.$$

EXERCISE 10-2   What is the length of the vector $\begin{pmatrix} 2 & 3 \end{pmatrix}$?

In the rectangular coordinate form, the dot product has a nice form. Consider two vectors $\vec{v}_1 = \begin{pmatrix} x_1 & y_1 \end{pmatrix}$ and $\vec{v}_2 = \begin{pmatrix} x_2 & y_2 \end{pmatrix}$ which form angles θ_1 and θ_2 with the positive x axis. Their dot product is found using polar coordinates:

$$
\begin{aligned}
\vec{v}_1 \cdot \vec{v}_2 &= \|\vec{v}_1\| \|\vec{v}_2\| \cos(\theta_1 - \theta_2) \\
&= \|\vec{v}_1\| \|\vec{v}_2\| (\cos \theta_1 \cos \theta_2 + \sin \theta_1 \sin \theta_2) \\
&= (\|\vec{v}_1\| \cos \theta_1)(\|\vec{v}_2\| \cos \theta_2) + (\|\vec{v}_1\| \sin \theta_1)(\|\vec{v}_2\| \sin \theta_2) \\
&= x_1 x_2 + y_1 y_2.
\end{aligned}
$$

EXAMPLE 10-2   Prove that the dot product is distributive.

Proof: Let $\vec{u} = \begin{pmatrix} x_0 & y_0 \end{pmatrix}$, $\vec{v} = \begin{pmatrix} x_1 & y_1 \end{pmatrix}$, and $\vec{w} = \begin{pmatrix} x_2 & y_2 \end{pmatrix}$. We have

$$\vec{u} \cdot (\vec{v} + \vec{w}) = x_0(x_1 + x_2) + y_0(y_1 + y_2) = (x_0 x_1 + y_0 y_1) + (x_0 x_2 + y_0 y_2) = (\vec{u} \cdot \vec{v}) + (\vec{u} \cdot \vec{w}),$$

as desired.

We can easily extend the coordinate representation into three (or more) dimensions. The dot product in three dimensions (**3D**) is

$$x_1 x_2 + y_1 y_2 + z_1 z_2,$$

and a similar expression holds in higher dimensions, even though we run out of letters.

EXERCISE 10-3   Show that $\begin{pmatrix} 1 & 17 & -3 & 2 \end{pmatrix}$ is perpendicular to $\begin{pmatrix} -6 & 1 & 5 & 2 \end{pmatrix}$.

The notion of vector addition gives us a swift, nice proof of the Triangle Inequality for complex numbers (page 90). If we view $\vec{v}$ and $\vec{w}$ as complex numbers v and w, so that $\vec{v} = \begin{pmatrix} v_1 & v_2 \end{pmatrix} \equiv v_1 + v_2 i$ and $\|\vec{v}\| = |v|$, the graph at right represents the addition $v + w$ in the complex plane. Since the vectors $\vec{v}$, $\vec{w}$, and $\vec{v} + \vec{w}$ form either a triangle or a straight line (when $\vec{v}$ and $\vec{w}$ are in the same direction), we have $\|\vec{v}\| + \|\vec{w}\| \geq \|\vec{v} + \vec{w}\|$ (since $\|\vec{v}\|$, $\|\vec{w}\|$, and $\|\vec{v} + \vec{w}\|$ are the sides

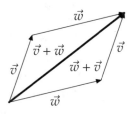

of a triangle, which may be degenerate). In complex number notation, this becomes $|v| + |w| \geq |v + w|$, and the equality condition of $v = cw$ follows from the observation that $\|\vec{v}\| + \|\vec{w}\| = \|\vec{v} + \vec{w}\|$ only if $\vec{v}$ and $\vec{w}$ are in the same direction, so $v_1 = cw_1$ and $v_2 = cw_2$.

10.4   What is a Matrix?

To understand what a matrix is, we will solve the following standard problem:

> *Given a point (x, y), what is the new point obtained after rotating (x, y) by an angle θ in the plane?*

We can do this using polar coordinates as we did on page 49. Here, we will rotate the point, not the axes, through an angle of θ counterclockwise. If the polar coordinates of the point are initially (r, α), then after the rotation the coordinates are $(r, \alpha + \theta)$. Then we can go back to rectangular coordinates. Let's call the new coordinates (x', y'); thus, we find

$$
\begin{aligned}
x' = r\cos(\alpha + \theta) &= r(\cos\alpha \cos\theta - \sin\alpha \sin\theta) \\
y' = r\sin(\alpha + \theta) &= r(\sin\alpha \cos\theta + \cos\alpha \sin\theta).
\end{aligned}
$$

Since $r\cos\alpha = x$ and $r\sin\alpha = y$ we can write these in terms of the original coordinates:

$$
\begin{aligned}
x' &= x\cos\theta - y\sin\theta \\
y' &= x\sin\theta + y\cos\theta.
\end{aligned} \tag{10.3}
$$

(Notice that these equations are different from those on page 49. This is because here we are rotating the point counterclockwise rather than the axes. We can see that the above equations are the same of those by noting that α on page 49 equals $-\theta$ here.) We have boiled the rotation down to a function from the old coordinates to the new coordinates. The functions for x' and y' are linear in x and y, so they are completely specified by four coefficients; we can use this to develop an efficient notation for the transformation.

If we write the old and new points as the vectors $\begin{pmatrix} x \\ y \end{pmatrix}$ and $\begin{pmatrix} x' \\ y' \end{pmatrix}$, then we can encapsulate the information in the transformation equations (10.3) with the form

$$
\begin{pmatrix} x' \\ y' \end{pmatrix} = \begin{pmatrix} \cos\theta & -\sin\theta \\ \sin\theta & \cos\theta \end{pmatrix} \begin{pmatrix} x \\ y \end{pmatrix}. \tag{10.4}
$$

Compare this closely to (10.3). The object by which we "multiply" the vector $\begin{pmatrix} x \\ y \end{pmatrix}$ is a **matrix**; each item in it is called an **entry**. Each entry corresponds to a particular coefficient in equations (10.3), as a comparison shows. The upper left entry is the coefficient from x to x', the upper right is from y to x', the lower left is from x to y', and the lower right is from y to y'.

We have gone from regarding the transformation (10.3) as transforming each coordinate according to an equation, to seeing it as the application of a transformation matrix to a vector. Let us examine the method by which, given only the *right* side of (10.4), we can get the left. In other words, given only the initial vector and the transformation matrix, how do we compute the transformed vector?

The answer is quite simple. To compute the first element of the new vector, we go across the first row of the matrix, multiplying the elements of the row by the corresponding elements of the vector. The resulting sum is the first element of the new vector. To compute the second element, we do the same with the second row of the matrix.

EXAMPLE 10-3   Let's carry out the process described above to multiply the vector $\begin{pmatrix} a \\ b \end{pmatrix}$ by the matrix $\begin{pmatrix} 2 & 3 \\ 4 & 5 \end{pmatrix}$. The first element of the product will be found by going across the top row of the matrix and down the vector to get $(2)(a) + (3)(b)$. The second element is formed with the second row of the matrix, going down the vector as before to get $(4)(a) + (5)(b)$. Thus we have

$$\begin{pmatrix} 2 & 3 \\ 4 & 5 \end{pmatrix} \begin{pmatrix} a \\ b \end{pmatrix} = \begin{pmatrix} 2a + 3b \\ 4a + 5b \end{pmatrix}.$$

EXERCISE 10-4   Find the product $\begin{pmatrix} 2 & -4 \\ -6 & 8 \end{pmatrix} \begin{pmatrix} 1 \\ -1 \end{pmatrix}$.

EXERCISE 10-5

   i. What is the effect of the matrix $\begin{pmatrix} 1 & 0 \\ 0 & -1 \end{pmatrix}$ on a general vector? Geometrically, what kind of a transformation is this?

   ii. Find the matrix which takes any vector to itself. This is called the **identity matrix**.

   iii. Can you guess what matrix multiplication looks like for 3D vectors?

Matrices are often named with letters, like vectors. Usually these are underlined, so the matrix named A is written $\underline{A}$. It is easy to verify that matrix multiplication of a vector is linear, meaning that $\underline{A}(\vec{v} + \vec{w}) = \underline{A}\vec{v} + \underline{A}\vec{w}$ and $\underline{A}(c\vec{v}) = c\underline{A}\vec{v}$.

EXERCISE 10-6   Verify that matrix multiplication of a vector is linear.

10.5   Matrix Multiplication

Once we understand the role of matrices as transformations of vectors, we can ask: what happens when we apply two transformations in a row? Say we have the vector $\begin{pmatrix} 1 \\ 1 \end{pmatrix}$, and we apply first the matrix $\begin{pmatrix} 3 & -4 \\ 5 & -6 \end{pmatrix}$, then the matrix $\begin{pmatrix} -1 & 2 \\ 3 & -4 \end{pmatrix}$. The result will be

$$\begin{pmatrix} -1 & 2 \\ 3 & -4 \end{pmatrix} \left[\begin{pmatrix} 3 & -4 \\ 5 & -6 \end{pmatrix} \begin{pmatrix} 1 \\ 1 \end{pmatrix} \right].$$

EXERCISE 10-7 If you still feel uncomfortable with multiplying a vector by a matrix, evaluate the above product explicitly.

Applying the matrices one at a time is fine; but suppose we wish to consider the two transformations as one, composite transformation? That is, we want to find a matrix $\underline{C}$ such that

$$\begin{pmatrix} -1 & 2 \\ 3 & -4 \end{pmatrix} \left[\begin{pmatrix} 3 & -4 \\ 5 & -6 \end{pmatrix} \begin{pmatrix} 1 \\ 1 \end{pmatrix} \right] = \underline{C} \begin{pmatrix} 1 \\ 1 \end{pmatrix}.$$

We shall define "matrix multiplication" so that the above holds with $\underline{C} = \begin{pmatrix} -1 & 2 \\ 3 & -4 \end{pmatrix} \begin{pmatrix} 3 & -4 \\ 5 & -6 \end{pmatrix}$, the product of the two matrices.

How shall we define this product matrix C? In general we have

$$\begin{pmatrix} a & b \\ c & d \end{pmatrix} \left[\begin{pmatrix} e & f \\ g & h \end{pmatrix} \begin{pmatrix} x \\ y \end{pmatrix} \right] = \begin{pmatrix} a & b \\ c & d \end{pmatrix} \begin{pmatrix} ex + fy \\ gx + hy \end{pmatrix}$$

$$= \begin{pmatrix} a(ex + fy) + b(gx + hy) \\ c(ex + fy) + b(gx + hy) \end{pmatrix}$$

$$= \begin{pmatrix} (ae + bg)x + (af + bh)y \\ (ce + dg)x + (cf + dh)y \end{pmatrix}$$

$$= \begin{pmatrix} ae + bg & af + bh \\ ce + dg & cf + dh \end{pmatrix} \begin{pmatrix} x \\ y \end{pmatrix}.$$

We shall thus *define* the product $\begin{pmatrix} a & b \\ c & d \end{pmatrix} \begin{pmatrix} e & f \\ g & h \end{pmatrix}$ to be the matrix $\begin{pmatrix} ae + bg & af + bh \\ ce + dg & cf + dh \end{pmatrix}$; then everything will work nicely.

If this seems like a rigged game, it is! We have chosen matrix multiplication so that it means something we want. Observe that the way to do matrix multiplication is the same as when we multiplied a vector by a matrix. In fact, if we consider only the first column of $\begin{pmatrix} e & f \\ g & h \end{pmatrix}$ and the first column of the product, we have matrix multiplication of a vector; the same is true for the second columns.

EXAMPLE 10-4 Find $\begin{pmatrix} -1 & 2 \\ 3 & -4 \end{pmatrix} \begin{pmatrix} 3 & -4 \\ 5 & -6 \end{pmatrix}$.

Solution: To get the top left entry in the product, we go across the top row of the first matrix and down the left column of the second, to get $(-1)(3) + (2)(5) = 7$. To get the top right entry, we go across the top row of the first matrix and down the right column of the seond, getting

$(-1)(-4) + (2)(-6) = -8$. To get the bottom left, we go across the bottom row of the first matrix and down the left column, getting $(3)(3) + (-4)(5) = -11$. To get the bottom right, we use the bottom row of the first matrix and the right column of the second, to get $(3)(-4) + (-4)(-6) = 12$. Thus the product is $\begin{pmatrix} 7 & -8 \\ -11 & 12 \end{pmatrix}$.

EXERCISE 10-8   Verify that column by column, matrix multiplication of matrices looks just like matrix multiplication of vectors.

EXAMPLE 10-5   By equation (10.4), a 90° rotation is given by $\begin{pmatrix} 0 & -1 \\ 1 & 0 \end{pmatrix}$, and a 180° rotation by $\begin{pmatrix} -1 & 0 \\ 0 & -1 \end{pmatrix}$. Doing one and then the other gives the transformation

$$\begin{pmatrix} -1 & 0 \\ 0 & -1 \end{pmatrix} \begin{pmatrix} 0 & -1 \\ 1 & 0 \end{pmatrix}.$$

To find the upper left entry in the product, go *across* the first row of $\begin{pmatrix} -1 & 0 \\ 0 & -1 \end{pmatrix}$ and *down* the first column of $\begin{pmatrix} 0 & -1 \\ 1 & 0 \end{pmatrix}$ to get $(-1)(0) + (0)(1) = 0$. For the upper right, go across the same row of the first matrix, but down the *second* column of the second, to get $(-1)(-1) + (0)(0) = 1$. For the bottom entries we do the same thing, but going across the second row of the first matrix. The result is $\begin{pmatrix} 0 & 1 \\ -1 & 0 \end{pmatrix}$.

EXERCISE 10-9   To what rotation does the product above correspond? Is this what you would expect?

EXERCISE 10-10   Evaluate $\begin{pmatrix} 2 & -3 \\ -4 & 5 \end{pmatrix} \begin{pmatrix} 1 & 1 \\ 2 & 3 \end{pmatrix}$.

EXERCISE 10-11   Geometrically, what do you get when you reflect through the x axis and then through the y axis? Show you get the right result in matrices by multiplying the matrix for x reflection, $\begin{pmatrix} -1 & 0 \\ 0 & 1 \end{pmatrix}$, by the matrix for y reflection.

Since matrix multiplication is transitive, $\underline{A}(\underline{BC}) = (\underline{AB})\underline{C}$. We usually just write $\underline{ABC}$ and do the multiplication in whichever order we want.

WARNING: It seems sensible that matrix multiplication would be commutative, so that $\underline{AB} = \underline{BA}$. However, this is NOT true!

EXERCISE 10-12   Show that matrix multiplication is not commutative by finding a simple counterexample.

Since we can multiply matrices, we can also take them to positive integral powers, just writing $\underline{AAAA}$ as $\underline{A}^4$, for example.

EXERCISE 10-13 Write down the matrix $\underline{A}$ for a rotation by 60°. Find $\underline{A}^6$ without any computation.

10.6   Matrices in Higher Dimensions

A 2×2 matrix has been used to represent a transformation from one 2D vector to another. If you thought about Exercise 10-5, you may have figured out how to extend this to 3D vectors. In three dimensional space each point has an x and y coordinate as in 2D, but also has a z coordinate to denote its distance above or below the xy plane. The positive x, y, and z axes are situated as shown.

Here a transformation from a vector $\begin{pmatrix} x & y & z \end{pmatrix}$ to a vector $\begin{pmatrix} x' & y' & z' \end{pmatrix}$ has the form $x' = ax + by + cz$, etc. There are nine coefficients to the transformation, that from x to x', from y to x', from z to x', from x to y', etc. (compare this to the discussion of 2×2 matrix entries on page 104.) We represent the coefficients in exactly the same way as for 2D matrices.

EXERCISE 10-14 Write down the 3×3 identity matrix.

EXAMPLE 10-6 We can easily write down the 3×3 matrix for a rotation by angle θ about the z axis. Clearly, the new z coordinate is the same as the old z coordinate, so the coefficient from z to z' is 1, while the coefficients from x and y to z' are 0 (no contribution). Also, neither x' nor y' is affected by z, so these two coefficients are 0. Finally, the other coefficients come from the standard rotation matrix of equation (10.4). The matrix is thus

$$\begin{pmatrix} \cos\theta & -\sin\theta & 0 \\ \sin\theta & \cos\theta & 0 \\ 0 & 0 & 1 \end{pmatrix}.$$

EXERCISE 10-15 Find the 3×3 matrix for:

   i. Rotation about the x axis.

   ii. Squashing all vectors to $\vec{0}$, the origin.

   iii. Reflection in the xy plane.

It is pretty simple to show that 3×3 matrices work the same as 2×2's in terms of associativity, noncommutativity, etc.

Since we can imagine vectors of more than 3 dimensions, we can similarly write down matrices which transform those vectors, such as 4×4, 5×5, etc. We can even write down matrices which are not square! For example, a 2×3 matrix (number of *rows* goes first) takes 3D vectors to 2D ones:

$$\begin{pmatrix} 1 & 2 & 3 \\ 4 & 5 & 6 \end{pmatrix} \begin{pmatrix} a \\ b \\ c \end{pmatrix} = \begin{pmatrix} a + 2b + 3c \\ 4a + 5b + 6c \end{pmatrix}. \tag{10.5}$$

All you need to remember is that to find an entry in the product, we go *across* the corresponding row and *down* the corresponding column. Study the above example if this is still unclear.

EXERCISE 10-16 Write down and multiply:

   i. Two 3×3 matrices.

   ii. A 2×4 and a 4×3 matrix.

   iii. A 1×3 and a 3×1 matrix. (To what does this correspond?) Compare the dimensions of the products to the dimensions of the original matrices in these three cases. Is there a pattern?

It seems strange, but only under certain circumstances can we multiply a $k \times l$ matrix by an $m \times n$ matrix. To see why, let the first matrix be $\underline{A}$ and the second $\underline{B}$.

EXAMPLE 10-7 Consider the multiplication $\underline{A}\vec{x}$. Find the dimensions of $\vec{x}$ and $\underline{A}\vec{x}$, where $\underline{A}$ is a $k \times l$ matrix.

Solution: In the multiplication we will be going across rows of $\underline{A}$ and down $\vec{x}$. Since $\underline{A}$ has l columns, each of its rows is l entries long. Thus $\vec{x}$ has l entries also, so is dimension l.

On the other hand, there will be one entry in the product $\underline{A}\vec{x}$ for each row of $\underline{A}$, as each entry in the product is formed by going across one row of $\underline{A}$. Thus the product will have k entries, so will be dimension k.

EXERCISE 10-17 Compare the preceding discussion to equation (10.5). Do the two agree?

For vectors $\vec{x}$ we have $(\underline{A}\underline{B})\vec{x} = \underline{A}(\underline{B}\vec{x})$, by associativity. Clearly $\vec{x}$ must be an n-dimensional vector if $\underline{B}$, which takes n-dimensional vectors to m-dimensional ones, can transform it. The product $\underline{B}\vec{x}$ will be m-dimensional. But this product must be l-dimensional to be transformed by $\underline{A}$! Thus we must have $m = l$.

Furthermore, the dimension of $\underline{A}\underline{B}\vec{x}$ will be k, since $\underline{A}$ was used last and its outputs are k-dimensional. Thus the product $\underline{A}\underline{B}$ takes n-dimensional vectors to k-dimensional ones, and must be a $k \times n$ matrix. It is this pattern that we were looking for in Exercise 10-16—go back and verify that it is true in those cases if you have not already.

10.7   Better Matrix Notation

Up to now we have written a general 2×2 matrix as $\underline{A} = \begin{pmatrix} a & b \\ c & d \end{pmatrix}$. A better way to write this is by labelling each entry by its row and column numbers. We would then write

$$\underline{A} = \begin{pmatrix} a_{11} & a_{12} \\ a_{21} & a_{22} \end{pmatrix}. \tag{10.6}$$

WARNING: As always with matrices, ROWS GO FIRST—for example, a_{42} is an entry in the fourth row, second column of $\underline{A}$, not the other way around.

We'll often use the a_{ij} notation because it is very efficient.

EXAMPLE 10-8 The 3×3 identity matrix is completely specified in this notation by

$$a_{ij} = \begin{cases} 1, & i = j \\ 0, & i \neq j \end{cases}.$$

Do you see why?

EXAMPLE 10-9 The product rule takes a nice form in this notation. Given $\underline{A}\underline{B} = \underline{C}$, with $\underline{A}$ an $l \times m$ matrix, $\underline{B}$ an $m \times n$, and $\underline{C}$ therefore a $l \times n$, we have

$$c_{ij} = a_{i1}b_{1j} + a_{i2}b_{2j} + \ldots + a_{im}b_{mj},$$

or to compress even more,

$$c_{ij} = \sum_{k=1}^{m} a_{ik}b_{kj}.$$

If these expressions are unclear, write $\underline{A}$ and $\underline{B}$ in the form (10.6) and multiply out to see. Try starting with small values, like $l = 2$, $m = 3$, $n = 4$.

EXERCISE 10-18 Express the matrix $\begin{pmatrix} 0 & 1 & 2 \\ -1 & 0 & 1 \\ -2 & -1 & 0 \end{pmatrix}$ in the manner of Example 10-8.

Problems to Solve for Chapter 10

155. Write down the 2D matrix for a rotation by $45°$.

156. Show how the multiplication of rotation matrices can be used to remember the trig identities $\sin(x + y) = \sin x \cos y + \sin y \cos x$ and $\cos(x + y) = \cos x \cos y - \sin x \sin y$.

157. Find the product

$$\begin{pmatrix} 2 & 1 & 9 \\ -6 & 0 & -3 \\ 1 & 3 & 2 \end{pmatrix} \begin{pmatrix} -2 & 11 & -1 \\ 4 & 4 & -3 \\ 3 & -2 & 1 \end{pmatrix}.$$

158. Three vertices of parallelogram $PQRS$ are $P(-3, -2)$, $Q(1, -5)$, $R(9, 1)$ with P and R diagonally opposite. What is coordinate S? (AHSME 1963)

159. Find the cosine of the angle between the vectors $\begin{pmatrix} 3 & 4 & 5 \end{pmatrix}$ and $\begin{pmatrix} -1 & 4 & 3 \end{pmatrix}$.

160. Matrix $\underline{A}$ has two rows, three columns. Matrix $\underline{B}$ has 4 rows, 2 columns. The existing product of these two matrices consists of how many elements? (MAΘ 1992)

161. Let $\underline{A}$ be the matrix

$$\begin{pmatrix} 15 & 2 \\ 6 & 7 \end{pmatrix}$$

and let x be the sum of the entries of a matrix $\underline{B}$ such that $\underline{AB} = \underline{BA}$. Find the smallest value of x over all matrices $\underline{B}$ whose entries are positive integers. (Mandelbrot #3)

162. What is the image of $\begin{pmatrix} 3 \\ 1 \\ 2 \end{pmatrix}$ under the mapping $\begin{pmatrix} 1 & 4 & 1 \\ -2 & 0 & 0 \\ 3 & 2 & -3 \end{pmatrix}$? (MAΘ 1991)

163. Find $\min f$ and $\max f$ where x and y are real numbers and

$$f(x, y) = 2 \sin x \cos y + 3 \sin x \sin y + 6 \cos x.$$

(M&IQ 1991)

──*the BIG PICTURE*─────

Imagine an atom (particle of matter) sitting in space. There are many possible "states" the atom could be in: vibrating fast or slow, spinning around in different ways, and so on. But as we pointed out in a *BIG PICTURE* in Volume 1, quantum mechanics can't tell us exactly which state the atom is in, just the *probabilities* of its being in each state. These probabilities are often thought of as a vector, $\vec{P} = \begin{pmatrix} P_1 & P_2 & P_3 & \cdots \end{pmatrix}$, where P_i is the probability of being in the *i*th state. So far we're on solid ground. But what if the atom has infinitely many possible states? Suddenly our nice, normal vector has become infinite-dimensional!

Now imagine a particle of light—a **photon**—flies onto the scene and our atom absorbs it. This will cause our atom to switch from its initial state to some other state. How do we know what other state? We don't! Again, we only know the probabilities. If the atom started in state *i*, there is some probability $A_{i\rightarrow 1}$ that it ends up in state 1, some probability $A_{i\rightarrow 2}$ that it ends up in state 2, and so on. (What does $A_{i\rightarrow i}$ represent?) Our original probability vector $\vec{P}$ thus transforms into a new probability vector $\vec{Q}$, which describes the probabilities after the absorption. How do we transform one vector to another? With a matrix, of course! We define a **transition matrix** $\underline{A}$, so that $\underline{A}\vec{P} = \vec{Q}$:

$$\begin{pmatrix} A_{1\rightarrow 1} & A_{2\rightarrow 1} & \cdots \\ A_{1\rightarrow 2} & A_{2\rightarrow 2} & \cdots \\ \vdots & \vdots & \ddots \end{pmatrix} \begin{pmatrix} P_1 \\ P_2 \\ \vdots \end{pmatrix} = \begin{pmatrix} Q_1 \\ Q_2 \\ \vdots \end{pmatrix}.$$

If you are familiar with the rules of probability, you might be able to understand this in more depth. Why, for example, is Q_1, the probability we end up in state 1, equal to $P_1 A_{1\rightarrow 1} + P_2 A_{2\rightarrow 1} + P_3 A_{3\rightarrow 1} + \cdots$? Can you see that we must have $P_1 + P_2 + P_3 + \cdots = Q_1 + Q_2 + Q_3 + \cdots = 1$?

To calculate the probability vectors and transition matrices takes some doing, but the mathematical apparatus of the infinite dimensional vectors involved is more or less the same as that for the humble 2D vectors we define in the text.

Chapter 11

Cross Products and Determinants

11.1 The Cross Product

We have seen in Chapter 10 that there is a connection between the dot product and vector *lengths*. We now define a special product between vectors which allows us to discuss *areas*.

So, given two 3D vectors $\vec{v}$ and $\vec{w}$, we shall define the **cross product** $\vec{v} \times \vec{w}$ to be the vector $\vec{x}$ such that

▷ $\vec{x}$ is perpendicular to both $\vec{v}$ and $\vec{w}$ (so that $\vec{x} \cdot \vec{v} = \vec{x} \cdot \vec{w} = 0$);

▷ the length of $\vec{x}$ is the area of the parallelogram spanned by $\vec{v}$ and $\vec{w}$, as in the figure at right.

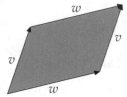

EXAMPLE 11-1 For any vectors $\vec{v}$ and $\vec{w}$, we have $(\vec{v} \times \vec{w}) \cdot \vec{v} = 0$, since we have defined the cross product to be such that $(\vec{v} \times \vec{w}) \perp \vec{v}$.

EXERCISE 11-1 What is the area of the parallelogram spanned by $\vec{v}$ and $\vec{w}$ in terms of $\|\vec{v}\|$, $\|\vec{w}\|$, and θ, the angle between the two vectors?

Given vectors $\vec{v}$ and $\vec{w}$, there are two vectors which satisfy our criteria for the cross product, one which points 'up' from the plane containing $\vec{v}$ and $\vec{w}$ and another which points 'down' from the plane. How do we know which vector is $\vec{v} \times \vec{w}$? There's no sound mathematical reason to choose one or the other, so we must adopt a convention which we can apply to any pair of vectors.

This brings to the dreaded **right hand rule**. This is nothing more than a way to remember in which of the two possible directions we choose our cross product to be.

▷ Consider the equation $\vec{v} \times \vec{w} = \vec{x}$. If you extend the index finger of your *right hand* along $\vec{v}$ and the middle finger along $\vec{w}$, then $\vec{x}$ will be along your thumb pointing perpendicular to the other two fingers.

EXAMPLE 11-2 If we take $\vec{v} = \begin{pmatrix} 0 & 1 & 0 \end{pmatrix}$ and $\vec{w} = \begin{pmatrix} 1 & 0 & 0 \end{pmatrix}$, then find $\vec{v} \times \vec{w}$.

Solution: Take the desired vector to be $\vec{x} = \begin{pmatrix} a & b & c \end{pmatrix}$. Then the dot products of $\vec{x}$ with $\vec{v}$ and $\vec{w}$ are a and b respectively; by the first condition on the cross product these must both equal zero, so $\vec{x} = \begin{pmatrix} 0 & 0 & c \end{pmatrix}$. By the second condition, the length $\|\vec{x}\| = |c|$ must be 1 (why?), so that c is ±1. The right hand rule tells us that $\vec{x}$ is pointing down, so $\vec{x} = \begin{pmatrix} 0 & 0 & -1 \end{pmatrix}$.

EXERCISE 11-2 As $\vec{v}$ stays fixed and $\vec{w}$ rotates in a full circle, describe the path followed by the tip of $\vec{v} \times \vec{w}$.

EXERCISE 11-3 Using the right hand rule, find the relationship between $\vec{v} \times \vec{w}$ and $\vec{w} \times \vec{v}$.

WARNING: Exercise 11-3 shows an important difference between the cross product and other products with which you are familiar. The cross product is NOT commutative; that is, $\vec{v} \times \vec{w} \neq \vec{w} \times \vec{v}$.

11.2   The Cross Product in Coordinates

Like the dot product, the cross product takes on a fairly simple form in the coordinate representation. If we take $\vec{v} = \begin{pmatrix} x_1 & y_1 & z_1 \end{pmatrix}$ and $\vec{w} = \begin{pmatrix} x_2 & y_2 & z_2 \end{pmatrix}$, then it can be shown that the vector

$$\vec{v} \times \vec{w} = \begin{pmatrix} (y_1 z_2 - y_2 z_1) & (z_1 x_2 - z_2 x_1) & (x_1 y_2 - x_2 y_1) \end{pmatrix} \tag{11.1}$$

has the desired properties. Since we have seen that there is only one vector satisfying all three defining conditions, this must be the desired cross product.

EXERCISE 11-4 Show that the vector $\vec{v} \times \vec{w}$ defined in (11.1) is perpendicular to both $\vec{v}$ and $\vec{w}$.

Although the cross product is not commutative, it is still linear, so $\vec{v} \times (\vec{w}_1 + \vec{w}_2) = (\vec{v} \times \vec{w}_1) + (\vec{v} \times \vec{w}_2)$ and $\vec{v} \times (c\vec{w}) = c(\vec{v} \times \vec{w})$. These properties can be easily verified using (11.1).

When we take the cross product of two vectors which are only two dimensional, we extend to three dimensions: we pretend that our vectors are actually three dimensional, with a z-component of 0. So if the vectors are $\begin{pmatrix} x_1 & y_1 \end{pmatrix}$ and $\begin{pmatrix} x_1 & y_2 \end{pmatrix}$, we write them as $\begin{pmatrix} x_1 & y_1 & 0 \end{pmatrix}$ and $\begin{pmatrix} x_1 & y_2 & 0 \end{pmatrix}$, tacking on a component of zero in the third dimension. We can then use (11.1).

EXERCISE 11-5 Use (11.1) to verify that the cross product of two 2D vectors points either straight up or straight down (in three dimensions).

11.3   The Determinant

We are now able to ask (and answer) a question which has been hanging about since the introduction of matrices, namely, is there a "size" for matrices? The size of a vector is simply its length. For matrices, however, the size depends on area, which we are only now ready to tackle.

A very common way to represent a vector is to break it down in terms of the fundamental unit vectors $\vec{i} = \begin{pmatrix} 1 & 0 \end{pmatrix}$ and $\vec{j} = \begin{pmatrix} 0 & 1 \end{pmatrix}$: $\begin{pmatrix} a & b \end{pmatrix} = a\vec{i} + b\vec{j}$. (Similarly, in 3D we have $\begin{pmatrix} a & b & c \end{pmatrix} = a\vec{i} + b\vec{j} + c\vec{k}$, where $\vec{k} = \begin{pmatrix} 0 & 0 & 1 \end{pmatrix}$.) Let us thus examine the action of a general 2D matrix $\underline{A} = \begin{pmatrix} a_{11} & a_{12} \\ a_{21} & a_{22} \end{pmatrix}$ on the unit vectors $\vec{i}$ and $\vec{j}$. We find

$$\underline{A}\vec{i} = \begin{pmatrix} a_{11} & a_{12} \\ a_{21} & a_{22} \end{pmatrix} \begin{pmatrix} 1 \\ 0 \end{pmatrix} = \begin{pmatrix} a_{11} \\ a_{21} \end{pmatrix} \quad \text{and} \quad \underline{A}\vec{j} = \begin{pmatrix} a_{11} & a_{12} \\ a_{21} & a_{22} \end{pmatrix} \begin{pmatrix} 0 \\ 1 \end{pmatrix} = \begin{pmatrix} a_{12} \\ a_{22} \end{pmatrix}.$$

Originally, $\vec{i}$ and $\vec{j}$ spanned a parallelogram (square) of area 1. After transforming by $\underline{A}$, the vectors span a parallelogram of area

$$\left| (\underline{A}\vec{i}) \times (\underline{A}\vec{j}) \right| = \left\| \begin{pmatrix} a_{11} \\ a_{21} \end{pmatrix} \times \begin{pmatrix} a_{12} \\ a_{22} \end{pmatrix} \right\| = \left| a_{11}a_{22} - a_{12}a_{21} \right|.$$

The quantity $a_{11}a_{22} - a_{12}a_{21}$ (no absolute value bars) is called the **determinant** of the 2D matrix $\underline{A}$, and is written $|\underline{A}|$ or $\det \underline{A}$. The determinant is thus the amount by which the area of the unit square is multiplied under transformation by $\underline{A}$. Since $|\underline{A}| = a_{11}a_{22} - a_{12}a_{21}$, we see that the determinant of a matrix can be negative. To what does this correspond? Since we've used cross products to find our determinant form, perhaps this sign change can be explained by them. A quick comparison of $|\underline{A}|$ to the cross product $(\underline{A}\vec{i}) \times (\underline{A}\vec{j})$ reveals that a negative determinant corresponds to a matrix which reverses the direction of the cross product of two vectors. (Compare $\vec{i} \times \vec{j}$ to $(\underline{A}\vec{i}) \times (\underline{A}\vec{j})$. When are they in the same direction? Opposite directions?)

How does the area of any other parallelogram change? Such a parallelogram is spanned by some two vectors $\vec{v}$ and $\vec{w}$; these vectors can be written as linear combinations $v_1\vec{i} + v_2\vec{j}$ and $w_1\vec{i} + w_2\vec{j}$, where v_1, v_2, w_1, and w_2 are real numbers.

EXERCISE 11-6   Find the area of the parallelogram spanned by $\vec{v}$ and $\vec{w}$ in terms of v_1, v_2, w_1, and w_2.

Under transformation by $\underline{A}$, $\vec{v}$ and $\vec{w}$ become $v_1\underline{A}\vec{i} + v_2\underline{A}\vec{j}$ and $w_1\underline{A}\vec{i} + w_2\underline{A}\vec{j}$, using the linearity of matrix multiplication. The area of the parallelogram spanned by these transformed vectors is then the absolute value of

$$(v_1\underline{A}\vec{i} + v_2\underline{A}\vec{j}) \times (w_1\underline{A}\vec{i} + w_2\underline{A}\vec{j}),$$

which by the linearity of the cross product is

$$(v_1w_2 - w_1v_2)(\underline{A}\vec{i} \times \underline{A}\vec{j}) + v_1w_1(\underline{A}\vec{i} \times \underline{A}\vec{i}) + v_2w_2(\underline{A}\vec{j} \times \underline{A}\vec{j}). \tag{11.2}$$

 EXERCISE 11-7   It looks like the coefficient of the first term in (11.2) should be $v_1w_2 + w_1v_2$, but we've written $v_1w_2 - w_1v_2$. Where does the $-$ sign come from?

EXERCISE 11-8   Prove that $\vec{v} \times \vec{v} = 0$ for any vector $\vec{v}$.

Using Exercise 11-8, equation (11.2) is simplified to

$$(v_1w_2 - v_2w_1)(\underline{A}\vec{i} \times \underline{A}\vec{j}) = |\underline{A}|(v_1w_2 - v_2w_1)\vec{k}, \tag{11.3}$$

which has a magnitude of $|\underline{A}|$ times the original area of the parallelogram! Thus *the area of any parallelogram is multiplied by $|\underline{A}|$ when transformed by $\underline{A}$.* (Again, negative $|\underline{A}|$ means the original parallelogram is 'flipped' by $\underline{A}$. Compare (11.3) to our description of negative determinants and cross products.) Even more strongly, since any area can be thought of as being covered by tiny little parallelograms, any area at all is multiplied by $|\underline{A}|$.

EXAMPLE 11-3 Find the determinant of $\begin{pmatrix} -2 & 2 \\ 1 & 3 \end{pmatrix}$.

Solution: The determinant is $(-2)(3) - (2)(1) = -\mathbf{8}$.

EXERCISE 11-9 Consider the rectangle formed by the points $(2,7)$, $(2,6)$, $(4,7)$, and $(4,6)$. Is it still a rectangle after transformation by $\begin{pmatrix} 3 & 1 \\ 2 & .5 \end{pmatrix}$? By what factor has its area changed?

EXERCISE 11-10 The circle with center $(-1,3)$ and radius 2 is transformed into some figure C by the matrix $\begin{pmatrix} 2 & 1 \\ -3 & 4 \end{pmatrix}$. Find the area of C.

The determinant is, it seems, a measure of how much a matrix stretches or squishes areas. What happens if we successively apply the transformations $\underline{A}$ and then $\underline{B}$? First an area K is multiplied by $|\underline{A}|$, then by $|\underline{B}|$, so the final area is $|\underline{B}|\,|\underline{A}|K$. On the other hand, we saw in Chapter 10 that we can view the successive transformations as a single, overall transformation $\underline{BA}$. Thus the area K is transformed to $|\underline{BA}|K$. Since the way of looking at the transformation (two separate or one compound) doesn't affect the final area, we must thus have

$$|\underline{BA}| = |\underline{B}|\,|\underline{A}|$$

for any two matrices $\underline{A}$ and $\underline{B}$.

EXERCISE 11-11 Find the determinant of the product

$$\begin{pmatrix} 2 & -3 \\ 7 & -4 \end{pmatrix} \begin{pmatrix} -5 & 1 \\ 3 & -1 \end{pmatrix} \begin{pmatrix} 2 & 6 \\ 0 & -4 \end{pmatrix}.$$

11.4 Determinants in Higher Dimensions

Determinants in dimensions greater than 2 can be defined by analogy. For example, the determinant of a 3×3 matrix is the amount by which the matrix stretches or squeezes *volumes*. The determinant of a general 3×3 matrix

$$\begin{pmatrix} a_{11} & a_{12} & a_{13} \\ a_{21} & a_{22} & a_{23} \\ a_{31} & a_{32} & a_{33} \end{pmatrix}$$

turns out (after some none-too-pleasant analytic geometry) to be

$$a_{11}a_{22}a_{33} + a_{12}a_{23}a_{31} + a_{13}a_{21}a_{32} - a_{12}a_{21}a_{33} - a_{13}a_{22}a_{31} - a_{11}a_{23}a_{32}.$$

As you can see, each three-term product contains one and only one element from each row and column; in fact, the sum contains *all* three-term products which satisfy this criterion. All that's left to understand is those strange +'s and −'s. Note that in each set of three the first indices are 1, 2, and 3 in that order, so the sign is determined from the second indices. In fact, if the order of the second indices is one switch away from the ordering 1, 2, 3 (e.g. $1, 2, 3 \to 2, 1, 3$) then the sign is −, and if it requires zero or two switches (e.g. $1, 2, 3 \to 2, 1, 3 \to 2, 3, 1$) then the sign is +.

EXAMPLE 11-4   We can use a simple shorthand to compute 3×3 determinants. Consider the determinant

$$\begin{vmatrix} 1 & 8 & -2 \\ 3 & -4 & 9 \\ 5 & -3 & 8 \end{vmatrix}.$$

(Note that the matrix is enclosed by vertical bars, rather than parentheses, to indicate the determinant.) We copy the first two columns on the other side of the bar, as:

$$\begin{array}{|ccc|cc|} 1 & 8 & -2 & 1 & 8 \\ 3 & -4 & 9 & 3 & -4 \\ 5 & -3 & 8 & 5 & -3 \end{array}$$

We can now get the determinant by forming products along all the long digonals of this grid. We add the products up, giving a + sign to those going down and to the right and a − sign to those going up and to the right. In this case, the diagonals going down yield $(1)(-4)(8) = -32$, $(8)(9)(5) = 360$, and $(-2)(3)(-3) = 18$. The diagonals going up, with their − signs, yield $-(5)(-4)(-2) = -40$, $-(-3)(9)(1) = 27$, and $-(8)(3)(8) = -192$. Adding up all these terms gives $-32 + 360 + 18 - 40 + 27 - 192 = \mathbf{141}$ as the determinant.

EXERCISE 11-12   Prove that the shorthand developed above works.

EXERCISE 11-13   Prove that multiplying all the entries in one row of $\underline{A}$ by c yields a matrix with determinant $c|\underline{A}|$.

EXERCISE 11-14   Matrix $\underline{B}$ is formed by multiplying all elements of $\underline{A}$ by c. Find the determinant $|\underline{B}|$ in terms of $|\underline{A}|$.

11.5   Minors

We have seen that there are simple forms for the 2×2 and 3×3 determinants. But what of the more complicated matrices of higher dimension? We start from the 3×3 determinant of matrix $\underline{A}$

$$\begin{vmatrix} a_{11} & a_{12} & a_{13} \\ a_{21} & a_{22} & a_{23} \\ a_{31} & a_{32} & a_{33} \end{vmatrix} = a_{11}a_{22}a_{33} - a_{11}a_{23}a_{32} + a_{12}a_{23}a_{31} - a_{12}a_{21}a_{33} + a_{13}a_{21}a_{32} - a_{13}a_{22}a_{31}.$$

Observe that the form of this determinant allows it to be broken down as

$$\begin{aligned} |\underline{A}| &= a_{11}(a_{22}a_{33} - a_{23}a_{32}) - a_{12}(a_{21}a_{33} - a_{23}a_{31}) + a_{13}(a_{21}a_{32} - a_{22}a_{31}) \\ &= a_{11}\begin{vmatrix} a_{22} & a_{23} \\ a_{32} & a_{33} \end{vmatrix} - a_{12}\begin{vmatrix} a_{21} & a_{23} \\ a_{31} & a_{33} \end{vmatrix} + a_{13}\begin{vmatrix} a_{21} & a_{22} \\ a_{31} & a_{32} \end{vmatrix}. \end{aligned}$$

The 3×3 determinant can be evaluated solely in terms of 2×2 determinants! (Verify this be inspection.) In fact, we can write this in other ways as well:

$$a_{13}\begin{vmatrix} a_{21} & a_{22} \\ a_{31} & a_{32} \end{vmatrix} - a_{23}\begin{vmatrix} a_{11} & a_{12} \\ a_{31} & a_{32} \end{vmatrix} + a_{33}\begin{vmatrix} a_{11} & a_{12} \\ a_{21} & a_{22} \end{vmatrix}$$

or

$$-a_{21}\begin{vmatrix} a_{12} & a_{13} \\ a_{32} & a_{33} \end{vmatrix} + a_{22}\begin{vmatrix} a_{11} & a_{13} \\ a_{31} & a_{33} \end{vmatrix} - a_{23}\begin{vmatrix} a_{11} & a_{12} \\ a_{31} & a_{32} \end{vmatrix},$$

to write two. (Verify these.) What are these forms? For each we have picked a row or column, and for each entry in the row or column multiplied the entry by the matrix formed by simply crossing out both the row and column in which the entry sits.

EXERCISE 11-15 The one thing left out of the discussion is the signs preceding the terms in the sums. Can you figure out how these signs are chosen?

We can immediately extend our observations to the case of any $n \times n$ matrix.

The step-by-step method to evaluate the determinant of any matrix.

1. Given an $n \times n$ matrix $\underline{A}$, go along any row or column, entry by entry.

2. For each entry a_{ij} in the row or column, find the determinant of the $(n-1) \times (n-1)$ matrix formed by crossing out the ith row and jth column of $\underline{A}$. Call this matrix $\underline{A}_{ij}$.

3. The determinant of $\underline{A}$ is the sum of $(-1)^{i+j}a_{ij}|\underline{A}_{ij}|$ for the entries in the chosen row or column.

This method is called **expansion by minors**, where the **minors** are the submatrices $\underline{A}_{ij}$ formed by crossing out the ith row and the jth column. Always remember to add the correct signs to the terms, as denoted by the $(-1)^{i+j}$ term in the sum.

EXERCISE 11-16 What does the matrix $a_{ij} = (-1)^{i+j}$ look like?

EXERCISE 11-17 We have seen by example that our method works for the 3×3 case. Show that it also works in the 2×2 case.

EXAMPLE 11-5 To make sure the explanation is clear, let's use minors on the 4×4 matrix

$$\begin{vmatrix} 1 & 3 & 5 & 7 \\ 2 & 1 & 0 & -1 \\ 2 & 4 & 6 & 8 \\ 6 & 5 & 3 & 2 \end{vmatrix}.$$

Let's use the third column, to make use of the 0. The expansion is

$$5\begin{vmatrix} 2 & 1 & -1 \\ 2 & 4 & 8 \\ 6 & 5 & 2 \end{vmatrix} - 0\begin{vmatrix} 1 & 3 & 7 \\ 2 & 4 & 8 \\ 6 & 5 & 2 \end{vmatrix} + 6\begin{vmatrix} 1 & 3 & 7 \\ 2 & 1 & -1 \\ 6 & 5 & 2 \end{vmatrix} - 3\begin{vmatrix} 1 & 3 & 7 \\ 2 & 1 & -1 \\ 2 & 4 & 8 \end{vmatrix}.$$

Evaluating the 3×3's this is $5(-6) - 0(\text{something}) + 6(5) - 3(0) = 0$.

EXERCISE 11-18 Write down a 3×3 determinant and evaluate it using expansion by minors. Evaluate it using the shortcut method to check your work.

≤ *EXERCISE 11-19* Use minors to evaluate the determinant of the **diagonal matrix**

$$\begin{pmatrix} a_{11} & 0 & 0 & \cdots & 0 \\ 0 & a_{22} & 0 & \cdots & 0 \\ \vdots & \vdots & \vdots & \ddots & \vdots \\ 0 & 0 & 0 & \cdots & a_{nn} \end{pmatrix}.$$

 ≤ *EXERCISE 11-20* How about of the **triangular matrix**

$$\begin{pmatrix} a_{11} & 0 & 0 & \cdots & 0 \\ a_{21} & a_{22} & 0 & \cdots & 0 \\ \vdots & \vdots & \vdots & \ddots & \vdots \\ a_{n1} & a_{n2} & a_{n3} & \cdots & a_{nn} \end{pmatrix}?$$

EXERCISE 11-21 Prove that any matrix with a row or column made up of all 0's has determinant 0.

It is important to realize that minors only gives us a way to go from an $n \times n$ determinant to n $(n-1) \times (n-1)$ determinants. Thus it is not perfect—to do a 6×6 matrix by the minors method would mean doing $6\ 5 \times 5$'s, or $30\ 4 \times 4$'s, or $120\ 3 \times 3$'s (which we could then do directly). In theory, we can (eventually) do any determinant this way. But as Example 11-5 shows, this is a lot of work, even for the 4×4 case.

11.6   Row and Column Operations

To think seriously about doing large determinants, we need a way to simplify them before we use minors. Luckily, there is such a method. It turns out that if we add any column to any other, the determinant is the same. What does "adding a column to another" look like? In the 3×3 case it could be

$$\begin{vmatrix} a_{11} & a_{12} & a_{13} \\ a_{21} & a_{22} & a_{23} \\ a_{31} & a_{32} & a_{33} \end{vmatrix} = \begin{vmatrix} a_{11} & a_{12} + a_{13} & a_{13} \\ a_{21} & a_{22} + a_{23} & a_{23} \\ a_{31} & a_{32} + a_{33} & a_{33} \end{vmatrix}.$$

The same works for subtraction, and for rows instead of columns. Moreover, it works for adding any multiple of a row or column.

To see why this is useful, let us redo Example 11-5, which was so messy using minors.

EXAMPLE 11-6 We evaluate the determinant

$$\begin{vmatrix} 1 & 3 & 5 & 7 \\ 2 & 1 & 0 & -1 \\ 2 & 4 & 6 & 8 \\ 6 & 5 & 3 & 2 \end{vmatrix}.$$

Let's subtract the first row from the third to get

$$\begin{vmatrix} 1 & 3 & 5 & 7 \\ 2 & 1 & 0 & -1 \\ 1 & 1 & 1 & 1 \\ 6 & 5 & 3 & 2 \end{vmatrix}.$$

Now adding twice the second row to the first row we get

$$\begin{vmatrix} 5 & 5 & 5 & 5 \\ 2 & 1 & 0 & -1 \\ 1 & 1 & 1 & 1 \\ 6 & 5 & 3 & 2 \end{vmatrix}.$$

We can then subtract five times the third row from the first to get

$$\begin{vmatrix} 0 & 0 & 0 & 0 \\ 2 & 1 & 0 & -1 \\ 1 & 1 & 1 & 1 \\ 6 & 5 & 3 & 2 \end{vmatrix},$$

which, upon expanding by minors along the first row, is clearly **0**.

We don't often get it quite so nice as this. Usually, we do have to expand one or more of the minors. But by forming a row or column which is mostly 0's, with only one or two nonzero terms, we can greatly reduce the number of minors we need to do.

EXERCISE 11-22 Do as little work as possible in evaluating the determinant

$$\begin{vmatrix} 17 & 23 & 23 & 23 \\ 17 & 17 & 23 & 23 \\ 17 & 17 & 17 & 23 \\ 17 & 17 & 17 & 17 \end{vmatrix}.$$

EXERCISE 11-23 Prove that any matrix with two identical rows or columns has determinant 0.

EXERCISE 11-24 Justify Exercises 11-13 and 11-14 in terms of minors.

EXAMPLE 11-7 Remembering the formula (11.1) for the cross product isn't so easy, but there is a very nice shorthand which does the trick. Recalling that the unit vectors are $\vec{i} = \begin{pmatrix} 1 & 0 & 0 \end{pmatrix}$, $\vec{j} = \begin{pmatrix} 0 & 1 & 0 \end{pmatrix}$, and $\vec{k} = \begin{pmatrix} 0 & 0 & 1 \end{pmatrix}$, we can write

$$\begin{pmatrix} x_1 & y_1 & z_1 \end{pmatrix} \times \begin{pmatrix} x_2 & y_2 & z_2 \end{pmatrix} = \begin{vmatrix} \vec{i} & \vec{j} & \vec{k} \\ x_1 & y_1 & z_1 \\ x_2 & y_2 & z_2 \end{vmatrix}.$$

There are many ways to see that this determinant is the cross product. For one thing, expansion by minors shows that it simplifies to $\vec{i}(y_1z_2 - z_1y_2) + \vec{j}(z_1x_2 - x_1z_2) + \vec{k}(x_1y_2 - y_1x_2)$, which is clearly equivalent to (11.1).

EXERCISE 11-25   Using the previous example, show that

$$\begin{pmatrix} x_0 & y_0 & z_0 \end{pmatrix} \cdot \left(\begin{pmatrix} x_1 & y_1 & z_1 \end{pmatrix} \times \begin{pmatrix} x_2 & y_2 & z_2 \end{pmatrix} \right) = \begin{vmatrix} x_0 & y_0 & z_0 \\ x_1 & y_1 & z_1 \\ x_2 & y_2 & z_2 \end{vmatrix}$$

for any vectors $\begin{pmatrix} x_0 & y_0 & z_0 \end{pmatrix}$, $\begin{pmatrix} x_1 & y_1 & z_1 \end{pmatrix}$, and $\begin{pmatrix} x_2 & y_2 & z_2 \end{pmatrix}$. This is a simple form for the **box product** defined in Chapter 12, and provides an easy way to measure the volume of any parallelepiped.

EXERCISE 11-26   Show that the cross product defined in Example 11-7 is perpendicular to both $\begin{pmatrix} x_1 & y_1 & z_1 \end{pmatrix}$ and $\begin{pmatrix} x_2 & y_2 & z_2 \end{pmatrix}$. (Use the previous exercise.)

11.7   The Inverse of a Matrix

We have discussed how, using repeated multiplications, we can find "powers" $\underline{A}^2, \underline{A}^3$, etc. of a matrix $\underline{A}$. We have had to wait for the determinant to define negative powers of matrices in a consistent way.

Given a real number $a \neq 0$, we always have $a^0 = 1$ and $a^{-1}a = 1$. For the $n \times n$ matrices, the equivalent to the real number 1 is the identity matrix $\underline{I}_n$. We thus define $\underline{A}^0 = \underline{I}_n$ for $|\underline{A}| \neq 0$. The restriction on the determinant of $\underline{A}$ is equivalent to the requirement $a \neq 0$ for real numbers. Why? Remember that $|\underline{AB}| = |\underline{A}||\underline{B}|$. We thus can expect that $|\underline{A}^n| = |\underline{A}|^n$. For $|\underline{A}| \neq 0$, we thus have $|\underline{A}|^0 = 1 = |\underline{A}^0| = |\underline{I}_n|$, which is correct. But for $|\underline{A}| = 0$, $|\underline{A}|^0 = 0^0$, which is undefined.

Once we have defined $\underline{A}^0$, we can define the **inverse** $\underline{A}^{-1}$ for $|\underline{A}| \neq 0$ to be the matrix $\underline{B}$ such that $\underline{AB} = \underline{I}_n$. We can show $\underline{A}$ commutes with its inverse by multiplying $\underline{AB} = \underline{I}_n$ by $\underline{B}$, yielding $\underline{BAB} = \underline{B}$. Hence, $(\underline{BA})\underline{B} = \underline{B}$, so that $\underline{BA}$ leaves $\underline{B}$ unchanged. Thus, we must have $\underline{BA} = \underline{I}_n = \underline{AB}$.

EXERCISE 11-27   Use the original, geometric definition of the determinant to show that a matrix with determinant 0 can't have an inverse.

EXAMPLE 11-8   Let's find the inverse of a 2×2 matrix $\underline{A} = \begin{pmatrix} a & b \\ c & d \end{pmatrix}$. Call the inverse $\begin{pmatrix} x & y \\ z & w \end{pmatrix}$, and write $\begin{pmatrix} a & b \\ c & d \end{pmatrix} \begin{pmatrix} x & y \\ z & w \end{pmatrix} = \underline{I}_2 = \begin{pmatrix} 1 & 0 \\ 0 & 1 \end{pmatrix}$. Performing the multiplication, we get $\begin{pmatrix} ax + bz & ay + bw \\ cx + dz & cy + dw \end{pmatrix} = \begin{pmatrix} 1 & 0 \\ 0 & 1 \end{pmatrix}$, so we have four equations: $ax + bz = 1$; $ay + bw = 0$; $cx + dz = 0$; $cy + dw = 1$. Solving these equations for x, y, z, w we get $x = d/(ad - bc) = d/|\underline{A}|$, $y = -b/|\underline{A}|$, $z = -c/|\underline{A}|$, $w = a/|\underline{A}|$. Thus the inverse of the general 2×2 matrix $\underline{A} = \begin{pmatrix} a & b \\ c & d \end{pmatrix}$ is given by

$$\underline{A}^{-1} = \frac{1}{|\underline{A}|} \begin{pmatrix} d & -b \\ -c & a \end{pmatrix}.$$

It is natural to ask whether there is a general prescription to find the inverse of a given matrix. There is, but it is quite a mess. We need first to define the **transpose** $\underline{A}^{\mathrm{T}}$ of a matrix $\underline{A}$, which is just the matrix obtained by flipping the matrix over its main diagonal:

$$\begin{pmatrix} 1 & 2 & 3 \\ 4 & 5 & 6 \\ 7 & 8 & 9 \end{pmatrix}^{\mathrm{T}} = \begin{pmatrix} 1 & 4 & 7 \\ 2 & 5 & 8 \\ 3 & 6 & 9 \end{pmatrix}.$$

(Another way to look at the transpose is that we have reversed the roles of rows and columns, so that every entry a_{ij} is replaced by a_{ji}.)

To find the inverse of the $n \times n$ matrix $\underline{A}$:

1. Replace each entry by the determinant of its minor.

2. Change the signs by multiplying each entry a_{ij} by $(-1)^{i+j}$, as was done for minors.

3. Divide by $|\underline{A}|$.

4. Transpose the matrix. The result is $\underline{A}^{-1}$.

Although this is very messy, often you are only asked to find one element of the inverse, which is much simpler, as in Example 11-9. Also, remember that the determinant of $\underline{A}^{-1}$ is $1/|\underline{A}|$, so you don't need to compute the inverse at all to compute its determinant!

EXERCISE 11-28 Show that the formula we obtained in Example 11-8 for the inverse of a 2×2 matrix agrees with the form we get using the general method.

EXAMPLE 11-9 Find the entry in the third row, second column of the inverse of

$$\begin{pmatrix} 4 & 8 & 7 \\ 2 & 3 & 11 \\ 6 & 3 & 1 \end{pmatrix}.$$

Solution: Since we will need the determinant, let's find that first. We subtract twice the second row from the first and three times the second row from the third to get

$$\begin{vmatrix} 4 & 8 & 7 \\ 2 & 3 & 11 \\ 6 & 3 & 1 \end{vmatrix} = \begin{vmatrix} 0 & 2 & -15 \\ 2 & 3 & 11 \\ 0 & -6 & -32 \end{vmatrix}.$$

Expanding by minors down the first column we have $-2 \begin{vmatrix} 2 & -15 \\ -6 & -32 \end{vmatrix}$, or 308. (Note how easy row operations make this; note also the sign due to the location of the 2.) Now the entry in the third row, second column of the inverse corresponds to the entry in the second row, third column of the matrix, because the last step is transposition. The entry we are interested in is thus the 11. Its minor is $\begin{pmatrix} 4 & 8 \\ 6 & 3 \end{pmatrix}$, with determinant -36. The sign changes because of the position of the 11, so we have 36. The entry in the inverse is just this divided by the determinant, or $36/308 = \mathbf{9/77}$.

EXERCISE 11-29 Use the general method to find the inverse of the 4×4 identity matrix. Is this what you expected?

EXERCISE 11-30 Practice by finding the inverse of a random 3×3 matrix. Check that the inverse times the original matrix gives I_3.

Just finding one entry of the inverse can require some work, so it is important to do as little as possible, using row and column operations to simplify the determinant and other shortcuts.

Once we have defined $\underline{A}^{-1}$, we define $\underline{A}^{-2} = (\underline{A}^{-1})^2$, etc. We can now take any integral power of a matrix with nonzero determinant.

Problems to Solve for Chapter 11

164. A is a 2 by 2 matrix whose entries are the first four prime numbers. What is the largest possible value of $\det A$? (MAΘ 1992)

165. Find the value of A if

$$A = \begin{vmatrix} 4 & 4 & -3 & 2 \\ -3 & -2 & 2 & 3 \\ 2 & 5 & 4 & -2 \\ 3 & -3 & -2 & 0 \end{vmatrix}.$$

(MAΘ 1992)

166. For what value of c will there be no inverse for the matrix

$$\begin{pmatrix} 1 & 4 & c \\ 2 & -1 & 7 \\ 3 & -2 & 11 \end{pmatrix}?$$

(MAΘ 1991)

167. Find the determinant of the product CBA, where $A = \begin{pmatrix} 2 & 1 \\ 3 & 4 \end{pmatrix}$, $B = \begin{pmatrix} 2 & 3 \\ 5 & 4 \end{pmatrix}$ and $C = \begin{pmatrix} 2 & 1 \\ 6 & 1 \end{pmatrix}$. (MAΘ 1991)

168. Evaluate the following determinant, giving the answer in factored form. (MAΘ 1991)

$$\begin{vmatrix} a & 1 & 1 & 1 \\ 1 & a & 1 & 1 \\ 1 & 1 & a & 1 \\ 1 & 1 & 1 & a \end{vmatrix}$$

169. If $\begin{vmatrix} W & X \\ Y & Z \end{vmatrix} = 4$, then find $\begin{vmatrix} 4W & 4X \\ 4Y & 4Z \end{vmatrix}$. (MAΘ 1991)

170. Evaluate the determinant below.

$$\begin{vmatrix} 3 & 1 & 1 & 1 & 1 & 1 \\ 3 & 3 & 1 & 1 & 1 & 1 \\ 3 & 3 & 3 & 1 & 1 & 1 \\ 3 & 3 & 3 & 3 & 1 & 1 \\ 3 & 3 & 3 & 3 & 3 & 1 \\ 3 & 3 & 3 & 3 & 3 & 3 \end{vmatrix}$$

(Mandelbrot #1)

171. If $A = \begin{pmatrix} 4 & 2 \\ 1 & 1 \end{pmatrix}$, then find A^{-2}. (MAΘ 1991)

172. Find a matrix whose determinant, when set equal to zero, represents the equation of a circle passing through the points $(-3, 1)$, $(2, 4)$, and $(5, -2)$. (MAΘ 1991)

Chapter 12

Analytic Geometry

12.1   Lines, Angles, and Distances

Let point A be $(x_1, 0)$ and point B be (x_2, y_2). Hence, we have

$$\tan\theta = \frac{BX}{AX} = \frac{y_2 - 0}{x_2 - x_1} = m,$$

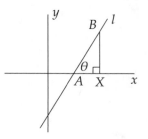

the slope of line l. From this we see that if line l makes an angle θ with the positive x axis, then $\tan\theta$ equals the slope of the line.

EXAMPLE 12-1   Find the slope of a line which makes a 120° angle with the positive x axis.

   Solution: Applying $\tan\theta = m$, which works perfectly fine for obtuse angles since the slopes of such lines are negative, we find that the slope of the line is $\tan 120° = m = -\sqrt{3}$.

How about two lines? Draw a horizontal line through the intersection point of lines l and n. Let α be the angle line l makes with the horizontal, β be the angle between l and n, and $\theta = \alpha + \beta$. Hence, if m_1 is the slope of l and m_2 is the slope of n, we have $\tan\alpha = m_1$ and $\tan\theta = m_2$ and

$$\tan\beta = \tan(\theta - \alpha) = \frac{\tan\theta - \tan\alpha}{1 + \tan\theta\tan\alpha} = \frac{m_2 - m_1}{1 + m_1 m_2}.$$

EXAMPLE 12-2   Find the acute angle made by the lines $2x - y = 3$ and $x - 3y = 4$.

   Solution: The slopes of the two lines are 2 and 1/3, so from the above discussion we find

$$\tan\theta = \frac{\frac{1}{3} - 2}{1 + (1/3)(2)} = -1.$$

Since $\tan\theta = -1$, the angle between the lines is 135°. WARNING: The problem asks for the acute angle, not the obtuse angle. Hence, our desired answer is $180° - 135° = \mathbf{45°}$. Keep an eye out for this; we can take the slopes of the line in either order, so $\tan\theta$ can be negative or positive, corresponding to the obtuse and acute angles between the lines, respectively.

EXERCISE 12-1   Find the tangent of the obtuse angle formed by $2x - 3y = 4$ and $x - 3y + 2 = 0$.

12.2   Parameters

Curves are really one-dimensional figures, so we should be able to describe them with a single variable instead of the usual x and y. Let's start with the unit circle,

$$x^2 + y^2 = 1.$$

We can describe this circle with one variable using trigonometry. Recall that we can let $x = \cos \theta$ and $y = \sin \theta$. Hence, as θ ranges from 0 to 2π, we trace out the entire circle. For this representation, we say that

$$\begin{aligned} x &= \cos \theta \\ y &= \sin \theta \end{aligned}$$

are the **parametric equations** that describe the circle $x^2 + y^2 = 1$. The dummy variable θ is called the **parameter**. This parametric description is useful not only because it has only one variable θ, but also because θ is unconstrained—it can take on any value. In our original (x, y) descriptions, only certain pairs (x, y) are on the circle.

Let's try a more complicated circle:

$$(x - 5)^2 + (y - 3)^2 = 16.$$

We wish to find a pair of functions such that $x = f(\theta)$ and $y = g(\theta)$ describe the above circle. Note that if we write $x = 5 + f_1(\theta)$ and $y = 3 + g_1(\theta)$, our circle becomes

$$[f_1(\theta)]^2 + [g_1(\theta)]^2 = 16.$$

This is highly suggestive of our initial circle, so we let $f_1(\theta) = 4\cos \theta$ and $g_1(\theta) = 4\sin \theta$, and our parametric representation of the circle is

$$\begin{aligned} x &= 5 + 4\cos \theta \\ y &= 3 + 4\sin \theta. \end{aligned}$$

EXAMPLE 12-3   Find a parametric description of the line $2x + 3y = 5$.

Solution: There are many possible representations; we find ours by solving the equation for y:

$$y = -\frac{2}{3}x + \frac{5}{3}.$$

Thus, one possible parametric description of the line is

$$\begin{aligned} x &= t \\ y &= -2t/3 + 5/3. \end{aligned}$$

EXERCISE 12-2 Find a parametric representation for the curve $9x^2 - 4y^2 - 72x + 16y + 164 = 0$.

EXAMPLE 12-4 Find a general parametric representation for the ellipse

$$\frac{(x-h)^2}{a^2} + \frac{(y-k)^2}{b^2} = 1.$$

Solution: Comparing this to the identity $\sin^2 \theta + \cos^2 \theta = 1$, we see that we can develop a parametric form by letting $(x-h)^2/a^2 = \sin^2 \theta$. Taking square roots, we find $x = h + a \sin \theta$. Similarly, we find $y = k + b \cos \theta$ to complete the problem. In the same method as above, we can use the identity $\sec^2 \theta - \tan^2 \theta = 1$ to develop a parameterization of a general hyperbola.

Just as important as finding parametric representations for curves is determining the original equation for a curve given the parametric equations describing it. Let's try an example.

Find the equation of a curve satisfying the parametric equations

$$x = 3 + \log t^2$$
$$y = 2 - \log t.$$

To get rid of our parameter, we combine the equations to eliminate t, or solve for the parameter in one equation and substitute in the other. When trigonometric functions of parameters occur, we can also use various identities to get rid of the parameters. In this case, we note the first equation is equivalent to $x = 3 + 2 \log t$. Now we can eliminate $\log t$ by multiplying the equation for y by 2 and adding the result ($2y = 4 - 2 \log t$) to the equation for x, yielding $x + 2y = 7$ as the desired equation.

EXAMPLE 12-5 Find the curve satisfying the parametric equations

$$x = \cos t - \sin t$$
$$y = \sin 2t.$$

Solution: Recall from our discussion of trigonometry that squaring the first equation gives

$$x^2 = (\cos t - \sin t)^2 = \cos^2 t - 2 \sin t \cos t + \sin^2 t = 1 - \sin 2t.$$

Since $\sin 2t = y$, the desired equation is $x^2 = 1 - y$, a parabola.

EXERCISE 12-3 Find the curve described by

$$x = (\sin^2 \theta)/(\cos \theta)$$
$$y = \cos \theta.$$

12.3   Vectors

First we'll run through a quick review of a few important concepts which we'll be using in this chapter. In the diagram, let O be the origin, $\vec{a}$ be the vector representing $\overrightarrow{OA}$, and $\vec{b}$ be the vector representing $\overrightarrow{OB}$. Since $\vec{a} \cdot \vec{b} = \|\vec{a}\|\|\vec{b}\| \cos \angle AOB$, we have

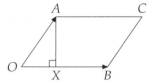

$$\vec{a} \cdot \vec{b} = (AO)(OB)\frac{OX}{AO} = (OB)(OX).$$

Thus the dot product of $\vec{a}$ and $\vec{b}$ is the length of $\vec{b}$ times the length of the projection of OA onto OB (segment OX above). Make sure you understand this interpretation of the dot product as a measure of projection. Finally, recall that $\vec{a}$ and $\vec{b}$ are perpendicular if and only if $\vec{a} \cdot \vec{b} = 0$. (To what projection does a negative dot product correspond? Draw two vectors which have a negative dot product and you'll see!)

EXAMPLE 12-6   Find the vector which is **normal**, or perpendicular, to the line $2x + 3y - 7 = 0$.

Solution: Consider two points (x_1, y_1) and (x_2, y_2) on the line. Hence, we have

$$2x_1 + 3y_1 - 7 = 0 \text{ and}$$
$$2x_2 + 3y_2 - 7 = 0.$$

Subtracting the first from the second

$$2(x_2 - x_1) + 3(y_2 - y_1) = \begin{pmatrix} 2 & 3 \end{pmatrix} \cdot \begin{pmatrix} x_2 - x_1 & y_2 - y_1 \end{pmatrix} = 0.$$

The second vector in the dot product is the vector in the direction of the line since (x_1, y_1) and (x_2, y_2) are on the line. Since the dot product is 0, the vector $\begin{pmatrix} 2 & 3 \end{pmatrix}$ is normal to the line.

Our work on this problem shows us how to determine the vector, $\vec{v}$ from point $P_1 = (x_1, y_1)$ to $P_2 = (x_2, y_2)$. In going from P_1 to P_2, the x-coordinate changes by $x_2 - x_1$ and the y-coordinate by $y_2 - y_1$. These changes give us our vector, $\vec{v} = \begin{pmatrix} x_2 - x_1 & y_2 - y_1 \end{pmatrix}$.

EXAMPLE 12-7   Find the distance from (x_0, y_0) to the line $Ax + By + C = 0$.

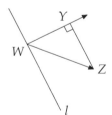

Solution: Let the line be line l in the diagram and the point be Z. Suppose point $W(x_1, y_1)$ lies on l. If we draw a line through Z parallel to l, the distance between the parallel line and l is the desired distance. In the diagram this line through Z intersects the normal to line l through W at Y. From this we see that the distance we seek is the length of the projection of $\overrightarrow{WZ}$ onto the normal $\vec{n}$ to line l through W. As in the prior example we can show that this normal is $\begin{pmatrix} A & B \end{pmatrix}$, and our distance is

$$\frac{|\overrightarrow{WZ} \cdot \vec{n}|}{\|\vec{n}\|} = \frac{|A(x_0 - x_1) + B(y_0 - y_1)|}{\sqrt{A^2 + B^2}} = \frac{|Ax_0 + By_0 - (Ax_1 + By_1)|}{\sqrt{A^2 + B^2}}.$$

Since (x_1, y_1) is on l, we have $Ax_1 + By_1 = -C$, and the distance is

$$\frac{|Ax_0 + By_0 + C|}{\sqrt{A^2 + B^2}}.$$

EXERCISE 12-4   In the previous example, why do we divide by $\|\vec{n}\|$ in determining the distance between the point and the line.

Now let's look at the cross product. First, $\vec{a} \times \vec{b}$ is a vector normal to the plane containing $\vec{a}$ and $\vec{b}$. The length of the cross product is found by

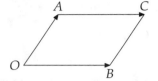

$$\|\vec{a} \times \vec{b}\| = \|\vec{a}\|\|\vec{b}\| \sin \angle AOB = (AO)(OB) \sin \angle AOB,$$

which is equal to the area of parallelogram $OACB$, where C is found by copying vector $\overrightarrow{OB}$ at A. Since $[ABO]$ is half of this parallelogram, we can find $[ABO]$ as half the magnitude of $\vec{a} \times \vec{b}$.

EXAMPLE 12-8   Find the area of the triangle with vertices $(5, 4)$, $(3, 6)$, and $(2, 1)$.

Solution: Let A, B, and C, respectively be the aforementioned vertices. Let's write them as three dimensional points with 0 in the z dimension (for example point A is $(5, 4, 0)$) so we can use cross products. Let C be the origin and $\vec{a}$ and $\vec{b}$ be $\overrightarrow{CA}$ and $\overrightarrow{CB}$. Hence, $\vec{a} = \begin{pmatrix} 5-2 & 4-1 & 0-0 \end{pmatrix} = \begin{pmatrix} 3 & 3 & 0 \end{pmatrix}$ and $\vec{b} = \begin{pmatrix} 1 & 5 & 0 \end{pmatrix}$. Thus, $\vec{a} \times \vec{b} = \begin{pmatrix} 0 & 0 & 12 \end{pmatrix}$. The magnitude of this is 12, so the area of the desired triangle is $12/2 = \textbf{6}$.

 EXERCISE 12-5   Prove, using the same approach as in the prior example, that the area of the triangle with vertices (x_1, y_1), (x_2, y_2), and (x_3, y_3) is the absolute value of

$$\frac{1}{2}\begin{vmatrix} x_1 & y_1 & 1 \\ x_2 & y_2 & 1 \\ x_3 & y_3 & 1 \end{vmatrix}.$$

 EXERCISE 12-6   Prove that if we have a convex polygon (meaning any segment connecting two points in the polygon is contained entirely within the polygon) with n vertices in order at (x_1, y_1), ..., (x_n, y_n), then we can find the area as follows. List the vertices vertically in order, putting the first point both first and last as in the middle two columns below, then find the products along diagonals as shown

$$
\begin{array}{ccccc}
 & x_1 & y_1 & & \\
 & x_2 & y_2 & & \\
x_2 y_1 & x_3 & y_3 & x_1 y_2 & \\
\vdots & \vdots & \vdots & \vdots & \\
x_{n-1} y_{n-2} & x_n & y_n & x_{n-2} y_{n-1} & \\
x_n y_{n-1} & x_1 & y_1 & x_{n-1} y_n & \\
x_1 y_n & & & x_n y_1 &
\end{array}
$$

Let S_l be the sum of the left column of products and S_r the sum of the right column. The area is then $|S_r - S_l|/2$. Hint: Prove it first for a triangle, then use induction.

We can also find the area of a polygon with lattice points (points with integer coefficients) as vertices using **Pick's Theorem**. Draw the polygon and let I be the number of lattice points entirely within the polygon (we'll call these interior points) and B be the number of points which lie on the boundary of polygon (which we'll call boundary points). Pick's Theorem states that the area contained in the polygon is

$$I + \frac{B}{2} - 1.$$

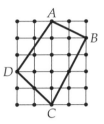

Suppose we are asked to find the area of $ABCD$ at right. There are 8 points inside $ABCD$ and 6 points on the boundary (the 4 vertices plus the points on BC and DC). By Pick's Theorem, the area is therefore $8 + 6/2 - 1 = 10$.

We'll prove Pick's Theorem for convex polygons through a series of steps. We'll start with rectangles, then move to right triangles, then any triangle, then finally convex polygons.

EXAMPLE 12-9 Prove that Pick's Theorem holds for a rectangle with sides of length a and b which are parallel to the coordinate axes.

Proof: The area of the rectangle is clearly ab, so we wish to prove that $I + B/2 - 1 = ab$. The interior points of the rectangle form an $a - 1$ by $b - 1$ grid, so $I = (a - 1)(b - 1)$. For the boundary there are 4 corners, $a - 1$ lattice points on each of one pair of sides and $b - 1$ lattice points on each of the other pair of sides. Hence, $B = 4 + 2(a - 1) + 2(b - 1)$. Thus, we have

$$I + B/2 - 1 = ab - a - b + 1 - (2 + a - 1 + b - 1) - 1 = ab,$$

as desired.

EXERCISE 12-7 Use the proven fact that Pick's Theorem is true for rectangles to prove that it works for right triangles which have legs parallel to the coordinate axes.

Now we're ready for the toughest part of our proof; showing that Pick's Theorem holds for *any* triangle with integer vertices.

We can inscribe any such triangle BEF in a rectangle such that the sides of the rectangle are parallel to the coordinate axes and one of the vertices of the triangle is a vertex of the rectangle as shown.

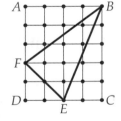

To prove Pick's Theorem for $\triangle BEF$ we'll apply Pick's Theorem to $ABCD$ and the three right triangles in $ABCD$ outside $\triangle BEF$. Let $I_\square$ and $B_\square$ be the number of interior points and boundary points of $ABCD$, respectively. Similarly, let $I_\triangle$ and $B_\triangle$ be the total number of interior and boundary points of *all three* right triangles and I_* and B_* be the number of interior and boundary points of $\triangle BEF$. To prove Pick's Theorem for $\triangle BEF$, we must show that $[BEF] = I_* + B_*/2 - 1$.

Since any interior point of $ABCD$ is either an interior point of one of the right triangles, a boundary point of $\triangle BEF$ besides one of the three vertices, or an interior point of $\triangle BEF$, we have

$$I_\square = I_\triangle + (B_* - 3) + I_*.$$

Similarly, any boundary point of one of the right triangles is either a boundary point of $ABCD$ or a boundary point of $\triangle BEF$, so we have

$$B_\triangle = B_\square + B_*.$$

Notice that in this equation we have counted the vertices of $\triangle BEF$ twice among the boundary points of the right triangles (once in $B_\square$ and once in B_*). This is necessary because each of these three vertices occur on two of the right triangles. Finally we are ready to evaluate the area of $\triangle BEF$ as the difference between the area of $ABCD$ and the area contained in the right triangles. Using Pick's Theorem, the area of $ABCD$ is $I_\square + B_\square/2 - 1$ and that of the right triangles is $I_\triangle + B_\triangle/2 - 3$, where we subtract 3 because we are applying Pick's Theorem 3 times. Hence we have

$$\begin{aligned}
[BEF] &= \left(I_\square + \frac{B_\square}{2} - 1\right) - \left(I_\triangle + \frac{B_\triangle}{2} - 3\right) \\
&= I_\triangle + B_* - 3 + I_* + \frac{B_\square}{2} - 1 - I_\triangle - \frac{B_\square + B_*}{2} + 3 \\
&= (I_* + I_\triangle - I_\triangle) + \left(B_* + \frac{B_\square}{2} - \frac{B_\square + B_*}{2}\right) + (3 - 3 - 1) \\
&= I_* + \frac{B_*}{2} - 1,
\end{aligned}$$

so we have proven that Pick's Theorem holds for any triangle $[BEF]$. Note that in this proof, we have assumed that none of the sides of $\triangle BEF$ are parallel to a coordinate axis. Can you use a similar argument to the one above to address the case of one of the sides of $\triangle BEF$ being parallel to a coordinate axis?

EXERCISE 12-8 Complete our proof of Pick's Theorem for convex polygons by showing that we can divide any n sided polygon into triangles, then apply Pick's Theorem to the triangles to show that it holds for the polygon.

EXERCISE 12-9 In our proof of Pick's Theorem we stated that any triangle can be inscribed in a rectangle such that the sides of the rectangle are parallel to the coordinate axes and one of the vertices of the triangle is a vertex of the rectangle. Prove that this is true.

EXERCISE 12-10 How can we extend our proof for convex polygons to prove Pick's Theorem for non-convex polygons?

12.4   Points, Lines, and Planes

If we are describing points in space we need three coordinates, two for the x and y directions as in two dimensional graphing, and a third for distance above or below the standard xy plane. As with two dimensions, we are often interested in finding the distance between two such points.

In the figure, let the points A and B be (x_1, y_1, z_1) and (x_2, y_2, z_2), respectively. The x, y, and z axes are also shown. We find the distance between A and B in much the same way as in two dimensions: using the Pythagorean Theorem. We draw a line through A parallel to the x axis and a line through B parallel to the z axis. We select points X and Y on these lines such that XY is parallel to the y axis. Since AX, XY, and BY are parallel to the coordinate axes, $\triangle AXY$ and $\triangle AYB$ are right triangles.

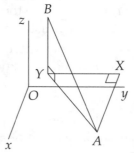

Clearly Y has the same x and y coordinate as B and the same z coordinate as A. Hence Y has coordinates (x_2, y_2, z_1) and similarly, X has coordinates

(x_2, y_1, z_1). Thus, X and A differ only in the x coordinate and $AX = |x_2 - x_1|$. Similarly, we find $XY = |y_2 - y_1|$ and $BY = |z_2 - z_1|$. From the Pythagorean Theorem we have

$$AY = \sqrt{AX^2 + XY^2} = \sqrt{(x_2 - x_1)^2 + (y_2 - y_1)^2};$$

we then apply the Pythagorean Theorem to triangle ABY to find

$$AB = \sqrt{AY^2 + BY^2} = \sqrt{(x_2 - x_1)^2 + (y_2 - y_1)^2 + (z_2 - z_1)^2}.$$

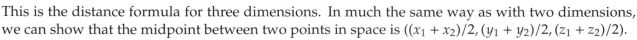

This is the distance formula for three dimensions. In much the same way as with two dimensions, we can show that the midpoint between two points in space is $((x_1 + x_2)/2, (y_1 + y_2)/2, (z_1 + z_2)/2)$.

How do we describe lines? Just as for lines in a plane, for lines in space we need a point on the line and a direction. For example, suppose we have a line through $(1, 2, 3)$ in the direction of $\vec{v}$, where $\vec{v} = \begin{pmatrix} 2 & 3 & 4 \end{pmatrix}$. Hence, $(1, 2, 3) + 2(2, 3, 4) = (5, 8, 11)$ is on the line, as is $(1, 2, 3) - 3(2, 3, 4) = (-5, -7, -9)$. In fact, we get a point on the line by adding any multiple $t\vec{v}$ of $\vec{v}$ to $(1, 2, 3)$. Our line then becomes

$$\begin{pmatrix} x \\ y \\ z \end{pmatrix} = \begin{pmatrix} 1 \\ 2 \\ 3 \end{pmatrix} + t \begin{pmatrix} 2 \\ 3 \\ 4 \end{pmatrix}.$$

Hence we have described the line as a set of parametric equations:

$$\begin{aligned} x &= 1 + 2t \\ y &= 2 + 3t \\ z &= 3 + 4t. \end{aligned}$$

If we solve each of these for t, we can write

$$t = \frac{x - 1}{2} = \frac{y - 2}{3} = \frac{z - 3}{4}.$$

In this notation, we don't need to include the t to describe the line.

EXERCISE 12-11 Find a parametric representation for the line through $(1, -1, 3)$ and $(2, 3, 1)$.

Let's try planes. An equation of the form $Ax + By = D$ describes a line in two dimensions, so it seems likely that an equation of the form $Ax + By + Cz = D$ describes a plane in three dimensions. This is correct, but why?

Suppose we know that our plane contains the point $(1, 2, 3)$ and is *perpendicular* to the direction $\vec{v} = \begin{pmatrix} 2 & 1 & 4 \end{pmatrix}$. (Why do we use a vector perpendicular to a plane to denote the plane's direction?) Consider any point (x, y, z) which is on the plane. The vector $\vec{w} = \begin{pmatrix} x - 1 & y - 2 & z - 3 \end{pmatrix}$ must be perpendicular to $\vec{v}$ since $\vec{w}$ is contained in the plane. Thus, we must have $\vec{w} \cdot \vec{v} = 0$, or

$$2(x - 1) + 1(y - 2) + 4(z - 3) = 0.$$

Our plane, then, is $2x + y + 4z = 16$. Notice that the coefficients match the directional components of the **normal vector**, $\vec{v}$. We can use this fact to quickly determine the equation of a plane. For example, if a plane contains $(2, 4, 1)$ and is normal to $\begin{pmatrix} -1 & 4 & 3 \end{pmatrix}$, the equation of the plane is $-x + 4y + 3z = c$ for some c. We find $c = 17$ by letting $(x, y, z) = (2, 4, 1)$, so the plane is $-x + 4y + 3z = 17$.

EXAMPLE 12-10   Find the equation of the plane passing through $(0, 3, -1)$, $(2, -1, 2)$, and $(1, -4, 0)$.

    Solution: Let the three given points be A, B, and C, respectively. We have three points, so we have enough to determine a plane; however, we don't have a direction. Since we have three points in the plane, we can find two vectors parallel to the plane, namely $\overrightarrow{AB}$ and $\overrightarrow{AC}$. Hence, the direction normal to the plane is given by the cross product:

$$\overrightarrow{AB} \times \overrightarrow{AC} = \begin{pmatrix} 2 & -4 & 3 \end{pmatrix} \times \begin{pmatrix} 1 & -7 & 1 \end{pmatrix} = \begin{pmatrix} 17 & 1 & -10 \end{pmatrix}.$$

Thus, we have

$$\begin{pmatrix} x & y-3 & z+1 \end{pmatrix} \cdot \begin{pmatrix} 17 & 1 & -10 \end{pmatrix} = 0,$$

so our plane is $17x + y - 10z = 13$.

EXERCISE 12-12   Find the plane through $(1, 2, 1)$, $(0, -3, 1)$, and $(-1, -2, 2)$.

 EXERCISE 12-13   Find the distance from the point (x_0, y_0, z_0) to the plane $Ax + By + Cz + D = 0$.

    Notice that we could also describe the plane in the example above as

$$\begin{pmatrix} x \\ y \\ z \end{pmatrix} = \begin{pmatrix} 0 \\ 3 \\ -1 \end{pmatrix} + u \begin{pmatrix} 2 \\ -4 \\ 3 \end{pmatrix} + v \begin{pmatrix} 1 \\ -7 \\ 1 \end{pmatrix}.$$

Since the two vectors $(2, -4, 3)$ and $(1, -7, 1)$ are parallel to the plane, we can add any multiples of these to the point $(0, 3, -1)$ in the plane to get other points in the plane. Hence, we can describe the plane with two parameters as

$$\begin{aligned} x &= 2u + v \\ y &= 3 - 4u - 7v \\ z &= -1 + 3u + v. \end{aligned}$$

We see from this that just as we can describe curves with a single parameter, we can describe surfaces with two.

    Finally we are ready for volumes. Let $A = (x_1, y_1, z_1)$, $B = (x_2, y_2, z_2)$, and $C = (x_3, y_3, z_3)$ be points in space and $\vec{a}$, $\vec{b}$, and $\vec{c}$ represent the vectors from O to A, B, and C, respectively. As discussed above, $\vec{a} \times \vec{b}$ is a vector normal to plane OAB whose length is the area of the parallelogram with sides OA and OB. Now, suppose we evaluate $\vec{c} \cdot (\vec{a} \times \vec{b})$. We can write this as $\|\vec{a} \times \vec{b}\|(\vec{c} \cdot \vec{n})$, where n is the **unit normal** to plane OAB, meaning it is the vector with length 1 in the direction of $\vec{a} \times \vec{b}$.

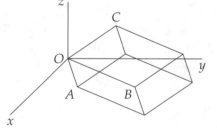

EXERCISE 12-14   Why does $\vec{c} \cdot (\vec{a} \times \vec{b}) = \|\vec{a} \times \vec{b}\|(\vec{c} \cdot \vec{n})$?

Since $\vec{c}\cdot\vec{n}$ is the length of the projection of c in the direction of n and $\|\vec{n}\| = 1$, this product is equal to the distance from C to plane OAB. Since $\|\vec{a}\times\vec{b}\|$ is the area of the parallelogram with sides OA and OB, the magnitude of the product $\|\vec{a}\times\vec{b}\|(\vec{c}\cdot\vec{n})$ is the volume of the parallelepiped with sides OA, OB, and OC. The product $\vec{c}\cdot(\vec{a}\times\vec{b})$ is often called the **box product** of the three vectors, and the magnitude is the same regardless of the order of $\vec{a}$, $\vec{b}$, and $\vec{c}$ in the product. Keep in mind that the product can be positive or negative, since the cross product of $\vec{a}$ and $\vec{b}$ may be on the same or opposite side of OAB as point C (depending on which of $\vec{a}$ and $\vec{b}$ comes first in the cross product).

EXERCISE 12-15   Prove that the box product $\vec{c}\cdot(\vec{a}\times\vec{b})$ has the same magnitude regardless of the order of $\vec{a}$, $\vec{b}$, and $\vec{c}$ in the product.

We can use this same approach to find the volume of the tetrahedron with vertices O, A, B, and C. This tetrahedron is a pyramid with base $\triangle AOB$ and altitude the same as that of the parallelepiped. Since the area of the triangle is half the area of the parallelogram with sides OA and OB and a pyramid has volume (1/3)(base area)(height), the volume of the tetrahedron is then $[\vec{c}\cdot(\vec{a}\times\vec{b})]/6$.

EXAMPLE 12-11   Find the volume of the tetrahedron with vertices at $(1,0,-2)$, $(2,3,1)$, $(2,1,-4)$, and $(-1,2,-1)$.

Solution: We can find the vectors $\vec{a}$, $\vec{b}$, and $\vec{c}$ above by designating one of the points as the origin O above and the other three as A, B, and C. Letting the first point be O, our vectors are $\vec{a} = \begin{pmatrix} 1 & 3 & 3 \end{pmatrix}$, $\vec{b} = \begin{pmatrix} 1 & 1 & -2 \end{pmatrix}$, and $\vec{c} = \begin{pmatrix} -2 & 2 & 1 \end{pmatrix}$. Instead of finding the cross product of the first two vectors then dotting the result with the third vector, we note that in the dot product $\vec{c}\cdot(\vec{a}\times\vec{b})$, we merely multiply the first component of $\vec{a}\times\vec{b}$ by -2, the second by 2 and the third by 1. (Why? Look at the components of $\vec{c}$.) Hence, rather than evaluating the cross product

$$\begin{vmatrix} \vec{i} & \vec{j} & \vec{k} \\ 1 & 3 & 3 \\ 1 & 1 & -2 \end{vmatrix},$$

we replace the $\vec{i}, \vec{j}, \vec{k}$ with the components of the third vector and we have

$$\vec{c}\cdot(\vec{a}\times\vec{b}) = \begin{vmatrix} -2 & 2 & 1 \\ 1 & 3 & 3 \\ 1 & 1 & -2 \end{vmatrix} = 26.$$

Hence, our desired volume is $26/6 =$ **13/3**.

EXERCISE 12-16   Show that the box product of any three vectors $\begin{pmatrix} x_1 & y_1 & z_1 \end{pmatrix}$, $\begin{pmatrix} x_2 & y_2 & z_2 \end{pmatrix}$, and $\begin{pmatrix} x_3 & y_3 & z_3 \end{pmatrix}$ is

$$\begin{vmatrix} x_1 & y_1 & z_1 \\ x_2 & y_2 & z_2 \\ x_3 & y_3 & z_3 \end{vmatrix}.$$

Use this to write a general formula for the volume of tetrahedron with vertices (x_1, y_1, z_1), (x_2, y_2, z_2), (x_3, y_3, z_3), and (x_4, y_4, z_4).

12.5   Curved Surfaces

The equation $x^2 + y^2 = r^2$ is a circle when plotted in a plane; however, if we consider this as an equation in three dimensions, we have no restriction on z. Hence, for every value of z we have a circle of radius r. The resulting graph is an infinite cylinder whose axis is the z axis and radius has length r. We can write this with parameters z and θ as

$$
\begin{aligned}
x &= r\cos\theta \\
y &= r\sin\theta \\
z &= z.
\end{aligned}
$$

 The parameters (r, θ, z) as defined above can be used to identify any point in space, just as polar coordinates (r, θ) locate any point in the plane. Thus these **cylindrical coordinates** are a new set of three dimensional coordinates, which can be used where convenient as an alternative to the Cartesian coordinates (x, y, z).

EXAMPLE 12-12   Express the Cartesian point $(3, 3, 3)$ in cylindrical coordinates.

Solution: The third coordinate remains the same, 3. The first two, $(3, 3)$, we put in polar coordinates as $r = 3\sqrt{2}$ and $\theta = 45°$. Hence, the point is $(3\sqrt{2}, 45°, 3)$.

EXERCISE 12-17   Express the cylindrical coordinate point $(3, 120°, -4)$ in rectangular coordiantes.

EXERCISE 12-18   What is the equation for a cylinder in cylindrical coordinates?

In the same way that a circle is the set of points equidistant from a given point in a plane, a sphere is the set of points equidistant from a given point in space. Let the center be (x_0, y_0, z_0) and the distance be ρ. From the distance formula, for any point (x, y, z) on the sphere we have

$$
\rho = \sqrt{(x - x_0)^2 + (y - y_0)^2 + (z - z_0)^2}.
$$

Squaring this we have the general form for a sphere: $(x - x_0)^2 + (y - y_0)^2 + (z - z_0)^2 = \rho^2$.

Having seen the parameterization for cylinders and knowing of the one for circles, we figure there must be some convenient parameterization for the sphere. We'll consider the sphere

$$
x^2 + y^2 + z^2 = \rho^2.
$$

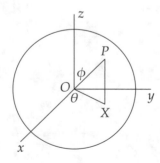

Connect any point P on the sphere with the origin O. Let ϕ be the angle formed by OP and the positive z axis, where $0 \le \phi \le \pi$. Hence, if the point is above the xy plane (i.e. the plane $z = 0$), we have $0 \le \phi \le \pi/2$, and if it is below, $\pi/2 \le \phi \le \pi$. We then let θ be the angle between the projection, OX, of OP onto the xy plane and the positive x axis, just as in polar and cylindrical coordinates. Since in the diagram $OP = \rho$ and $\angle POX = 90° - \phi$, we find $PX = \rho\sin(90° - \phi) = \rho\cos\phi$ and $OX = \rho\cos(90° - \phi) = \rho\sin\phi$. If we then project OX onto the x axis, we find that the x coordinate is

$(OX)(\cos\theta) = \rho\cos\theta\sin\phi$ and the y coordinate is $\rho\sin\theta\sin\phi$. Hence, we describe the sphere as

$$
\begin{aligned}
x &= \rho\cos\theta\sin\phi \\
y &= \rho\sin\theta\sin\phi \\
z &= \rho\cos\phi.
\end{aligned}
$$

These are **spherical coordinates**. For any point P, ϕ is the angle OP makes with the positive z axis, θ is the angle the projection of OP onto the xy plane makes with the positive x axis, and ρ is the length of OP.

EXERCISE 12-19 Prove that $x^2 + y^2 + z^2 = \rho^2$ for our spherical parameterization above.

EXAMPLE 12-13 Express the point $(-2\sqrt{2}, 2\sqrt{2}, 4)$ in spherical coordinates.

Solution: Finding ρ is easy:

$$
\rho = \sqrt{x^2 + y^2 + z^2} = \sqrt{(-2\sqrt{2})^2 + (2\sqrt{2})^2 + 4^2} = 4\sqrt{2}.
$$

Since $z = \rho\cos\phi = 4\sqrt{2}\cos\phi$, we find $\cos\phi = \sqrt{2}/2$ and $\phi = 45°$. Finally, the value of θ is the same as when we put $(-2\sqrt{2}, 2\sqrt{2})$ in polar coordinates, or $135°$, since the point is in the second quadrant and $\tan\theta = -1$. Hence, the point is $(\rho, \theta, \phi) = (\mathbf{4\sqrt{2}, 135°, 45°})$.

EXAMPLE 12-14 Express the cylinder $x^2 + y^2 = 1$ in spherical coordinates.

Solution: Since $x = \rho\cos\theta\sin\phi$ and $y = \rho\sin\theta\sin\phi$, we have

$$
x^2 + y^2 = \rho^2\cos^2\theta\sin^2\phi + \rho^2\sin^2\theta\sin^2\phi = \rho^2\sin^2\phi,
$$

so our equation is $\rho^2\sin^2\phi = 1$.

EXERCISE 12-20 Find the equation of a sphere with center at the origin in spherical coordinates.

EXERCISE 12-21 What is the graph of $\rho = \rho_1$, where ρ_1 is a constant? How about $\theta = \theta_1$? And $\phi = \phi_1$?

EXERCISE 12-22 What geometrical figure is described by the equation $x^2 + y^2 = z^2$?

12.6 Using Analytic Geometry

Although it's usually a painful process, some geometry problems can be attacked by labelling the given figures in the plane and using algebra. We'll just do an example here to show you how analytical geometry can be useful.

EXAMPLE 12-15 The sides AD and BC of a convex quadrilateral $ABCD$ are extended to meet at E. Let H and G be the midpoints of BD and AC, respectively. Find the ratio of the area of the triangle EHG to that of the quadrilateral $ABCD$. (Canada 1978)

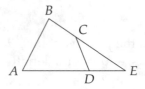

Solution: Let A be the origin, B be (a, b), C be (c, d), and point D be $(1, 0)$. Since point E is on the x axis, it is the point on line BC where $y = 0$. Since the line through B and C is

$$y - b = \frac{d - b}{c - a}(x - a),$$

the coordinates of E are $((ad - bc)/(d - b), 0)$. Since G and H are the midpoints of AC and BD, they have coordinates $(\frac{c}{2}, \frac{d}{2})$ and $(\frac{a+1}{2}, \frac{b}{2})$, respectively. Using our methods from earlier in the chapter to find the area of a triangle, we have

$$
\begin{aligned}
[ABCD] &= [AEB] - [CDE] \\
&= \frac{1}{2}\begin{vmatrix} 0 & 0 & 1 \\ \frac{ad-bc}{d-b} & 0 & 1 \\ a & b & 1 \end{vmatrix} - \frac{1}{2}\begin{vmatrix} c & d & 1 \\ 1 & 0 & 1 \\ \frac{ad-bc}{d-b} & 0 & 1 \end{vmatrix} \\
&= (bc - ad + d)/2
\end{aligned}
$$

and

$$
\begin{aligned}
[GEH] &= \frac{1}{2}\begin{vmatrix} \frac{c}{2} & \frac{d}{2} & 1 \\ \frac{ad-bc}{d-b} & 0 & 1 \\ \frac{a+1}{2} & \frac{b}{2} & 1 \end{vmatrix} \\
&= (bc - ad + d)/8
\end{aligned}
$$

Hence, $[GEH] = [ABCD]/4$ and our desired ratio is **1/4**.

WARNING: Don't fall into the trap of using analytical geometry often to solve normal geometry problems. It is rarely the best way to go. For those of you who really like the concepts of analytical geometry, there is a happy medium between coordinate geometry and Euclidean principles: the use of vectors.

12.7   Vectors and Geometry Problems

First we'll do a review of vector addition and subtraction. In the diagram, suppose we are interested in adding vectors $\overrightarrow{OA}$ and $\overrightarrow{OB}$. (Remember that the tail of the vector comes first in writing the vector, as in $\overrightarrow{OB}$.) If we let O be the origin, we can write the two vectors as $\vec{A}$ and $\vec{B}$. 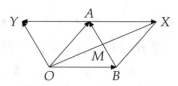 To add these, we copy vector $\vec{B}$ with A as its tail forming $\overrightarrow{AX}$. The result of the addition $\vec{A} + \vec{B}$ is the vector from our original starting point, O, to the final point, X, or

$$\vec{A} + \vec{B} = \overrightarrow{OX}.$$

Notice that in finding $\vec{A} + \vec{B}$, we start from O, travel in the magnitude and direction of $\vec{A}$, then travel $\vec{B}$. Similarly, to find $\vec{A} - \vec{B}$, we go from O to A, then starting from A we go in the direction and magnitude of $-\vec{B}$, or $\overrightarrow{AY}$ in the diagram. The result is $\overrightarrow{OY}$. Since $AY \parallel BO$ and $AY = BO$, quadrilateral $OBAY$ is a parallelogram. Hence, $\overrightarrow{OY}$ has the same magnitude and direction as $\overrightarrow{BA}$. Thus, we can represent the vector from B to A as $\vec{A} - \vec{B}$.

EXERCISE 12-23 Show that for points A, B, and C, we can write $\overrightarrow{AB} + \overrightarrow{BC} = \overrightarrow{AC}$.

EXERCISE 12-24 What is $\overrightarrow{AB} - \overrightarrow{AC}$?

There is one last important relation to take from this initial diagram. Since $OAXB$ is a parallelogram, point M, the intersection of the diagonals, is the midpoint of AB and OX. Since $\overrightarrow{OM}$ is in the same direction as $\overrightarrow{OX}$ and $OX = 2(OM)$, we have

$$\overrightarrow{OM} = \frac{\overrightarrow{OX}}{2} = \frac{\vec{A} + \vec{B}}{2}.$$

EXAMPLE 12-16 With respect to some arbitrary origin, points A, B, and C are represented by $\vec{A}$, $\vec{B}$, and $\vec{C}$. Find vector representations of the sides and medians of $\triangle ABC$.

Solution: Side AB is represented by the vector from A to B, or $\vec{B} - \vec{A}$ by the discussion above. Similarly, the other two sides are $\vec{C} - \vec{B}$ and $\vec{A} - \vec{C}$. (The negatives of any of these three are also valid representations of the sides.) As for the median from point A, we know it connects A to the midpoint of BC. We can represent the midpoint, M, of BC as $\vec{M} = (\vec{B} + \vec{C})/2$. Hence, we have

$$\overrightarrow{AM} = \vec{M} - \vec{A} = \frac{\vec{B} + \vec{C} - 2\vec{A}}{2}.$$

The other medians are found in the same way.

EXERCISE 12-25 Let X be a point on AB such that $AX = 2(BX)$. Find a vector representation for $\vec{X}$ in terms of $\vec{A}$ and $\vec{B}$.

EXAMPLE 12-17 Let the sides AB, BC, and AC of $\triangle ABC$ be c, a, and b, respectively, and the foot of the angle bisector from A be point D. Prove that

$$\vec{D} = \frac{b\vec{B} + c\vec{C}}{b + c}.$$

Proof: In working the previous exercise, you should have found that the vector representation of a point X on segment YZ such that $XY = y$ and $XZ = z$ is

$$\vec{X} = \frac{z\vec{Y} + y\vec{Z}}{y + z}.$$

Applying this to point D on BC, we have

$$\vec{D} = \frac{(BD)\vec{C} + (CD)\vec{B}}{BD + CD}.$$

We need to relate BD and CD to the sides of the triangle, so we turn to the Angle Bisector Theorem, which gives $BD/CD = AB/AC = c/b$. Dividing the top and bottom of our fraction for $\vec{D}$ by CD, we find

$$\vec{D} = \frac{(c/b)\vec{C} + \vec{B}}{c/b + 1} = \frac{c\vec{C} + b\vec{B}}{c + b}.$$

We can use vectors to determine intersections. For example, how can we represent the centroid of a triangle with vectors? Let $\vec{G}$ be the vector representing the centroid, and the midpoints of BC and AC be at M and N, respectively. Since G is on AM and BN, we know that $\overrightarrow{AG}$ is in the same direction as $\overrightarrow{AM}$ and $\overrightarrow{BG}$ is in the same direction as $\overrightarrow{BN}$. Here's the key: if vectors $\vec{x}$ and $\vec{y}$ are in the same direction, then there is some constant c such that $\vec{x} = c\vec{y}$. (Why?) Hence, there is some pair of constants c_1 and c_2 such that $\overrightarrow{AG} = c_1\overrightarrow{AM}$ and $\overrightarrow{BG} = c_2\overrightarrow{BN}$, or

$$\vec{G} - \vec{A} = c_1\left(\frac{\vec{B} + \vec{C}}{2} - \vec{A}\right)$$

$$\vec{G} - \vec{B} = c_2\left(\frac{\vec{A} + \vec{C}}{2} - \vec{B}\right).$$

Since $\vec{G}$ must be the same in both of these, we find

$$\vec{G} = c_1\left(\frac{\vec{B} + \vec{C}}{2} - \vec{A}\right) + \vec{A} = c_2\left(\frac{\vec{A} + \vec{C}}{2} - \vec{B}\right) + \vec{B}.$$

Since $\vec{A}$, $\vec{B}$, and $\vec{C}$ are arbitrary, the coefficients of these must be the same on both sides of the equality above. Matching coefficients of $\vec{C}$, we have $c_1 = c_2$, and matching those of $\vec{A}$ or $\vec{B}$, we find they both equal 2/3. Putting these back in the above expression for $\vec{G}$, we have

$$\vec{G} = \frac{\vec{A} + \vec{B} + \vec{C}}{3}$$

as our representation of the centroid of $\triangle ABC$.

Let's try altitudes now. Let H be the orthocenter of $\triangle ABC$. Since the line from A through H is perpendicular to BC, the vector $\vec{H} - \vec{A}$ must be normal to $\vec{B} - \vec{C}$. Vectors which are perpendicular have a dot product of 0 (remember this, it's a very good way to use vectors), so we can write

$$(\vec{H} - \vec{A}) \cdot (\vec{B} - \vec{C}) = (\vec{H} - \vec{B}) \cdot (\vec{C} - \vec{A}) = (\vec{H} - \vec{C}) \cdot (\vec{A} - \vec{B}) = 0. \qquad (12.1)$$

Now we appear stuck. There's no obvious simple way to find $\vec{H}$. This leads us to yet another clever technique when working with vectors. We can choose *any origin we want* when working with vectors, so we should choose an origin which simplifies our problem. In most triangle problems, this convenient origin is the circumcenter of the triangle, because in this case, $\vec{A}$, $\vec{B}$, and $\vec{C}$ all have the same length (because the circumcenter of a triangle is equidistant from the vertices of the triangle). Now let's re-examine the equations (12.1) and try guessing a form of $\vec{H}$. The best one that stands out is simply $\vec{H} = \vec{A} + \vec{B} + \vec{C}$ since it is symmetric (since $\vec{A}$, $\vec{B}$, and $\vec{C}$ are arbitrary, symmetric forms are a good place to start). Thus, we find

$$(\vec{H} - \vec{A}) \cdot (\vec{B} - \vec{C}) = (\vec{B} + \vec{C}) \cdot (\vec{B} - \vec{C}) = \vec{B} \cdot \vec{B} - \vec{B} \cdot \vec{C} + \vec{C} \cdot \vec{B} - \vec{C} \cdot \vec{C}.$$

Since $\vec{B} \cdot \vec{C} = \vec{C} \cdot \vec{B}$ and $\vec{x} \cdot \vec{x} = \|\vec{x}\|^2$, we find $(\vec{H} - \vec{A}) \cdot (\vec{B} - \vec{C}) = \|\vec{B}\|^2 - \|\vec{C}\|^2 = 0$, since $\vec{B}$ and $\vec{C}$ have the same length. Similarly, the other two expressions are also 0 and we find that

$$\vec{H} = \vec{A} + \vec{B} + \vec{C}$$

is the vector representation of the orthocenter of a triangle when the origin is taken to be the circumcenter.

From this proof we see the importance of cleverly choosing the origin. (The circumcenter is usually best for triangles.) The following example shows how vectors can be used to simplify seemingly complicated problems.

EXAMPLE 12-18 Vertex A of the acute triangle ABC is equidistant from the circumcenter O and the orthocenter H. Determine all possible values for the measure of angle A. (IMO 1989)

Solution: Letting the circumcenter be the origin of our vector system, we can write the restriction that O and H are equidistant from A as $\|\vec{A} - \vec{O}\| = \|\vec{A}\| = \|\vec{A} - \vec{H}\|$. Squaring this and noting that $\|\vec{A}\| = \|\vec{B}\| = \|\vec{C}\| = R$, the circumradius, and that $\vec{H} = \vec{A} + \vec{B} + \vec{C}$, we have

$$R^2 = \|\vec{A} - \vec{O}\|^2 = \|\vec{A} - \vec{H}\|^2 = \|\vec{B} + \vec{C}\|^2 = (\vec{B} + \vec{C}) \cdot (\vec{B} + \vec{C}).$$

Expanding the right side and noting that

$$a^2 = \|\vec{B} - \vec{C}\|^2 = (\vec{B} - \vec{C}) \cdot (\vec{B} - \vec{C}) = \|\vec{B}\|^2 + \|\vec{C}\|^2 - 2\vec{B} \cdot \vec{C},$$

where a is the length of side BC, we find

$$R^2 = \|\vec{B}\|^2 + 2\vec{B} \cdot \vec{C} + \|\vec{C}\|^2 = \|\vec{B}\|^2 + \|\vec{C}\|^2 + \|\vec{B}\|^2 + \|\vec{C}\|^2 - a^2 = 4R^2 - a^2.$$

Hence, $a/R = \sqrt{3}$ and from the law of sines we have $a/R = 2\sin A$, so $\sin A = \sqrt{3}/2$ and $\angle A = 60°$ is the only possible value of $\angle A$.

EXERCISE 12-26 Use the result of Example 12-17 to show that if I is the incenter of $\triangle ABC$ with $a = BC$, $b = AC$, and $c = AB$, then

$$\vec{I} = \frac{a\vec{A} + b\vec{B} + c\vec{C}}{a + b + c}.$$

EXAMPLE 12-19 Prove that if the vectors from the origin O to points A and C are $\vec{A}$ and $\vec{C}$, respectively, then

$$(\vec{A} - \vec{C}) \cdot (\vec{A} - \vec{C}) = \|\vec{A}\|^2 + \|\vec{C}\|^2 + \|\vec{A}\|\|\vec{C}\|$$

implies that $\angle AOC = 120°$.

Proof: Applying the law of cosines to $\triangle AOC$, we have

$$AC^2 = OA^2 + OC^2 - 2(OA)(OC)\cos\angle AOC.$$

Since AC is represented by $\vec{A} - \vec{C}$, we have $AC^2 = \|\vec{A} - \vec{C}\|^2 = (\vec{A} - \vec{C})\cdot(\vec{A} - \vec{C})$. Similarly, we have $OA = \|\vec{A}\|$ and $OC = \|\vec{C}\|$. Making these substitutions in our law of cosines, we have

$$(\vec{A} - \vec{C})\cdot(\vec{A} - \vec{C}) = \|\vec{A}\|^2 + \|\vec{C}\|^2 - 2\|\vec{A}\|\|\vec{C}\|\cos\angle AOC.$$

Comparing this to the expression in the problem, we find $\cos\angle AOC = -1/2$, so $\angle AOC = 120°$. When working with vectors, keep an eye out for expressions like the one in this problem so you can identify $120°$ angles.

EXERCISE 12-27 In the spirit of the above problem, what do we know about $\angle AOC$ if

$$(\vec{A} - \vec{C})\cdot(\vec{A} - \vec{C}) = \|\vec{A}\|^2 + \|\vec{C}\|^2 - \|\vec{A}\|\|\vec{C}\|?$$

Finally, let's take a look at how we can use vectors on three dimensional problems. As we discussed in Volume 1, most three dimensional problems are merely two dimensional problems in hiding. The solution to the problem can be found by choosing the correct two dimensional cross section. There are some (but not too many) more complicated problems which cannot be solved with planar cross sections, but most of these are a bit beyond the scope of our discussion. We will, however, introduce the use of vectors to solve some of these problems.

EXAMPLE 12-20 Let G be the centroid of face BCD of regular tetrahedron $ABCD$. Prove that AG is perpendicular to BCD.

Proof: For each point X, let the vector $\vec{X}$ represent the vector from the origin to X. Since G is the centroid of $\triangle BCD$, we have

$$\vec{G} = \frac{\vec{B} + \vec{C} + \vec{D}}{3}.$$

In order to prove that AG is perpendicular to face BCD, we must show that $\overrightarrow{AG}$ is perpendicular to some vector in the plane BCD. One such vector in the plane BCD is $\vec{B} - \vec{C}$, the vector from C to B. Hence, we must show that $(\overrightarrow{AG})\cdot(\vec{B} - \vec{C}) = 0$. Now we choose the origin to simplify the problem. We let point A be the origin because then $\overrightarrow{AG} = \vec{G}$, and vectors $\vec{B}$, $\vec{C}$, and $\vec{D}$ represent the edges from A to the other vertices of the tetrahedron. Hence, we have

$$(\overrightarrow{AG})\cdot(\vec{B} - \vec{C}) = \left(\frac{\vec{B} + \vec{C} + \vec{D}}{3}\right)\cdot(\vec{B} - \vec{C}) = \frac{1}{3}\left(\vec{B}\cdot\vec{B} - \vec{C}\cdot\vec{C} + \vec{B}\cdot\vec{D} - \vec{C}\cdot\vec{D}\right).$$

How do we evaluate each of these terms? First note that the lengths of $\vec{B}$, $\vec{C}$, and $\vec{D}$ are the same. Let this length be x. Hence, $\vec{B}\cdot\vec{B} = \vec{C}\cdot\vec{C} = x^2$. Since the faces of $ABCD$ are equilateral triangles, $\vec{B}\cdot\vec{D} = \vec{C}\cdot\vec{D} = x^2\cos 60° = x^2/2$. Making these substitutions in the above expression yields

$$(\overrightarrow{AG})\cdot(\vec{B} - \vec{C}) = 0,$$

as desired. Hence, the line from a vertex to the centroid of the opposite face of a regular tetrahedron is the altitude from that vertex to the opposite face.

EXAMPLE 12-21 Point X is such that

$$\vec{X} = \frac{\vec{A} + \vec{B} + \vec{C} + \vec{D}}{4}$$

represents the vector from the origin to X. A segment from each vertex of tetrahedron $ABCD$ is drawn to the centroid of the opposite face. Prove that X is on all four of these segments, thus showing that they are concurrent. The point at the head of $\vec{X}$ defined above is called the **centroid** of the tetrahedron.

Proof: Let G be the centroid of face BCD. To show that X is on AG, we must prove that $\vec{X} - \vec{A}$ and $\vec{G} - \vec{A}$ are in the same direction. To prove these vectors are in the same direction we must show that there is some constant such that $\vec{X} - \vec{A} = c(\vec{G} - \vec{A})$. Writing these vectors in terms of the vertices, we find

$$\vec{X} - \vec{A} = \frac{\vec{A} + \vec{B} + \vec{C} + \vec{D}}{4} - \vec{A} = \frac{\vec{B} + \vec{C} + \vec{D} - 3\vec{A}}{4};$$

$$\vec{G} - \vec{A} = \frac{\vec{B} + \vec{C} + \vec{D}}{3} - \vec{A} = \frac{\vec{B} + \vec{C} + \vec{D} - 3\vec{A}}{3}.$$

Hence, we have $\vec{X} - \vec{A} = (3/4)(\vec{G} - \vec{A})$. Thus, X is on AG and we can also show that X is on each of the other 3 similarly defined segments, so all four of these segments are therefore concurrent. Furthermore, the point X divides each segment in the ratio $3 : 1$, just like the centroid of an equilateral triangle divides each median in the ratio $2 : 1$.

EXERCISE 12-28 If $ABCD$ is a regular tetrahedron, what can we say about the altitudes of $ABCD$ based on the prior example?

EXERCISE 12-29 Complete our analogy of the point X in the above example in a regular tetrahedron to the centroid of an equilateral triangle. What is the ratio of the radius of the sphere inscribed in regular tetrahedron $ABCD$ to the altitude length of $ABCD$? How about the radius of the circumscribed sphere?

EXERCISE 12-30 Find the altitude length, the volume, the radius of the inscribed sphere, and the radius of the circumscribed sphere of a regular tetrahedron with side length 6.

Problems to Solve for Chapter 12

173. Find the volume of the tetrahedron with vertices $A(0, -1, 3)$, $B(3, 2, 1)$, $C(1, -1, 2)$, and $D(2, 3, 1)$. (MAΘ 1991)

174. If $x = 1 + 2^p$ and $y = 1 + 2^{-p}$, then find y in terms of x. (AHSME 1970)

175. Find the volume of the region satisfying $0 \le z \le 6$ and $x^2 + y^2 \le z^2$.

176. Given a point P in the octant of space where $x, y, z > 0$, the line connecting point P with the origin makes angles θ_1 with the z axis, θ_2 with the x axis, and θ_3 with the y axis. Given that $\cos \theta_1 = R$ and $\cos \theta_2 = S$, find $\cos \theta_3$. (MAΘ 1992)

177. Find a parametric representation of the line through $(1, 2, 3)$ and $(-2, -1, -3)$.

178. If A, B, C, D are four points in space such that

$$\angle ABC = \angle BCD = \angle CDA = \angle DAB = \pi/2,$$

prove that A, B, C, D lie in a plane. (Canada 1976)

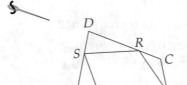

179. Find k if P, Q, R, and S are points on the sides of quadrilateral $ABCD$ so that

$$\frac{AP}{PB} = \frac{BQ}{QC} = \frac{CR}{RD} = \frac{DS}{SA} = k,$$

and the area of quadrilateral $PQRS$ is exactly 52% of the area of quadrilateral $ABCD$. (USAMTS 3)

180. There are two spherical balls of different sizes lying in two corners of a rectangular room, each touching two walls and the floor. If there is a point on each ball which is 5 inches from each wall which that ball touches and 10 inches from the floor, then find the sum of the diameters of the balls. (AHSME 1977)

181. Let P be a point on hypotenuse AB (or its extension) of isosceles right triangle ABC. Prove that for all such P, $2CP^2 = AP^2 + PB^2$. (AHSME 1969)

182. Find the volume of the region in space defined by $|x + y + z| + |x + y - z| \le 8$, where $x, y, z \ge 0$. (Mandelbrot #1)

183. In right-angled parallelepiped $ABCDA_1B_1C_1D_1$ diagonal AC_1 is perpendicular to the plane containing triangle A_1BD. Prove that $ABCDA_1B_1C_1D_1$ is a cube. (M&IQ 1992)

184. The altitudes of a tetrahedron $ABCD$ are extended externally to points E, F, G, and H respectively, where $AE = k/h_a$, $BF = k/h_b$, $CG = k/h_c$, and $DH = k/h_d$. Here, k is a constant and h_a denotes the length of the altitude of $ABCD$ from vertex A, etc. Prove that the centroid of the tetrahedron $EFGH$ coincides with the centroid of $ABCD$. (Canada 1982)

Chapter 13

Equations and Expressions

13.1 Linear Equations

In the first volume we solved linear equations in one variable and systems of equations in two variables. Since $x + y + z = 6$ describes a whole plane, there are clearly infinitely many solutions to this equation. What if we add another equation, like in the system below:

$$\begin{aligned} x + y + z &= 6 \\ x + 3y + 2z &= 15? \end{aligned}$$

How does this system differ from the systems of two equations we examined in Volume 1? There are 3 variables among the equations rather than 2. If a point (x, y, z) satisfies both of these, then it must be on both of the planes they represent in three dimensional Cartesian space. Hence, it is on the line which is the intersection of the planes. Since a line also contains infinitely many points, we once again can't find a finite number of solutions to the system. Let's try adding another equation, so we have the system

$$\begin{aligned} x + y + z &= 6 \\ x + 3y + 2z &= 15 \\ 2x - 2y + 3z &= -9. \end{aligned}$$

Since any solution to the first two equations lies on the line formed by the intersection of the corresponding planes, the simultaneous solution to all three equations is the intersection of this line with the third plane. In what ways can a line intersect a plane? The intersection can be a line (if the line is in the plane), a point (the most common), or no intersection (if the line is parallel to the plane).

Since we know how to solve a two variable, two equation system, we solve the three equation system by reducing it to a two variable one. We do this by eliminating z. This technique is the same as in Volume 1. If we multiply the first equation by 2 and the second by -1, our system is

$$\begin{aligned} 2x + 2y + 2z &= 12 \\ -x - 3y - 2z &= -15 \\ 2x - 2y + 3z &= -9. \end{aligned}$$

Now we add the first equation to the second, yielding

$$2x + 2y + 2z = 12$$
$$x - y = -3$$
$$2x - 2y + 3z = -9.$$

We write the first equation back in its original form (just divide by 2), then multiply it by 3 and the last equation by -1 so we can eliminate z from that one too:

$$3x + 3y + 3z = 18$$
$$x - y = -3$$
$$-2x + 2y - 3z = 9.$$

Now we add the first equation to the third, which gives us

$$3x + 3y + 3z = 18$$
$$x - y = -3$$
$$x + 5y = 27.$$

Now neither of the last two equations has a z. We can solve these last two equations to find $x = 2$ and $y = 5$. We're not done though because we must go back and find z. Putting these x and y values back into the first equation, we find $z = -1$; thus, our answer is $(x, y, z) = (\mathbf{2, 5, -1})$. The method we have used is exactly the same as the elimination we used for systems of two equations in two variables (just a hair more complicated).

Notice that for 3 variables, we need at least 3 equations to determine a single solution. If we have less than three equations, there will always be infinitely many solutions. Compare this to the two variable case. If we only have one equation, say $x + y = 1$, there are clearly infinitely many solutions.

If we have three equations do we always have a single solution? No! Remember from our two variable systems, that sometimes no solution exists (when the two lines are parallel), and sometimes there are infinitely many solutions (when the lines are the same). Similarly, with three equations and variables, two planes may be parallel, or one plane may be parallel to the intersection line of the other two. In these cases, there are no solutions since there is no point where all three planes intersect. Furthermore, the third plane might contain the entire intersection line of the other two planes. Here, there are infinitely many solutions (every point on the line is on all three planes).

EXERCISE 13-1 Take three sheets of paper and investigate all the ways three planes can intersect (or not intersect) each other. Determine how many solutions there are to the system of equations representing the planes in each case. (For example, if all three sheets meet at a single point and not a line, there is only one solution.)

EXAMPLE 13-1 Solve the following system of equations:

$$x + y + 3z = 2$$
$$x - 2y + 2z = 1$$
$$2x - y + 5z = 3.$$

Solution: First we eliminate x from the second equation by subtracting the first from the second, yielding

$$x + y + 3z = 2$$
$$-3y - z = -1$$
$$2x - y + 5z = 3.$$

Now we use the first equation to eliminate x from the last by multiplying the first equation by 2 and subtracting the result from the third equation. This process yields

$$x + y + 3z = 2$$
$$-3y - z = -1$$
$$-3y - z = -1.$$

The last two equations are the same. Have we made a mistake? No. Any solution to these two equations is a simultaneous solution to all three equations. Since these two equations are the same, there are infinitely many pairs (y, z) which satisfy them both, so there are **infinitely many** solutions (x, y, z) to the system they form.

EXERCISE 13-2 Name a few points which are solutions to the above system of equations.

EXERCISE 13-3 What would the solution to the prior example be if the third equation were $2x - y + 5z = 4$ instead?

EXERCISE 13-4 Why did we choose to eliminate x from the equations first rather than eliminating z as in our initial example?

Rather than carrying around all the x's, y's, and z's, mathematicians have developed a shorthand, methodical way to solve these (and much bigger) systems of linear equations. For this technique, called **Gaussian elimination**, we copy the coefficients of our equations and the answers into a matrix as shown below, where each row of the matrix represents one of the equations. The system

$$x + y + z = 4$$
$$x - 2y + 3z = 4$$
$$-2x - 3y + z = -1$$

becomes

$$\begin{pmatrix} 1 & 1 & 1 & 4 \\ 1 & -2 & 3 & 4 \\ -2 & -3 & 1 & -1 \end{pmatrix},$$

where the coefficients of x are in the first column, those of y in the second, those of z in the third, and the constants (which are always placed on the other side of the equal sign) are in the fourth column. We solve the system by first eliminating x from the last two equations through standard matrix row operations. This is just like the operations we did to simplify determinants. If we add twice the first row of the matrix to the third row, we get

$$\begin{pmatrix} 1 & 1 & 1 & 4 \\ 1 & -2 & 3 & 4 \\ 0 & -1 & 3 & 7 \end{pmatrix}.$$

Notice that the bottom left element is 0, so we have eliminated x from that equation. We eliminate x from the middle equation by subtracting the first row from the second, which leaves

$$\begin{pmatrix} 1 & 1 & 1 & 4 \\ 0 & -3 & 2 & 0 \\ 0 & -1 & 3 & 7 \end{pmatrix}.$$

Finally, we eliminate y from the last equation by multiplying the last row by 3,

$$\begin{pmatrix} 1 & 1 & 1 & 4 \\ 0 & -3 & 2 & 0 \\ 0 & -3 & 9 & 21 \end{pmatrix},$$

and then subtracting the second row from the resulting third row. Our final matrix then is

$$\begin{pmatrix} 1 & 1 & 1 & 4 \\ 0 & -3 & 2 & 0 \\ 0 & 0 & 7 & 21 \end{pmatrix}.$$

If we convert this back into equations, we have

$$\begin{aligned} x + y + z &= 4 \\ -3y + 2z &= 0 \\ 7z &= 21 \end{aligned}$$

 The last equation immediately gives us z, which we can use in the second to get y, then the first to get x. Make sure you see how this method is the same as our elimination technique. WARNING: Gaussian elimination works only if the coefficient of x is nonzero in the first equation. If it is zero, you can't use the first row to eliminate x from the other two equations. (Do you see why?) In such a case, you need to let the first row represent one of the other equations.

EXAMPLE 13-2   What if Gaussian elimination results in

$$\begin{pmatrix} 1 & 1 & 1 & 4 \\ 0 & -3 & 2 & 0 \\ 0 & 0 & 0 & 0 \end{pmatrix}?$$

How about

$$\begin{pmatrix} 1 & 1 & 1 & 4 \\ 0 & -3 & 2 & 0 \\ 0 & 0 & 0 & 4 \end{pmatrix}?$$

Solution: For the first matrix, the corresponding equations are

$$\begin{aligned} x + y + z &= 4 \\ -3y + 2z &= 0 \\ 0 &= 0. \end{aligned}$$

The last equation is always true. The second equation gives us infinitely many pairs (y, z) which we can use to find x's, so there are infinitely many solutions. For the second matrix, the equations are

$$\begin{aligned} x + y + z &= 4 \\ -3y + 2z &= 0 \\ 0 &= 4. \end{aligned}$$

Although again we can use the second to find infinitely many pairs (y, z) and use these to get x's, none of the resulting triplets (x, y, z) will solve the last equation, which is clearly never true. Since the last equation can't ever be true, there is no point where all three can simultaneously be true. Hence, there are no solutions to this system.

EXERCISE 13-5 Use Gaussian elimination to solve the system

$$\begin{aligned} 4x + 2y + z &= 3 \\ 2x - 3y + z &= 6 \\ x - 3y + 2z &= 6. \end{aligned}$$

You may think three variable systems are simple enough to do without Gaussian elimination, and the authors would certainly agree with you; however, as the systems get larger, the need for a methodical approach like Gaussian elimination increases drastically (most notably if you have such large systems that you need to program a computer to solve them—Gaussian elimination gives a nice algorithmic routine).

A different approach to equation solving is to express a system of equations as $\underline{A}\vec{x} = \vec{b}$, where $\underline{A}$ is a matrix representing the coefficients in the equations, $\vec{x}$ represents the variables, and $\vec{b}$ the constants. Take the system

$$\begin{aligned} x + 2y - 3z &= 6 \\ 4x + y - 2z &= 7 \\ -x + y - 3z &= 3. \end{aligned}$$

We can represent this as

$$\begin{pmatrix} 1 & 2 & -3 \\ 4 & 1 & -2 \\ -1 & 1 & -3 \end{pmatrix} \begin{pmatrix} x \\ y \\ z \end{pmatrix} = \begin{pmatrix} 6 \\ 7 \\ 3 \end{pmatrix},$$

because multiplying the two matrices on the left gives

$$\begin{pmatrix} x + 2y - 3z \\ 4x + y - 2z \\ -x + y - 3z \end{pmatrix} = \begin{pmatrix} 6 \\ 7 \\ 3 \end{pmatrix},$$

which is the initial system of equations. If we can find $\underline{A}^{-1}$, then we can solve the system of equations by multiplying both sides of $\underline{A}\vec{x} = \vec{b}$ by $\underline{A}^{-1}$, which gives $\underline{A}^{-1}\underline{A}\vec{x} = \underline{A}^{-1}\vec{b}$, so

$$\vec{x} = \underline{A}^{-1}\vec{b}.$$

Hence, we can solve the system of equations $A\vec{x} = \vec{b}$ uniquely if and only if A is invertible. If A is not invertible, then we can't find a unique solution to the system of equations. This isn't the best method to solve systems of linear equations because inverting large matrices is a painful process; however, it does give us a good way to check if there is a solution.

Recall that a matrix is invertible if and only if its determinant is nonzero. Returning to the above system, since

$$\begin{vmatrix} 1 & 2 & -3 \\ 4 & 1 & -2 \\ -1 & 1 & -3 \end{vmatrix} = 12,$$

the inverse of A exists, and the system has a single solution.

EXAMPLE 13-3   Find all values of a such that the system

$$\begin{aligned} ax + 2y + 3z &= 1 \\ 2x + ay - 3z &= 4 \\ 3x - y + 2z &= -5 \end{aligned}$$

cannot be solved for a unique solution (x, y, z).

Solution: Writing the system as $A\vec{x} = \vec{b}$, we find the determinant of A as

$$\begin{vmatrix} a & 2 & 3 \\ 2 & a & -3 \\ 3 & -1 & 2 \end{vmatrix} = 2a^2 - 12a - 32.$$

Setting this equal to zero, we find that the desired values of a are $a = \mathbf{8}$ and $a = \mathbf{-2}$. (Try them and see if there are any solutions (x, y, z) when a has these values.)

Speaking of bigger systems, what happens if we have more variables, like $w + x + y + z = 7$? How many linear equations do we need in four variables to have a chance at finding a unique (i.e. there's only one) solution? For two variables, we need 2 equations; for three variables, we need 3. It stands to reason that for four variables, we need 4 equations. Try to extend our earlier arguments for why we need 3 equations for three variables to figure out why we need 4 equations for 4 variables.

Four variable and larger systems are usually too tedious to solve by hand. Linear equations in many (by many we mean hundreds, or even thousands) variables are very common, so solving them is very important, but for this task we usually (always) use a computer. There are some larger systems which are solvable by hand, though, and these are the topic of the next section.

13.2   Convenient Systems

Some systems of equations have such a nice form that there's a slick and easy way to solve them. We'll start with a continuation of the last section. Solve the following system:

$$\begin{aligned}
2v + w + x + y + z &= 4 \\
v + 2w + x + y + z &= 5 \\
v + w + 2x + y + z &= 6 \\
v + w + x + 2y + z &= 7 \\
v + w + x + y + 2z &= 8.
\end{aligned}$$

Before you start the tedious process of Gaussian elimination or the excruciating method of variable elimination, take a close look at the left side of the equations. They are very similar. This is our big tip-off that there's a slicker way to attack the problem. The key is finding a useful way to combine the equations. In such a symmetric looking system, the idea that stands out is simply adding the equations. If we add them all together we find

$$6v + 6w + 6x + 6y + 6z = 30,$$

so that $v + w + x + y + z = 5$. How does this help? Look at the first equation. We have

$$2v + w + x + y + z = v + (v + w + x + y + z) = 4.$$

We found that the quantity in parentheses is 5, so the equation becomes $v + 5 = 4$, or $v = -1$. We can use the same method to find the other variables, so that $(v, w, x, y, z) = (-1, 0, 1, 2, 3)$. Not too tough.

EXERCISE 13-6 Find (w, x, y, z) if

$$\begin{aligned}
w + x + y &= 20 \\
w + x + z &= 22 \\
w + y + z &= 24 \\
x + y + z &= 36.
\end{aligned}$$

This method is not restricted to linear systems. Try

$$\begin{aligned}
a(a + b) &= 108 \\
b(a + b) &= \frac{297}{4}.
\end{aligned}$$

Seeing the nice pattern on the left we try adding the equations, from which we have

$$a(a + b) + b(a + b) = (a + b)(a + b) = 108 + \frac{297}{4} = \frac{729}{4}.$$

Since $(a + b)^2 = 729/4$, we can take the square root to find $a + b = \pm 27/2$. First we try $a + b = 27/2$. Substituting this for $a + b$ in the first equation gives

$$a\left(\frac{27}{2}\right) = 108,$$

from which $a = 8$ and then $b = 11/2$. Similarly, if $a + b = -27/2$, we find $a = -8$ and $b = -11/2$. Thus, we find the two solutions using a little craftiness.

EXERCISE 13-7 Solve the following system of equations:

$$
\begin{aligned}
xy &= 12\sqrt{6} \\
yz &= 54\sqrt{2} \\
zx &= 48\sqrt{3}.
\end{aligned}
$$

At the end of the chapter, you'll have a little more practice in attacking these 'convenient' systems. If you see a nice patterned system of equations, there's usually some way to combine the equations through addition or multiplication to make finding the answer easy.

13.3 Symmetric Expressions and Advanced Factorizations

In the first volume, we investigated the sum and difference of two squares and of two cubes. For a quick review, we'll list these relationships:

$$
\begin{aligned}
a^2 + b^2 &= (a+b)^2 - 2ab \\
a^2 - b^2 &= (a-b)(a+b) \\
a^3 + b^3 &= (a+b)(a^2 - ab + b^2) \\
a^3 - b^3 &= (a-b)(a^2 + ab + b^2).
\end{aligned}
$$

We can extend the difference factorizations to any power n:

$$
a^n - b^n = (a-b)(a^{n-1} + a^{n-2}b + a^{n-3}b^2 + \cdots + ab^{n-2} + b^{n-1}),
$$

and the sum factorizations to any odd power $2n+1$:

$$
a^{2n+1} + b^{2n+1} = (a+b)(a^{2n} - a^{2n-1}b + a^{2n-2}b^2 - \cdots - ab^{2n-1} + b^{2n}).
$$

We know to look for these factorizations from the fact that $a = b$ and $a = -b$ are clearly solutions of $a^n - b^n = 0$ and $a^{2n+1} + b^{2n+1} = 0$, respectively. (Why?)

EXERCISE 13-8 Prove the above factorizations for $a^n - b^n$ and $a^{2n+1} + b^{2n+1}$ using sums of geometric series.

We also looked in Volume 1 at squares and cubes of binomials, for example

$$
\begin{aligned}
(a+b)^2 &= a^2 + 2ab + b^2 \\
(a-b)^2 &= a^2 - 2ab + b^2 \\
(a+b)^3 &= a^3 + 3a^2b + 3ab^2 + b^3 \\
(a-b)^3 &= a^3 - 3a^2b + 3ab^2 - b^3.
\end{aligned}
$$

What if we introduce more variables? For example, what is $(a + b + c)^2$? Let's multiply it out:

$$
\begin{aligned}
(a + b + c)^2 &= (a + b + c)(a + b + c) \\
&= a(a + b + c) + b(a + b + c) + c(a + b + c) \\
&= a^2 + ab + ac + ba + b^2 + bc + ca + cb + c^2 \\
&= a^2 + b^2 + c^2 + 2(ab + bc + ca).
\end{aligned}
$$

Another way we can find this product is to realize that in the expansion of $(a + b + c)(a + b + c)$ all the resulting terms will be squares of the variables (like a^2) or products of two of them (like ab). The squares can only occur in one way, but the products of two variables can happen in two ways; for example, ab can be made by taking an a from the first $(a + b + c)$ and a b from the second or by taking b from the first and a from the second. Hence, the coefficient of ab is 2. Following this logic, the product is $a^2 + b^2 + c^2 + 2(ab + bc + ca)$ since the squares occur once and the products twice.

EXAMPLE 13-4 Find $(a + b + c)^3$ using the above logic.

Solution: Write the product as

$$
(a + b + c)(a + b + c)(a + b + c).
$$

What types of terms can we have in the product? All terms will involve the product of three variables. Some terms will be cubes, like a^3. Others will be one variable times the square of another, like ab^2. Still others are the product of all three, or abc. Consider the cubes first. Each can only occur once, so the expansion contains $a^3 + b^3 + c^3$. For the terms like ab^2, the a can come from any of the three terms and the b's then come from the other two terms. Hence, ab^2 occurs three times, as does ba^2, bc^2, etc. Finally, we check out abc. We have 3 choices for the source of a, leaving 2 choices for the source of b, and only 1 for that of c. Hence, abc occurs 6 times. Putting this all together, we have

$$
(a + b + c)(a + b + c)(a + b + c) = a^3 + b^3 + c^3 + 3(ab^2 + ba^2 + ac^2 + ca^2 + bc^2 + cb^2) + 6abc.
$$

How can we be sure we have all the terms? If we take the product of three quantities which each contain three terms, we should have $(3)(3)(3) = 27$ terms. Above, we have 3 cubes, 3 each of the terms like ab^2, and 6 abc's. Thus, there are $3 + 3(6) + 6 = 27$ terms, so we found them all. If you're skeptical, go ahead and multiply the product out completely and find out how the terms above arise.

EXERCISE 13-9 Find $(a + b + c + d)^3$.

Reciprocal expressions are also very common. Let's take a look. Write

$$
\frac{1}{x} + \frac{1}{y} + \frac{1}{z}
$$

with a common denominator. The common denominator is xyz; expressing each term with this denominator we have

$$
\frac{1}{x} + \frac{1}{y} + \frac{1}{z} = \frac{yz + xz + xy}{xyz}.
$$

EXERCISE 13-10 Express

$$\frac{1}{x^2yz} + \frac{1}{y^2zw} + \frac{1}{z^2wx} + \frac{1}{w^2xy}$$

with a common denominator.

EXERCISE 13-11 If $x + y + z = 6$ and $xyz = 2$, then find

$$\frac{1}{xy} + \frac{1}{yz} + \frac{1}{zx}.$$

13.4 More Polynomials

We'll start with a problem. Find x, y, and z if

$$\begin{aligned} x + y + z &= 7 \\ xy + yz + zx &= -14 \\ xyz &= -120. \end{aligned}$$

Seeing all of these symmetric sums, we might think to try some of the principles of the last section; however, we've seen these expressions before. On page 60 we saw symmetric sums relating roots to equations. In fact, from the given equations, we can deduce that x, y, and z are the roots of the polynomial

$$t^3 - 7t^2 - 14t + 120 = 0.$$

(Make sure you see how x, y, and z being the roots of this polynomial leads to the above system of equations.) To find x, y, and z, we just factor using our polynomial solving techniques:

$$t^3 - 7t^2 - 14t + 120 = (t - 5)(t - 6)(t + 4) = 0.$$

Hence, x, y, and z are 5, 6, and −4.

EXERCISE 13-12 How many solutions (x, y, z) are there to the above system?

EXAMPLE 13-5 Find all (a, b, c) if

$$\begin{aligned} 2a + 3b + c &= 11 \\ 6ab + 2ac + 3bc &= 24 \\ abc &= -6. \end{aligned}$$

   Solution: These aren't the nice symmetric equations we saw in our discussion of coefficients and roots of a polynomial. We can make $2a + 3b + c$ a symmetric sum by letting $x = 2a$ and $y = 3b$. We must also make these substitutions in the other two equations. Letting $a = x/2$ and $b = y/3$, they become

$$\begin{aligned} x + y + c &= 11 \\ xy + cx + yc &= 24 \\ (xyc)/6 &= -6. \end{aligned}$$

Writing the last equation as $xyc = -36$, we find that we've made our desired three symmetric equations. We won't always be able to do this, but it's worth a shot. Thus, x, y, and c are the roots of

$$t^3 - 11t^2 + 24t + 36 = 0.$$

Factoring this yields

$$(t - 6)(t - 6)(t + 1) = 0,$$

so the x, y, and c are 6, 6, and −1. So which one's which? Like you should have seen in the previous exercise, we have to try all possible ways. If we let $(x, y, c) = (6, 6, -1)$, we find $(a, b, c) = (3, 2, -1)$. If we let $(x, y, c) = (6, -1, 6)$, we find $(a, b, c) = (3, -1/3, 6)$, and finally, for $(x, y, c) = (-1, 6, 6)$, we have $(a, b, c) = (-1/2, 2, 6)$. These are the three solutions for a, b, and c.

We're not done with polynomials yet! How many points do we need to determine the graph of a line? Right, just two. How about a quadratic? We need three. For example, if the points are $(1, 5)$, $(2, 11)$, and $(-1, -1)$, we write the quadratic as $y = ax^2 + bx + c$ and using the three points, we write

$$
\begin{aligned}
a + b + c &= 5 \\
4a + 2b + c &= 11 \\
a - b + c &= -1.
\end{aligned}
$$

Using the techniques from the first section of this chapter, we find that $(a, b, c) = (1, 3, 1)$, so our quadratic is $y = x^2 + 3x + 1$. Thus, if three points on one quadratic are the same as three points on another, then the two quadratics must be the same. For the same reason, four points determine a cubic, five determine a quartic, etc.

In the same spirit as above, what can we say about a linear equation with two different roots? Let the equation be $ax + b = 0$ and the roots be x_1 and x_2. Thus, we have

$$
\begin{aligned}
ax_1 + b &= 0 \quad \text{and} \\
ax_2 + b &= 0.
\end{aligned}
$$

Subtracting, we have $a(x_1 - x_2) = 0$, so since x_1 and x_2 are different, a must be 0 and so must b. Thus, if we find a linear equation with two different roots, the equation is 0 everywhere.

Extending the above argument, we find that any quadratic with three distinct roots is everywhere 0, any cubic with four distinct roots is everywhere 0, and so on. So what kind of problem does this help us on?

Prove that

$$\frac{1}{a(a - b)(a - c)} + \frac{1}{b(b - c)(b - a)} + \frac{1}{c(c - a)(c - b)} = \frac{1}{abc}$$

for all sets of distinct nonzero numbers $\{a, b, c\}$. (M&IQ 1993)

Rather than showing that the left side equals $1/abc$, we show that

$$\frac{1}{a(a - b)(a - c)} + \frac{1}{b(b - c)(b - a)} + \frac{1}{c(c - a)(c - b)} - \frac{1}{abc} = 0.$$

Writing the left side with the common denominator $abc(a-b)(a-c)(b-c)$, we have

$$\frac{bc(b-c)-ac(a-c)+ab(a-b)-(a-b)(a-c)(b-c)}{abc(a-b)(a-c)(b-c)}.$$

We can show that this is 0 by showing that the numerator is 0. Look at the numerator as a polynomial in c, meaning let a and b be constants and c be a variable, or

$$f(c)=bc(b-c)-ac(a-c)+ab(a-b)-(a-b)(a-c)(b-c).$$

Since each term in $f(c)$ has degree 2 in c, meaning that the power of c in each is at most c^2 (for example, the first term $bc(b-c)$ is b^2c-bc^2), $f(c)$ is a quadratic. If we can show that this quadratic has 3 different roots, then $f(c)=0$ for all c. First let $c=a$; then we have

$$f(a)=ba(b-a)-a^2(0)+ab(a-b)-(a-b)(0)(b-a)=0,$$

so a is a root of $f(c)$. Similarly, $f(b)=0$ and $f(0)=0$. Since a, b, and 0 are three distinct roots of the quadratic $f(c)$, $f(c)=0$ everywhere, or

$$bc(b-c)-ac(a-c)+ab(a-b)-(a-b)(a-c)(b-c)=0.$$

Thus

$$\frac{bc(b-c)-ac(a-c)+ab(a-b)-(a-b)(a-c)(b-c)}{abc(a-b)(a-c)(b-c)}=0,$$

and we have proven the identity.

Of course, you could use a ton of algebra to prove this identity, but this method is much faster for complex identities. Simpler identities are easier to prove with direct algebra.

EXERCISE 13-13 Prove that

$$\frac{b+c}{(a-b)(a-c)}+\frac{c+a}{(b-c)(b-a)}+\frac{a+b}{(c-a)(c-b)}=0$$

for all sets of distinct nonzero numbers $\{a,b,c\}$.

13.5 Squares and Cubes

In Volume 1, we used squaring and cubing to solve equations with the variable inside the square root or the cube root. For example, to solve

$$\sqrt[3]{x+3}=2,$$

we cube the equation to find $x+3=8$, so $x=5$.

These techniques are useful for other types of problems as well. For example, simplify $\sqrt{6+\sqrt{11}}-\sqrt{6-\sqrt{11}}$. First we try to simplify $\sqrt{6+\sqrt{11}}$ using techniques from Volume 1. For example, we can write $\sqrt{4 + 2\sqrt{3}} = 1 + \sqrt{3}$. Unfortunately, we can't find a nice neat square root like this for $\sqrt{6 + \sqrt{11}}$. Instead, let

$$x = \sqrt{6 + \sqrt{11}} - \sqrt{6 - \sqrt{11}}.$$

To clear out the square roots, square both sides, leaving

$$x^2 = 6 + \sqrt{11} - 2\sqrt{36 - 11} + 6 - \sqrt{11} = 12 - 10 = 2.$$

Hence, $x = \sqrt{2}$. (Why not $x = -\sqrt{2}$?)

Squaring or cubing often simplifies equations involving radicals, so try it when all else fails.

13.6   Using Graphing

We'll cover a whole genre of problems with a simple example.

> *For how many positive numbers x does $\cos x = x/8$?* (MAΘ 1987)

We can't possibly hope to actually find the solutions, but even a rough sketch will enable us to count the solutions. We graph $y = \cos x$ (solid line) and $y = x/8$ (dashed line). Where these graphs meet, we have $\cos x = x/8$ and hence a solution to our equation. There are three intersections of the graphs, so there are 3 solutions.

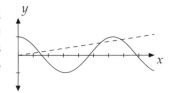

Problems to Solve for Chapter 13

185. If $a \neq b$, $a^3 - b^3 = 19x^3$, and $a - b = x$, find a in terms of x. (AHSME 1975)

186. Solve the system of equations

$$\begin{aligned}
(x + y)(x + y + z) &= 66 \\
(y + z)(x + y + z) &= 99 \\
(z + x)(x + y + z) &= 77.
\end{aligned}$$

(M&IQ 1992)

187. If a, b, and c are real numbers such that $a^2 + b^2 + c^2 = 1$, then what is the minimum value of $ab + bc + ca$? (MAΘ 1987)

188. Find the prime factorization of $2^{22} + 1$. (MAΘ 1991)

189. Four positive integers are given. We select any three of these integers, find their arithmetic average, and add this result to the fourth integer. In this way, the numbers 29, 23, 21, and 17 are obtained. What are the four original numbers? (AHSME 1955)

190. Simplify the product below. (AHSME 1981)

$$\left(\frac{1}{x + y + z}\right)\left(\frac{1}{x} + \frac{1}{y} + \frac{1}{z}\right)\left(\frac{1}{xy + yz + zx}\right)\left(\frac{1}{xy} + \frac{1}{yz} + \frac{1}{zx}\right).$$

191. Evaluate

$$\frac{\sqrt{\sqrt{5}+2}+\sqrt{\sqrt{5}-2}}{\sqrt{\sqrt{5}+1}}-\sqrt{3-2\sqrt{2}}.$$

(AHSME 1976)

192. Find all ordered triples (x, y, z) which satisfy

$$
\begin{aligned}
x + y - z &= 0 \\
zx - xy + yz &= 27 \\
xyz &= 54.
\end{aligned}
$$

(Mandelbrot #1)

193. The simultaneous system below has no solution for what real values of n?

$$
\begin{aligned}
nx + y &= 1 \\
ny + z &= 1 \\
x + nz &= 1
\end{aligned}
$$

(AHSME 1973)

194. Prove that it is not possible to assign the integers $1, 2, 3, \ldots, 20$ to the twenty vertices of a regular dodecahedron so that the five numbers at the vertices of each of the twelve pentagonal faces have the same sum. (USAMTS 1)

195. Consider the system of equations:

$$
\begin{aligned}
a_1 + 8a_2 + 27a_3 + 64a_4 &= 1 \\
8a_1 + 27a_2 + 64a_3 + 125a_4 &= 27 \\
27a_1 + 64a_2 + 125a_3 + 216a_4 &= 125 \\
64a_1 + 125a_2 + 216a_3 + 343a_4 &= 343.
\end{aligned}
$$

These four equations determine a_1, a_2, a_3, and a_4. Show that

$$a_1(x+1)^3 + a_2(x+2)^3 + a_3(x+3)^3 + a_4(x+4)^3 \equiv (2x+1)^3,$$

i.e., these two polynomials are identically the same. Use this to show that $a_1 + a_2 + a_3 + a_4 = 8$ and that $64a_1 + 27a_2 + 8a_3 + a_4 = 729$. (Mandelbrot #3)

196. In a rectangular solid, the area of the top face is 135, the area of the front face is 30, and the area of the right face is 50. Find the volume of the solid. (MAΘ 1990)

197. Prove the identity

$$\frac{bc(b+c)}{(a-b)(a-c)} + \frac{ca(c+a)}{(b-c)(b-a)} + \frac{ab(a+b)}{(c-a)(c-b)} = a+b+c$$

for distinct nonzero numbers a, b, and c. (M&IQ 1993)

198. Factor the expression $x^2 - y^2 - z^2 + 2yz + x + y - z$ completely. (AHSME 1963)

199. If a, b, and c are non-zero real numbers such that

$$\frac{a+b-c}{c} = \frac{a-b+c}{b} = \frac{-a+b+c}{a},$$

then find all possible values of

$$\frac{(a+b)(b+c)(c+a)}{abc}.$$

(AHSME 1978)

200. Find $5a + 7b + 9c$ if a, b, and c satisfy the equations

$$
\begin{aligned}
ab &= 2(a+b) \\
bc &= 3(b+c) \\
ca &= 4(c+a).
\end{aligned}
$$

(USAMTS 1)

201. Find x^2 if $\sqrt[3]{x+9} - \sqrt[3]{x-9} = 3$. (AHSME 1963)

202. Reduce the fraction

$$\frac{a^2 + b^2 - c^2 + 2ab}{a^2 + c^2 - b^2 + 2ac}.$$

(AHSME 1960)

203. Find the sum $\sqrt[3]{5 + 2\sqrt{13}} + \sqrt[3]{5 - 2\sqrt{13}}$.

204. If $xyz = x^3 + y^3 + z^3 = 4$ and $xy^2 + x^2y + yz^2 + y^2z + zx^2 + z^2x = 12$, then find the real value of $xy + yz + zx$. (Mandelbrot #3)

205. Let $g(x) = x^5 + x^4 + x^3 + x^2 + x + 1$. What is the remainder when the polynomial $g(x^{12})$ is divided by the polynomial $g(x)$? (AHSME 1977)

206. Find all triples of positive real numbers (x, y, z) which satisfy the following system:

$$
\begin{aligned}
\sqrt[3]{x} - \sqrt[3]{y} - \sqrt[3]{z} &= 16 \\
\sqrt[4]{x} - \sqrt[4]{y} - \sqrt[4]{z} &= 8 \\
\sqrt[6]{x} - \sqrt[6]{y} - \sqrt[6]{z} &= 4.
\end{aligned}
$$

(MOP)

207. Prove that the equation $4a^2 + 4a = b^2 + b$ has no positive integer solutions (a, b). (Canada 1977)

208. Find the positive integer solutions (x, y) of the equation $x^2 + 3 = y(x + 2)$. (M&IQ 1992)

209. Let a, b, and c be real numbers such that

$$(bc - a^2)^{-1} + (ca - b^2)^{-1} + (ab - c^2)^{-1} = 0.$$

Prove that

$$a(bc - a^2)^{-2} + b(ca - b^2)^{-2} + c(ab - c^2)^{-2} = 0.$$

(IMO 1985)

the BIG PICTURE

Mathematics is generally seen as a European endeavor, passed from the Greeks to the Romans to the Europeans of the Renaissance, and this is reflected in the nomenclature we use. However, many of the discoveries we now refer to by European names we actually anticipated by Indian or Chinese mathematicians.

For example, the "Gaussian elimination" we used in this chapter to solve sets of linear equations was used in the Chinese *Nine Chapters on the Mathematical Art*, written around 250 B.C.! (Gauss lived around 1800.) Amazingly, the Chinese work used notation very similar to what we use today, forming the coefficients into a grid and using operations to simplify the grid.

Similarly, the "Pascal's Triangle" which puts the binomial coefficients into a simple triangular pattern was developed in China, in almost exactly its modern form, as early as 1100. (Pascal lived in the 1600's.) Another modern method anticipated by the Chinese was "Horner's method," a simple numerical algorithm for finding the roots of a polynomial which was rediscovered by Horner in the 1800's.

So why don't we call these formulas and methods by more accurate names? This is an intricate historical question, but the simple answer is that not enough cultural exchange took place with China for Chinese methods to diffuse west. It is for similar reasons that the math developed by the Maya culture of Mexico never interacted with the stream from which modern math came. On the other hand, a great deal of Indian, Arabic, and Egyptian math came to Europe through trade. Hence the name *algebra*, from the Arabic *al-jabr*. The Arabs preserved and extended the methods of the Greeks; Ptolemy's major work in astronomy is still known as *Almagest*, Arabic for "the great work." Both the Arabs and Indians had the quadratic formula, and much geometry lost to Europe.

While historians of math universally acknowledge the contributions and achievements of the mathematicians of other cultures, those contributions still get the short shrift in nomenclature. Except for the odd Brahmagupta's or Chinese Remainder Theorem, our mathematical names come almost entirely from European rediscoverers.

Chapter 14

Inequalities

In Volume 1 we discussed how to work with inequalities which are *sometimes* true. For example, $x > 0$ is only true when x is positive. In this chapter, we will work with inequalities which are *always* true, like the Trivial Inequality we discussed in Volume 1, $x^2 \geq 0$ for all real numbers x. Many readers will likely have never seen anything like the problems at the end of this chapter before. For this reason (and because inequality problems are lots of fun), we have gathered many problems to try out. Once you've learned how to work with inequalities, you'll likely find them as interesting as we do.

14.1 Trivial Inequality Revisited

The square of any real number is nonnegative. It's that simple. For example,

Prove that $\cos 2\theta + \sin^2 \theta$ is nonnegative for all angles θ.

Our strategy here is to manipulate the given expression to the square of a real quantity. Since

$$\cos 2\theta + \sin^2 \theta = \cos^2 \theta - \sin^2 \theta + \sin^2 \theta = \cos^2 \theta,$$

and $\cos^2 \theta \geq 0$ because $\cos^2 \theta$ is the square of $\cos \theta$, we conclude that $\cos 2\theta + \sin^2 \theta \geq 0$.

EXERCISE 14-1 Prove that $4x^2 - 12xy + 9y^2 \geq 0$ for all real number pairs (x, y).

EXAMPLE 14-1 Find the minimum value of $x^2 + 2x + 2$.

Solution: Since $x^2 + 2x + 2 = (x + 1)^2 + 1$, the minimum is **1** because $(x + 1)^2 \geq 0$.

EXERCISE 14-2 Show that $(x^2 + 1)(y^2 + 1) \geq (xy + 1)^2$ for all x and y.

The Trivial Inequality is the most basic general (i.e. always true) inequality, and can be used in many, many ways. If no method is clear in solving an inequality problem, this is often the best place to start.

14.2   Arithmetic Mean-Geometric Mean Inequality

The Arithmetic Mean-Geometric Mean Inequality, commonly called AM-GM, states that the arithmetic mean of a set of positive numbers is greater than or equal to the geometric mean of those numbers. Recall that the arithmetic mean of a set of n numbers is the sum of the numbers divided by n and the geometric mean is the nth root of the product of the numbers. Hence, we can write

$$\frac{a_1 + a_2 + a_3 + \cdots + a_n}{n} \geq \sqrt[n]{a_1 a_2 a_3 \cdots a_n},$$

for positive numbers $a_1, a_2, a_3, \ldots, a_n$.

    WARNING: AM-GM only works if all the numbers are positive! Can you find a counterexample if some are negative?

EXAMPLE 14-2   Prove the AM-GM Inequality for $n = 2$.

    Solution: With $n = 2$, AM-GM asserts that for positive numbers a and b,

$$\frac{a + b}{2} \geq \sqrt{ab}.$$

This brings us to a most important inequality solving technique: working backwards. We use reversible steps to manipulate what we're trying to prove into something that's easy to prove. For the given problem, we start by multiplying both sides by 2 and squaring, yielding

$$a^2 + 2ab + b^2 \geq 4ab.$$

Subtracting $4ab$ from both sides, we have $a^2 - 2ab + b^2 \geq 0$. The left side of this is just $(a - b)^2$, which as the square of a real number is clearly always nonnegative.

    WARNING: A key aspect of working backwards is checking that the logic works when used in reverse order. Thus we must check that we can start from $(a - b)^2 \geq 0$, which we know is true, to obtain $(a + b)/2 \geq \sqrt{ab}$, which we want to prove is true. The only step that we may balk at is taking the square root of both sides of $a^2 + 2ab + b^2 \geq 4ab$ to get $(a + b) \geq 2\sqrt{ab}$; we can do this because we restrict a and b to positive numbers.

    When writing proofs for papers or contests, you should present your solution working forwards, even if you find the solution working backwards.

    As the above proof suggests, many problems which can be solved with AM-GM can also be handled using the Trivial Inequality and lots of algebra. In general, this is not recommended, because AM-GM and the other inequalities we'll introduce in this chapter reduce the amount of work enormously.

    To prove the AM-GM Inequality, we'll start with a lemma.

        Lemma. *Suppose x and y are positive real numbers such that $x > y$. If we decrease x and increase y by some positive quantity ϵ such that $x - \epsilon \geq y + \epsilon$, then $(x - \epsilon)(y + \epsilon) > xy$. Hence, by subtracting ϵ from x and adding it to y, we leave the average of the two numbers unchanged while increasing their product.*

The proof of the lemma is pretty simple. We wish to show that $(x - \epsilon)(y + \epsilon) - xy > 0$. Expanding the product $(x - \epsilon)(y + \epsilon)$, we find that

$$(x - \epsilon)(y + \epsilon) - xy = (x - y)\epsilon - \epsilon^2$$

Since $x - \epsilon \geq y + \epsilon$, we have $x - y \geq 2\epsilon$, so

$$(x - \epsilon)(y + \epsilon) - xy \geq 2\epsilon^2 - \epsilon^2 = \epsilon^2 \geq 0.$$

Hence, we conclude that $(x - \epsilon)(y + \epsilon) \geq xy$.

Now on to our proof of AM-GM. Suppose $a_1, a_2, \ldots, a_n$ are positive real numbers with average A and product P. If all the a_i are equal, then both the arithmetic mean and the geometric mean are equal to A. (Why?) Suppose not all a_i equal A. Let a_j be the one number closest to A without being equal to A. Without loss of generality, let $a_j < A$. Since the average of the numbers is A, there is some member of the set of numbers greater than A. Let a_k be the greatest of these numbers. Clearly we must have $a_k - A \geq A - a_j$ since a_j is closer to A than any other a_i not equal to A.

We now use our lemma. Replace a_j with A and a_k with $a_k - (A - a_j)$. Note that $a_k - (A - a_j) \geq a_j + (A - a_j)$, so we can apply our lemma with $(A - a_j)$ as our ϵ. By our lemma, the average of the numbers in the new set is the same, but the product is now higher. If we continue this process, we make one of the members of the set equal to A with each application of the process. Hence, in some finite number of steps, we will make all the numbers equal to A. Thus, we prove that of all sets of positive numbers with average A, the set with maximum product has all elements equal to A. Thus, the maximum possible value of the geometric mean of the set is A. This maximum *only* occurs when all elements equal A (since if one or more are not equal to A, the product of the numbers can be increased by the process above).

Note that we have made a big deal of when the equality holds (meaning the equality portion of the nonstrict inequality occurs). This is a very important part of inequality problems, so don't overlook it.

One very useful technique in applying AM-GM is breaking the question into parts.

EXAMPLE 14-3 Prove that for all positive numbers x, y, and z,

$$x^2 + y^2 + z^2 \geq xy + yz + xz.$$

Proof: Seeing the sum on the greater than side, we may think to try AM-GM directly, but this yields $(x^2 + y^2 + z^2)/3 \geq \sqrt[3]{x^2 y^2 z^2}$, which clearly isn't too helpful. If we look at the less than side, we see products of two numbers, which suggests using AM-GM on just x^2 and y^2, yielding $(x^2 + y^2)/2 \geq xy$. Similarly, we can show $(x^2 + z^2)/2 \geq xz$ and $(y^2 + z^2)/2 \geq yz$. Adding these three inequalities gives $x^2 + y^2 + z^2 \geq xy + xz + yz$ as desired. Notice how we divided the inequality to be proven into three separate inequalities.

EXERCISE 14-3 When does equality hold in the previous example?

EXAMPLE 14-4 Show that

$$x^2 y^2 + x^2 z^2 + y^2 z^2 \geq x^2 yz + xy^2 z + xyz^2.$$

Solution: Seeing the products like x^2y^2 on the left side, we may be tempted to try AM-GM, yielding

$$\frac{x^4 + y^4}{2} \geq x^2 y^2.$$

WARNING: Why is this not likely to be useful? Because in the expression we are trying to prove, x^2y^2 is on the *greater* side rather than the *lesser* side like in our above AM-GM result. Don't spend too long chasing dead ends like this. With AM-GM the solution is usually pretty straightforward. Since this problem looks similar in form to the last one, let's try the same technique. We use AM-GM on x^2y^2 and x^2z^2 to get

$$\frac{x^2y^2 + x^2z^2}{2} \geq \sqrt{(x^2y^2)(x^2z^2)}.$$

Notice that the x^2y^2 is now on the greater side as desired. Simplifying the right side gives $(x^2y^2 + x^2z^2)/2 \geq x^2yz$. Aha! Just like last time, we can do this twice more and add the three resulting inequalities to prove the given inequality. (When does equality occur?)

EXERCISE 14-4 Show that $\frac{a}{b} + \frac{b}{a} \geq 2$ for all positive pairs (a, b), and find where equality holds.

14.3   Cauchy's Inequality

Recall from our discussion of vectors that the dot product of two vectors $\vec{x}$ and $\vec{y}$ is

$$\vec{x} \cdot \vec{y} = \|x\| \, \|y\| \cos \theta,$$

where θ is the angle between the two vectors. Since $\cos \theta \leq 1$, $\|x\| \, \|y\| \cos \theta \leq \|x\| \, \|y\|$. Thus, $\vec{x} \cdot \vec{y} \leq \|x\| \, \|y\|$. Writing $\vec{x}$ and $\vec{y}$ in terms of their Cartesian coordinates, they are $\begin{pmatrix} x_1 & x_2 & \cdots & x_n \end{pmatrix}$ and $\begin{pmatrix} y_1 & y_2 & \cdots & y_n \end{pmatrix}$. Using these coordinates and squaring both sides of the inequality $\vec{x} \cdot \vec{y} \leq \|x\| \, \|y\|$, we have

$$(x_1y_1 + x_2y_2 + \cdots + x_ny_n)^2 \leq (x_1^2 + x_2^2 + \cdots + x_n^2)(y_1^2 + y_2^2 + \cdots + y_n^2).$$

This very important inequality is called **Cauchy's Inequality**, or sometimes the Cauchy-Schwarz Inequality.

EXAMPLE 14-5 Use the above proof to determine the equality condition for Cauchy's Inequality.

Solution: The inequality entered our problem when we noted that $\cos \theta \leq 1$. Thus, equality holds only if $\cos \theta = 1$, or $\theta = 0°$. In this case, $\vec{x}$ and $\vec{y}$ are in the same direction so the ratio of the components of $\vec{x}$ to the components of $\vec{y}$ is constant, or

$$\frac{x_1}{y_1} = \frac{x_2}{y_2} = \cdots = \frac{x_n}{y_n}.$$

EXERCISE 14-5 Prove that

$$(a_1x + b_1)^2 + (a_2x + b_2)^2 + (a_3x + b_3)^2 + \cdots + (a_nx + b_n)^2 \geq 0$$

and use this fact to prove Cauchy's Inequality. Hint: Write the left side as a quadratic equation in x and note that a quadratic equation is nonnegative for all x if and only if the discriminant is nonpositive.

As the form of Cauchy's Inequality suggests, it is most obviously useful for problems involving products of sums or squares of sums.

EXAMPLE 14-6 Prove that

$$1^2 + 2^2 + \cdots + n^2 \geq \frac{(1 + 2 + \cdots n)^2}{n}$$

for all integers $n \geq 1$.

Proof: Seeing the square of a sum, we think of Cauchy's Inequality. We multiply both sides by n to isolate the square of a sum as in Cauchy's Inequality, leaving

$$(1^2 + 2^2 + \cdots + n^2)(n) \geq (1 + 2 + \cdots + n)^2.$$

If we write n as $(1^2 + 1^2 + \cdots + 1^2)$, we have

$$(1^2 + 2^2 + \cdots + n^2)(1^2 + 1^2 + \cdots + 1^2) \geq (1 + 2 + \cdots + n)^2,$$

which is true by Cauchy's Inequality. (Note once again how we have worked backwards to solve this problem. Show that each of the steps we have taken is reversible.)

EXAMPLE 14-7 Show that if α and β are angles in the first quadrant, then

$$\left(\frac{\cos^3 \alpha}{\cos \beta} + \frac{\sin^3 \alpha}{\sin \beta} \right) \cos(\alpha - \beta) \geq 1.$$

(Mandelbrot #3)

Proof: Writing $\cos(\alpha - \beta) = \cos \alpha \cos \beta + \sin \alpha \sin \beta$, the left hand side becomes

$$\left(\frac{\cos^3 \alpha}{\cos \beta} + \frac{\sin^3 \alpha}{\sin \beta} \right) (\cos \alpha \cos \beta + \sin \alpha \sin \beta).$$

Seeing the product of sums, we apply Cauchy:

$$\left(\frac{\cos^3 \alpha}{\cos \beta} + \frac{\sin^3 \alpha}{\sin \beta} \right) (\cos \alpha \cos \beta + \sin \alpha \sin \beta) \geq$$

$$\left(\sqrt{\left(\frac{\cos^3 \alpha}{\cos \beta} \right) (\cos \alpha \cos \beta)} + \sqrt{\left(\frac{\sin^3 \alpha}{\sin \beta} \right) (\sin \alpha \sin \beta)} \right)^2.$$

The lesser side is

$$\left(\sqrt{\cos^4 \alpha} + \sqrt{\sin^4 \alpha} \right)^2 = \left(\cos^2 \alpha + \sin^2 \alpha \right)^2 = 1,$$

so we have our desired inequality.

14.4   Maximization and Minimization

In algebra class you were probably asked a question like 'If Farmer Bob has 40 feet of fence, what is the largest rectangular field that Farmer Bob can fence off?' You were then taught to let x and y be the dimensions of the field, so $2x + 2y = 40$. The area is $xy = x(20 - x)$, and you completed the square to find

$$\text{Area} = -(x - 10)^2 + 100.$$

By the Trivial Inequality the maximum area is 100 and occurs when $x = y = 10$, or when the field is a square. This is a fine approach, but what if we were told that Farmer Bob has 96 square inches of wrapping paper and asked to find the volume of the largest rectangular box he can wrap with the paper. Now we have three variables and our completing the squares method isn't quite as helpful.

For these **optimization** (either minimization or maximization) problems, we can often apply AM-GM, Cauchy's Inequality, or the Trivial Inequality. For Farmer Bob's wrapping problem, we let x, y, and z be the dimensions of the box. The surface area of the box is to be covered by the paper, so

$$2(xy + yz + zx) = 96.$$

We wish to maximize xyz. Applying AM-GM to the three terms in the sum above, we have

$$\frac{xy + yz + zx}{3} \geq \sqrt[3]{(xy)(yz)(zx)} = (xyz)^{2/3}.$$

Using our first equation, we find $xyz \leq 64$, so 64 is the maximum volume. (How did we know to get xyz on the lesser side?) Applying the equality condition for AM-GM we further find that the box attains this maximum volume when $xy = yz = zx$, or $x = y = z = 4$. Thus, the box of maximum volume is a cube.

WARNING: Although boxes are usually cubes and rectangles usually squares in this type of problem, don't assume this will be the case every time. You must use the equality conditions of inequality to *prove* it. Furthermore, your assumption may not always be correct!

It is very important to show that equality can be attained, because if it cannot, then we haven't found the maximum. For example, if we are told that x is a two digit number and asked to find its maximum value, we cannot assume from the true statement $x \leq 100$ that 100 is the maximum, because 100 cannot be attained. Thus, optimization problems are two part problems: show that the desired quantity can be no higher or lower than the optimal value, and show that the optimal value can be attained.

EXAMPLE 14-8   If $xyz = 27$ and x, y, and z are positive, find the minimum value of $x + y + z$.

Solution: Since we are minimizing, we want $x + y + z$ on the greater side. (Why?) Using AM-GM we have
$$\frac{x + y + z}{3} \geq \sqrt[3]{xyz} = 3.$$

Hence $x + y + z \geq 9$, where equality is attained when $x = y = z = 3$. Thus, our minimum value is **9**.

EXERCISE 14-6   Find the maximum value of xyz if $2x + y + z = 12$.

We are sometimes interested in finding the smallest or the largest member of a set. We denote the smallest number in set A by $\min A$ and the largest by $\max A$. Hence, by $\min\{x, y, z\}$, we mean the smallest of the numbers x, y, and z. Furthermore, by $\max\min\{x, y, z\}$, we mean consider all sets $\{x, y, z\}$, find the minimum element of each set, then find the maximum of all these minimum elements.

EXAMPLE 14-9 If $x + y = 4$, find $\max\min\{x, y\}$.

Solution: Without loss of generality, let $x \geq y$. Hence $\min\{x, y\} = y$. Thus, we are trying to maximize y such that $y \leq x$ and $x + y = 4$. Since $x + y \geq y + y = 2y$, we have $4 \geq 2y$, so $y \leq 2$. Thus, the maximum value of y is **2**. We must show that this value can be attained, which it can when $x = y = 2$.

EXERCISE 14-7 We might try to use the above "without loss of generality let $x \geq y$" approach on the following:

If $2x + y = 4$, find $\max\min\{x, y\}$.

Could we? Why or why not?

14.5 Geometry and Inequalities

Because there are so many symmetric expressions in geometry, such as Heron's formula or the perimeter of a triangle, there are very many inequalities which can be derived with the help of geometrical principles. One purely geometric tool which is often useful in attacking geometric inequalities is the **Triangle Inequality**, which states that the sum of any two sides of a triangle is greater than the third side. (Prove this inequality!) Since the Triangle Inequality is a strict inequality in geometry (meaning there can never be equality), it is generally not useful on nonstrict inequality problems.

This section will mostly be examples, with a few helpful hints scattered about. In these problems, you will need to use many geometric relations as well as the Triangle Inequality, the other inequalities in this chapter, and the ever important fact that $\cos\theta$ and $\sin\theta$ are less than or equal to 1.

EXAMPLE 14-10 Prove that the cube of the perimeter of a triangle is greater than or equal to 108 times the product of its area and its circumradius.

Proof: First we write out what we are asked to prove:

$$(a + b + c)^3 \geq 108[ABC]R.$$

Seeing the product $[ABC]R$, we recall that $4[ABC]R = abc$, so our expression becomes

$$(a + b + c)^3 \geq 27abc.$$

Taking the cube root and dividing by 3 we have

$$\frac{a + b + c}{3} \geq \sqrt[3]{abc},$$

which is true by AM-GM. (Are all of our steps reversible?)

EXERCISE 14-8   Use the previous result to prove that $p^3 = 108[ABC]R$ if and only if $\triangle ABC$ is equilateral.

EXAMPLE 14-11   Show that if a quadrilateral is cyclic with consecutive sides a, b, c, and d and diagonals p and q, then

$$pq \leq \sqrt{(a^2 + b^2)(c^2 + d^2)}.$$

(ARML 1987)

   Proof: From Ptolemy's Theorem (page 35) we have $ac + bd = pq$; hence the above expression becomes $(ac + bd) \leq \sqrt{(a^2 + b^2)(c^2 + d^2)}$. Squaring this inequality, we have

$$(a^2 + b^2)(c^2 + d^2) \geq (ac + bd)^2,$$

which is just Cauchy's Inequality and therefore true.

   As you do more work with geometric inequalities, you'll find that knowing the few important ways to find the area of a triangle is very useful in solving geometric inequalities.

14.6   Wrap-Up and Parting Hints

Most of the very important inequality solving techniques are discussed among the previous sections, but there are still a couple approaches we haven't seen.

  ▷ If $A \geq B$ and $B \geq C$, then $A \geq C$. Sometimes you may find it necessary to use an intermediate expression, like B above, to show that $A \geq C$.

  ▷ If A and B are positive and $1/A \geq 1/B$, then $B \geq A$. Sometimes you will be given an inequality whose denominators are easier to work with than the numerators. Take reciprocals and reverse the inequality sign; perhaps this will simplify the problem.

  ▷ Don't forget the Triangle Inequality for complex numbers when faced with $|x + y|$! Remember that $|x + y| \leq |x| + |y|$.

EXAMPLE 14-12   As a parting shot, we introduce a few more advanced inequalities. We have introduced the arithmetic mean and the geometric mean, but we can also define a **harmonic mean** (HM) as the reciprocal of the average of the reciprocals, and a **root mean square** (RMS) as the square root of the average of the squares. For any set of positive numbers $\{a_1, a_2, \ldots .a_n\}$, we then have

$$\text{RMS} \geq \text{AM} \geq \text{GM} \geq \text{HM},$$

or

$$\sqrt{\frac{a_1^2 + a_2^2 + \cdots + a_n^2}{n}} \geq \frac{a_1 + a_2 + \cdots + a_n}{n} \geq \sqrt[n]{a_1 a_2 \cdots a_n} \geq \frac{n}{\frac{1}{a_1} + \frac{1}{a_2} + \cdots + \frac{1}{a_n}}.$$

   We can extend this discussion past the root mean square to even higher powers to obtain the Power Mean Inequality, which states that if $m > n$, then

$$\sqrt[m]{\frac{a_1^m + a_2^m + \cdots + a_k^m}{k}} \geq \sqrt[n]{\frac{a_1^n + a_2^n + \cdots + a_k^n}{k}}.$$

EXERCISE 14-9 Write the Power Mean Inequality in summation notation.

EXERCISE 14-10 Show that for $m = 2$, $n = 1$, the Power Mean Inequality is merely RMS $\geq$ AM.

Problems to Solve for Chapter 14

If inequalities are new to you, be patient. It takes practice to get good at them!

210. If x and y are real and $x^2 + y^2 = 1$, compute the maximum value of $(x + y)^2$. (ARML 1985)

211. Let $xyz = 1$ for positive x, y, z. Show that $\min\{x + y, x + z, y + z\}$ has no maximum value. (Mandelbrot #1)

212. Show that if α and β are first quadrant angles and

$$\left(\frac{\cos^3 \alpha}{\cos \beta} + \frac{\sin^3 \alpha}{\sin \beta} \right) \cos(\alpha - \beta) = 1,$$

then $\alpha = \beta$. (Mandelbrot #3)

213. If A, B, C, and D are positive numbers such that $A + 2B + 3C + 4D = 8$, then what is the maximum value of $ABCD$? (MAΘ 1991)

214. For positive x, y, z such that $xyz = 1$, use the AM-GM Inequality to show that $\min \max\{x + y, x + z, y + z\} = 2$. (Mandelbrot #1)

215. For positive x, y, z such that $x + y + z = 3$, show that $\max \min\{xy, xz, yz\} = 1$. (Mandelbrot #1)

216. Show that for any two positive real numbers a and b,

$$\frac{a + b}{2} - \sqrt{ab} \geq \sqrt{\frac{a^2 + b^2}{2}} - \frac{a + b}{2},$$

by showing that this inequality is equivalent to

$$\frac{(a + b)^2}{2} \geq \sqrt{(2ab)(a^2 + b^2)}$$

and then using the AM-GM Inequality. (Mandelbrot #1)

217. Let $r_1, r_2, \ldots, r_n$ be n real numbers each greater than zero. Prove that for any real number $x > 0$,

$$(x + r_1)(x + r_2) \cdots (x + r_n) \leq \left(x + \frac{r_1 + r_2 + \cdots + r_n}{n} \right)^n.$$

(Mandelbrot #3)

218. What is the smallest positive integer n such that $\sqrt{n} - \sqrt{n - 1} < .01$? (AHSME 1978)

219. Let x be a real number and let $f(x) = \sum_{i=1}^{10} |x - F_i|$, where F_i is the ith Fibonacci number; i.e. $F_1 = F_2 = 1$ and $F_n = F_{n-1} + F_{n-2}$ for $n > 2$. Find the minimum value of $f(x)$. (USAMTS 2)

220. Let $r_1, r_2, \ldots, r_n$ be n real numbers each greater than zero. Prove that for any real number $x > 0$,

$$(x + r_1)(x + r_2) \cdots (x + r_n) \geq \left(x + \sqrt[n]{r_1 r_2 \cdots r_n}\right)^n.$$

(Mandelbrot #3)

221. If $x^3 - 12x^2 + ax - 64$ has real, nonnegative roots, find a. (Mandelbrot #1)

222. Prove that $\sqrt{n} \leq \sqrt[n]{n!}$ for every positive integer n. (USAMTS 1)

223. Let a, b, c, and d be the areas of the triangular faces of a tetrahedron, and let h_a, h_b, h_c, and h_d be the corresponding altitudes of the tetrahedron. If V denotes the volume of the tetrahedron, prove that

$$(a + b + c + d)(h_a + h_b + h_c + h_d) \geq 48V.$$

(USAMTS 3)

224. Find the smallest integer n such that

$$\left(x^2 + y^2 + z^2\right)^2 \leq n\left(x^4 + y^4 + z^4\right)$$

for all real numbers x, y, and z. (AHSME 1977)

225. Cars A and B travel the same distance. Car A travels half the *distance* at u miles per hour and half at v miles per hour. Car B travels half the *time* at u miles per hour and half at v miles per hour. The average speed of Car A is x miles per hour and that of Car B is y miles per hour. Prove that $x \leq y$. (AHSME 1973)

226. Prove that the product of two sides of a triangle is always greater than the product of the diameters of the inscribed circle and the circumscribed circle. (IMO 1985)

227. Triangle ABC has side lengths $AB = 6$, $AC = 5$, and $BC = 4$. A point P in the interior of $\triangle ABC$ is a distance l from BC, a distance m from AB, and a distance n from AB. If $l^2 + m^2 + n^2 = 225/44$, then find l. (Mandelbrot #2)

228. Show that for all positive a and b with root mean square RMS, arithmetic mean AM, geometric mean GM, and harmonic mean HM, we have RMS − AM ≥ GM − HM. (Mandelbrot #1)

229. If a, b, and c are each positive and $a + b + c = 6$, show that

$$\left(a + \frac{1}{b}\right)^2 + \left(b + \frac{1}{c}\right)^2 + \left(c + \frac{1}{a}\right)^2 \geq \frac{75}{4}.$$

(ARML 1987)

230. At a wedding reception n guests have assembled into m groups to converse. (The groups are not necessarily equal sized.) The host is preparing m square cakes, each with an ornate ribbon adorning its perimeter, to serve to the m groups. No guest is allowed to have more than 25 cm^2 of cake. Prove that no more than $20\sqrt{mn}$ cm of ribbon is needed to embellish the m cakes. (Mandelbrot #3)

231. Let $ABCD$ be a tetrahedron having each sum of opposite edges equal to 1. Prove that

$$r_A + r_B + r_C + r_D \le \frac{\sqrt{3}}{3},$$

where r_A, r_B, r_C, r_D are the inradii of the faces, equality holding if $ABCD$ is regular. (IMO 1986)

232. The circumcircle k of acute $\triangle ABC$ has radius r. The bisectors of the angles of the triangle intersect the circle again in the points A', B' and C'. If P and Q are the areas of $\triangle ABC$ and $\triangle A'B'C'$, respectively, prove the inequality $16Q^3 \ge 27r^4P$. (IMO 1989)

233. Prove that if $x_i > 0$ for all i then

$$\left(x_1^{19} + x_2^{19} + \cdots + x_n^{19}\right)\left(x_1^{93} + x_2^{93} + \cdots + x_n^{93}\right) \ge$$
$$\left(x_1^{20} + x_2^{20} + \cdots + x_n^{20}\right)\left(x_1^{92} + x_2^{92} + \cdots + x_n^{92}\right),$$

and find when equality holds. (Mandelbrot #3)

234. Let M be an interior point of the triangle ABC such that $\angle AMC = 90°$, $\angle AMB = 150°$, and 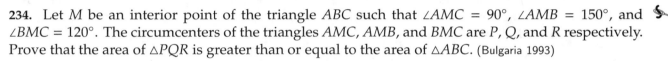 $\angle BMC = 120°$. The circumcenters of the triangles AMC, AMB, and BMC are P, Q, and R respectively. Prove that the area of $\triangle PQR$ is greater than or equal to the area of $\triangle ABC$. (Bulgaria 1993)

Chapter 15

Combinatorics

15.1 Identities

Combinatorics is the science of counting. A large part of this science is the establishment of **identities**, which allow a complex expression to be written much more simply. For example, in Volume 1, we used sets to show that for any n,

$$\binom{n}{0} + \binom{n}{1} + \binom{n}{2} + \cdots + \binom{n}{n} = 2^n. \tag{15.1}$$

This identity allows us to replace the complicated left hand side of (15.1) with the terse right side.

In this chapter we'll look at some of the prettier and more useful combinatorial identities.

15.2 Pascal's Identity

Consider a set of n objects. In how many ways can we choose k of them? If you have read Volume 1, you should know that we can do it in

$$\binom{n}{k} = \frac{n!}{k! \, (n-k)!}$$

ways.

However, we need not be so direct about things. Consider some particular one of the n objects, and call it A. Then we can choose k objects *including* A in only $\binom{n-1}{k-1}$ ways, because after including A, we must pick $k-1$ of the remaining $n-1$ to include in our k.

EXERCISE 15-1 In how many ways can we choose k objects *not including* A?

Since our final group of k objects either contains A or doesn't, we can choose the group in $\binom{n-1}{k-1} + \binom{n-1}{k}$ ways. But we can also pick the group in $\binom{n}{k}$ ways by our original argument! We thus have

$$\binom{n-1}{k-1} + \binom{n-1}{k} = \binom{n}{k}$$

for any n and k. This is called **Pascal's identity** (though it was evidently known in much of Asia at least 300 years before Pascal observed it).

EXAMPLE 15-1 Let's try a concrete example. With $n = 6$ and $k = 4$, Pascal's identity asserts that $\binom{5}{3} + \binom{5}{4} = \binom{6}{4}$. Calculating the combinations (do it yourself), this becomes $10 + 5 = 15$, which is true.

EXERCISE 15-2 Test some more possible n and k.

EXERCISE 15-3 Make sure you understand the argument by which we derived Pascal's identity; arguments like this are very common. What happens if $k = 0$?

One interesting thing about combinatorial identities is that once you understand them, you can usually prove them in at least two extremely different ways. For example, Pascal's identity can be confirmed by going directly back to the definition of $\binom{n}{k}$:

$$
\begin{aligned}
\binom{n-1}{k-1} + \binom{n-1}{k} &= \frac{(n-1)!}{(k-1)!\,(n-k)!} + \frac{(n-1)!}{k!\,(n-k-1)!} \\
&= (n-1)! \left[\frac{k}{k!\,(n-k)!} + \frac{n-k}{k!\,(n-k)!} \right] \\
&= (n-1)!\,\frac{n}{k!\,(n-k)!} \\
&= \frac{n!}{k!\,(n-k)!} \\
&= \binom{n}{k},
\end{aligned}
$$

where we have used the fact that $r! = r(r-1)!$ in going from the first to the second line. Isn't that slick? We now have two equally good, but utterly different, arguments which lead to the same identity. Make sure you understand both—that your mind can easily shift gears from the counting argument to the algebraic argument.

EXAMPLE 15-2 Let's look at another example of proofs of different types. Consider a group of n people from which we want to form a k-member committee with m leaders. We can choose k people to be on a committee in $\binom{n}{k}$ ways, then choose the m committee leaders in $\binom{k}{m}$ ways. Or, we can choose the m leaders *first* in $\binom{n}{m}$ ways and then choose the remaining $k - m$ committee members from the $n - m$ remaining people in $\binom{n-m}{k-m}$ ways. Since both methods will give us all the committees, we have the identity

$$
\binom{n}{k}\binom{k}{m} = \binom{n}{m}\binom{n-m}{k-m}. \tag{15.2}
$$

We can prove this identity in a purely algebraic way as well. We just expand all the terms of (15.2) using the definition of $\binom{n}{k}$, so that the identity we want to prove is

$$
\frac{n!}{k!\,(n-k)!}\,\frac{k!}{m!\,(k-m)!} = \frac{n!}{m!\,(n-m)!}\,\frac{(n-m)!}{(k-m)!\,(n-k)!}.
$$

Since after a little cancellation the two sides have all the same terms in their numerators and denominators, they must clearly be equal.

15.3 More Identities

Pascal's Identity is one of the two most fundamental combinatorial identities. The other we encountered in Volume 1:

$$\binom{n}{k} = \binom{n}{n-k}.$$

EXERCISE 15-4 Develop both a counting and an algebraic argument to prove this identity.

From just these two basic identities, we can derive quite a few others. For example, suppose we apply Pascal's identity not just once, but many times, writing

$$
\begin{aligned}
\binom{n}{k} &= \binom{n-1}{k} + \binom{n-1}{k-1} \\
&= \binom{n-1}{k} + \binom{n-2}{k-1} + \binom{n-2}{k-2} \\
&= \binom{n-1}{k} + \binom{n-2}{k-1} + \binom{n-3}{k-2} + \binom{n-3}{k-3}
\end{aligned}
\tag{15.3}
$$

and so on. We can continue this way, expanding the last term with Pascal's identity, until the last term is $\binom{n-k}{k-k} = \binom{n-k}{0} = \binom{n-k-1}{0}$, at which point we stop. We have thus proven the identity

$$\binom{n}{k} = \binom{n-1}{k} + \binom{n-2}{k-1} + \binom{n-3}{k-2} + \cdots + \binom{n-k-1}{0}. \tag{15.4}$$

EXERCISE 15-5 Try some n and k to test (15.4). Why is the identity obvious if $k = n - 1$?

EXAMPLE 15-3 Since our identities are getting very long and taking up a lot of space, we can use the space-saving $\sum$ notation to write them more easily. Convince yourself that

$$\binom{n}{k} = \sum_{i=0}^{k} \binom{n-1-i}{k-i}$$

is equivalent to (15.4).

Suppose we again apply Pascal's identity repeatedly as in equations (15.3), but this time to the term we left alone in that expansion. We thus write

$$
\begin{aligned}
\binom{n}{k} &= \binom{n-1}{k} + \binom{n-1}{k-1} \\
&= \binom{n-2}{k} + \binom{n-2}{k-1} + \binom{n-1}{k-1} \\
&= \binom{n-3}{k} + \binom{n-3}{k-1} + \binom{n-2}{k-1} + \binom{n-1}{k-1}
\end{aligned}
$$

and so on; the process will terminate when we have

$$\binom{n}{k} = \binom{k-1}{k-1} + \binom{k}{k-1} + \binom{k+1}{k-1} + \cdots + \binom{n-1}{k-1}. \tag{15.5}$$

Applying Pascal's identity in a slightly different way, we achieve a completely different identity!

EXERCISE 15-6 Try some values of n and k to verify (15.5). Why is the identity obvious if $k = 1$?

EXAMPLE 15-4 Evaluate $S = \binom{n}{1} + 2\binom{n}{2} + 3\binom{n}{3} + \cdots + n\binom{n}{n}$.

Solution: We use an old trick from Volume 1: writing the sum backwards yields

$$S = n\binom{n}{n} + (n-1)\binom{n}{n-1} + (n-2)\binom{n}{n-2} + \cdots + \binom{n}{1},$$

which after applying the identity $\binom{n}{k} = \binom{n}{n-k}$ to each term in the sum becomes

$$S = n\binom{n}{0} + (n-1)\binom{n}{1} + (n-2)\binom{n}{2} + \cdots + \binom{n}{n-1}.$$

We add this to the original series to get

$$2S = n\binom{n}{0} + n\binom{n}{1} + n\binom{n}{2} + \cdots + n\binom{n}{n-1} + n\binom{n}{n}.$$

Using the identity (15.1), we then have $2S = n2^n$, or $S = n2^{n-1}$.

15.4 Block Walking

In the derivations of the identities (15.4) and (15.5), we have gotten very far from the elegant counting arguments by which we proved Pascal's identity. It's a good idea to keep pure counting techniques in mind, even when algebraic methods (like the repeated application of Pascal's identity) work fine; counting arguments often point the way to new results.

On the other hand, counting arguments can get messy. To reduce complication, we'll introduce a new tool: **Pascal's triangle**. Pascal's triangle is formed like this:

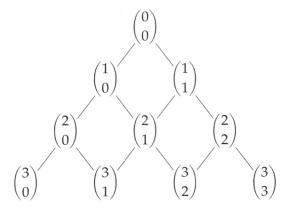

Pascal's triangle is interesting for several reasons, but the biggest is that because of Pascal's identity, each element is equal to the sum of the elements above and to the right and above and to the left. Thus in the diagram above, each element is the sum of the elements above it and with lines connecting to it. Rather than computing all the $\binom{n}{k}$'s directly, we can use this simple rule to write out the elements by simple addition.

EXERCISE 15-7 Write out the first four rows of Pascal's triangle explicitly. Use the rule above to extend the triangle several more rows.

EXERCISE 15-8 Why is Pascal's triangle symmetric right-to-left?

EXERCISE 15-9 Find the sum of the elements in the first, second, third, and fourth rows of Pascal's triangle. Is there a pattern? Does it correlate to anything you have seen? Why does this happen?

EXAMPLE 15-5 Combinatorial identities can be thought of as relationships between elements of Pascal's triangle. For example, the identity (15.5) asserts that the sum of the elements denoted by ∘ at right equals the element denoted by •. (The ×'s denote elements not taking part in the identity.) See if you can draw pictures of other identities you have seen—such mental pictures may be easier to remember than a cumbersome formula.

```
                    ×
                 ×     ∘
              ×     ∘     ×
           ×     ∘     ×     ×
        ×     ∘     ×     ×     ×
     ×     ×     •     ×     ×     ×
```

The importance of Pascal's triangle in combinatorics is twofold. First, it can be used to look for and test possible identities, without the grind of multiplying out the $\binom{n}{k}$'s. Second, it can be used to prove identities through the method known as **block walking**.

The key to block walking is to imagine taking a walk on Pascal's Triangle. Starting at $\binom{0}{0}$, we proceed strictly downward along the lines drawn in the picture of Pascal's triangle above. At each junction, we can choose to go left or right; the element $\binom{n}{k}$ is attained after n downward moves by k right decisions and $n - k$ left decisions. (Verify this yourself.)

The key question is, in how many ways can we walk to the position $\binom{n}{k}$? Since we need to choose k right decisions out of n total decisions, we can do it in $\binom{n}{k}$ ways!

EXERCISE 15-10 Prove the same thing (that we can walk to $\binom{n}{k}$ in $\binom{n}{k}$ ways) by induction.

So what does it matter how many ways we can walk to $\binom{n}{k}$? It allows us to make complicated counting arguments with the notion of walks as a simplifying crutch. For example, consider the identity (15.5), which we drew in Example 15-5 above. In terms of block walking, the identity asserts that the sum of the number of walks to the ∘'s is equal to the number of walks to the •. We can prove this by observing that at each ∘, we can branch right only once more if we hope to get to the •. Thus the ∘'s can be thought of as all possible positions of the *last* right branching we make. Since there must be one and only one last right branching, the sum of the numbers of walks to the ∘'s must equal the number of walks to the •.

EXERCISE 15-11 Prove the identity (15.4) by a block walking argument.

EXAMPLE 15-6 Prove that

$$\sum_{k=0}^{n} \binom{n}{k}^2 = \binom{2n}{n}. \tag{15.6}$$

Proof: In walking from $\binom{0}{0}$ to $\binom{2n}{n}$, we must pass through the nth row of the triangle, say at $\binom{n}{k}$. The number of ways to go from $\binom{n}{k}$ on to $\binom{2n}{n}$ is $\binom{n}{n-k}$, since we need to make $n - k$ right branches out of the n total branches we have left. Thus the total number of ways to get to $\binom{2n}{n}$ passing through $\binom{n}{k}$ is $\binom{n}{k}\binom{n}{n-k} = \binom{n}{k}\binom{n}{k} = \binom{n}{k}^2$. Since we could pass through the nth row at any position k, we then have

$$\binom{2n}{n} = \binom{n}{0}^2 + \binom{n}{1}^2 + \cdots + \binom{n}{n}^2,$$

which is equivalent to what we were trying to prove.

EXERCISE 15-12 Prove **Vandermonde's identity**,

$$\sum_{k=0}^{r} \binom{m}{k}\binom{n}{r-k} = \binom{m+n}{r}, \tag{15.7}$$

and show that (15.6) is a special case of this result. (Be careful, since r might be greater than m or n.)

EXAMPLE 15-7 Block walking is not the only way to visualize combinatorical arguments. In Example 15-2, we used a **committee selection** model to prove an identity. We could just as well have used this model to prove (15.7). Notice that the single term $\binom{m+n}{r}$ is the number of ways to pick an r-member committee from $m + n$ people. Each term of the sum is the way to pick such an r-member committee from $m + n$ people provided exactly k of the people are among a specific group of m people. (We choose k of the these m, and the other $r - k$ from the remaining n, for a total of $\binom{m}{k}\binom{n}{r-k}$.) Since the number of members of the committee which are from the first m can be anywhere from 0 up to r, the sum over all such numbers must equal the total number of ways to form the committee. If $r > m$ or $r > n$ some possible committee choices will be impossible—we can't take i people from the set of n if $i > n$—but in these cases the corresponding $\binom{n}{i}$ in the sum will be zero, so such cases are well accounted for. (If you have trouble following our arguments, try letting m of the people be female and n be male.)

Obviously there are other models which might be useful in proving combinatorial identities. Try to devise one which allows you to form a clear mental picture of what's going on. (One advantage of block walking is that you can draw a *physical* picture of what's happening.)

15.5 The Binomial Theorem

One very special combinatorial identity results when we expand an expression like $(x + y)^4$. The fourth power means we are multiplying $(x + y)$ together four times, so the expression can also be written

$$(x + y)(x + y)(x + y)(x + y).$$

Writing it in this form allows us to use the distributive law to find the product. Each term in the expanded version will have either an x or a y from each $(x + y)$ in the product; for example, the term $xxxx$ or x^4 will arise when we take the x every time.

Since each term will consist of four letters, one from each $(x + y)$, the terms of the resulting sum can only be x^4, x^3y, x^2y^2, xy^3, or y^4. Because the sum of the x and y exponents is 4 in each case, we can write each type of term as x^ky^{4-k} for some k between 0 and 4.

Each combination of letters can have a different coefficient, however. For example, to form xy^3 we need to take one x and three y's. This can happen in four ways, since the x can come from any of the four $(x + y)$'s: the possible orders are $xyyy$, $yxyy$, $yyxy$, and $yyyx$. Thus the final sum will contain the term $4xy^3$.

In general, for a term x^ky^{4-k}, we need to pick k x's from the four $(x + y)$'s and take y's from the others. By elementary counting, there are $\binom{4}{k}$ ways to choose the x's, so the term $\binom{4}{k}x^ky^{4-k}$ is what will appear in the final sum. The full expansion will thus be

$$(x + y)^4 = \binom{4}{4}x^4 + \binom{4}{3}x^3y + \binom{4}{2}x^2y^2 + \binom{4}{1}x^1y^3 + \binom{4}{0}y^4.$$

EXERCISE 15-13   To test the validity of this combinatorial approach, we can expand $(x + y)^4$ in a different way: write $(x + y)^4 = (x + y)^2(x + y)^2$, expand both squares, and multiply. Try it this way, and see if your answer agrees with the expansion above.

EXERCISE 15-14   Write the expansion above in $\sum$ form.

EXERCISE 15-15   Suppose I said: "For a term x^ky^{4-k}, we need to pick $4 - k$ y's and take x's for the rest. We can do this in $\binom{4}{4-k}$ ways, so the term that should appear in the final sum is $\binom{4}{4-k}x^ky^{4-k}$, not $\binom{4}{k}x^ky^{4-k}$ as was claimed above." Is something wrong with my logic, or is the discussion above in error?

It's clear that we can extend our argument for $(x + y)^4$ to any power. We write

$$(x + y)^n = \underbrace{(x + y)(x + y)(x + y) \cdots (x + y)}_{n \text{ times}},$$

so that a term x^ky^{n-k} is formed by choosing k x's from the n $(x + y)$'s. This can be done in $\binom{n}{k}$ ways, so the term in the final sum will be $\binom{n}{k}x^ky^{n-k}$. Thus we can write $(x + y)^n$ as

$$\binom{n}{n}x^n + \binom{n}{n-1}x^{n-1}y + \binom{n}{n-2}x^{n-2}y^2 + \cdots + \binom{n}{1}xy^{n-1} + \binom{n}{0}y^n, \tag{15.8}$$

or more concisely as

$$(x + y)^n = \sum_{k=0}^{n} \binom{n}{n-k}x^{n-k}y^k. \tag{15.9}$$

This expansion is the **Binomial Theorem** for the integral power n.

EXAMPLE 15-8 Evaluate $(x + y)^5$.

Solution: Since $\binom{5}{0} = \binom{5}{5} = 1$, $\binom{5}{1} = \binom{5}{4} = 5$, and $\binom{5}{2} = \binom{5}{3} = 10$, we have

$$(x + y)^5 = x^5 + 5x^4y + 10x^3y^2 + 10x^2y^3 + 5xy^4 + y^5.$$

EXERCISE 15-16 Show that the Binomial Theorem gives the correct expansions for $n = 1, 2$, and 3.

EXAMPLE 15-9 Find the 12th term of $(2r - 5s)^{18}$.

Solution: The first term is $\binom{18}{18}(2r)^{18}$. The second term is $\binom{18}{17}(2r)^{17}(-5s)$. The third term is $\binom{18}{16}(2r)^{16}(-5s)^2$. Do you see a pattern? The kth term is $\binom{18}{18-k+1}(2r)^{18-k+1}(-5s)^{k-1}$, so the 12th term is

$$\binom{18}{18 - 12 + 1}(2r)^{18-12+1}(-5s)^{12-1} = \binom{18}{7}(2r)^7(-5s)^{11}.$$

WARNING: As you can see, the 12th term is not the same as the term with exponent 12 for either of the variables! Since both "find the kth term. . . " and "find the term whose exponent of x is k. . . " questions are common, make sure you know the difference, and how to deal with either one.

EXERCISE 15-17 Prove that the Binomial Theorem can be written

$$(x + y)^n = \sum_{k=0}^{n} \binom{n}{k} x^{n-k} y^k.$$

How is this different from equation (15.9)? Does this or equation (15.9) correspond better to the form (15.8)?

EXERCISE 15-18 Use the Binomial Theorem to

    i. expand $(x + 2y)^4$.

    ii. find the coefficient of x^4 in $(x + 2)^7$.

    iii. find the constant term in the expansion of $\left(x^2 + \dfrac{1}{x}\right)^6$.

    iv. find the sum of the coefficients in the expansion of $(a + b)^{10}$. (MAΘ 1991)

EXAMPLE 15-10 The Binomial Theorem is a good way to prove certain identities. For example, we can immediately get back the identity (15.1) by cleverly substituting $x = y = 1$ in the Binomial Theorem. We then have

$$(1 + 1)^n = 2^n = \binom{n}{0} + \binom{n}{1} + \binom{n}{2} + \cdots + \binom{n}{n},$$

as desired.

EXERCISE 15-19 What do we get when we take $x = 1$ and $y = -1$ in the Binomial Theorem? Show that this result can be derived in a simpler way if n is odd.

EXERCISE 15-20 Evaluate the sum

$$\sum_{k=0}^{n} 2^k \binom{n}{k}.$$

EXAMPLE 15-11 A fairly simple extension of the Binomial Theorem is to expressions like $(x + y + z + w)^{10}$. As with the binomial case, each term in the expansion will be of degree 10, since it will draw one letter each from the ten $(x + y + z + w)$'s being multiplied together. To find the coefficient of one such term $x^a y^b z^c w^d$, where $a + b + c + d = 10$, we need to think of in what ways such a term can arise. Let's look at the particular case of $x^2 y^3 z w^4$. In the expansion

$$\underbrace{(x + y + z + w)(x + y + z + w)\cdots(x + y + z + w)}_{\text{10 terms}},$$

$x^2 y^3 z w^4$ could be $xxyyyzwwww$ or $xyzwwxywyw$ or any other such expression. The number of such expressions is the number of ways to rearrange the letters in the "word" $xxyyyzwwww$. In Volume 1 we showed that this number is

$$\frac{10!}{2!\,3!\,1!\,4!},$$

so this is the coefficient of the term $x^2 y^3 z w^4$.

EXERCISE 15-21 What is the coefficient of $x^4 y z^3 w^2$ in the same expansion as above?

EXERCISE 15-22 Find the coefficient of abc^2 in the expansion of $(a + b + c + d)^4$.

 EXERCISE 15-23 Write down the expansion of $(x + y + z)^n$ in $\sum$ notation. (You'll need more than one $\sum$.)

Problems to Solve for Chapter 15

Note: many of these problems are good exercises in the use of $\sum$ notation. Try to use them to become more comfortable with this very versatile notation.

235. Find the sum $\binom{100}{1} + 2\binom{100}{2} + 3\binom{100}{3} + \cdots + 100\binom{100}{100}$. (MAΘ 1991)

236. Evaluate $\sum_{k=0}^{n} \binom{n}{k}\binom{m}{k}$ for fixed m and n.

237. Evaluate

$$\sum_{i=1}^{10}\sum_{k=1}^{i} \binom{i}{k}.$$

(MAΘ 1992)

238. In the expansion of $(xy - 2y^{-3})^{16}$, find the coefficient of the term that does not contain y. (MAΘ 1991)

239. Show that $\displaystyle\sum_{k=m}^{n} \binom{k}{r} = \binom{n+1}{r+1} - \binom{m}{r+1}$. for integers $r < m < n$.

240. Evaluate $44\binom{45}{0} + 43\binom{45}{1} + 42\binom{45}{2} + \cdots + 0\binom{45}{44} - \binom{45}{45}$. (MAΘ 1992)

241. (Mandelbrot #1)

i. Given a row of $n + k + 1$ blocks, show that there are $\binom{n+k}{n-1}$ groups of n blocks which include the first block.

ii. Show that there are $\binom{n+k+1-m}{n-1}$ groups of n blocks which include the mth block (with the first block being on the far left) but no blocks to the left of the mth block.

iii. Use these to prove that

$$\binom{n-1}{0} + \binom{n}{1} + \binom{n+1}{2} + \cdots + \binom{n+k}{k+1} = \binom{n+k+1}{k+1}.$$

242. Find the sum of the coefficients of $(a + b + c + d)^{10}$.

243. Prove that $\displaystyle\sum_{k=1}^{m} \binom{n+k-1}{k} = \sum_{k=1}^{n} \binom{m+k-1}{k}$.

244. Find the sum of the last three digits of 19^{92}. (MAΘ 1992)

245. Prove that $\displaystyle\sum_{k=0}^{n-1}(-1)^k \binom{n}{k+1} = 1$.

246. Evaluate $\binom{n}{1} + 3\binom{n}{3} + 5\binom{n}{5} + \cdots$ in closed form.

247. Evaluate $\displaystyle\sum_{k=1}^{n} \binom{n}{k}\binom{n}{k-1}$.

248. For fixed n, maximize the quantity $\binom{2n+k}{n}\binom{2n-k}{n}$.

249. Prove that $\displaystyle\sum_{k=0}^{m} \binom{n}{k}\binom{n-k}{m-k} = 2^m \binom{n}{m}$ for $m < n$.

250. Find the sum

$$\binom{22}{10}\binom{15}{0} + \binom{22}{9}\binom{15}{1} + \binom{22}{8}\binom{15}{2} + \cdots + \binom{22}{0}\binom{15}{10}.$$

Chapter 16

Sequences and Series

16.1 Fractions in Other Bases

In Volume 1 we examined how to express integers in other bases, but what about fractions? The places after the decimal point in a base ten number represent $1/10$, $1/100$, $1/1000$, etc., so the places after the decimal point in base k represent $1/k$, $1/k^2$, $1/k^3$, etc. For example, to find 0.112_3 as a base 10 fraction, we simply add $1(1/3) + 1(1/9) + 2(1/27) = 14/27$.

EXAMPLE 16-1 Find $0.\overline{324}_5$ as a base 10 fraction.

Solution: In Volume 1 we evaluated repeating decimals by multiplying by the appropriate power of 10 and subtracting. Since we are using base 5, we multiply by a power of 5 instead. Since the repeating group is of length 3, we use 5^3, so

$$
\begin{aligned}
x &= 0.324324324\ldots \\
125x &= 324.324324324\ldots.
\end{aligned}
$$

Subtracting the first from the second (and remembering that the expressions on the right are in base 5, we have $124x = 324_5 = 89$, so $x = \mathbf{89/124}$.

Getting to base 10 from some other base is pretty easy, but writing a given fraction as a decimal in some other base isn't always so simple.

Let's try writing $1/2$ in base 3. Since $1/2$ is more than $1/3$ but less than $2(1/3)$, the first decimal place is 1. This leaves $1/2 - 1/3 = 1/6$ for the remainder. Again $2(1/9) > 1/6 > 1/9$, so the next decimal place is 1 also, leaving $1/6 - 1/9 = 1/18$ for the rest. Continuing in this manner, we keep getting ones seemingly forever. This leads us to suspect that $1/2 = 0.\overline{1}_3$. Using our above method to evaluate $0.\overline{1}_3$, we find that it indeed equals $1/2$.

This example gives us a general method for writing a fraction in base k. Evaluate each of the successive decimal places until the decimal either terminates or a pattern emerges. If we find a pattern, we must then show that our suspected decimal does in fact equal the desired fraction.

EXAMPLE 16-2 Find 5/6 as a base 5 decimal.

Solution: The first decimal place is 4, leaving $5/6 - 4(1/5) = 1/30$. Since $1/30 < (1/5)^2$, the next decimal place is 0. Since $1/30 > 4(1/5)^3$, the next place is 4, leaving $1/750$ for the rest. Thus, the following decimal is 0 (since $1/750 < 1/625$), and we begin to see the pattern $0.404040\ldots$. We can quickly verify that $0.\overline{40}_5 = 5/6$.

16.2 Σome Σpecial Σeries

When faced with a sum, we would usually be much happier with a **closed form**, a simple formula without dots or $\sum$'s. For example, given $1 + 2 + 3 + \cdots + n$, we can easily use the formula for the sum of an arithmetic series to get

$$1 + 2 + 3 + \cdots + n = \frac{n}{2}(n+1) = \frac{n(n+1)}{2}. \tag{16.1}$$

This simple form provides an instant answer if someone asks you to find $1 + 2 + \cdots + 1001$. Rather than do the thousand-term summation, you just plug 1001 in for n to get $(1001)(1002)/2$. That's the beauty of a closed form.

EXERCISE 16-1 Write down the closed forms for $2 + 4 + 6 + \cdots + 2n$ and $1 + 3 + 5 + \cdots + (2n - 1)$.

Having gotten those three out of the way, let's consider something meatier:

$$S(n) = 1 + 4 + 9 + \cdots + n^2 = \sum_{i=1}^{n} i^2.$$

None of the techniques we used in Volume 1 seem to work very well here. A different method will do it, and give some practice in using $\sum$ notation at the same time. We need to use the basic combinatorial identity

$$\binom{k}{k} + \binom{k+1}{k} + \binom{k+2}{k} + \cdots \binom{n}{k} = \binom{n+1}{k+1},$$

derived on page 172.

How does the combinatorial sum relate? If we write

$$i^2 = i^2 + i - i = i(i-1) + i = 2\binom{i}{2} + i,$$

the connection becomes more clear. We then have

$$\sum_{i=1}^{n} i^2 = \sum_{i=1}^{n}\left[2\binom{i}{2} + i\right]$$
$$= 2\sum_{i=1}^{n}\binom{i}{2} + \sum_{i=1}^{n} i.$$

These sums may be simplified using the combinatorial identity above to get

$$\sum_{i=1}^{n} i^2 = 2\binom{n+1}{3} + \binom{n+1}{2}$$
$$= \frac{n(n+1)(2n+1)}{6}.$$

Can you follow the transition from the next-to-last to the last step?

We can, in principle at least, extend this type of argument to find $\sum i^r$ for any integer r. All we need is to find an expression for i^r as $a_r\binom{i}{r} + a_{r-1}\binom{i}{r-1} + \cdots + a_1\binom{i}{1}$. (In the proof above for $r = 2$, we had $a_2 = 2$ and $a_1 = 1$, though we concealed the structure somewhat by using just i instead of $\binom{i}{1}$.) We can always do this, by expanding the combinatorial terms and equating coefficients in the polynomial which results, if we put in enough time and effort.

EXAMPLE 16-3 One case for which it is worthwhile to put in the effort is for $r = 3$. We need to find $a_1, a_2,$ and a_3 so that

$$i^3 = a_3\binom{i}{3} + a_2\binom{i}{2} + a_1\binom{i}{1}.$$

Expanding, this is

$$i^3 = \frac{a_3}{6}(i)(i-1)(i-2) + \frac{a_2}{2}(i)(i-1) + a_1 i.$$

We could expand the products and equate coefficients of i^3, i^2, and i, but there's a slicker way to find $a_1, a_2,$ and a_3. Since the above relation must hold for all positive i, we choose $i = 1$, so $1^3 = 0 + 0 + a_1$, or $a_1 = 1$. Similarly, $i = 2$ gives $8 = 0 + a_2 + 2a_1$, so $a_2 = 6$. Finally $i = 3$ gives $27 = a_3 + 3a_2 + 3a_1$, or $a_3 = 6$. Thus,

$$\sum_{i=1}^{n} i^3 = 6\sum_{i=1}^{n}\binom{i}{3} + 6\sum_{i=1}^{n}\binom{i}{2} + \sum_{i=1}^{n}\binom{i}{1} = 6\binom{n+1}{4} + 6\binom{n+1}{3} + \binom{n+1}{2}.$$

 EXERCISE 16-2 Simplify the expression above to show

$$\sum_{i=1}^{n} i^3 = \left(\binom{n+1}{2}\right)^2.$$

16.3   The Fibonacci Numbers

The sequences we have seen up to now have all had their nth term defined as a function of n. However, some sequences are not so simple. For these, the nth term can only be defined in terms of the previous terms. Such a sequence is called **recursive**. We have actually already seen some recursions. For example, the definition of an arithmetic sequence by

$$x_1 = a;$$
$$x_n = x_{n-1} + d, \qquad n > 1;$$

is a recursive definition. In this case, however, we can also find the **closed form** $x_n = a + (n - 1)d$. A closed form cannot contain other terms of the sequence or summation symbols; unfortunately, in many cases one either does not exist, or is terribly complicated. In such circumstances we have to stick to recursion.

By far the most important recursion is the **Fibonacci numbers**. The definition is extremely simple: each term is the sum of the previous two. To start off, we use two 1's. The sequence thus goes

$$1, 1, 2, 3, 5, 8, 13, \ldots$$

EXERCISE 16-3 Write down the next few terms of the sequence.

Let's make the definition of the Fibonacci numbers more precise. The Fibonacci numbers are a sequence F_k, $k = 0, 1, 2, \ldots$, such that $F_0 = F_1 = 1$ and for $k > 1$, $F_k = F_{k-1} + F_{k-2}$.

The Fibonacci numbers have tons of interesting properties. For example, consider the limit as $k \to \infty$ of the ratio F_k/F_{k-1}. We write

$$\phi = \lim_{k \to \infty} \frac{F_k}{F_{k-1}} = \lim_{k \to \infty} \frac{F_{k-1} + F_{k-2}}{F_{k-1}} = 1 + \lim_{k \to \infty} \frac{F_{k-2}}{F_{k-1}} = 1 + \frac{1}{\phi}, \tag{16.2}$$

where the last step is the only tricky one. Since k is going to infinity, if the limit ϕ exists at all, it is the same for k as for $k - 1$. Thus, in the limit, the ratio F_{k-2}/F_{k-1} equals the ratio F_{k-1}/F_k, or $1/\phi$. This may seem fishy, but it is entirely rigorous, IF THE LIMIT ϕ EXISTS. We *assume* here that it does, because the Fibonaccis seem fairly well-behaved; to prove that fact is more complicated. Thus be warned that there is a missing proof to make all this rigorous.

With that warning in mind, we can go on to do what equation (16.2) begs us to do: solve for ϕ. Multiplying by ϕ (assuming ϕ to be nonzero) and rearranging, the equation $\phi = 1 + 1/\phi$ becomes $\phi^2 - \phi - 1 = 0$. By the quadratic formula, we get

$$\phi = \frac{1 + \sqrt{5}}{2}.$$

This is the "golden ratio," called this because it has certain interesting properties and because the Greeks felt the most aesthetically pleasing rectangles had the ratio of sides $1 : \phi$. (You can even today find many rectangular objects which have been made in the golden ratio.)

EXERCISE 16-4 The quadratic equation for ϕ, $\phi^2 - \phi - 1 = 0$, has two roots. Why did we choose the one we did as the desired value?

There are many other interesting facts about the Fibonacci numbers. For example, it is relatively simple to prove that

$$F_{n+1}F_{n-1} = F_n^2 - (-1)^n. \tag{16.3}$$

You can easily verify that this works for small n; we'll prove it by induction. For the base case, we have $F_0 F_2 = 2 = 1^2 + 1 = F_1^2 - (-1)^1$. To do the inductive step we assume the relation holds for $n - 1$, so that

$$F_n F_{n-2} = F_{n-1}^2 - (-1)^{n-1},$$

or

$$F_{n-1}^2 - F_n F_{n-2} = (-1)^{n-1} = -(-1)^n. \tag{*}$$

We wish to use this to show that the relation holds for n. We have

$$
\begin{aligned}
F_{n+1}F_{n-1} &= (F_n + F_{n-1})(F_n - F_{n-2}) \\
&= F_n^2 + F_{n-1}(F_n - F_{n-2}) - F_n F_{n-2}.
\end{aligned}
$$

Since $F_n - F_{n-2} = F_{n-1}$, by (*) we have

$$F_{n+1}F_{n-1} = F_n^2 + F_{n-1}^2 - F_n F_{n-2} = F_n^2 - (-1)^n,$$

as desired.

EXERCISE 16-5   Prove the following Fibonacci identities.

   i. $F_n = F_{n-2} + F_{n-3} + \cdots + F_0 + 1$

  ii. $F_0^2 + F_1^2 + \cdots + F_n^2 = F_n F_{n+1}$

 iii. $F_0 + F_2 + F_4 + \cdots + F_{2n} = F_{2n+1}$

Perhaps the most interesting Fibonacci identity of all is that F_n can be written as a sum of $\binom{n}{k}$'s:

$$F_n = \binom{n}{0} + \binom{n-1}{1} + \binom{n-2}{2} + \cdots \tag{16.4}$$

We can prove this is an especially simple way. First observe that (16.4) holds for $n = 0$ and $n = 1$; we get $F_0 = \binom{0}{0} = 1$ and $F_1 = \binom{1}{0} = 1$. Then we show that the sum on the right side of (16.4) satisfies the Fibonacci relation:

$$
\begin{aligned}
&\left[\binom{n-1}{0} + \binom{n-2}{1} + \binom{n-3}{2} + \cdots\right] + \left[\binom{n}{0} + \binom{n-1}{1} + \binom{n-2}{2} + \cdots\right] \\
&= \binom{n}{0} + \left[\binom{n-1}{0} + \binom{n-1}{1}\right] + \left[\binom{n-2}{1} + \binom{n-2}{2}\right] + \cdots \\
&= \binom{n+1}{0} + \binom{n}{1} + \binom{n-1}{2} + \cdots
\end{aligned}
$$

We have used Pascal's identity to get from the second to the third line. Since Pascal's identity $\binom{n}{k} = \binom{n-1}{k-1} + \binom{n-1}{k}$ holds for any n and k, even if $k > n$, we don't have to worry about where the sums end.

Because the combinatorial sum in (16.4) satisfies the Fibonacci relation and matches F_n for $n = 0$ and 1, it must be identical to F_n for all n.

16.4   Dealing with Recurrences

A general recurrence relation tends to be a fairly complicated beast, but a knowledge of how they work often makes it possible to derive facts about them.

A common problem is to take a recurrence relation, like $x_k = x_{k-1} + x_{k-2}$, and find a closed form expression for the nth term. If we could do this, we could find the nth term by plugging n directly into some formula, rather than first having to compute the first $n - 1$ terms using the recurrence formula.

However, this simple-seeming request leads to difficult problems. To see this, let's try to find a closed form for F_n, the nth Fibonacci number. One method is to make the guess that the Fibonacci sequence $\{F_n\}$ can be written as the sum of two geometric sequences $\{ar^n\}$ and $\{bs^n\}$, so that $F_n = ar^n + bs^n$ for all n. The sum must satisfy the Fibonacci relation $F_{k-1} + F_k = F_{k+1}$, so we have

$$ar^{k-1} + bs^{k-1} + ar^k + bs^k = ar^{k+1} + bs^{k+1}. \tag{16.5}$$

You might be able to solve this with some effort, but a simpler way exists. We can rewrite (16.5) as

$$ar^{n-1} + ar^n - ar^{n+1} = -bs^{n-1} - bs^n + bs^{n+1},$$

or

$$ar^{n-1}(1 + r - r^2) = -bs^{n-1}(1 + s - s^2). \tag{16.6}$$

Since $r \neq s$ by the assumption that we have different geometric series, the only way the two sides of (16.6) can be equal for all n is if $1 + r - r^2 = 1 + s - s^2 = 0$.

EXERCISE 16-6 Why can't the two sides of (16.6) be equal for all n unless they are both equal to 0?

We have thus shown that both r and s satisfy the quadratic equation $x^2 - x - 1 = 0$. Solving this equation by the quadratic formula, we thus find

$$r = \frac{1 + \sqrt{5}}{2} \quad \text{and} \quad s = \frac{1 - \sqrt{5}}{2}.$$

EXERCISE 16-7 Check by hand that r and s above satisfy $x^2 - x - 1 = 0$.

Our choices of r and s force the summed sequence $\{ar^n + bs^n\}$ to satisfy the Fibonacci relation, *no matter what a and b are.* We can thus construct lots of sequences which satisfy the relation just by choosing different a and b.

EXERCISE 16-8 Suppose we take $a = b = 1$. Write down the terms of $\{ar^n + bs^n\}$ for $n = 0, 1, 2$, and 3 and show that they do satisfy the Fibonacci relation.

EXAMPLE 16-4 What are a and b for the Fibonacci series? We set

$$ar^0 + bs^0 = a + b = F_0 = 1$$

and

$$ar^1 + bs^1 = a\left(\frac{1 + \sqrt{5}}{2}\right) + b\left(\frac{1 - \sqrt{5}}{2}\right) = F_1 = 1$$

and solve the resulting system of equations. Using the first equation to write $b = 1 - a$, the second equation gives

$$a\left(\frac{1 + \sqrt{5}}{2}\right) + (1 - a)\left(\frac{1 - \sqrt{5}}{2}\right) = 1,$$

which yields $a = (1 + \sqrt{5})/2\sqrt{5}$. Substituting this into the first equation yields $b = (-1 + \sqrt{5})/2\sqrt{5}$.

Using Example 16-4, we can now write down the general closed form for the Fibonacci sequence as

$$F_n = ar^n + bs^n = \left(\frac{1+\sqrt{5}}{2\sqrt{5}}\right)\left(\frac{1+\sqrt{5}}{2}\right)^n + \left(\frac{-1+\sqrt{5}}{2\sqrt{5}}\right)\left(\frac{1-\sqrt{5}}{2}\right)^n$$

$$= \frac{1}{\sqrt{5}}\left[\left(\frac{1+\sqrt{5}}{2}\right)^{n+1} - \left(\frac{1-\sqrt{5}}{2}\right)^{n+1}\right].$$

This is called **Binet's formula** for the Fibonacci sequence.

EXERCISE 16-9 Show that Binet's formula gives the correct values for F_0, F_1, and F_2. (You should have already calculated r^2, r^3, s^2, and s^3 for Exercise 16-8.)

EXERCISE 16-10 Consider a sequence $\{G_n\}$ with $G_{k+1} = G_k + 2G_{k-1}$ for $k \geq 1$, with $G_0 = 0$ and $G_1 = 1$. Find the general term G_n in closed form.

 EXERCISE 16-11 What changes would we have to make to our scheme to handle a three-term recursion relation like $X_{k+1} = \alpha X_k + \beta X_{k-1} + \gamma X_{k-2}$?

16.5   Dealing with Sums

 We are often asked to add up a series (especially an infinite one), with no other information to go on. To do this for arbitray series can require complicated maneuvering, as for the derivation of $\sum_{i=1}^{n} i^2$. The vast majority of sums are too hard to do at all! Many are on the border: someone has done them, but only with a lot (perhaps years) of work. A classic example of this kind is the simple-seeming sum $\sum_{i=1}^{\infty} \frac{1}{i^2}$, for which the answer is the unfathomable $\frac{\pi^2}{6}$. The moral: don't spend too long with a sum unless you have good reason to believe it is doable.

As an example of a common method, consider the series

$$\sum_{i=1}^{n} \frac{1}{i(i+1)} = \frac{1}{1\cdot 2} + \frac{1}{2\cdot 3} + \frac{1}{3\cdot 4} + \cdots + \frac{1}{n\cdot(n+1)}$$

This is the simplest example of a **telescoping series**, so called because the series can be made to fold up like a telescope, leaving only a couple of terms behind. The key is the **partial fraction decomposition**

$$\frac{1}{n(n+1)} = \frac{1}{n} - \frac{1}{n+1}.$$

Verify that this equality is valid. Once you accept that, we can write the series as

$$\left(\frac{1}{1} - \frac{1}{2}\right) + \left(\frac{1}{2} - \frac{1}{3}\right) + \left(\frac{1}{3} - \frac{1}{4}\right) + \cdots + \left(\frac{1}{n-1} - \frac{1}{n}\right) + \left(\frac{1}{n} - \frac{1}{n+1}\right).$$

If we now cancel all the terms which come in both as + and −, we are left with only

$$\frac{1}{1} - \frac{1}{n+1} = \frac{n}{n+1}.$$

Expanding the terms a bit has allowed us to roll the entire series up into two terms.

The method of partial fractions is a crucial one in analyzing series. Here we'll discuss how to do this for expressions of the form $(ax + b)/(x - c)(x - d)$, since these are the most commonly occurring expressions in sums requiring partial fractions.

Find the partial fraction decomposition of

$$\frac{2x - 1}{x^2 - 4x + 3}.$$

The first step is factoring the denominator as $(x - 3)(x - 1)$. We can then express the given fraction as a sum of terms whose numerators are constants and denominators are the factors $x - 1$ and $x - 3$, or

$$\frac{2x - 1}{(x - 1)(x - 3)} = \frac{A}{x - 1} + \frac{B}{x - 3}.$$

We only need these two terms because rational expressions which sum to $(2x - 1)/(x - 1)(x - 3)$ must have common denominator $(x - 1)(x - 3)$; hence the denominator of each term in the sum must be a factor of $(x - 1)(x - 3)$.

We now find A and B by multiplying the above equation by $(x - 1)(x - 3)$ to get $2x - 1 = A(x - 3) + B(x - 1)$. Letting $x = 1$, we find $1 = -2A$, or $A = -1/2$. Letting $x = 3$, we find $5 = 2B$, or $B = 5/2$. Thus we have

$$\frac{2x - 1}{(x - 1)(x - 3)} = \frac{-1/2}{x - 1} + \frac{5/2}{x - 3}.$$

We can extend our process to any rational expression $f(x)/g(x)$, where f and g are polynomials with rational coefficients such that $\deg f < \deg g$ by first factoring $g(x)$ into unfactorable linear and quadratic expressions with rational coefficients. We then equate $f(x)/g(x)$ to a sum of terms, where the terms are determined by the factors of $g(x)$.

For each linear factor $x - c$ of $g(x)$, we have a term of the form $a_i/(x - c)$; for each quadratric factor there is a term of the form $(a_i x + a_j)/(x^2 + cx + d)$. The only subtlety comes in the case of repeated factors. If the factor $h(x)$ occurs n times, then we will have the n terms $a_1/h(x)$, $a_2/(h(x))^2$, $a_3/(h(x))^3, \ldots, a_n/(h(n))$. Once we've found all our terms, we then find all our unknown a_i's as we did above; multiply both sides of $f(x)/g(x) =$ (sum of terms) by $g(x)$ and cleverly choose x's.

Many complicated sums can be analyzed with suitably involved partial fraction decompositions and telescoping. Even products can telescope, as the first example shows.

EXERCISE 16-12 Find $\displaystyle\sum_{n=1}^{\infty} \frac{n}{(n + 1)(n + 2)}$. (MA$\Theta$ 1992)

EXAMPLE 16-5 Evaluate $\displaystyle\prod_{n=1}^{13} \frac{n(n + 2)}{(n + 4)^2}$. (Mandelbrot #2)

Solution: Let's expand the $\prod$ notation to get

$$\frac{(1)(3)}{(5)(5)} \cdot \frac{(2)(4)}{(6)(6)} \cdot \frac{(3)(5)}{(7)(7)} \cdots \frac{(13)(15)}{(17)(17)}.$$

What cancels? In the numerator of the product there are one 1, one 2, two 3's, two 4's, two 5's, two each of 6 through 13, one 14, and one 15. In the denominator there are two each of 5 through 17. Thus everything cancels except for

$$\frac{1 \cdot 2 \cdot 3 \cdot 3 \cdot 4 \cdot 4}{14 \cdot 15 \cdot 16 \cdot 16 \cdot 17 \cdot 17} = \frac{3}{7 \cdot 5 \cdot 16 \cdot 17 \cdot 17} = \frac{3}{161840}.$$

EXAMPLE 16-6 Telescoping isn't the only general method for evaluating sums. In fact, the solution to this one looks quite a bit like our standard methods from Volume 1:

Find $\sum_{n=1}^{\infty} \frac{2n}{3^{n+1}}$. (MAΘ 1990)

Solution: We call the sum S, so that

$$S = \frac{2}{9} + \frac{4}{27} + \frac{6}{81} + \frac{8}{243} + \cdots$$

We then divide S by 3, to get

$$S/3 = \frac{2}{27} + \frac{4}{81} + \frac{6}{243} \cdots$$

The clever part is to subtract the series for $S/3$ from that for S, to get a pure geometric series:

$$
\begin{aligned}
S - S/3 = 2S/3 &= \frac{2}{9} + \frac{2}{27} + \frac{2}{81} + \frac{2}{243} + \cdots \\
&= \frac{2/9}{1 - (1/3)} \\
&= \frac{1}{3},
\end{aligned}
$$

so $S = 3(1/3)/2 = \mathbf{1/2}$.

EXERCISE 16-13 Do the previous example in another way, by writing

$$\sum_{n=1}^{\infty} \frac{2n}{3^{n+1}} = \frac{2}{3} \sum_{n=1}^{\infty} \sum_{m=n}^{\infty} \frac{1}{3^m}$$

and evaluating the second summation first. (Make sure you see the clever way in which the double sum is equal to the single sum!)

16.6   The Binomial Theorem Revisited

Recall the Binomial Theorem, which allows us to expand any positive integral power of a binomial expression like $(x + y)$:

$$(x + y)^n = \binom{n}{0} x^n y^0 + \binom{n}{1} x^{n-1} y^1 + \cdots + \binom{n}{n} x^0 y^n.$$

Of course, this gives no information about expansions like $(x + y)^{1/2}$, or $(x + y)^{-1}$. After all, what is $\binom{1/2}{3}$? $\binom{-1}{7}$?

It turns out, however, that there is an extension of the Binomial Theorem to cover just such weird cases. The key to writing down the new theorem is to define quantities $\binom{n}{k}$ where n is not a positive integer. To make this new definition correspond well to the old definition, we write the old definition in a new way:

$$\binom{n}{k} = \frac{n!}{k!\,(n-k)!} = \frac{n(n-1)(n-2)\cdots(n-k+1)}{k!}$$

Since there is no satisfactory definition of the factorial $n!$ if n is not a positive integer, the first definition $n!/k!(n-k)!$ won't do us any good. But suppose we try to blindly use the alternate way of writing $\binom{n}{k}$ for $n = 1/2, k = 3$. We get

$$\frac{(1/2)(1/2-1)(1/2-2)}{3!} = \frac{(1/2)(-1/2)(-3/2)}{6} = \frac{1}{16},$$

which is a perfectly reasonable result! This second way of writing $\binom{n}{k}$ allows us to define it for any n.

WARNING: Although n can be any real number in the new expression for $\binom{n}{k}$, k must still be a nonnegative integer, since we have a $k!$ in the definition. Also, note that $\binom{n}{0} = 1$ for all n. As a final warning, if n is not a positive integer we must abandon any hope of connecting $\binom{n}{k}$ to real combinatorial actions like picking k things from a set of n.

EXAMPLE 16-7 Evaluate $\binom{7/3}{4}$.

Solution: We have
$$\binom{7/3}{4} = \frac{(7/3)(7/3-1)(7/3-2)(7/3-3)}{4!} = \frac{(7/3)(4/3)(1/3)(-2/3)}{24} = -\frac{7}{243}.$$

EXERCISE 16-14 Evaluate $\binom{-3}{4}$ and $\binom{-7/3}{3}$.

EXERCISE 16-15 Use our new definition to look at $\binom{n}{k}$, where n is a positive integer and $k > n$.

EXERCISE 16-16 Simplify $\binom{-1}{n}$.

EXAMPLE 16-8 Show that if n and r are positive integers, then

$$\binom{-n}{r} = (-1)^r \binom{n+r-1}{r}.$$

Proof: We simply write out $\binom{-n}{r}$ as

$$
\begin{aligned}
\binom{-n}{r} &= \frac{[-n][-(n+1)][-(n+2)]\cdots[-(n+r-1)]}{r(r-1)(r-2)\cdots 1} \\
&= \frac{(-1)^r(n)(n+1)(n+2)\cdots(n+r-1)}{r!} \\
&= \frac{(-1)^r(n+r-1)!}{(n-1)!\,r!} \\
&= (-1)^r \binom{n+r-1}{r},
\end{aligned}
$$

and we're done!

Using our new definition of $\binom{n}{k}$, we now can write the statement of the expanded Binomial Theorem: for *any real number n*,

$$(x + y)^n = \binom{n}{0}x^n y^0 + \binom{n}{1}x^{n-1}y^1 + \binom{n}{2}x^{n-2}y^2 + \cdots$$

This looks suspiciously like the original Binomial Theorem! The only difference is that instead of showing the expanded series as terminating at some point, it keeps on going. This is because, if n is not a positive integer, the terms

$$\frac{n}{1}, \frac{n(n-1)}{2}, \frac{n(n-1)(n-2)}{6}, \cdots$$

will never hit zero.

   If n *is* a positive integer, then at some point the fractions will have an $(n - n)$ term on top, and will thus all be zero. Thus for positive integers n, we get back the familiar, terminating version.

EXAMPLE 16-9 Calculate $1.2^{-1/3}$ to a few decimal places.

Solution: From the general Binomial Theorem we have

$$
\begin{aligned}
(1 + .2)^{-1/3} &= \binom{-1/3}{0}(1^{-1/3})(.2)^0 + \binom{-1/3}{1}(1^{-4/3})(.2)^1 + \cdots \\
&= (1)(1)(1) + (-1/3)(1)(.2) + (2/9)(1)(.04) + \cdots \\
&= 1 - .0666 + .0088 - \cdots \\
&\approx \mathbf{0.9422}.
\end{aligned}
$$

While not exactly right, this approximation is pretty close to the actual value.

EXERCISE 16-17 Estimate $1/(2.12)^2$ using the general Binomial Theorem.

   As with any infinite series, we have to consider **convergence** carefully when using the general Binomial Theorem. That is, does our sum add up to a finite result or does it just get bigger and bigger as more terms are added on? Remember that the terms of a series must tend to 0 if it is to converge, although just because the terms tend to 0, the series doesn't have to converge. Way out in the series created by the Binomial Theorem, the term looks like

$$\binom{n}{\text{large \#}}x^{n-\text{large \#}}y^{\text{large \#}},$$

or

$$\binom{n}{\text{large \#}}x^n\left(\frac{y^{\text{large \#}}}{x^{\text{large \#}}}\right).$$

Since x^n is fixed, and $\binom{n}{\text{large \#}}$ tends to a finite limit as the large number gets big (we won't prove this here, as it's off the track a good bit), the important term is the last term. This term will tend to 0 if $|x| > |y|$, but won't if $|x| \le |y|$. Thus, in order for the series to converge, we must have $|x| > |y|$.

WARNING: Although $|x| > |y|$ forces the terms of the series to tend to 0, this does not in itself assure that the series converges. (Always keep in mind the series $1 + \frac{1}{2} + \frac{1}{3} + \cdots$, which diverges even though its terms tend to 0.) The binomial series does converge as long as $|x| > |y|$, but this requires proof (which we won't get into here).

EXAMPLE 16-10 The Binomial Theorem allows us to make quick estimates of many square roots, fractions, etc. For example, consider $\frac{1}{n+\epsilon}$, where ϵ is small compared to n. (This Greek letter, pronounced EP-si-lon, is often called upon for the low-status job of representing a small number.) By the Binomial Theorem we have

$$\frac{1}{n+\epsilon} = (n+\epsilon)^{-1} = \binom{-1}{0} n^{-1} \epsilon^0 + \binom{-1}{1} n^{-2} \epsilon^1 + \binom{-1}{2} n^{-3} \epsilon^2 + \cdots$$

Since the terms in the series expansion get smaller and smaller, using more and more terms will give a better and better approximation to the true value of $\frac{1}{n+\epsilon}$. Taking only the first two terms yields the so-called **first-order approximation**

$$(n+\epsilon)^{-1} \approx n^{-1} - \epsilon n^{-2} = \frac{n - \epsilon}{n^2}.$$

The order of the approximation is the highest power of ϵ which appears, which is why this one is called first order.

EXERCISE 16-18 Find the exact value of $1/101$ using a calculator, then compare to the first order approximation, which you can do by hand. (Hint: use $A = 100$ and $\epsilon = 1$.) Was the extra precision worth digging out the calculator?

EXERCISE 16-19 Guess what a second order approximation to $(n+\epsilon)^{-1}$ would be. How about "zero-th" order?

EXERCISE 16-20 Find a first order approximation to $\sqrt{A^2 + \epsilon}$ and use it to calculate $\sqrt{17}$ without a calculator.

16.7 Harmonic Sequences

In Volume 1 we discussed arithmetic and geometric sequences. In particular, these sequences have the property that any element a_n is the arithmetic or geometric mean of the two adjacent terms a_{n-1} and a_{n+1}. (Make sure you see why this is so.)

But the arithmetic and geometric means aren't the only types of means. In particular, suppose we construct a **harmonic sequence**, where every term is the *harmonic* mean of its neighbors:

$$a_n = \frac{2}{\frac{1}{a_{n-1}} + \frac{1}{a_{n+1}}}.$$

If we invert both sides of this equation, we have

$$\frac{1}{a_n} = \frac{\frac{1}{a_{n-1}} + \frac{1}{a_{n+1}}}{2},$$

so that $1/a_n$ is the arithmetic mean of $1/a_{n-1}$ and $1/a_{n+1}$! Thus a harmonic sequence can be formed by taking the reciprocals of the terms of an arithmetic sequence.

EXAMPLE 16-11   Since $1, 3, 5, \ldots$ is an arithmetic sequence, $\frac{1}{1}, \frac{1}{3}, \frac{1}{5}, \ldots$ is a harmonic sequence.

EXERCISE 16-21   Which are harmonic sequences?

     i. $2, 1, \frac{2}{3}, \frac{1}{2}, \ldots$

     ii. $\frac{1}{4}, \frac{3}{10}, \frac{3}{8}, \frac{1}{2}, \ldots$

     iii. $\frac{1}{2}, \frac{1}{4}, \frac{1}{8}, \frac{1}{16}, \ldots$

Problems to Solve for Chapter 16

251. If the sum of the first $3n$ positive integers is 150 more than the sum of the first n positive integers, then find the sum of the first $4n$ positive integers. (AHSME 1970)

252. In the harmonic sequence $6, 3, 2, \frac{3}{2}, \frac{6}{5}, \ldots$, what will the eighth term be? (MAΘ 1990)

253. Evaluate $\sum_{k=1}^{10} k^2 + k + 1$. (MAΘ 1991)

254. Express in simplest form:

$$\left(1 + \frac{1}{2}\right)\left(1 + \frac{1}{3}\right)\left(1 + \frac{1}{4}\right)\left(1 + \frac{1}{5}\right)\left(1 + \frac{1}{6}\right)\left(1 + \frac{1}{7}\right).$$

(MATHCOUNTS 1988)

255. Given $a_0 = 1$, $a_1 = 3$, and the general relation $a_n^2 - a_{n-1}a_{n+1} = (-1)^n$ for $n \geq 1$, find a_3. (AHSME 1958)

256. What is the sum of all proper fractions with a denominator less than or equal to 30? (MATHCOUNTS 1988)

257. Evaluate $\dfrac{1}{2 \cdot 4} + \dfrac{1}{4 \cdot 6} + \dfrac{1}{6 \cdot 8} + \cdots + \dfrac{1}{18 \cdot 20}$. (MATHCOUNTS 1989)

258. Evaluate the infinite product

$$2^{1/3}4^{1/9}8^{1/27}16^{1/81} \ldots$$

(Mandelbrot #1)

259. If $a_{n+1} = 2a_n - 3a_{n-1}$, where $a_1 = 2$ and $a_2 = -1$, then find a_5. (MAΘ 1991)

260. Compute the sum

$$\frac{1}{\sqrt{2}+\sqrt{1}} + \frac{1}{\sqrt{3}+\sqrt{2}} + \frac{1}{\sqrt{4}+\sqrt{3}} + \cdots + \frac{1}{\sqrt{25}+\sqrt{24}}$$

261. For a finite sequence $A = (a_1, a_2, \ldots, a_n)$ of numbers, the *Cesaro sum* of A is defined to be

$$\frac{S_1 + S_2 + \cdots + S_n}{n},$$

where $S_k = a_1 + a_2 + \cdots + a_k$. If the Cesaro sum of the 99-term sequence $(a_1, a_2, \ldots, a_{99})$ is 1000, what is the Cesaro sum of the 100-term sequence $(1, a_1, a_2, \ldots, a_{99})$? (AHSME 1992)

262. Given that $v_1 = 2$, $v_2 = 4$ and $v_{n+1} = 3v_n - v_{n-1}$, prove that $v_n = 2F_{2n-2}$, where the terms F_n are the Fibonacci numbers.

263. Evaluate $\sum_{k=1}^{\infty} \frac{k^2}{2^k}$. (Mandelbrot #2)

264. Find the sum $\sum_{n=3}^{\infty} \frac{4}{(4n-3)(4n+1)}$. (MAΘ 1990)

265. In terms of $p = \sum_{k=1}^{\infty} \frac{1}{k^2}$ and $q = \sum_{k=1}^{\infty} \frac{1}{k^3}$, evaluate $\sum_{j=1}^{\infty} \sum_{k=1}^{\infty} \frac{1}{(j+k)^3}$. (Mandelbrot #3)

266. Simplify the product $\left(1 - \frac{1}{3}\right)\left(1 - \frac{1}{4}\right)\left(1 - \frac{1}{5}\right) \cdots \left(1 - \frac{1}{n}\right)$. (AHSME 1959)

267. If n is a multiple of 4, evaluate the sum $1 + 2i + 3i^2 + \cdots + (n+1)i^n$. (AHSME 1964)

268. Given $f(0) = 3$, $f(1) = -1$, and $f(n) = f(n-2) - f(n-1)$, find $f(100)$ in terms of the Fibonacci numbers $(F_0, F_1, \ldots, F_{101})$, where $F_n = F_{n-1} + F_{n-2}$ and $F_0 = F_1 = 1$. (MAΘ 1992)

269. Consider the following triangle of integers, where each number below the apex of the triangle is the sum of the three numbers which are above it to the left, directly above it, and above it to the right. (Empty spaces count as zeroes.) Show that from the third row on, each row contains at least one even number. (USAMTS 1)

$$
\begin{array}{ccccccccc}
 & & & & 1 & & & & \\
 & & & 1 & 1 & 1 & & & \\
 & & 1 & 2 & 3 & 2 & 1 & & \\
 & 1 & 3 & 6 & 7 & 6 & 3 & 1 & \\
1 & 4 & 10 & 16 & 17 & 16 & 10 & 4 & 1
\end{array}
$$

270. Prove the identity

$$\frac{1(2)}{2} + \frac{2(3)}{2} + \frac{3(4)}{2} + \cdots + \frac{n(n+1)}{2} = 1(n) + 2(n-1) + \cdots + (n-1)(2) + n(1)$$

where n is any positive integer. (M&IQ 1991)

271. Define two sequences of rational numbers as follows: let $a_0 = 2$ and $b_0 = 3$, and recursively define $a_n = \frac{a_{n-1}^2}{b_{n-1}}$ and $b_n = \frac{b_{n-1}^2}{a_{n-1}}$. Find b_8, leaving your answer in the exponential form m^n/p^q. (Mandelbrot #2)

272. Find the coefficient of the fourth term of $(1 - 2x)^{1/3}$. (MAΘ 1991)

273. For a sequence $u_1, u_2, \dots$, define $\Delta^1(u_n) = u_{n+1} - u_n$ and, for all integers $k > 1$, $\Delta^k(u_n) = \Delta^1(\Delta^{k-1}(u_n))$. If $u_n = n^3 + n$, then find the smallest k such that $\Delta^k(u_n) = 0$ for all n. (AHSME 1976)

274. If $R_n = \frac{1}{2}(a^n + b^n)$, where $a = 3 + 2\sqrt{2}$, $b = 3 - 2\sqrt{2}$, and $n = 0, 1, 2, \dots$, then find the units digit of R_{12345}. (AHSME 1990)

275. If the sequence $\{a_n\}$ is recursively defined by $a_1 = 2$, and $a_{n+1} = a_n + 2n$ for $n \geq 1$ then find a_{100}. (AHSME 1984)

276. Let a sequence $\{u_n\}$ be defined by $u_1 = 5$ and the relation $u_{n+1} - u_n = 3 + 4(n - 1)$, $n = 1, 2, 3, \dots$. If u_n is expressed as a polynomial in n, what is the algebraic sum of its coefficients? (AHSME 1969)

277. Find $\displaystyle\sum_{n=0}^{\infty} \frac{\sin(nx)}{3^n}$ if $\sin x = 1/3$ and $0 \leq x \leq \pi/2$. (MAΘ 1992)

278. Let $a_1 < a_2 < a_3 < \dots < a_n < \dots$ be positive integers such that $a_{2n} = a_n + n$ for $n = 1, 2, 3, \dots$ It is known that if a_n is a prime number, then n is a prime number. Find, with proof, a_{1993}. (Bulgaria 1993)

279. Let n be a positive integer and let a_n denote the number of positive integers which can be formed whose digits are chosen from $1, 3, 4$ and the sum of whose digits are equal to n. Prove that a_{2n} is a perfect square for every n. (Bulgaria 1993)

280. A collection of $2n$ letters contains 2 each of n different letters. The collection is partitioned into n pairs, each pair containing 2 letters which may be the same or different. Denote the number of distinct partitions by u_n. (Partitions differing in the order of the pairs in the partition or in the order of the two letters in the pairs are not considered distinct.) Prove that $u_{n+1} = (n + 1)u_n - (n(n - 1)/2)u_{n-2}$. (IMO 1985)

281. A sequence of numbers $a_1, a_2, a_3, \dots$ satisfies $a_1 = 1/2$ and $a_1 + a_2 + \dots + a_n = n^2 a_n$ for $n \geq 1$. Find a_n in terms of n. (Canada 1975)

the BIG PICTURE

Mathematics is often seen as a rigid, step-by-step discipline. But the creation of mathematics usually proceeds in a haphazard, seat-of-the-pants manner. Consider this derivation by Euler. Prominent mathematicians of the 1700's, including Gottfried Wilhelm Leibniz and James Bernoulli, had tried and failed to evaluate the infinite series

$$\frac{1}{1^2} + \frac{1}{2^2} + \frac{1}{3^2} + \cdots ,$$

but Euler finally did it. He used an expression which will be familiar to students of calculus,

$$\sin x = x - \frac{x^3}{3!} + \frac{x^5}{5!} - \cdots$$

The zeroes of $\sin x$ are 0, $\pm\pi$, $\pm 2\pi$, etc., so Euler made the leap of claiming that the polynomial on the right hand side can be factored as

$$x - \frac{x^3}{3!} + \frac{x^5}{5!} - \cdots = x \left(1 - \frac{x}{\pi}\right)\left(1 + \frac{x}{\pi}\right)\left(1 - \frac{x}{2\pi}\right)\left(1 + \frac{x}{2\pi}\right)\cdots ,$$

since both sides are 0 at the same places. Dividing both sides by x and simplifying the right side, we get

$$1 - \frac{x^2}{3!} + \frac{x^4}{5!} - \cdots = \left(1 - \frac{x^2}{\pi^2}\right)\left(1 - \frac{x^2}{4\pi^2}\right)\left(1 - \frac{x^2}{9\pi^2}\right)\cdots$$

The constant terms of both sides agree, both being 1, so this crazy procedure might be valid. Setting the x^2 coefficients equal, we have

$$-\frac{1}{6} = -\frac{1}{\pi^2} - \frac{1}{4\pi^2} - \frac{1}{9\pi^2} - \cdots ,$$

or, multiplying both sides by $-\pi^2$,

$$\frac{\pi^2}{6} = \frac{1}{1^2} + \frac{1}{2^2} + \frac{1}{3^2} + \cdots$$

And that's it! Later, of course, the proof had to be tightened up and made rigorous, but as it stands the derivation is a testament to the power of unfettered creativity in mathematics.

Chapter 17

Counting in the Twilight Zone

In Volume 1 we examined a great many counting methods, but all were based on the rock of common sense. In this chapter we will look at counting methods which go far beyond common sense, and thus allow the counting of far more interesting things.

17.1   One to One

We will escape the realm of common sense with the help of the obvious-seeming proposition that *if a one to one correspondence can be drawn between the members of two groups, the two groups are equal in size*. Recall that **one to one** (also written 1-1 or 1 : 1) means that each object in either group corresponds to one and only one object in the other.

EXAMPLE 17-1   Prove that the number of integers greater than 0 and less than 100 equals the number of integers greater than 100 and less than 200.

Proof: For any integer n in the first group (so $0 < n < 100$) the corresponding integer in the second group will be $n + 100$. Clearly $100 < n + 100 < 200$. It is clear that every integer n in the first group has a single counterpart $n + 100$ in the second, and that every integer m in the second group has a single counterpart $m - 100$ in the first group. Thus the correspondence is one to one, and the two groups of numbers are the same size.

17.2   Clever Correspondences

Like any obvious statement, the one to one correspondence principle is useless taken by itself. It must be coupled with a clever correspondence if it is to have any power.

A common example is of the form:

> A dog trainer wants to buy 8 dogs all of which are either cocker spaniels, Irish setters, or Russian wolfhounds. In how many ways can she make the choice?

The problem is an example of making *selections with repetition*, because we can choose as many as we wish from each category. At face value it doesn't seem any harder than many problems we tackled in Volume 1. However, if you try it you'll see it's much harder.

EXERCISE 17-1 Think about the problem until you see why it can't easily be done with our previous methods.

Our problem can be solved with a neat one to one correspondence. Namely, for each choice of 8 dogs we can write a sequence like

$$ddd\_dd\_ddd.$$

The number of d's before the first __ represents the number of spaniels, the number in the middle the number of setters, and the number after the second __ the number of wolfhounds.

EXAMPLE 17-2 To what choice of dog varieties does the sequence above correspond?

Solution: Since there are three d's before the first __, we have three spaniels. Since there are two d's in the middle, there are two setters. Since there are three d's at the end, there are three wolfhounds. (Note that this is in fact a legal sequence since exactly eight dogs are accounted for.)

EXERCISE 17-2 Prove that we can write exactly one sequence for each choice of dogs, and that each sequence corresponds to exactly one choice of dogs. What happens in the case that there are zero dogs of some variety? Is this OK?

Since we have established in Exercise 17-2 a one to one correspondence between choices of dogs and sequences, all we have to count is the number of sequences. But counting the sequences is easy, since each sequence is just a matter of choosing two positions for the __'s out of 10 total positions. (There are 10 positions because we have 8 d's and 2 __'s.) The number of ways to choose 2 positions out of 10 is $\binom{10}{2} = 45$.

EXERCISE 17-3 Find (and prove) a simple formula for the number of ways to buy n dogs if there are r varieties to choose from.

EXERCISE 17-4 Prove that the number you found in the previous exercise is equal to the number of solutions in nonnegative integers of $x_1 + x_2 + \cdots + x_r = n$.

There are many other ways to set up one to one correspondences; in general, when a problem looks too difficult by other methods, look for a correspondence to a simpler problem. It will in general require some creativity on your part to come up with the particular correspondences which do the job, but you'll get a feel for what works with experience.

EXAMPLE 17-3 In how many ways may five people be seated in a row of twenty chairs given that no two people may sit next to one another?

Solution: Consider some arrangement of the five people as specified, then take one chair out from between each pair of people. What you're left with is a unique arrangement of 5 people in 16 chairs *without restrictions.* Similarly, starting with an unrestricted arrangement of 5 people in 16 chairs, adding a chair between each pair of people gives a unique arrangement of 5 non-adjacent people in 20 chairs. (Convince yourself of these two assertions.) Thus there is a one to one correspondence between the restricted 20-chair arrangements of the problem and unrestricted 16-chair arrangements. The number of unrestricted 16-chair arrangements is the number of ways to choose 5 chairs out of 16, or $\binom{16}{5}$.

EXAMPLE 17-4 How many nonnegative integer solutions are there to $x_1 + x_2 + x_3 \leq 50$?

Solution: We have seen how to solve $x_1 + x_2 + \cdots + x_r = n$, but the inequality complicates the problem. We might be tempted to successively solve $x_1 + x_2 + x_3 = 50$, then $x_1 + x_2 + x_3 = 49$, and so on, then try to simplify the sum of the results. But creative thinking yields a different way: just put as much of the 50 as is desired into $x_1 + x_2 + x_3$, and put the rest into a new variable y. With this idea, it becomes clear that a one to one correspondence exists between nonnegative solutions of our inequality and nonnegative solutions of the equality $x_1 + x_2 + x_3 + y = 50$, which by Exercises 17-3 and 17-4 has $\binom{53}{3}$ solutions.

17.3   Easy as . . .

In the first volume we used sets and Venn diagrams to attack problems like:

> There are 100 students taking language classes at Austin High School. If 60 are taking German and 75 are taking Spanish and these are the only languages taught, how many students take both Spanish and German?

Let's try a new approach. Say there are x students taking both languages. We could try counting the number of students taking languages by just adding the number of students in each language, or $60 + 75 = 135$. Since we know there are 100 students taking languages, we have made a mistake. Our error is in counting students taking both languages twice, once for German and once for Spanish. Thus, we must subtract from 135 the number of students taking both languages so that we only count them once. Hence, the total number of students taking language classes is $135 - x$. Setting this equal to 100 we find $x = 35$.

This is the heart of the **Principle of Inclusion-Exclusion**, or PIE: if we count something twice, subtract it once so we only count it once. It's that simple! When we move from two classes to three, the counting becomes a bit trickier, but the concept is the same. For example, let's call the classes A, B, and C and let the number of students in each be #(A), #(B), and #(C), respectively. To take care of overcounting students in both classes A and B, we must subtract the number of students in both classes, which we'll call #($A \cap B$). Similarly, we subtract the number of students in both B and C and in both A and C, for a total of

$$\#(A) + \#(B) + \#(C) - \#(A \cap B) - \#(A \cap C) - \#(B \cap C)$$

students. To convince yourself that this takes care of students enrolled in two classes, pretend you are in exactly two of the classes. How many times are you added to the total? Subtracted? How many times are you counted?

Now what if you're in all three classes? You're added three times and subtracted three times, so you're not counted at all! To take care of this, we must add back the number of students in all three classes. This makes our total number of students

$$\#(A) + \#(B) + \#(C) - \#(A \cap B) - \#(A \cap C) - \#(B \cap C) + \#(A \cap B \cap C).$$

EXERCISE 17-5 Again, pretend you are in 1, 2, or 3 classes and make sure that the aforementioned method only counts you once no matter how many times you are added or subtracted.

EXERCISE 17-6 What if there were 4 classes? How about 5 classes?

EXAMPLE 17-5 How many positive integers less than or equal to 1000 do not have 2, 3, or 5 among their prime factors?

Solution: We count the number of positive integers less than or equal to 1000 which do have 2, 3, or 5 among their prime factors and subtract that number from 1000 to find how many do not. There are $1000/2 = 500$ multiples of 2, $\lfloor 1000/3 \rfloor = 333$ multiples of 3 and $1000/5 = 200$ multiples of 5 in this range, for a total of $500 + 333 + 200 = 1033$ positive integers less than or equal to 1000 with 2, 3, or 5 as a factor. We've obviously overlooked something. We've badly overcounted, because many numbers are multiples of more than just one of these three numbers. Applying the Principle of Inclusion-Exclusion, we subtract from 1033 the number of multiples of both 2 and 3, of both 2 and 5, and of both 3 and 5. Finally, we then add to the result the number of integers which are multiples of all three.

Any number which is a multiple of 2 and 3 is a multiple of $(2)(3) = 6$, since 2 and 3 have no common nontrivial factors. Hence, we seek the multiples of 6, 10, 15, and $2(3)(5) = 30$. There are $\lfloor 1000/6 \rfloor = 166$ multiples of 6, $\lfloor 1000/10 \rfloor = 100$ multiples of 10, $\lfloor 1000/15 \rfloor = 66$ multiples of 15, and $\lfloor 1000/30 \rfloor = 33$ multiples of 30. By PIE, there are

$$1033 - 166 - 100 - 66 + 33 = 734$$

integers less than or equal to 1000 with 2, 3, or 5 among their factors. Hence, there are $1000 - 734 = \mathbf{266}$ integers in that range which are not multiples of 2, 3, or 5.

EXERCISE 17-7 Suppose there is some number of objects placed in n categories $A_1, A_2, \ldots, A_n$, where each object may be in more than one category. Let $\#(A_i)$ be the number of objects in category A_i. Suppose $\#(A_i)$ is the same for all i, $\#(A_i \cap A_j)$ is the same for all distinct pairs (i, j), $\#(A_i \cap A_j \cap A_k)$ is the same for all triples (i, j, k), etc. Show that the Principle of Inclusion-Exclusion gives

$$\#(A_1 \cup A_2 \cup A_3 \cup \cdots \cup A_n) = \binom{n}{1}\#(A_1) - \binom{n}{2}\#(A_1 \cap A_2) + \binom{n}{3}\#(A_1 \cap A_2 \cap A_3)$$

$$- \binom{n}{4}\#(A_1 \cap A_2 \cap A_3 \cap A_4) + \cdots + (-1)^n \binom{n}{n}\#(A_1 \cap A_2 \cap \cdots \cap A_n).$$

This application of the Principle of Inclusion-Exclusion is very useful in problems containing symmetry.

EXAMPLE 17-6 There are four baskets numbered from 1 to 4 and four balls numbered from 1 to 4. Each basket is allowed to have at most two balls. In how many ways can the balls be placed in the baskets such that no ball has the same number as the basket it is in?

Solution: This problem has symmetry, so we apply the concepts of the previous exercise. First we count the number of ways to put the balls in the baskets with no restrictions. There are 4! ways to put the balls in 4 different baskets. There are $\binom{4}{1}\binom{4}{2}(3)(2)$ ways to put two balls in one basket and the others in their own baskets (4 ways to pick the basket with two balls, 6 ways to pick the balls in that basket, $(3)(2)$ ways to put the other balls in different baskets). Finally, we can put two balls each in two baskets in $\binom{4}{2}\binom{4}{2}$ ways (6 ways to pick the two non-empty baskets and 6 ways to distribute the balls among these baskets). Hence there are $24 + 144 + 36 = 204$ ways to put the balls in the baskets.

To solve the problem, we will count the ways the balls can be put in the baskets such that at least one ball has the same number as the basket that holds it. Let #(i) be the number of ways to fill the baskets such that basket i holds ball i. From the previous exercise, we seek the quantity

$$\binom{4}{1}\#(1) - \binom{4}{2}\#(1 \cap 2) + \binom{4}{3}\#(1 \cap 2 \cap 3) - \binom{4}{4}\#(1 \cap 2 \cap 3 \cap 4).$$

For the first, after we put ball 1 in basket 1, we can either put another ball in that basket or put all the balls in the other baskets. The former can be done in $\binom{3}{1}(3^2) = 27$ ways (3 ways to pick the other ball in basket 1, 3^2 ways to put the other balls in the other baskets); the latter can be done in $\binom{3}{1}\binom{3}{2}(2) + 3! = 24$ ways, where we divide this into the case of two of the balls in one of the other three baskets and the case of the other three being in different baskets. For #($1 \cap 2$) we put balls 1 and 2 in baskets 1 and 2. The other two balls can be put in the baskets in $2 + (2)(2)(2) + (2)(2) = 14$ ways, where we consider the cases of putting 2, 1, or 0 of the remaining balls in the first two baskets. (Make sure you see this.) The last two are easy. After we put 3 balls in the right baskets, the other has four choices and we can only get them all right in 1 way. Putting these in our above expression, there are

$$4(27 + 24) - 6(14) + 4(4) - 1(1) = 135$$

ways to put the balls in the baskets so that at least one ball is in the right basket. This leaves $204 - 135 = \mathbf{69}$ ways of filling the baskets so that no ball has the same number as they basket that holds it.

This is a very complicated counting problem, and you may argue that you would be better off just listing the possibilities and counting. Using the Principle of Inclusion-Exclusion is better than listing and counting because it's awfully hard to tell if we've listed all the possibilities, and as the number of possibilities gets large (what if there were 6 balls and 6 baskets), the listing and counting method becomes very unreliable.

17.4   Generating Functions

When it comes to counting, **generating functions** are the cleverest thing there is. The idea of generating functions is that functions can be manipulated in various ways which combinatorial quantities cannot, so to examine the properties of some combinatorial function $A(k)$, we instead look at the function

$$A(0) + A(1)x + A(2)x^2 + A(3)x^3 + \cdots,$$

where the coefficient $A(k)$ of x^k is the number of ways event k can occur. Perhaps the simplest example of a useful generating function is

$$\binom{n}{0} + \binom{n}{1}x + \binom{n}{2}x^2 + \cdots + \binom{n}{n}x^n,$$

where we let $A(k) = \binom{n}{k}$ for some fixed n. We could say that this is the generating function for the number of ways we can get k heads when flipping n different coins. The power of writing this as a function is that we can use the Binomial Theorem to convert the function to the simple $(x + 1)^n$. In Chapter 15, we saw that this function can then be used to rapidly get identities like $\binom{n}{0} + \binom{n}{1} + \cdots + \binom{n}{n} = 2^n$, $\binom{n}{1} + \binom{n}{3} + \cdots = \binom{n}{0} + \binom{n}{2} + \cdots$, and so on.

Another type of generating function can be used to look at distribution problems. For example, suppose we let $A(k)$ be the number of ways in which we can collect \$$k$ from 5 people if each person gives either 0, 1, or 3 dollars. Rather than writing out the generating function, we consider the generating function for each person individually. Any single person has 1 way to give \$0, 1 way to give \$1, no ways to give \$2, 1 way to give \$3, and no ways to give anything larger, so the individual generating function is $(1x^0 + 1x^1 + 1x^3)$. The reason the individual function is interesting is that the overall generating function can be found by *multiplying the individual functions together!*

Why? Consider some set of possible contributions, say \$1, \$3, \$3, \$0, \$3. This corresponds to the set of generating terms

$$x^1 \cdot x^3 \cdot x^3 \cdot x^0 \cdot x^3;$$

that is, there is a one to one correspondence between sets of contributions and generating terms in the product. Since we want to count every set of contributions once, we want to count every generating term once. Multiplying the individual functions together does exactly this, by the distributive property! Hence the kth term of the expansion of

$$(1 + x + x^3)(1 + x + x^3)(1 + x + x^3)(1 + x + x^3)(1 + x + x^3) = (1 + x + x^3)^5$$

will give the number of ways to collect \$$k$ from the five people.

EXERCISE 17-8 The argument above, that the overall generating function can be found by multiplying the individual generating functions, is the linchpin of everything we'll do with generating functions. Make sure you understand it well right now, or the rest of this section won't make sense.

EXAMPLE 17-7 Ten people with one dollar each and one person with three dollars get together to buy an eight-dollar pizza. In how many ways can they do it?

Solution: Each of the ten people with one dollar contributes a generating function $(1 + x)$, and the last person contributes $(1 + x + x^2 + x^3)$. Thus the overall generating function is

$$(1 + x)^{10}(1 + x + x^2 + x^3).$$

By the Binomial Theorem, this becomes

$$\left(1 + \binom{10}{1}x + \binom{10}{2}x^2 + \cdots + \binom{10}{10}x^{10}\right)(1 + x + x^2 + x^3).$$

Recall that we are interested in an eight dollar total contribution, which means we want the coefficient of x^8. By the distributive property, the sum becomes

$$(1 + x + x^2 + x^3) + \binom{10}{1}(x + x^2 + x^3 + x^4) + \cdots + \binom{10}{10}(x^{10} + x^{11} + x^{12} + x^{13}),$$

and the coefficient of the x^8 term is

$$\binom{10}{5} + \binom{10}{6} + \binom{10}{7} + \binom{10}{8}.$$

EXERCISE 17-9 Write down a factored generating function for the number of solutions of $e_1 + e_2 + e_3 = k$, where e_1 is even, e_2 odd, and e_3 prime.

In dealing with generating functions, we use several identities for simplification. The Binomial Theorem is often key, as are the geometric series identities

$$1 + x + x^2 + x^3 + \cdots = \frac{1}{1 - x} \tag{17.1}$$

and

$$1 + x + x^2 + \cdots + x^r = \frac{1 - x^{r+1}}{1 - x}. \tag{17.2}$$

For example, consider distributing 23 toys among 6 children such that no child gets more than 5 or less than 2 toys. Each child contributes a generating function $x^2 + x^3 + x^4 + x^5$, so the overall generating function is

$$(x^2 + x^3 + x^4 + x^5)^6 = x^{12}(1 + x + x^2 + x^3)^6.$$

By identity (17.2), the sum $1 + x + x^2 + x^3$ is equal to $(1 - x^4)/(1 - x)$, so our generating function is $x^{12}(1 - x^4)^6(1 - x)^{-6}$. We get rid of the x^{12} by noting that the coefficient of x^{23} in $x^{12}(1 - x^4)^6(1 - x)^{-6}$ is the same as the coefficient of x^{11} in $(1 - x^4)^6(1 - x)^{-6}$. By the Binomial Theorem, once for the positive exponent $n = 6$ and once for the negative exponent $n = -6$, we expand this latter product into

$$\left[\binom{6}{0} - \binom{6}{1}x^4 + \binom{6}{2}x^8 - \cdots + \binom{6}{6}x^{48}\right]\left[\binom{-6}{0} - \binom{-6}{1}x + \binom{-6}{2}x^2 - \cdots\right].$$

All that's left is to find the coefficient of x^{11}. This is simple, because the only contributing terms are $-\binom{6}{0}\binom{-6}{11}$, $\binom{6}{1}\binom{-6}{7}$, and $-\binom{6}{2}\binom{-6}{3}$. Thus the coefficient of the x^{11} term, and therefore the number of ways to perform the required task, is

$$-\binom{6}{0}\binom{-6}{11} + \binom{6}{1}\binom{-6}{7} - \binom{6}{2}\binom{-6}{3}.$$

EXERCISE 17-10 In how many ways can we get a sum of 25 when 10 distinct dice are rolled?

17.5 Partitions

One of the most beautiful applications of generating functions is in counting **partitions**, ways to split an integer into parts. (For example, some partitions of 5 are $3 + 1 + 1$, $4 + 1$, $3 + 2$, and 5.) There is no simple formula for the general partition problem, as you'll discover if you try to find one, but generating functions provide an interesting window into the general problem and many variations.

To find a generating function for the number of partitions of n, you might think that it suffices to consider that each contributing number can be 0, 1, 2,..., so that each contributor has an individual generating function $(1 + x + x^2 + \cdots)$. However, this is no good because it considers $1 + 2$ and $2 + 1$ as different partitions (and furthermore, we don't know how many contributors there are)! Instead, we realize that a partition is just a list of numbers: the partition $4 + 3 + 3 + 1$ of 11, for example, is equivalent to the description "one 1, two 3's, one 4." Thus we let number of 1's in the partition be one contributor, the number of 2's be a contributor, and so on. The 1's, then, contribute an individual generating function $1 + x + x^2 + \cdots$, where the 1 corresponds to zero 1's in the partition, the x to one 1, the x^2 to two 1's, and so on.

EXERCISE 17-11 Find the individual generating function for the number of 2's in the partition.

Since the number of k's in the partition contributes an individual generating function $1 + x^k + x^{2k} + \cdots$, the overall generating function is

$$(1 + x + x^2 + \cdots)(1 + x^2 + x^4 + \cdots)(1 + x^3 + x^6 + \cdots) \cdots \qquad (17.3)$$

EXERCISE 17-12 Expand the product above up to the x^4 term. Show that the coefficient of x^1 is the number of partitions of 1, the coefficient of x^2 is the number of partitions of 2, and similarly for 3 and 4.

EXAMPLE 17-8 Using the geometric series formula, the factor $1 + x^k + x^{2k} + \cdots$ equals $1/(1 - x^k)$. Thus the generating function (17.3) can also be written

$$\frac{1}{(1 - x)(1 - x^2)(1 - x^3) \cdots}$$

Once we can find a generating function for the general partition problem, we can easily specialize it. How many ways can n be partitioned into 2's, 3's and 4's? The individual generating functions are $1 + x^2 + x^4 + \cdots$, $1 + x^3 + \cdots$, and $1 + x^4 + \cdots$, so the overall generating function is

$$(1 + x^2 + x^4 + \cdots)(1 + x^3 + x^6 + \cdots)(1 + x^4 + x^8 + \cdots) = \frac{1}{(1 - x^2)(1 - x^3)(1 - x^4)}.$$

How many ways can n be partitioned with at most two of any integer? The individual generating functions are $1 + x + x^2$, $1 + x^2 + x^4$, $1 + x^3 + x^6$, and so on, so the overall generating function is

$$(1 + x + x^2)(1 + x^2 + x^4)(1 + x^3 + x^6) \cdots$$

Granted that evaluating the nth coefficient of such generating functions, which must be done to get a numerical answer, is not easy; however, mere possession of the generating function can allow interesting analysis.

EXAMPLE 17-9 Prove that the number of partitions of n in which no part appears exactly once is equal to the number of partitions in which no part is congruent to 1 or 5 (mod 6).

Solution: We find the two generating functions separately and prove they are equal. For the first one, the individual generating function for the number of 1's becomes $1 + x^2 + x^3 + x^4 + \cdots$. We must delete the x because it corresponds to exactly one 1, a situation forbidden by the problem. Similarly we must delete the second term of each individual generating function in (17.3), so the overall generating function is

$$(1 + x^2 + x^3 + \cdots)(1 + x^4 + x^6 + \cdots)(1 + x^6 + x^9 + \cdots)\cdots,$$

which using the geometric series formula is

$$\left(1 + \frac{x^2}{1-x}\right)\left(1 + \frac{x^4}{1-x^2}\right)\left(1 + \frac{x^6}{1-x^3}\right)\cdots$$

$$= \frac{1 - x + x^2}{1-x} \cdot \frac{1 - x^2 + x^4}{1-x^2} \cdot \frac{1 - x^3 + x^6}{1-x^3}\cdots$$

$$= \frac{(1 - x + x^2)(1 + x)}{(1-x)(1+x)} \cdot \frac{(1 - x^2 + x^4)(1 + x^2)}{(1-x^2)(1+x^2)}\cdots$$

$$= \frac{1 + x^3}{1-x^2} \cdot \frac{1 + x^6}{1-x^4} \cdot \frac{1 + x^9}{1-x^6}\cdots$$

$$= \frac{1}{1-x^2} \cdot \frac{1}{1-x^3} \cdot \frac{1}{1-x^4} \cdot \frac{1}{1-x^6} \cdot \frac{1}{1-x^8}\cdots,$$

where the last equality is found by cancelling each $1 + x^{3k}$ in the numerator with a $1 - x^{6k} = (1 + x^{3k})(1 - x^{3k})$ farther out in the denominator, leaving a $1 - x^{3k}$ in the denominator. All that's left in the denominator when we're through is $1 - x^k$ for all k not congruent to 1 or 5 (mod 6). (Confirm these calculations yourself.) Hence this is exactly the generating function for the number of partitions into parts not congruent to 1 or 5 (mod 6), so the generating functions are equal and we're done.

As you've seen, effective use of generating functions requires quite a bit of skill with series manipulation. With practice, these operations will become easy. Once you've learned calculus, come back to the study of generating functions (a college discrete mathematics book may help); the operations of integration and differentiation vastly widen the scope of generating function applications.

17.6 Counting on Graphs

We'll start with a basic grid counting problem. Suppose Andy the Ant sits at point 1 and wishes to go to point 20 but can only walk down or to the right. If Andy can only turn at other numbered points, how many different paths can Andy take from 1 to 20?

$$
\begin{array}{ccccc}
1 & 2 & 3 & 4 & 5 \\
6 & 7 & 8 & 9 & 10 \\
11 & 12 & 13 & 14 & 15 \\
16 & 17 & 18 & 19 & 20
\end{array}
$$

One such path is 1-6-11-16-17-18-19-20. Clearly to go from 1 to 20, Andy must take 7 steps, 3 down and 4 to the right. Our problem is to count the number of orders in which Andy can take three steps to the right out of seven steps. Thus, our answer is simply $\binom{7}{3} = 35$.

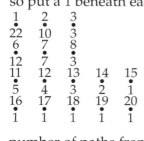

Now suppose Anna the Anteater comes and sits on point 5, so that Andy can't safely go to point 4, 5, 9, or 10. How many paths can Andy take now? Our problem isn't so simple, because many of Andy's earlier paths are disallowed.

Notice that any successful path must go through either point 2 or point 6. Hence, if we let #(i) be the number of paths from point i to point 20, we have #(1) = #(2) + #(6). Instead of working forward in this manner, let's work backwards. For example, for each of the points on the bottom row there is only 1 path to point 20, so put a 1 beneath each of these vertices.

There's only one succesful path from 15, but from point 14 we can go through either point 15 or point 19. Similarly, for any point i, the number of paths from i to 20 is the sum of the numbers of paths from the point directly to the right of i and from the point below i. Thus, we put a 2 below point 14, a 3 below 13, and so on filling out next to the last row. To go from point 8 to point 20, we must go first to point 13, so there are 3 paths from point 8 to 20. Continuing as before, we fill out the grid with numbers representing the number of paths from each point to point 20. Thus, we find our desired answer is 22.

EXERCISE 17-13 Can we use our backwards counting approach on three-dimensional grid problems?

Nearly every problem involving counting on a grid can be solved working backwards as we did in counting Andy's paths which avoid Anna the Anteater; however, the recursive method we have used for these grids is applicable to other types of problems as well.

EXERCISE 17-14 Mike starts at one corner of a tetrahedron. In a *move*, he walks along any edge to a different corner. In how many ways can he end up where he started after 6 moves?

17.7 Counting Infinite Sets

One really astounding consequence of the one-to-one correspondence principle is that it allows us to "count" infinite sets. Even though there is no finite number which equals the size of an infinite set, we can use one-to-one correspondences to show that certain sets are the same size, or that one set is bigger than another.

One usual example of an infinite set is the positive integers,

$$\{1, 2, 3, 4, \ldots\}.$$

However, we can place the set of *all* integers in correspondence with the positive integers, like so:

$$
\begin{array}{ccccccccccc}
1 & 2 & 3 & 4 & 5 & 6 & 7 & 8 & 9 & 10 & 11 & \ldots \\
0 & 1 & -1 & 2 & -2 & 3 & -3 & 4 & -4 & 5 & -5 & \ldots
\end{array}
$$

Since they can be placed in correspondence, the set of all integers is the same size as the set of positive integers, even though the positive integers are wholly contained by the integers! How can this be? When dealing with infinite sets, such oddities are not rare.

WARNING: Never say *there are the same number of positive integers as all integers*; there is no meaning to the phrase *the number of positive integers*. Refer only to the sizes of the sets involved.

EXERCISE 17-15 Show that the sets of odd and even positive integers each have the same size as the set of all positive integers.

EXAMPLE 17-10 Even the set of all positive rational numbers, which seems immensely larger than the set of positive integers, is actually the same size. We make the correspondence by writing the rationals in a grid:

$$\begin{array}{cccc}
\frac{1}{1} & \frac{1}{2} & \frac{1}{3} & \frac{1}{4} & \cdots \\[4pt]
\frac{2}{1} & \frac{2}{2} & \frac{2}{3} & \frac{2}{4} & \cdots \\[4pt]
\frac{3}{1} & \frac{3}{2} & \frac{3}{3} & \frac{3}{4} & \cdots \\[4pt]
\frac{4}{1} & \frac{4}{2} & \frac{4}{3} & \frac{4}{4} & \cdots \\[4pt]
\vdots & \vdots & \vdots & \vdots & \ddots
\end{array}$$

We can create a similar grid for the positive integers by filling up along the diagonals as follows:

$$\begin{array}{cccc}
1 & 2 & 4 & 7 & \cdots \\
3 & 5 & 8 & 12 & \cdots \\
6 & 9 & 13 & 18 & \cdots \\
10 & 14 & 19 & 25 & \cdots \\
\vdots & \vdots & \vdots & \vdots & \ddots
\end{array}$$

We then correspond each rational to the integer in the corresponding place in the grid.

Given all these examples, you might be starting to think that any infinite set can be placed in one-to-one correspondence with the positive integers. Not so. The set of real numbers is larger than the set of positive integers, as was proven by Georg Cantor in the late 1800's. His famous **diagonal proof** is one of the classic beautiful proofs of math.

The proof goes as follows. Assume that we can list all the real numbers one after the other. We will show that there is one real number which is not in the list, contradicting the assertion that we have listed them all. Let the list be as follows, where each a_{ij} is a single digit:

$$a_{10}.a_{11}a_{12}a_{13}\ldots$$
$$a_{20}.a_{21}a_{22}a_{23}\ldots$$
$$a_{30}.a_{31}a_{32}a_{33}\ldots$$
$$\vdots \quad \vdots \quad \vdots \quad \vdots$$

Now form a new number as follows: let b_1 be any digit which is different from a_{11}; let b_2 be any digit which is different from a_{22}; b_3 different from a_{33}; and so on. Consider the number

$$x = 0.b_1b_2b_3b_4\ldots$$

Clearly x is different from $a_{10}.a_{11}a_{12}\ldots$, since they differ in the first place after the decimal ($b_1 \neq a_{11}$). Similarly, x is different from $a_{20}.a_{21}a_{22}\ldots$, since $b_2 \neq a_{22}$. In like manner, x must be different from every number in our list. Thus x is not in our list, so our original assertion that the list contained all the real numbers must have been false.

In other words, we can't list the real numbers in correspondence with the positive integers, for no such list can contain all the reals. There is no way to correspond the real numbers to the positive integers: the set of reals is larger. This should be surprising—two infinite sets which are not the same size?! Sets which can be corresponded to the positive integers are called **countably infinite**, while sets which cannot be so corresponded are called **uncountable**.

EXAMPLE 17-11   With infinity, we invariably get strangeness. One bizarre result is that the set of all real numbers is the same size as the set of real numbers in any finite range, say $(-1, 1)$.

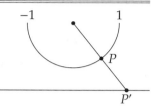

The one-to-one correspondence can be seen geometrically in the picture at right, where we have wrapped the segment around into a semicircle. Each point P on the segment is paired in a 1-1 manner with a point P' on the real number line by drawing the line shown.

Those with a more analytic bent might like the following correspondence better. We take

$$x \longleftrightarrow \tan(\pi x/2),$$

where x is in the range $(-1, 1)$, so $\pi x/2$ spans the period $(-\pi/2, \pi/2)$ of tangent and $\tan(\pi x/2)$ thus spans the entire range $(-\infty, \infty)$.

EXERCISE 17-16   Given two segments of lengths a and b, give both a geometric and an analytic proof that the two sets of points are the same size.

EXAMPLE 17-12   An even more surprising result is that there are equally many points in a *square* as there are in a line segment! Let the square have vertices $(0,0)$, $(1,0)$, $(1,1)$, and $(0,1)$; then every point inside has coordinates (x, y) with $0 < x, y < 1$. Similarly let the line segment be the interval $(0, 1)$, so that every point is associated with a number z, $0 < z < 1$.

How can we draw a 1-1 correspondence between pairs (x, y) and numbers z? To go from the pair to the number, we consider the decimal expansions $0.x_1x_2 \ldots$ and $0.y_1y_2 \ldots$ of x and y, and let $(x, y) \to z = 0.x_1y_1x_2y_2 \ldots$. Clearly for each pair there is one, and only one, number z. To go from the number to the pair we do this backwards: write $z = 0.z_1z_2 \ldots$ and take $z \to (x, y) = (0.z_1z_3z_5 \ldots, 0.z_2z_4z_6 \ldots)$. Clearly for each z there is one and only one pair. Since the correspondence thus determined is 1-1, there are equally many points in a line segment (area = 0) as in a square (area = 1)! (Of course, visualizing the correspondence is a bit difficult. . .)

Problems to Solve for Chapter 17

282. Five balls are numbered 1 to 5. Three boxes are numbered 1 to 3. How many distinct ways can the balls be put in the boxes if two boxes have two balls each and the other box has the remaining ball? (MAΘ 1992)

283. How many positive integers less than 101 are multiples of 5 or 7, but not both? (Mandelbrot #1)

284. In how many ways can 3 squares be chosen from a 5 by 5 grid so that no two chosen squares are in the same row or column? (Mandelbrot #3)

285. Lines $L_1, L_2, \ldots, L_{100}$ are distinct. All lines L_{4n}, n a positive integer, are parallel to each other. All lines L_{4n-3}, n a positive integer, pass through a given point A. Find the maximum number of points of intersection of pairs of lines from the complete set $\{L_1, L_2, \ldots, L_{100}\}$. (AHSME 1976)

286. How many solutions in *positive* integers are there to $x_1 + x_2 + \cdots + x_8 = 19$?

287. Let the set $S = \{a_1, a_2, a_3, \ldots, a_{12}\}$, where all 12 elements are distinct. We wish to form sets each of which contain one or more elements of set S with the restriction that the subscript of each element in a specific set must be an integral multiple of the smallest subscript in the set (e.g. the sets $\{a_2, a_4, a_{10}\}, \{a_6, a_{12}\}, \{a_9\}$ are all acceptable.) How many such sets can be formed? (MAΘ 1991)

288. In how many ways can 3 Americans, 4 Germans, 2 Frenchmen, and 3 Russians sit around a circular table if those of the same country sit together? (MAΘ 1991)

289. On their return to land, the seven exiles from Gilligan's Island, as well as Gilligan's pet ape, are seated in a row for a welcome home meal. In how many ways can the eight be seated if Ginger is tactfully seated next to neither Gilligan nor his ape? (Mandelbrot #3)

290. Twenty chairs are set up in a row for the Princeton garlic-eating contest. Only five eaters attend the competition, but none will sit next to any other. In how many ways can the eaters be seated? (Mandelbrot #3)

291. Points in a grid are numbered as shown. Movements from point number A to point number B can only be made if $B > A$ and the two points are in the same row or column. Find the total number of ways to go from point 1 to point 30. (MAΘ 1992)

292. How many lines in a three-dimensioinal rectangular coordinate system pass through four distinct points of the form (i, j, k), where i, j, and k are positive integers not exceeding four? (Can you generalize this to $i, j, k \leq n$?) (AHSME 1981)

1	2	3	4	5
10	9	8	7	6
11	12	13	14	15
20	19	18	17	16
21	22	23	24	25
30	29	28	27	26

293. Six people sat down along one side of a banquet table completely ignoring their name cards. In how many ways could this have been done so that no person was seated where his/her name card was placed? (MAΘ 1992)

294. Find generating functions for

i. the number of partitions of a number into even integers.

ii. the number of partitions of a number into different odd integers.

iii. the number of ways to give a dollar amount of change with standard U.S. bills ($1, $5, $10, $20, $50, or $100).

iv. the number of integer solutions of $2x + 3y + 7z = n$ with $z < 4$.

295. When $(a + b + c + d)^{10}$ is expanded and like terms combined, how many terms are in the result? (MAΘ 1992)

296. For any set S, let $|S|$ denote the number of elements in S, and let $n(S)$ be the number of subsets of S, including the empty set and the set S itself. If A, B, and C are sets for which

$$n(A) + n(B) + n(C) = n(A \cup B \cup C) \quad \text{and} \quad |A| = |B| = 100,$$

then what is the minimum possible value of $|A \cap B \cap C|$? (AHSME 1991)

297. Suppose that 7 boys and 13 girls line up in a row. Let S be the number of places in the row where a boy and a girl are standing next to each other. For example, for the row *GBBGGGBGBGGGBGBGGBGG* we have $S = 12$. If all possible orders of these 20 people are considered, what is the average value of S? Can you generalize this result to a group of m boys and n girls? (AHSME 1989)

298. Let n be an even integer not less than 4. A cube with edge n in length (briefly, an n-cube) is constructed from n^3 unit cubes (briefly, u-cubes). There are $\frac{n^3}{4}$ different colors given and exactly 4 u-cubes are colored in each of these given colors. Prove that one can choose n u-cubes of different colors, no two of which are in the same level (a level is a set of n^2 u-cubes whose centers lie in a plane parallel to one of the faces of the n cube). (M&IQ 1991)

299. A walk consists of a sequence of steps of length 1 taken in directions north, south, east, or west. A walk is *self-avoiding* if it never passes through the same point twice. Let $f(n)$ denote the number of n-step self-avoiding walks which begin at the origin. Show that $2^n < f(n) \leq 4 \cdot 3^{n-1}$. (Canada 1979)

300. Let n be a fixed positive integer. Find the sum of all positive integers with the following property: In base 2, it has exactly $2n$ digits consisting of n 1's and n 0's. (The first digit cannot be 0.) (Canada 1991)

the BIG PICTURE

Georg Cantor, who came up with the modern way of identifying infinite sets using 1-1 correspondences and discovered uncountable sets, discovered other weird things as well. One of the weirdest is the **Cantor set**. To construct a Cantor set we start with an ordinary segment and cut out the middle third. We then cut out the middle thirds of each subsegment which remains, leaving four smaller segments. We continue cutting out middle thirds forever, as shown.

We can compute the length of the Cantor set: at each step the length is multiplied by 2/3, so the final length is (2/3)(2/3)(2/3) ⋯, which tends to 0. But just because its length is 0 doesn't mean it contains no points! Consider our segment to be a number line from 0 to 1, where each decimal is written in base 3. In taking out the first middle third, we take out all decimals which start with 0.1 . . ., leaving in those which start 0.0 . . . or 0.2 . . .. Similarly, taking out the second middle thirds gets rid of those numbers which start 0.01 . . . or 0.21 . . ., leaving those which start 0.00 . . ., 0.02 . . ., 0.20 . . ., or 0.22 . . .. Continuing in this manner, the Cantor set contains *all numbers whose base-3 decimal representation contains no 1's.* The set is far from being empty.

The Cantor set actually contains as many points as the entire line segment! We can set up the 1-1 correspondence as follows. Any number in the Cantor set has a decimal representation made up of 0's and 2's. Convert all the 2's to 1's and consider this new representation as a base-2 decimal representation. In this way, every number in the Cantor set corresponds to a number in $(0,1)$. Similarly, every number in $(0,1)$ corresponds to a number in the Cantor set, by doing the reverse process: write the decimal in base 2, convert 1's to 2's, and think of the new decimal as a base-3 representation. This is a one to one correspondence, so the sets of points are the same size.

So the Cantor set has length 0, but as many points as the entire segment $(0,1)$. (Think this one over a little before you buy it!)

Chapter 18

Again and Again

18.1   Repeats

Often in math we have an opportunity to repeat the same operation more than once. For example, multiplication is just repeated addition, as $2 \times 5 = 2 + 2 + 2 + 2 + 2$, and powers are repeated multiplication: $2^5 = 2 \times 2 \times 2 \times 2 \times 2$. We can extend this progression a step further by considering repeated powers, like

$$2^{2^{2^{2^{2}}}}.$$

Similarly, we can construct **continued fractions**, like

$$2 + \cfrac{1}{2 + \cfrac{1}{2 + \cfrac{1}{2 + \frac{1}{2}}}},$$

or **continued roots**, like

$$\sqrt{2 + \sqrt{2 + \sqrt{2 + \sqrt{2 + \sqrt{2}}}}}.$$

EXERCISE 18-1   Evaluate the continued power, fraction, and root above.

18.2   Off to Infinity

Somewhat surprisingly, continued expressions are often easiest to deal with when they are *infinite*, rather than finite. For example, the finite continued root above can only be evaluated with a calculator, while the infinite version

$$\sqrt{2 + \sqrt{2 + \cdots}}$$

is handled easily with a straight calculation. We write

$$x = \sqrt{2 + \sqrt{2 + \cdots}},$$

so that (this is the clever part)

$$x = \sqrt{2 + x}.$$

We then have only to square both sides to obtain the quadratic $x^2 = 2+x$, which factors as $(x-2)(x+1)$, for solutions of $x = 2$ and $x = -1$. Since -1 is not a reasonable solution (and is thus **extraneous**), the infinite continued root is equal to 2.

EXERCISE 18-2   Evaluate the following.

  i. $2 + \cfrac{1}{2 + \cfrac{1}{2+\frac{1}{2+\cdots}}}$

  ii. $2 + \cfrac{1}{3 + \cfrac{1}{2+\frac{1}{3+\cdots}}}$

18.3   Rational Continued Fractions

We will focus on continued fractions, as they are much more tractable than continued powers or roots. To narrow the scope even more, we will look only at those continued fractions in which the numerators of all the fractions are 1's; that is, those that look like

$$a_1 + \cfrac{1}{a_2 + \cfrac{1}{a_3+\cdots}},$$

which we call **proper**. We'll also require all the a_i to be positive integers.

    Proper continued fractions are like decimal expansions in an important way: every rational number has a representation as a finite proper continued fraction, and every irrational as an infinite one. For example, let's write down such a representation for the fraction $\frac{85}{26}$.

    We will be a little careful and worry about the **uniqueness** of our representation. (In other words, is the representation we write down the only valid one, or are there others?) We need only to notice that every expression $\frac{1}{\text{something}}$ is less than 1. Since we have

$$\frac{85}{26} = a_1 + \frac{1}{\text{something}}$$

with a_1 a positive integer, a_1 must be the integer part of $\frac{85}{26}$, or 3. We then have

$$\frac{85}{26} = 3 + \frac{7}{26} = 3 + \cfrac{1}{\frac{26}{7}} = a_1 + \cfrac{1}{a_2 + \cfrac{1}{\text{something}}},$$

or

$$\frac{26}{7} = a_2 + \frac{1}{\text{something}}.$$

EXERCISE 18-3   Convince yourself that a_1 had to equal 3 in the foregoing equations by seeing what would have happened if it had equalled 2 or 4.

Again, a_2 must be the integer part of $\frac{26}{7}$ because $\frac{1}{\text{something}}$ is less than 1. Thus $a_2 = 3$, and

$$3 + \frac{5}{7} = a_2 + \cfrac{1}{a_3 + \cfrac{1}{\text{something}}}.$$

Continuing in the same way, a_3 must be the integer part of $\frac{7}{5}$, or 1, a_4 must be the integer part of $\frac{5}{2}$, or 2, and a_5 must be the integer part of $\frac{2}{1}$, or 2. At this point there is nothing else left, so the complete fraction is

$$3 + \cfrac{1}{3 + \cfrac{1}{1 + \cfrac{1}{2 + \frac{1}{2}}}}.$$

EXERCISE 18-4   Verify from scratch that the fraction above does equal $\frac{85}{26}$.

EXERCISE 18-5   Find the continued fraction expansions of $\frac{147}{29}$, $\frac{29}{7}$, and $\frac{70}{12}$.

Now let's reconsider the question of the uniqueness of our representation. At first glance, it seems like we never had any leeway in choosing the a_i. However, there is one choice which we have overlooked. Instead of taking $a_5 = 2$, we could have taken $a_5 = 1$ and $a_6 = 1$, so that $a_5 + \frac{1}{a_6} = 1 + \frac{1}{1} = 2$. Thus our continued fraction could also be written

$$3 + \cfrac{1}{3 + \cfrac{1}{1 + \cfrac{1}{2 + \cfrac{1}{1 + \frac{1}{1}}}}}.$$

Up to this somewhat trivial modification, the proper continued fraction decomposition of a rational number is unique.

EXAMPLE 18-1   Let's streamline our procedure for finding the continued fraction expansion of a rational number b_1. First, we take $a_1 = \lfloor b_1 \rfloor$. Then $a_2 = \lfloor 1/(b_1 - a_1) \rfloor = \lfloor b_2 \rfloor$, where we define $b_2 = 1/(b_1 - a_1)$. Similarly, $a_3 = \lfloor 1/(b_2 - a_2) \rfloor$, $a_4 = \lfloor 1/(b_3 - a_3) \rfloor$, and so on. For each i, $b_i = 1/(b_{i-1} - a_{i-1})$ and $a_i = \lfloor b_i \rfloor$.

EXERCISE 18-6   Recall from Volume 1 that $x - \lfloor x \rfloor = \{x\}$, the fractional part of x. Simplify the above formulas using this notation.

18.4   Real Continued Fractions

We can easily extend the work of the previous section to writing down proper continued fractions for real numbers as well. For example, take $b_1 = \sqrt{2} = 1.4142\ldots$. We compute the coefficients in the same way as for a rational number: $a_1 = \lfloor b_1 \rfloor = 1$, $a_2 = \lfloor 1/(b_1 - a_1) \rfloor = \lfloor 2.4142\ldots \rfloor = 2$, and so on.

EXERCISE 18-7 Prove that the continued fraction expansion of an irrational number cannot terminate.

EXERCISE 18-8 Find the first few terms in the proper continued fraction expansion of $\pi = 3.14159265\ldots$ A calculator is handy, though not necessary.

EXERCISE 18-9 Develop a quick method to find terms of continued fractions on a calculator. Only a few steps should be necessary for each term.

The continued fraction for an irrational number is always infinite. If we consider the various fractions obtained by terminating the continued fraction at some point, these rational numbers will converge to the irrational number as the number of terms included increases. For example, we have

$$\sqrt{2} = 1 + \cfrac{1}{2 + \cfrac{1}{2 + \cfrac{1}{2 + \cdots}}}$$

as you should be able to verify fairly easily. If we terminate the continued fraction after the first 1, we get 1. After the first 2, we get $1 + \frac{1}{2} = 1.5$. After the second 2, we get $1\frac{2}{5} = 1.4$. After the third 2, $1\frac{5}{12} = 1.417$. And so on.

EXERCISE 18-10 Find the first few convergent fractions in the proper continued fraction for π which you wrote down in Exercise 18-8.

EXAMPLE 18-2 It's too difficult to prove here, but the continued fraction expansion of any irrational square root $\sqrt{n}$ is periodic. For example, let's compute the continued fraction for $\sqrt{17}$. We have $\lfloor \sqrt{17} \rfloor = 4 = a_1$; $\lfloor 1/.1231 \rfloor = \lfloor 8.1231 \rfloor = 8$ so $a_2 = 8$; $\lfloor 1/.1231 \rfloor = \lfloor 8.1231 \rfloor = 8$ so $a_3 = 8$; and so on. Thus the continued fraction expansion is

$$\sqrt{17} = 4 + \cfrac{1}{8 + \cfrac{1}{8 + \cfrac{1}{8 + \cdots}}},$$

which is periodic with period 1.

Convergents

The fraction obtained by cutting off a continued fraction after k steps are called the kth **convergent** C_k. For example, in the continued fraction for $\sqrt{17}$, $C_1 = 4$, $C_2 = 4 + \cfrac{1}{8} = \cfrac{33}{8}$, and $C_3 = 4 + \cfrac{1}{8 + \frac{1}{8}} = 4 + \cfrac{8}{65} = \cfrac{268}{65}$.

To get a handle on convergents, we can create two sequences P_k and Q_k such that $C_k = P_k/Q_k$ in lowest terms. Since $C_1 = a_1$, we immediately have $P_1 = a_1$ and $Q_1 = 1$. Similarly, since $C_2 = a_1 + \cfrac{1}{a_2} = \cfrac{a_2 a_1 + 1}{a_2}$, we have $P_2 = a_2 a_1 + 1$ and $Q_2 = a_2$. We won't prove it here, but it can be shown that for $k > 2$, we have the recursions

$$\begin{aligned} P_k &= a_k P_{k-1} + P_{k-2} \\ Q_k &= a_k Q_{k-1} + Q_{k-2}. \end{aligned}$$

EXAMPLE 18-3 The third convergent of a generic continued fraction is

$$C_3 = a_1 + \cfrac{1}{a_2 + \frac{1}{a_3}} = a_1 + \frac{a_3}{a_2 a_3 + 1} = \frac{a_1 a_2 a_3 + a_1 + a_3}{a_2 a_3 + 1},$$

yielding $P_3 = a_1 a_2 a_3 + a_1 + a_3 = a_3(a_2 a_1 + 1) + a_1 = a_3 P_2 + P_1$ and $Q_3 = a_3 a_2 + 1 = a_3 Q_2 + Q_1$.

EXERCISE 18-11 Prove that $P_k Q_{k+1} - P_{k+1} Q_k = (-1)^k$.

Problems to Solve for Chapter 18

301. Solve for $x > 0$:

$$e^{x^{e^{x^{e^{x^{\cdot^{\cdot^{\cdot}}}}}}}} = 2.$$

(MAΘ 1990)

302. Find $\displaystyle\sum_{k=1}^{11} c_k^2$, where

$$c_n = n + \cfrac{1}{2n + \cfrac{1}{2n + \dots}}.$$

(Mandelbrot #3)

303. Find the continued fraction expansion for a number of the form $\sqrt{k^2 + 1}$. What is its period?

304. Find the infinite continued fraction for the *golden ratio* $\phi = (1 + \sqrt{5})/2$ and the first five convergents.

305. Find the sum of A and B in simplest terms if

$$A = \sqrt{6 + 2\sqrt{5}} - \sqrt{6 - 2\sqrt{5}}$$

and

$$B = A - \cfrac{1}{A - \cfrac{1}{A - \frac{1}{A - \dots}}}.$$

Chapter 19

Probability

Many probability problems are merely a pair of counting problems: we count the number of possibilities and the number of desired outcomes and we're done. Many others are simple applications of multiplication. Both of these methods, as well as casework, are addressed at length in Volume 1. While some of the questions at the end of the chapter require these methods, we will concentrate primarily on new material here.

19.1 Review, Definitions, and Notation

The probability the event A occurs is written $P(A)$. Similarly, the probability that event A does *not* occur is $P(A')$, where A' is read 'not A.' (Sometimes 'not A' is written $\overline{A}$.) Since A either happens or it doesn't, $P(A) = 1 - P(A')$.

If we are given two events A and B, the probability that they *both* occur is $P(A \cap B)$, where the $\cap$ means 'and.' The probability that *at least one* of the events occurs is $P(A \cup B)$, where the $\cup$ means 'or.'

Two events are called **uncorrelated** (or **independent**) if they have no bearing on each other. For example, two consecutive flips of a coin are uncorrelated because the result of the second flip in no way depends on the first flip. The probability of two uncorrelated events both occurring is the product of the probabilities of each event, or

$$P(A \cap B) = P(A) \cdot P(B)$$

for uncorrelated events A and B.

Two events are called **mutually exclusive** if both events cannot *simultaneously* occur. Thus, rolling a 1 on a die and rolling a 2 on a die are mutually exclusive for a single roll, since we can't roll both a 1 and a 2 on the same roll. For mutually exclusive events, the probability of one or the other occurring is the sum of the probabilities of each of the two events, or

$$P(A \cup B) = P(A) + P(B).$$

Make sure you understand these results before you go on. Don't bog yourself down too much with symbols; let common sense be your guide. Probability is mostly about thinking, and using symbols excessively will often lead you astray.

19.2　Going a Step Further

Let's try applying the principles of the previous section to the following problem.

> *What is the probability of rolling an even number or a multiple of 3 on a single roll of a six-sided die?*

Since P(even number) = 3/6 = 1/2 and P(multiple of 3) = 2/6 = 1/3, we may think our desired probability is 1/2 + 1/3 = 5/6. We would be wrong. Applying counting principles to solve the problem, we have 4 desired outcomes {2, 3, 4, 6} out of 6 possible, for a probability of 4/6 = **2/3**. What happened?

We went wrong in adding the probabilities of the two events. We cannot do so because they are *not* mutually exclusive; a roll of 6 satisfies both categories and hence we cannot simply apply our addition principle. The problem can be solved in much the same way as we attacked similar problems in counting—using the Principle of Inclusion-Exclusion. The probability of either event A or event B occurring is the probability of A plus that of B *minus* the probability of both happening, or

$$P(A \cup B) = P(A) + P(B) - P(A \cap B).$$

EXERCISE 19-1　How does the above formula reduce to our simple addition rule if A and B are mutually exclusive events?

EXERCISE 19-2　Find a similar expression to the one above for $P(A \cup B \cup C)$.

19.3　Geometry and Probability

While probability and geometry seem to be on opposite ends of the mathematical spectrum, there are a couple classes of problems in which they go hand in hand. Most probability problems involving geometry are clearly geometry problems; the problem itself involves squares or circles or other figures. Other problems which require a geometric approach are far more subtle. As an example of the former type, consider the following problem.

> *A point is chosen at random inside a circle of radius 2. What is the probability that the point is within one unit of the center of the circle?*

First we draw the problem. The region of all possible points is circle A and the region of all desireable points is circle B. The probability is merely the ratio of the area of the desired region to the area of the possible region, or $\pi/4\pi = \mathbf{1/4}$.

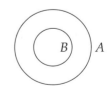

EXERCISE 19-3　A point is chosen at random inside a square which has side length 4. What is the probability that the point is within 1 inch of a side of the square?

In other problems, the necessity of geometry is much less apparent. Try this one:

> *A woman arrives at an airport between 11 and 12 o'clock. She waits for her husband for 10 minutes and if he doesn't arrive, she hails a taxi (and he's in a lot of trouble!). Her husband shows up at the airport at some time between 11 and 11:50. He waits for 20 minutes and if his wife hasn't shown up, he goes home (and he's in a lot of trouble!). What is the probability that the woman rides home with her husband?*

Try this problem before reading further; you'll find that our current library of methods are largely useless. Why? It's because we are dealing with continuous quantities rather than discrete (i.e. countable) ones. We can't investigate cases because there are infinitely many cases. For example, the man could show up at 11:01:52 or 11:01:53 or any other second, or millisecond, or *any* fraction of a second. This is our main clue to use geometry.

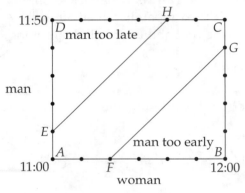

We can best describe all times between 11 and 12 o'clock by denoting 11:00 and 12:00 as two points on a number line and letting all points between represent times between 11 and 12. This is line AB in the diagram. If we plot the man's times (from 11:00 to 11:50) vertically (from A to D), we create a grid of all possible pairings of their arrival times. For example, point E represents the man arriving at 11:10 and the woman arriving at 11:00.

The space of all possible points is the rectangle $ABCD$. Now we must find all those points for which the woman meets her husband. Suppose the man arrives at 11:00. The woman can then arrive at any time from 11:00 to 11:20 and still meet her husband. Thus, the entire segment AF is in the desired region. (The circular points mark off 10 minute intervals.) If the man arrives x minutes after 11:00, the woman can arrive as late as $x + 20$ minutes after 11:00 and still meet her husband. This correlates to line FG in the figure. Similarly, she can arrive up to $x - 10$ minutes before her husband (since she'll wait for at most 10 minutes). This corresponds to EH in the diagram. The area above EH corresponds to the man arriving after the woman has left and the portion to the right of FG represents the man showing up too early and leaving. Make sure you see both of these.

If we let each 10 minute interval be a segment of length 1, so that $AD = 5$ and $AB = 6$, the area of the possible region is $[ABCD] = 30$ and that of the desired region is $[EAFGCH] = [ABCD] - [FBG] - [HDE] = 30 - 8 - 8 = 14$. Hence, our probability is $14/30 = \mathbf{7/15}$.

EXERCISE 19-4 Reread the previous problem. What does CG represent? How about CH? Do not proceed until you understand the problem entirely.

EXERCISE 19-5 Two numbers (not necessarily integers) are chosen at random between 0 and 10. What is the probabilty that they differ by no more than 5?

EXERCISE 19-6 How would the previous exercise change if it read 'Two integers are chosen...' instead?

Determining whether or not to use geometry is usually pretty easy. If the problem involves discrete choices, meaning that there are a countable number of cases, then graphing is not the right way to go. Graphing is useful for problems involving continuous quantities, such as arrival times or real numbers (as opposed to integers). The problems don't always involve areas; sometimes we use merely lengths or even volumes. Finally, take your time in determining the desired region; this is usually the most difficult part of the problem.

19.4 Conditional Probability

Welcome to Let's Make a Deal! In one of the boxes A, B, and C is $1,000,000$! Which box do you choose? You choose box C, a most splendid choice I must say. I'm going to help you out now. I'm gonna let you know one of the boxes which does not contain the money. I peek in the boxes and announce that box A does not contain the big bucks. Now, if you want to change and take box B, that's fine. What will you do, keep C or try B instead?

This is a loose formulation of the *Monty Hall problem*. At first glance, you might say that the money is equally likely to be in B or C, so changing doesn't help at all; however, consider the probability of winning this game. If you never change, the only way you win is that you chose the right box first, a 1/3 chance. If you change instead, you will always win if you pick a *wrong* box first, because after I expose one wrong box, the other unchosen box is a winner. Since you have a 2/3 chance of picking the wrong box initially, you have a 2/3 chance of winning *if you accept my offer to switch boxes*. Amazing, seems impossible, but true. Try the game on a few friends and convince yourself that it pays to change when given the option.

EXERCISE 19-7 Still not convinced? Suppose there are 1000 boxes. You pick one, and I name 998 of the boxes losers. Are you still going to stick with your choice or are you going to take the one unchosen box I conspicuously skipped over?

This is an example of **conditional probability**, in which we are given some known facts in addition to the basic problem. In the Monty Hall problem, the basic problem is choosing the right box, while the additional fact is knowing an unchosen box which does not have the money. Let's try another problem.

> *Suppose I have two cards, one with a blue side and a red side and the other with two red sides. I choose one at random and place it on the table. The top is red. What is the probability that the other side is also red?*

The answer is *not* 1/2! We must consider all cases which satisfy our given fact that the side we see is red. There are three, not two, cases: each side of the two sided red card (these are two different cases) and the one red side of the blue and red card. Clearly the third case will not be red on the other side, while each of the first two cases will reveal a red side when the card is flipped. Since each of the three cases is equally likely, our probability is **2/3** because we have 2 successes out of 3 possibilities.

Let's formalize our discussion a bit before proceeding. When we are asked to find the probability that event A occurs given that event B has occurred, we consider only those cases where B happens and find in what portion of those event A occurs as well. We write the probability that A happens, given that B is true, as $P(A|B)$. We can write

$$P(A|B) = \frac{P(A \cap B)}{P(B)},$$

since our desired probability is the ratio of the portion of cases where both A and B are true ($P(A \cap B)$) to the portion of cases in which B is true ($P(B)$). We don't always need to use this formula to solve conditional probability problems, but it is often very useful. Many problems can be solved by merely counting the number of cases in which B occurs and those in which both A and B occur as we did in the Monty Hall and card problems. WARNING: This simple counting approach only works if all cases are equally likely. Later in the chapter we will discuss an example in which we *must* use the formula rather than limiting our case search to those in which B is true.

Trying the formula on our card example, event B is 'a given side is red' and event A is 'both sides are red.' Thus, $P(A \cap B) = 1/2$ (since 1/2 of the cards with a red side have two red sides) and $P(B) = 3/4$ (since 3 out of 4 sides are red). Notice that we determine these two probabilities independently. Finally, we find $P(A|B) = (1/2)/(3/4) = 2/3$. Make sure you see the difference between $P(A \cap B)$ and $P(A|B)$. The former is the probability that a card with a red side has two red sides, while the latter is the probability that the both sides are red given that a *specific* side is red. The difference is subtle, but very significant.

Comparing our two methods of solving the card problem, we see that the formula for conditional probability allows us to find the probability with a few short computations rather than using casework. In many problems, such as the following example, the formula is much easier to use than casework.

EXAMPLE 19-1   Bag X has 5 white marbles and 2 black marbles. Bag Y has 3 white marbles and 5 black marbles. A bag is chosen at random and a marble taken from the bag. The marble is white; what is the probability that the bag was bag X?

Solution: Event B is 'the ball is white,' while event A is 'bag X is chosen.' Thus,

$$P(A \cap B) = P(\text{bag } X) \cdot P(\text{white ball from bag } X) = (1/2)(5/7) = 5/14.$$

For the probability of choosing a white ball, we must consider the mutually exclusive events of the ball coming from bag X and coming from bag Y. Thus,

$$P(B) = P(\text{white from } X) + P(\text{white from } Y) = \left(\frac{1}{2}\right)\left(\frac{5}{7}\right) + \left(\frac{1}{2}\right)\left(\frac{3}{8}\right) = \frac{61}{112}.$$

Hence, the probability that the bag was bag X given that the ball chosen is white is

$$P(A|B) = \frac{P(A \cap B)}{P(B)} = \frac{5/14}{61/112} = \frac{40}{61}.$$

WARNING: A very common mistake on problems like the previous example is to reason that there are 5 white marbles in bag X and 3 in bag Y, so the probability that the marble came from bag X is 5/8. This is NOT a sound argument because each marble is not equally likely to be chosen! (Why?) Don't make the same mistake. What if there were 7000 black marbles in bag X along with the 5 white ones? The likelihood that one of the white balls in bag X is chosen is now very, very small.

Perhaps geometry can help convince the skeptics. Considering our bags and balls, draw two congruent rectangles of area 1 to represent our bags. (The rectangles are equal because the bags are equally likely to be chosen.) Split the top rectangle, corresponding to bag X, into 7 equal rectangles, one for each ball. Similarly split the bottom rectangle, bag Y, into 8 rectangles. Shade rectangles corresponding to the black marbles. Then $P(A \cap B)/P(B)$ is the ratio of the white area in the top rectangle to the total white area, or

$$\frac{P(A \cap B)}{P(B)} = \frac{\frac{5}{7}}{\frac{5}{7} + \frac{3}{8}} = \frac{40}{61}.$$

Note that the small rectangles in the bottom do not equal those in the top. (What happens when there are 7000 black and 5 white marbles in bag X?) Remember, this is not a technique, but rather a tool to help you understand how conditional probability works.

EXERCISE 19-9   Suppose only one percent of the population has the disease mathphoberia. We design a test which diagnoses the disease successfully in afflicted patients 90% of the time. Unfortunately, 20% of the time it reports that the person has mathphoberia, when in fact they don't. The test reports that I have mathphoberia. What is the probability that the test is correct? How can we improve the accuracy of our testing procedure?

Conceptually, conditional probability can be very difficult to handle if it's new to you. Be skeptical; it took me quite a while to convince myself that conditional probability indeed 'works.'

Problems to Solve for Chapter 19

306. Find the probability that the ace of spades lies next to the jack of diamonds in an ordinary deck of 52 playing cards. (MAΘ 1991)

307. There are 4 black marbles and 2 white marbles in bag A. In bag B, there are 3 black and 5 white marbles. A bag is randomly chosen and a marble is chosen from the bag. The marble is black; what is the probability that it came from bag A? (MAΘ 1992)

308. In the World Series, two teams play each other repeatedly until one team has won a total of 4 games, then the Series ends. If each team is equally likely to win each game, what is the probability that the Series ends in exactly 6 games? (MAΘ 1992)

309. If three successive rolls of a die are all greater than three, what is the probability that they are all the same? (MAΘ 1990)

310. A circular coin of radius 1 cm. is dropped near the center of a chessboard (8 squares on a side) comprised of squares with sides of 2 cm. What is the probability that the coin lands so that it is entirely within one square? (That is, it may touch but not cross any of the lines.) A line is considered to have zero width. (MAΘ 1990)

311. If a number is selected at random from the set of all five-digit numbers in which the sum of the digits is equal to 43, what is the probability that this number will be divisible by 11? (AHSME 1970)

312. Three balls marked 1, 2, and 3 are placed in an urn. One ball is drawn, its number recorded, and then the ball is returned to the urn. This process is repeated and then repeated once more, and each ball is equally likely to be drawn on each occasion. If the sum of the numbers recorded is 6, what is the probabilty that the ball numbered 2 was drawn all three times? (AHSME 1983)

313. In an obscure card game, each player is dealt six cards from a standard deck of 52 cards. If a player receives exactly two fives, she wins. What is the probability of being dealt a winning hand? (Leave your answer as a product of combinations.) (MAΘ 1990)

314. A class contains 5 boys and 5 girls. For the class banquet, they select seats at random around a circular table that seats 10. What is the probability that some two girls will sit next to one another? (MAΘ 1991)

315. On the average, one-fifth of Alabamians are compulsive liars; the rest always tell the truth. Sam asks three Alabamians if it is raining, and all say yes. What is the probability that it is in fact raining? (Don't take offense; both of the authors are from 'Bama!) (Mandelbrot #3)

316. Some people play poker with two jokers in a 54-card deck. (The jokers are used as wild cards; they can represent any card.) Under these conditions what is the probability of being dealt five of a kind in a hand of five cards? (MAΘ 1990)

317. An integer is chosen at random from $\{x \mid 0 < x \le 500\}$. Find the probability that this integer is divisible by 7 or 11. (MAΘ 1991)

318. A screen covering the front of a fireplace has wires 1 mm in diameter, spaced in a mesh that has 5 mm square openings between the wires. A spark 2 mm in diameter pops out of the fire and heads directly toward the screen. What is the probability that the spark misses the wires? (MAΘ 1987)

319. If P is a point randomly placed on AB with a midpoint M, what is the probability that AP, PB, and AM can be made to form a triangle? (MAΘ 1991)

320. The amount 2.5 is split into two nonnegative real numbers uniformly at random, for instance, into 2.143 and .357, or into $\sqrt{3}$ and $2.5 - \sqrt{3}$. Then each number is rounded to its nearest integer, for instance, 2 and 0 in the first case above, 2 and 1 in the second. What is the probability that the two integers sum to 3? (AHSME 1987)

321. A point P is chosen at random in the coordinate plane. What is the probability that the unit circle with center P contains exactly two lattice points in its interior? (Mandelbrot #2)

322. Three points A, B, and C are selected at random on the circumference of a circle. Find the probability that the points lie on a semicircle. (MAΘ 1991)

323. Three numbers are chosen at random between 0 and 1. What is the probability that the difference between the greatest and the least is less than 1/3? (Mandelbrot #3)

Chapter 20

Find It and Make It

This chapter deals with locus and construction problems. These geometry problems are the true test of your knowledge of the very fundamentals of geometry, as the solutions to these problems rely on the basics which make geometry 'work.'

20.1   Locus

Just as a number which satisfies an equation is called a solution to the equation, the set of points which satisfies a set of criteria is called the **locus** of the criteria. One example of a locus is a circle; it is the set of all points in a plane equidistant from a given point. Before we move on to more difficult loci, we'll examine a few more simple examples like the circle.

Suppose we remove the 'in a plane' constraint on our set of points equidistant from a given point. The resulting locus is a sphere rather than a circle. Generally, there's a considerable difference between a three dimensional locus and two dimensional one. Most problems are two dimensional, and in this book you can assume the problem is two dimensional unless we state differently.

Now that we've done one point, let's try two. What is the locus of all points which are equidistant from two given points? That is, given points A and B, find all points C such that $AC = CB$. Clearly the midpoint of AB is one such point, but are there any others? If so, how can we describe them?

 Let M be the midpoint of AB and point C be a point such that $AC = BC$. By SSS congruency, we have $\triangle AMC \cong BMC$ so that $\angle AMC = \angle BMC$. Since AMB is a straight line, $\angle AMC = \angle BMC = 90°$. Hence any point C that satisfies $AC = BC$ is on the perpendicular bisector of AB. Does this mean that we can conclude that our desired locus is the perpendicular bisector of AB? NO! We've only proven that every point in the locus is on the perpendicular bisector; we have *not* proved that every point on the perpendicular bisector is in the locus. (Make sure you see the distinction.) Fortunately this is very easy to prove in the given problem. Again let M be the midpoint of AB, and let D be some point on the perpendicular bisector of AB. Since $DM = DM$, $AM = BM$, and $\angle AMD = \angle BMD$, we have $\triangle AMD \cong \triangle BMD$ and $AD = BD$. Hence, all points on the perpendicular bisector are in the locus. *Now* we can conclude that the locus is the perpendicular bisector of the segment.

Locus problems are two-part problems! Once we have decided that the locus is Γ (we often choose a symbol to represent the locus; capital Greek letters are often chosen for this because Greek letters are fun and lowercase ones usually stand for angles), we must prove that every point that satisfies the restrictions of the problem is on Γ, and then prove that every point on Γ satisfies the problem. Two parts; when doing a proof involving a locus you must not forget to do both.

Let's consider points equidistant from lines. In a plane, the set of points equidistant from a given line l is a pair of lines parallel to l. In space, the locus of points equidistant from a line becomes a cylinder. Stepping up to two lines, we find that the locus of points which are equidistant from non-parallel lines l and m is the pair of angle bisectors of the angles formed by l and m.

EXERCISE 20-1 Given lines l and m which intersect at O, prove that the locus of all points C such that the distances from C to l and m are the same is the pair of angle bisectors of the angles formed by l and m at O.

EXERCISE 20-2 What is the locus of all points in space equidistant from a given plane?

Although our introductory examples of locus problems are pretty simple, locus problems can get quite tough very quickly. Thus we'll talk about how to attack more difficult locus problems. First, play with the restraints of the problem until you can develop at least a guess of what the locus might be. This is best done by finding a few points (a simple sketch will do) on the locus. A pattern will usually emerge. Above, if we found a few points equidistant from A and B, we would find that the locus looked like a line. Once you have a guess, try to prove you are right. This is usually the hard part.

We'll show you how to develop this thought process by going through a few examples.

> *Let P be an interior point of a circle other than the center K. Take all chords of the circle which pass through P and determine their midpoints. What is the locus of these midpoints?* (AHSME 1975)

First let's find a few of these midpoints. Drawing the chord through P and K, we find that K is in the locus. Drawing the chord through P perpendicular to PK (i.e. a diameter), we find that P is in the locus (since a diameter perpendicular to a chord bisects the chord). If we sketch a few more points, the locus appears to be a curve of some sort. Remember this: if the locus appears to be a curve, it is very likely a circle or some portion thereof! After drawing a few more points, it seems our desired circle may be the circle with PK as its diameter.

We resort to fundamentals to prove our guess. Consider the shown chord with midpoint A. Recall that the perpendicular bisector of any chord of a circle passes through the center of the circle. Hence, the perpendicular through A passes through K. Since $\angle PAK = 90°$, $\angle PAK$ is inscribed in the semicircular arc $\overarc{PK}$. From this we see that any point on the locus is on the circle with diameter PK.

We must also show that any point on this circle is in the locus. Let A be any point on the circle. If we draw the chord BC through A perpendicular to AK, the line will pass through P (since the line is perpendicular to chord AK of the circle with diameter PK, it must also pass through P). Since the line through the center K is perpendicular to chord BC at A, it bisects BC. Hence, A is the midpoint of a chord which passes through P and thus is in our locus. We have finally completed our proof that the locus is the circle with diameter PK.

There are several lessons to take from this proof. First is the 'guess and prove' method we used: we experimented until we found what the locus was likely to be; then we proved what the locus was. Second, curved loci are usually circles or portions of circles. Finally, we saw a very effective method of proving a locus is a circle. We used the notion that all angles inscribed in the same arc are equal. In fact, we used this notion in reverse. We found a whole family of equal angles (in this case right angles like ∠*PAK*) whose sides intersect at *P* and *K*; we then deduced that the vertices of these angles must all be on the same circle. We will examine this concept further below.

EXAMPLE 20-1   If points *A* and *B* are fixed, find the locus of all points *C* such that ∠*ACB* = α, for some fixed angle α.

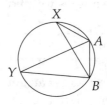

Solution: Consider points *X* and *Y* which are in the locus and on the same 'side' of *AB*. Since ∠*AXB* = ∠*AYB*, *X*, *Y*, *A*, and *B* are concyclic. Similarly, we can show that all points in the locus on the same 'side' of *AB* as *X* are on the same circle as *X*, *A*, and *B*. Proving the second part of our locus problem, that all the points on major arc $\overgroup{AXB}$ are in the locus, is pretty simple. Any point *Z* on this arc is such that ∠*AZB* = ∠*AXB* = α, so that *Z* is in the locus. Hence, we may be tempted to say that the circumcircle of △*AXB* is the locus. We would be wrong.

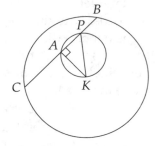

In the above diagram, points on minor arc $\overgroup{AB}$ are *not* in the locus. On that side of *AB*, we have another major arc as part of the locus and the whole locus is as shown at the right. Note that if α = 90°, the locus becomes the circle with diameter *AB*. (Why?)

WARNING: Always make sure you check all points on a circle to see if they are indeed in the locus; often one or more particular points will need to be omitted from the locus. In this example, our proof covers all points on the shown arcs *except A* and *B*. Taking these points into special consideration, we find that they are not in the locus. (Why?)

The method of equal inscribed angles is not the only useful method to prove that a locus is a circle. An equally useful and more fundamental technique is the very definition of a circle: prove that every point in the locus is equidistant from a given point. In the earlier example in the text we can do this by letting *M* (not shown) be the midpoint of *PK*. From right triangle *PAK*, since *AM* is the median to the hypotenuse *PK*, *AM* = *PM*. Similarly, all points on the locus are *PM* away from point *M*, so that the circle with radius *PM* and center *M* passes through all the points in the locus.

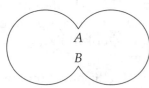

Stay patient with locus problems. Remember that most of your fundamental tools, even analytic geometry, can be useful, most notably all your knowledge about circles.

EXAMPLE 20-2   Points *A* and *B* are 5 units apart. How many lines in a given plane containing *A* and *B* are 2 units from *A* and 3 units from *B*? (AHSME 1990)

Solution: Any line which is two points away from *A* is tangent to the circle with radius 2 and center *A*. Likewise any line 3 units from *B* is tangent to the circle with radius 3 and center *B*. (This is a good way to view distances from points to lines in general.) Drawing the two circles, we note that the desired lines are those lines which are tangent to both circles. Since *AB* = 5, the circles are externally tangent, so there are only **3** common tangents.

EXERCISE 20-3 Segment *AB* is a fixed diameter of a circle whose center is *O*. From some point *C* on the circle, a chord *CD* is drawn perpendicular to *AB*. Let *P* be the intersection of the bisector of ∠*OCD* and the circle which is not point *C*. Find the locus of *P* as *C* covers all points on the circle except *A* and *B*. (AHSME 1951)

20.2   Construction

Like locus problems, constructions will make you use the fundamentals of geometry to do at first seemingly simple tasks which can grow more and more complex. Construction problems involve creating a specific figure using only a straightedge and a compass. Many sources, including this book, will use 'ruler' interchangibly with 'straightedge;' whichever tool you use, you cannot use it to make measurements. The ruler in construction problems is used only to make straight lines.

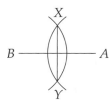

Like we did in the previous section, we'll start with the basics. How would you find the midpoint of a given segment with just a ruler and compass? (Remember, no measuring allowed!) Let the segment be *AB*. Use your compass to draw a circular arc with center *A* as shown and then draw a circle *with this same radius* and center *B*. Let the intersection points of these circles be *X* and *Y*. Since the original arcs were of equal circles, *X* and *Y* are midway between *A* and *B*. Hence, the intersection *XY* and *AB* is the midpoint of *AB*. (We also see that *XY* is the perpendicular bisector of *AB*.)

EXERCISE 20-4 With a real ruler and compass, execute this construction.

EXAMPLE 20-3 Construct the angle bisector of a given angle.

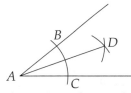

Solution: We'll take a very similar approach to the one we used to find the perpendicular bisector. Let *A* be the vertex of the angle. Draw an arc with center *A* intersecting the sides of the angle at *B* and *C*. Since the angle bisector is equidistant from the sides of the angle, we draw arcs of *equal* radius centered at *B* and *C*. Let the intersection of these arcs be *D*. We claim that *AD* is the angle bisector.

However, a claim isn't good enough; we have to prove it. Since they are radii of the same circle, *AC* = *AB*. As radii of equal circles, we have *BD* = *CD*. Since *AD* = *AD*, we then have △*ABD* ≅ △*ACD* by SSS congruency. Thus, we find ∠*BAD* = ∠*CAD*, and *AD* bisects ∠*BAC*. Like locus problems, constructions are two part problems: find and describe the construction, then prove that it works.

There is a certain battery of standard constructions which you need to know to attack construction problems. When working on more advanced problems, you can assume these basic construction methods work without proof. The authors strongly recommend that you actually do the constructions as we go.

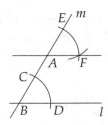

We'll start with parallel lines. Suppose we are given a line *l* and a point *A* through which we wish to draw a line parallel to *l*. We do this by using the angle equalities we know hold when parallel lines are cut by a transversal. Hence, we first draw any transversal *m* through *A* intersecting *l* at *B*. We make a parallel line by copying the angle formed by *m* and *l* at *B* to an angle at *A*.

To copy the angle, we first draw an arc centered at *B* which intersects *m* and *l* at *C* and *D* as shown. Draw an arc of equal radius with center *A* and let its intersection with *m* be *E*. We complete our copying by drawing an arc with center *E* and radius *CD*. This arc intersects the arc we drew with center *A* at point *F*. Since *AE* = *BC*, *AF* = *BD*, and *EF* = *CD*, we have copied △*BCD* at point *A*. Hence, ∠*EAF* = ∠*CBD* and *BD* ∥ *AF*. Remember this construction not only for the parallel line construction, but also for the method of copying an angle.

Perpendicular lines are a bit easier. First, for drawing a perpendicular to line *l* through a point *A* on line *l*, we draw a circle with center *A* and let the points where the circle intersects *l* be *B* and *C*. The perpendicular bisector of *BC* passes through *A* and is our desired line. Similarly, if we want a perpendicular line through point *D* not on line *m*, we draw a circle with center *D* that intersects line *m*. Call the intersection points *E* and *F*.

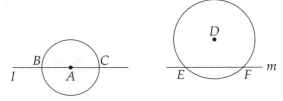

Again, the perpendicular bisector of *EF* is the desired perpendicular line through *D*. Since we know how to construct a perpendicular bisector, we know how to draw a perpendicular line.

The ruler and the compass are the tools of the trade, and the above methods are your primary weapons. Once you can complete the following exercise, you can learn how to attack almost any problem.

EXERCISE 20-5   Draw a triangle and construct its incenter, circumcenter, centroid, orthocenter, incircle, and circumcircle. *Don't go on until you can do this problem entirely.*

EXERCISE 20-6   Given a segment *AB*, construct a square with *AB* as one of its sides and another square with *AB* as one of its diagonals.

EXAMPLE 20-4   How would you construct a 45° angle?

Solution: Construct a square as in the previous exercise, then draw a diagonal. The diagonal forms 45° angles with the sides.

EXERCISE 20-7   Given a segment of length 1, construct a segment of length $\sqrt{17}$.

When solving more difficult construction problems, your initial tool should be your brain and perhaps your pencil. Leave the compass and ruler alone until you make some headway in solving the problem. Construction problems are geometry problems first, drawing problems second.

One very important technique in attacking constructions is that of *relaxing a constraint*. In introducing this concept, we will solve a problem used by Samuel Vandervelde to introduce constructions for the 1993-94 Mandelbrot Competition.

> Given △*ABC*, with ∠*C* obtuse, construct a square *PQRS* such that *P* and *Q* are on *AB*, *R* is on *BC*, and *S* is on *AC*.

After staring at the problem for a while as written, nothing stands out.

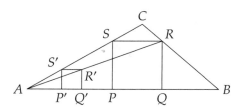

Let's try an easier problem instead, that of constructing a square with three of the vertices on △ABC. We *relax the constraint* that R be on BC. Let P'Q'R'S' be a square such that P' and Q' are on AB and S' is on AC.

We construct this square by picking a point S' on AC and drawing a perpendicular line to AB which meets AB at P'. The side of the square then has length P'S'. Construct the rest of the square as in Exercise 20-6. If we construct a bunch of these squares, we'll see that the upper right corners (the R''s) appear collinear. Let's see. Continue AR' to meet BC at R and draw rectangle PQRS by drawing RS ∥ AB and RQ and SP perpendicular to AB. From the many parallel lines in the diagram, we have △AS'R' ~ △ASR and △R'Q'A ~ △RQA. Hence,

$$\frac{RQ}{R'Q'} = \frac{RA}{R'A} = \frac{RS}{R'S'}.$$

Since S'R' = R'Q', we have RS = RQ and rectangle PQRS is a square. Thus, by relaxing a constraint (that R be on BC), we have found a construction: choose any point S' on AC and draw the perpendicular to AB meeting AB at P'. Use S'P' to complete the construction of square P'Q'R'S'. Draw ray AR' to find R on BC, then construct PQRS by drawing lines through R parallel and perpendicular to AB.

Notice how in this construction we have used many of our basic geometry tools. As you become more proficient at constructions, you will add more elementary constructions to your arsenal, which you can then employ with little brain-racking. These basic constructions include the construction of squares, special angles (such as 60° or 30°), equilateral triangles, and other regular polygons.

EXAMPLE 20-5 Find four points on segment AB which divide AB into five segments of equal length.

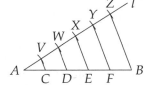

Solution: There's no clear way to split the segment into 5 equal pieces, but we can create a new segment AZ chopped into five equal pieces by drawing line l through A and making five equal arcs as shown. We first draw a circle with center A and arbitrary radius AV. We then draw a circle with center V and radius AV, thus finding W. Going on, we find X, Y, and Z, as well. Now we have a segment, AZ, which is divided into 5 equal segments. We use this to split AB into 5 equal parts by drawing ZB, then constructing lines parallel to ZB through Y, X, W, and V. The intersections of these lines with AB form the desired points.

We prove that this construction works by noting that

$$△ACV ~ △ADW ~ △AEX ~ △AFY ~ △ABZ.$$

Since AV = VW = WX = XY = YZ, we deduce that AC = CD = DE = EF = FB, as desired.

EXERCISE 20-8 How can we adapt the construction in the previous example to find point P on AB such that AP/PB = p/q for any pair of integers (p, q)?

Once again, don't reach for your ruler and compass as soon as you see a construction problem. Treat it like a geometry problem, find the solution, then break out the toys to see if your method works. Constructions are a lot of fun and can be wonderfully challenging. As you continue your study in geometry, keep the challenge of construction always in your mind; every once in a while you will stumble on a diagram whose construction may very well be more interesting than the intended problem or lesson.

Problems to Solve for Chapter 20

324. What is the locus of the vertices of all possible triangles that have the same base and a fixed area? (MAΘ 1991)

325. Giovanni finds a treasure map on which a large circle is drawn. Written on the map is the inscription, "Ye shall find the great treasure buried at the center of the circle!!" Unfortunately, the center is not marked on the map. How can Giovanni find the treasure without digging hundreds of holes?

326. Construct an equilateral triangle.

327. What is the locus of the centers of all circles of given radius a, in the same plane, passing through a fixed point? (AHSME 1960)

328. How many points are equidistant from a circle and two parallel tangents to the circle? (AHSME 1969)

329. Construct a 30° angle.

330. How did Bob manage to fill exactly 9 liters of water into his 12 liter rectangular box aquarium using only one chalk mark on the edge of the aquarium as a measuring tool? (i.e. Bob has no way of measuring volumes of water, he must use his geometric intuition.) (M&IQ 3)

331. Given a circle and its center, construct an equilateral triangle inscribed in the circle.

332. Consider triangle ABC with base AB fixed in length and position. As the vertex C moves on a straight line, what is the locus of the centroid of the triangle? (AHSME 1962)

333. What is the locus of the midpoint of a line segment that is drawn from a given external point P to a given circle with center O and radius r? (AHSME 1954)

334. In circle O, G is a moving point on diameter AB. AA' is drawn perpendicular to AB and equal to AG. BB' is drawn perpendicular to AB, on the same side of diameter AB as AA', and equal to BG. Let O' be the midpoint of $A'B'$. Then, as G moves from A to B, what is the locus of O'? (AHSME 1957)

335. Given three non-collinear points A, B, C, construct a circle with center C such that the tangents from A and B to the circle are parallel. (Canada 1970)

336. Let AC be a given segment in the plane. What is the set of all points B in the plane not on line AC such that $\angle ABC > \angle BAC$? (Mandelbrot #2)

337. Point A is on circle Γ, point G is inside this circle. Construct points B and C on Γ such that G is the centroid of $\triangle ABC$. (M&IQ 1992)

338. Prove that the locus of all points which have the same power with respect to two given circles is a straight line. Remember that the power of a point P with respect to a circle O is found by drawing a line through P intersecting circle O at X and Y. The power of point P is then $(PX)(PY)$.

339. In any triangle there is a point X which is the point of intersection of three circles of equal radii, each of which is internally tangent to two sides of a given triangle. Describe a method by which X may be constructed (by ruler and compass alone!). (USAMTS 2)

340. Let A, B be adjacent vertices of a regular n-gon ($n \geq 5$) in the plane having center O. A triangle XYZ, which is congruent to and initially coincides with OAB, moves rigidly in the plane in such a way that Y and Z each trace out the whole boundary of the polygon, X remaining inside the polygon. Find the locus of X. (IMO 1986)

the BIG PICTURE

Constructions were a special fascination for the ancient Greeks. Pursuing solutions of construction problems led them to much of the geometry they discovered, and they were very successful in solving those constructions.

It was thus all the more galling not to be able to achieve certain seemingly simple constructions. Three problems particularly remained out of reach. One: given a cube, construct another cube with twice the volume, or **doubling the cube**. Two: given a circle, construct a square with the same area, or **squaring the circle**. Three: given any angle, trisect it, or **trisecting the angle**.

The Greeks had good reason to think these problems were solvable, because all follow in an obvious manner from very simple constructions. For example, doubling a square is quite easy: if the square has side s, take the diagonal (length $\sqrt{2}\,s$) as the side of a new square with area $2s$. Similarly, bisecting an angle is a simple task, as is triangling a square.

However, no Greek was able to solve any of the problems, nor was anyone else up to the 1800's. At that time, all three constructions were shown to be impossible. How? Pierre Wantzel, a French civil engineer, showed in 1837 that given a reference segment of length 1, a length is constructible if and only if it is the root of an unfactorable rational polynomial whose degree is a power of 2. Thus $\sqrt{2}$, the side of a doubled square, is constructible since it is a root of $x^2 = 2$, with degree 2. On the other hand $\sqrt[3]{2}$, the side of a doubled cube, cannot be constructed since it is a root of $x^3 = 2$, of degree 3.

If a general angle can be trisected, then a 60° angle can be trisected. Trisecting such an angle gives a 20° angle, which can then be made to give a segment of length $\cos 20°$, by creating a right triangle with hypotenuse 1 and one angle 20°. Doubling this segment, a trivial operation, would then yield a segment of length $2\cos 20°$. However, this length is not constructible since it satisfies the unfactorable equation $x^3 - 3x - 1 = 0$, of degree 3. (Prove this with basic trig operations.) Thus a 60° angle can't be trisected, so a general angle certainly can't either (though certain special angles, like 90°, can).

For the circle-squaring, we would need a square with side $\sqrt{\pi}$, assuming the radius of the circle was 1. The number $\sqrt{\pi}$ was later shown to be **transcendental**, meaning it satisfies *no* polynomial with rational coefficients. Thus $\sqrt{\pi}$ certainly can't satisfy a polynomial with rational coefficients whose degree is a power of 2, so the circle can't be squared. The three famous Greek problems all turned out to have no solution.

Chapter 21

Collinearity and Concurrency

21.1 Three Points and a Line

A•

B•   C•

D•

E•

F•

How many points do we need to draw a line? Easy, two. What if we have three points? How can we tell if all three are on the same line or not? Sometimes it's very easy; for example, the points A, B, and C in the diagram at left are clearly not on the same line. However, in some cases it is not so clear. Points D, E, and F may be **collinear**, meaning all on the same line, but they may not. Just as 1.414 is not quite $\sqrt{2}$, "they look collinear" is not the same "they are collinear." In this section we examine techniques to prove three points are collinear.

There are many ways to prove that three points are collinear. We'll start with a method we mentioned in Volume 1. On shown segment AC, $AB + BC = AC$ if and only if point B is on segment AC. This method is clearly most useful for problems involving lengths.

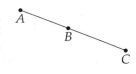

EXERCISE 21-1 Prove that point B is on segment AC if and only if $AB + BC = AC$.

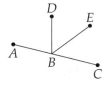

Another collinearity method borrowed from the very basics of geometry is the fact that a straight angle has a measure of 180°. In the diagram, point B is on AC if and only if

$$\angle ABD + \angle DBC = 180°.$$

We don't have to split this into just two angles; we could use point E as well, for which we need

$$\angle ABD + \angle DBE + \angle EBC = 180°$$

to ensure collinearity. Despite its simplicity, this method is very useful.

EXAMPLE 21-1 Given two lines l and m which are tangent to circle O at X and Y, prove that O, X, and Y are collinear if and only if $l \parallel m$.

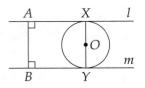

Solution: Points X, Y, and O are collinear if and only if $\angle XOY = 180°$. Suppose l and m are not parallel and intersect at some point Z. Then $ZXOY$ is a quadrilateral whose interior angles must have sum 360°. Since $\angle OXZ = \angle OYZ = 90°$, we must have $\angle XOY + \angle XZY = 180°$. The condition $\angle XZY \neq 0°$ implies $\angle XOY < 180°$, so X, O, and Y cannot be on the same line if l and m are not parallel. If l and m are parallel, draw segment AB as shown. Adding the angles of pentagon $ABYOX$ and setting the sum equal to 540°, we find $\angle YOX = 180°$, so that Y, O, and X are collinear.

In this problem, the result is fairly obvious; however, in many, and perhaps most, the result will not be so obvious and you will have to make very accurate diagrams to convince yourself that it is indeed true. And you'll need even more accurate proofs to convince everyone else!

EXERCISE 21-2 Given line AC and point B on the line, show that points D, E, and B in the diagram are collinear if and only if $\angle DBA = \angle EBC$. This is yet another simple result borrowed from basic geometry: the notion that vertical angles are equal. Can it also be used to prove collinearity?

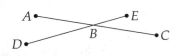

EXAMPLE 21-2 Consider point P on the circumcircle of $\triangle ABC$. Let points D, E, and F be the feet of the perpendicular segments drawn from P to AB, AC, and BC, respectively (where the sides are extended if necessary). Prove that D, E, and F are collinear. The line through these points is called the **Simson line** of point P with respect to $\triangle ABC$.

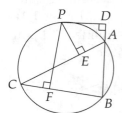

Proof: We will prove that D, E, and F are collinear by showing that $\angle DEA = \angle FEC$ and then using the result of the prior exercise. First, since P is on the circumcircle of $\triangle ABC$,

$$\angle APC = 180° - \angle B.$$

Look closely at quadrilaterals $ADPE$, $PFBD$, and $PEFC$. All three quadrilaterals are cyclic, the first two because they have opposite angles which sum to 180° and the last because $\angle PEC = \angle PFC$. Remember, lots of perpendicular lines usually means lots of cyclic quadrilaterals! From quadrilateral $PDBF$,

$$\angle DPF = 180° - \angle B = \angle APC.$$

Removing the shared angle $\angle APF$ from these two equal angles leaves $\angle FPC = \angle APD$. From quadrilaterals $ADPE$ and $EPCF$, we find

$$\angle FEC = \angle FPC = \angle APD = \angle AED,$$

from which we deduce that D, E, and F are collinear. Challenge: can you prove that the feet of the altitudes from P to the sides of $\triangle ABC$ are collinear *only* if P is on the circumcircle of $\triangle ABC$?

The next two techniques for proving collinearity involve slightly more advanced methods. The first method relies upon the use of vectors and the second was brought to us by Menelaus of Alexandria, who used it well over 1800 years ago.

The use of vectors in proving collinearity is very simple, so if you understand vectors, you can easily add this to your arsenal. Choose an arbitrary origin O. Let the vectors from O to the points X, Y, and Z be $\vec{x}$, $\vec{y}$, and $\vec{z}$, respectively. If $\vec{y} - \vec{x}$ and $\vec{z} - \vec{x}$ are in the same direction, then X, Y and Z are collinear. (Why?)

EXERCISE 21-3 How can we tell if $\vec{y} - \vec{x}$ and $\vec{z} - \vec{x}$ are in the same direction?

EXERCISE 21-4 What happens if we choose X to be the origin? Does this simplify our problem?

Now we have reached **Menelaus's Theorem**, which states that if X, Y, and Z on the sides BC, CA, and AB (extended if necessary) of $\triangle ABC$ are collinear, then

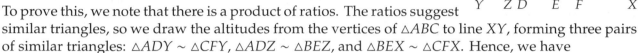

$$\frac{AZ}{BZ} \cdot \frac{BX}{CX} \cdot \frac{CY}{AY} = 1.$$

To prove this, we note that there is a product of ratios. The ratios suggest similar triangles, so we draw the altitudes from the vertices of $\triangle ABC$ to line XY, forming three pairs of similar triangles: $\triangle ADY \sim \triangle CFY$, $\triangle ADZ \sim \triangle BEZ$, and $\triangle BEX \sim \triangle CFX$. Hence, we have

$$\frac{CY}{AY} = \frac{CF}{AD}, \quad \frac{AZ}{BZ} = \frac{AD}{BE}, \quad \text{and} \quad \frac{BX}{CX} = \frac{BE}{CF}.$$

Multiplying these gives the desired relation. To prove the converse, that the relation in the theorem implies that X, Y, and Z are collinear, we introduce Isaac Newton's concept of directed segments. In using directed segments ratios of segments on the same line are given a sign, positive or negative, depending on whether or not the segments 'point' in the same direction. For example, AB/ZB is considered positive since $\overrightarrow{AB}$ and $\overrightarrow{ZB}$ are in the same direction while AB/BZ is negative because $\overrightarrow{AB}$ and $\overrightarrow{BZ}$ are in opposite directions. (Don't get too wrapped up in the notion of directed segments. We'll only use it for this proof.)

EXERCISE 21-5 Some sources quote Menelaus's Theorem using the expression

$$\frac{AZ}{ZB} \cdot \frac{BX}{XC} \cdot \frac{CY}{YA} = -1.$$

How can this be?

Moving on to our proof, we will show that YZ and BC intersect at the point X which satisfies Menelaus's Theorem. Let this intersection point be X', where X is a point on BC that, along with Y and Z on AC and AB respectively, satisfies

$$\frac{BX}{CX} \cdot \frac{CY}{AY} \cdot \frac{AZ}{BZ} = 1.$$

Since Y and Z are on AC and AB, and X' is on both YZ and BC, we also have

$$\frac{BX'}{CX'} \cdot \frac{CY}{AY} \cdot \frac{AZ}{BZ} = 1.$$

Combining these we find

$$\frac{BX}{CX} = \frac{BX'}{CX'}.$$

If these ratios both equal 1, then we are done, since the above equality will then imply that X and X' are both the midpoint of BC. If the constant ratio is not 1, then we have another problem.

EXERCISE 21-6   Ignoring the notion of directed segments, prove that if $c \neq 1$ and $c > 0$ then there are two points X' on BC such that $BX'/CX' = c$.

EXERCISE 21-7   Now let's use directed segments. Prove that there is only one point X' such that $BX'/CX' = c$, where c is any real number.

Applying the previous exercises to $BX/CX = BX'/CX'$, we deduce that X and X' must be the same point. Thus, if X, Y, and Z satisfy Menelaus's Theorem, then they are collinear.

This converse is a useful tool in proving collinearity. Problems involving lengths, ratios (similar triangles or power of a point), and diagrams which are similar to the one on page 235 (this is often the biggest tip-off) are excellent candidates for Menelaus's Theorem.

EXAMPLE 21-3   Let I be the intersection of angle bisectors BY and CZ and let X the foot of the angle bisector of $\angle A$. Use Menelaus's Theorem and the Angle Bisector Theorem to prove that A, I, and X are collinear.

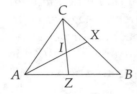

Proof: Although we discussed a much less complicated way to prove this fact in Volume I, this is an excellent exercise in the use of Menelaus's Theorem. The diagram shown is very suggestive. To use Menelaus, we must show that

$$\frac{CX}{BX} \cdot \frac{BA}{ZA} \cdot \frac{ZI}{CI} = 1,$$

where A, I, and X are the points on the sides of $\triangle ZBC$. From the Angle Bisector Theorem, we have $CX/BX = AC/AB$ (since X is the foot of the angle bisector from A) and $ZI/CI = BZ/BC$ (since BI bisects $\angle CBZ$ of $\triangle BZC$). Hence

$$\frac{CX}{BX} \cdot \frac{BA}{ZA} \cdot \frac{ZI}{CI} = \frac{AC}{AB} \cdot \frac{BA}{ZA} \cdot \frac{BZ}{BC} = \frac{(AC)(BZ)}{(BC)(AZ)} = 1,$$

where this last equality is a result of the Angle Bisector Theorem applied to bisector CZ, from which $AC/BC = AZ/BZ$. Thus A, I, and X are collinear.

 EXERCISE 21-8   Why can't we use $ZI/CI = AZ/AC$ from the Angle Bisector Theorem applied to bisector AI of triangle ACZ as a step in the last example?

21.2   Three Lines and a Point

Any group of three or more lines which pass through the same point are called **concurrent**. Some important examples of concurrent lines were discussed in Volume 1 when we introduced the angle bisectors, the perpendicular bisectors, the medians, and the altitudes of a triangle. In showing the concurrency of some of these, we used a couple very basic techniques which we'll now quickly review.

In working with angle bisectors and perpendicular bisectors, we used the most elementary technique: we showed that due to the properties of the circumcenter (its being equidistant from the three vertices), it must be on each of the three perpendicular bisectors. We showed a similar proof for the angle bisectors. For the medians, we used analytic geometry. This approach is usually very algebraic and should be avoided if possible. In this section we'll develop a technique similar to Menelaus's Theorem that will more easily prove that the medians are concurrent.

First, however, we'll look at using our collinearity techniques to prove concurrency. Suppose we wish to show that lines *AB*, *CD*, and *EF* are concurrent. Rather than viewing this as a concurrency problem, we can let *I* be the intersection of *CD* and *EF* and prove that *A*, *B*, and *I* are collinear. Hence, all three lines pass through *I*. Once we've changed our concurrency problem to a collinearity one, we can apply all of the techniques from the previous section.

EXAMPLE 21-4 Prove that the altitudes of a triangle are concurrent.

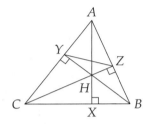

Proof: Let *H* be the intersection of altitudes *CZ* and *BY*. Connect *A* to *H* and draw the altitude from *H* to *X*. We wish to show that *A*, *H*, and *X* are collinear, so that *AX* is a straight line through *H* perpendicular to *BC*. We will do this by showing that $\angle CAH = 90° - \angle ACX$, then setting the sum of the interior angles of quadrilateral *AHXC* equal to 360°, thus finding that $\angle AHX = 180°$. First note that $\angle YBC = 90° - \angle ACB$. Now we need to show that $\angle CAX = \angle YBC$. Lots of perpendicular lines means cyclic quadrilaterals! Since $\angle CYB = \angle CZB$, quadrilateral *YZBC* is cyclic, so

$$\angle CZY = \angle YBC.$$

Since $\angle AYB + \angle AZC = 180°$, *AYHZ* is cyclic and

$$\angle CAH = \angle YAH = \angle HZY = \angle CZY = \angle YBC = 90° - \angle ACX.$$

As we mentioned before, we can now set the sum of the interior angles of quadrilateral *AHXC* equal to 360° to determine that $\angle AHX = 180°$. Thus, the altitudes of any triangle are concurrent.

EXERCISE 21-9 In the previous problem, we went to seemingly great lengths to prove $\angle HAC = 90° - \angle ACX$. Why can't we just argue that from right triangle *AXC*, $\angle HAC = 90° - \angle ACX$?

EXERCISE 21-10 Use one of our collinearity methods to prove that the medians of a triangle are concurrent.

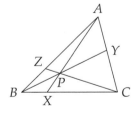

We've saved the best for last; we are now ready for **Ceva's Theorem**. The importance of this theorem is reflected in the fact that lines from a vertex of a triangle to the opposite side of the triangle are called **cevians** in honor of Giovanni Ceva, who first proved the theorem. The theorem, which closely resembles Menelaus's Theorem, states that if cevians *AX*, *BY*, and *CZ* of △*ABC* are concurrent, then

$$\frac{AZ}{ZB} \cdot \frac{BX}{XC} \cdot \frac{CY}{YA} = 1.$$

To prove Ceva's Theorem, we use a couple of concepts we learned in Volume 1. First, the ratio of the bases of two triangles with equal altitudes equals the ratio of the areas of the triangles. Second, if $a/b = c/d$, then $a/b = c/d = (a - c)/(b - d)$. (If these are new to you, prove them before proceeding.)

Now we interpret one of the ratios in terms of areas:

$$\frac{AZ}{ZB} = \frac{[ACZ]}{[BCZ]} = \frac{[ZAP]}{[ZBP]} = \frac{[ACZ] - [ZAP]}{[BCZ] - [ZBP]} = \frac{[APC]}{[BPC]}.$$

Similarly, we determine that

$$\frac{BX}{XC} = \frac{[BAP]}{[APC]} \quad \text{and} \quad \frac{CY}{YA} = \frac{[BPC]}{[BAP]}.$$

Multiplying these three relations gives the desired result and completes the proof of Ceva's Theorem.

The most useful aspect of Ceva's Theorem is its converse, which states that if cevians AX, BY, and CZ satisfy

$$\frac{AZ}{ZB} \cdot \frac{BX}{XC} \cdot \frac{CY}{YA} = 1,$$

then they are concurrent.

EXERCISE 21-11 Prove the converse of Ceva's Theorem using exactly the same technique we used to prove Menelaus's Theorem.

EXERCISE 21-12 Why do you think some sources quote Menelaus's Theorem as we showed in Exercise 21-5?

EXAMPLE 21-5 Prove that AD, BE, and CF are concurrent if and only if

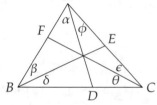

$$(\sin \alpha)(\sin \delta)(\sin \epsilon) = (\sin \beta)(\sin \theta)(\sin \phi),$$

where all angles are as measured in the diagram.

Proof: Seeing sines, we think to use the law of sines. Seeing concurrency and products of three quantities, we think of Ceva's Theorem. Hence, we use the law of sines to relate the angles in the diagram to the lengths which appear in Ceva's Theorem. Applying the law of sines to $\triangle ADB$ gives $\sin \alpha / BD = \sin B / AD$, so that $\sin \alpha = (\sin B)(BD/AD)$. Doing the same for the other 5 angles in our desired equation, the equation becomes

$$\frac{BD \sin B}{AD} \cdot \frac{EC \sin C}{BE} \cdot \frac{AF \sin A}{CF} = \frac{AE \sin A}{BE} \cdot \frac{BF \sin B}{CF} \cdot \frac{CD \sin C}{AD}.$$

Cancelling like crazy and dividing by $(AE)(BF)(CD)$, we have

$$\frac{BD}{CD} \cdot \frac{EC}{AE} \cdot \frac{AF}{BF} = 1,$$

so we have shown that the expression in Ceva's Theorem is equivalent to our expression in sines in the given problem. Hence

$$(\sin \alpha)(\sin \delta)(\sin \epsilon) = (\sin \beta)(\sin \theta)(\sin \phi)$$

is a necessary and sufficient condition for concurrency. We'll call this the sine form or the angle form of Ceva's Theorem.

EXAMPLE 21-6 Prove that the altitudes of any triangle are concurrent.

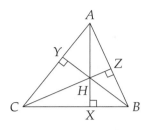

Proof: From right triangle ACX, $CX = AC \cos C$. If we do the same for each of the other 5 segments which appear in Ceva's Theorem, we find

$$\frac{AZ}{ZB} \cdot \frac{BX}{XC} \cdot \frac{CY}{YA} = \frac{AC \cos A}{BC \cos B} \cdot \frac{AB \cos B}{AC \cos C} \cdot \frac{BC \cos C}{AB \cos A} = 1,$$

so by Ceva's Theorem, the altitudes must be concurrent. The point of concurrency, the **orthocenter**, is usually called H as in the diagram.

EXERCISE 21-13 Use Ceva's Theorem to show that the medians of any triangle are concurrent. Do the same for the angle bisectors.

Ceva's Theorem is an extremely useful technique to prove concurrency. It is obviously most useful in problems involving triangles, so whenever you have a concurrency problem involving cevians, try using Ceva's Theorem and the many tools you know to evaluate ratios of lengths (trigonometry, similar triangles, the Angle Bisector Theorem, and so on). Like Menelaus's Theorem, it's pretty obvious when to use Ceva; however, it's sometimes challenging to show that the product of the ratios is unity.

Problems to Solve for Chapter 21

341. Suppose that in the diagram, $\alpha = \theta$, $\beta = \epsilon$, and $\delta = \phi$. Prove that in this case AD, BE, and CF are the altitudes of $\triangle ABC$ and use the sine form of Ceva's Theorem to show that the altitudes are concurrent.

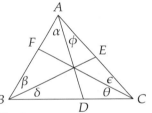

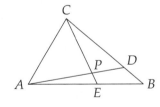

342. In triangle ABC, lines CE and DA are drawn so that

$$\frac{CD}{DB} = \frac{3}{1} \quad \text{and} \quad \frac{AE}{EB} = \frac{3}{2}.$$

Let $r = CP/PE$, where P is the intersection point of CE and AD. Find r.
(AHSME 1963)

343. Let points D, E, and F be on sides BC, AC, and AB, respectively. Let point D' be on BC such that D' is on the line formed by reflecting line AD through the angle bisector of $\angle A$, and similarly define BE' and CF'. Prove that if AD, BE, and CF are concurrent, then so are the lines AD', BE', and CF'.
(Mandelbrot #2)

344. Let CH be the altitude in the acute triangle ABC. The points X, Z, and Y lie on the lines CA, CH, and CB, respectively, in such a manner that $AX = AC$, $BY = BC$, and $HZ = HC$. Prove that X, Y, and Z are collinear.
(M&IQ 1992)

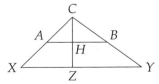

345. Point D is chosen on side BC of $\triangle ABC$ such that the incircles of $\triangle ACD$ and $\triangle ABD$ are tangent at G. (Mandelbrot #1)

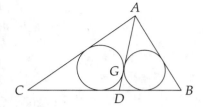

    i. Let line *l* be the angle bisector of ∠*ABC*, line *m* be the angle bisector of ∠*ACB*, and line *n* be the perpendicular to *BC* at point *D*. Prove that lines *l*, *m*, and *n* are concurrent.

    ii. In △*ABC*, suppose that points *H* and *I* are defined on segments *AC* and *AB* in the same manner as *D* was defined on *BC* above. Prove that the lines *AD*, *BH*, and *CI* are concurrent.

346. Prove that the lines through *A* and the incenter of △*ABC*, through *B* and the circumcenter of △*ABC*, and through *C* and the orthocenter of △*ABC* are concurrent if and only if $\cos^2 A = (\cos B)(\cos C)$. (Mandelbrot #2)

347. Prove that the orthocenter, the centroid, and the circumcenter of any triangle are collinear. This line is called the **Euler line** of the triangle. Prove also that the distance from the centroid to the orthocenter is twice its distance from the circumcenter.

348. Three circles are drawn which intersect pairwise as shown. Prove that *AD*, *BE*, and *CF* are concurrent.

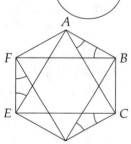

349. Given a triangle *ABC* and external points *X*, *Y*, and *Z* such that ∠*BAZ* = ∠*CAY*, ∠*CBX* = ∠*ABZ*, and ∠*ACY* = ∠*BCX*, prove that *AX*, *BY*, and *CZ* are concurrent. (IMO 1985)

350. The convex hexagon *ABCDEF* is such that angles *ABF*, *BAC*, *ECD*, *BDC*, *AEF*, and *EFD* all have equal measure. Prove that sides *AF*, *DE*, and *BC* have equal length. (MOP)

Chapter 22

Geometry Tidbits

This chapter contains several advanced concepts in geometry problem solving. Rather than put little
needles all over the chapter, we warn you now that most of this chapter is quite challenging.

22.1   Projections

In Volume 1 we discussed distortions, in which we stretched a figure in one dimension. We found that a distortion doesn't preserve length or area, but it does preserve *ratios* of lengths (in the same direction) and areas. For example, if triangle ABC is distorted to make $AB'C'$ as shown, we don't have $[ABC] = [AB'C']$; however, $[ABC]/[ABD] = [AB'C']/[AB'D']$.

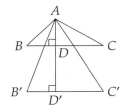

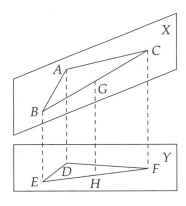

A **projection** is very similar to a distortion; in a projection, we map a figure in one plane into a figure in another plane. In the simplest type of projection, we project $\triangle ABC$ in plane X onto $\triangle DEF$ in plane Y by pretending that there is a large 'sun' directly above the planes such that $\triangle DEF$ is the 'shadow' of $\triangle ABC$. Thus, AD is perpendicular to plane Y, as are CF and BE. Because of these perpendicularities, this type of projection is called an **orthogonal projection**. To better understand orthogonal projections, draw a triangle on a clear piece of plastic or glass with a thick marker. Go outside when the sun is overhead and see what kind of shadows the triangle makes as you move it around. You should notice that the results of an orthogonal projection are exacly the same as a distortion.

As with distortions, orthogonal projections do not preserve lengths but they do preserve ratios of lengths and ratios of areas. For example, in our figure, $BG/GC = EH/HF$ and $[ABG]/[AGC] = [DEH]/[DHF]$. This preservation of ratios of lengths can be seen by first raising plane Y until point B coincides with point E. The similar triangles BGH and BCF will then give the desired result.

EXERCISE 22-1   Note in the diagram that the lengths whose ratio is preserved are lengths of segments with the same orientation. Construct an example to show that if two coplanar segments do not have the same orientation, then their projections do not necessarily have the same ratio as the original segments.

EXERCISE 22-2 Must we make similar orientation restrictions for the ratio of areas?

Now the important question: what good are orthogonal projections? The answer to this is the preservation of ratios. Using this property, we can project complicated figures into simple ones to solve problems.

EXAMPLE 22-1 Prove that the area of an ellipse with major axis and minor axis of lengths $2a$ and $2b$, respectively, is $ab\pi$.

Proof: We do this by projecting the ellipse into a figure whose area we can find, namely a circle with diameter $2b$. To take advantage of the constant ratio of areas, we must have some other relevant figure projected along with the ellipse. For this example, we consider the triangle formed by the endpoints of the major axis and one endpoint of the minor axis. Let this triangle be ABC and its projection be $A'B'C'$. Hence we have $[ABC] = ab$ and $[A'B'C'] = b^2$. (Why?) Since orthogonal projections preserve ratio of areas, we have

$$\frac{\text{Area of ellipse}}{[ABC]} = \frac{\text{Area of circle}}{[A'B'C']}.$$

Since the area of the circle is $b^2\pi$, we quickly find that the area of the ellipse is $ab\pi$.

EXAMPLE 22-2 Find the maximum value for the area of a triangle inscribed in an ellipse with minor axis 1 and major axis 100. (Mandelbrot #2)

Solution: Dealing with inscribed figures in an ellipse can be pretty tricky, so we perform an orthogonal projection to map the ellipse to a circle with diameter 1. Let ABC be the triangle of maximum area inscribed in the circle and $\triangle DEF$ be the triangle inscribed in the ellipse whose projection is $\triangle ABC$. Since the ratio of areas is preserved, $\triangle DEF$ must be the largest possible triangle inscribed in the ellipse. Now our problem is finding the maximum area of a triangle inscribed in a circle of diameter 1. This is just an equilateral triangle, which has area $3\sqrt{3}/16$. From the preservation of ratios, we have

$$\frac{[ABC]}{\text{Area of circle}} = \frac{[DEF]}{\text{Area of ellipse}}.$$

Thus,

$$[DEF] = \frac{(3\sqrt{3}/16)[(1/2)(100/2)\pi]}{\pi/4} = \frac{75\sqrt{3}}{4}.$$

EXERCISE 22-3 Could we have used an orthogonal projection to project the ellipse in the previous exercise into a circle with radius 100 rather than radius 1?

Orthogonal projections are generally most useful when we can project odd shapes, such as an ellipse, into regular ones, like a circle. As you will see in one of the problems at the end of the chapter, orthogonal projections can also be used to attack three-dimensional problems by projecting planar parts of the figure in the problem.

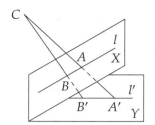

Orthogonal projections are not the only projections possible. Suppose that rather than a large sun shining directly above our plane, we have just a single point of light. The result, called a **central projection**, is shown in the figure. Point C is the **center of projection**, or the point of light. The **images** of the projections of A and B are A' and B', respectively.

If instead of light emanating from a point we take consider parallel beams of light, we get a **parallel projection**. Note that orthogonal projections are parallel projections in which the projection rays (lines AA' and BB') are perpendicular to the plane of the image, i.e. AA' is perpendicular to plane Y.

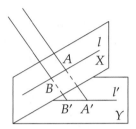

EXAMPLE 22-3 In parallel projections, ratios of lengths and areas are preserved, just as in orthogonal projections. This is proven in the same manner as we did with orthogonal projections, using the parallel rays and similar triangles.

EXERCISE 22-4 Construct an example to show that central projections do not preserve ratios of lengths.

In general, the most useful projection is the orthogonal projection; however, make sure you understand the other types of projection as well.

22.2 Inversion

Inversion with respect to a circle is one of the most bizarre useful geometric transformations. Let the circle about which we are inverting have center O and radius R. The image of a point P is the point P' on ray $\overrightarrow{OP}$ such that $OP \cdot OP' = R^2$. To get a handle on what this does, let's investigate what happens to a few particular points.

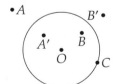

First consider point C on the circle. Since $OC = R$, $OC' = R^2/OC = R$ as well. Hence, the image of C is itself. Now try point A, outside the circle. Since $OA > R$, $OA' = R^2/OA < R$. Thus, A' is inside the circle on ray $\overrightarrow{OA}$. Similarly, we can show that the image of B, a point inside the circle, is outside the circle. What about the image of O? Since $OO = 0$, the image of O must be infinitely far away from O. We call this image the **point at infinity**. Similarly, the image of the "point at infinity" is O.

EXERCISE 22-5 Investigate the "point at infinity" concept. Let the radius be 10 and find the length of OA' if $OA = 1$, $OA = 0.1$, etc., and if $OA = 100$, $OA = 1000$, etc.

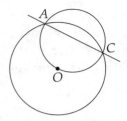

Extending these basic examples, we see that the image of the circle we are inverting about is the circle itself. By moving point *A* along the line through *O* and *A* in the diagram, we find that the image of any line through the origin is that line itself. Let's investigate the line through points *A* and *C* on the circle. Points on chord *AC* map to $\overset{\frown}{AC}$ outside circle *O*. Points on the line past *C* map to $\overset{\frown}{OC}$ and those on the line past *A* map to $\overset{\frown}{OA}$. We find (though we haven't proven this) that the inverse of a line which does not pass through the center of a circle is a circle which passes through the center of inversion. Going backwards, the image of a circle through the center of inversion is a line. Simliarly, we can find that the image of any circle not passing through the center of inversion is also a circle.

EXAMPLE 22-4   Prove that the image of a line intersecting the circle of inversion but not passing through the center is a circle and not some other strange curve.

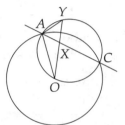

Proof: We'll first deal with the portion of the image outside circle *O*. Let point *X* be some point on chord *AC* with image *Y*. We wish to show that point *Y* lies on the circle which passes through *A*, *C*, and *O* (since these three points are clearly on the image). By the definition of inversion, $OY/OA = OA/OX$. Thus by SAS similarity, $\triangle XOA \sim \triangle AOY$, and $\angle CAO = \angle AYO$. Since $\triangle OAC$ is isosceles, we have $\angle ACO = \angle CAO = \angle AYO$; hence, *YAOC* is a cyclic quadrilateral. From this, we find that any point on chord *AC* has an image on the circumcircle of $\triangle ACO$.

Once again using the definition of inversion, for points outside the circle we have $OX/OC = OC/OY$ and $OA/OX = OY/OA$. From this we see that

$$\triangle OCX \sim \triangle OYC \quad \text{and} \quad \triangle OAX \sim \triangle OYA.$$

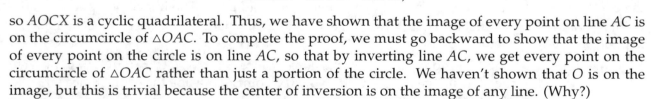

These relations give us

$$\angle OCX = \angle OYC = \angle OAX,$$

so *AOCX* is a cyclic quadrilateral. Thus, we have shown that the image of every point on line *AC* is on the circumcircle of $\triangle OAC$. To complete the proof, we must go backward to show that the image of every point on the circle is on line *AC*, so that by inverting line *AC*, we get every point on the circumcircle of $\triangle OAC$ rather than just a portion of the circle. We haven't shown that *O* is on the image, but this is trivial because the center of inversion is on the image of any line. (Why?)

Read through this proof closely; it shows why inversion works. It should also convince you that cyclic quadrilaterals are an excellent problem solving aid. Don't get too intimidated by this proof; using inversion generally isn't this tough. Furthermore, as you've seen throughout *the ART of PROBLEM SOLVING* many of the tools which we use 'easily' have very complicated proofs.

EXERCISE 22-6   Given a point *P* outside circle *O*, construct the point which is the inversion of point *P* with respect to *O*.

Inversion is a pretty complex process; what can we use it for? One answer to that is shown in the proof above: we can convert cyclic quadrilateral problems to collinearity problems. For example, in the proof above, proving that three points are collinear is equivalent to proving that their images are all on the same circle with the center of inversion. Thus, if we are asked to show that three points are collinear, we can instead perform an inversion with respect to some circle and show that the image points and the center of inversion are concyclic. Clearly, such a method is only useful in problems involving circles. Inversion problems are quite rare, so don't dive into inversion until after you've tried other approaches. However, playing with inversion is fun, so take the time to invert all sorts of figures and see what results!

22.3 Homothecy

In Volume 1 we discussed dilations and stated that a figure and its image under dilation are **homothetic**, meaning that all lines through corresponding points of the two figures share a common point.

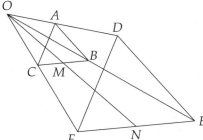

In the figure, triangles ABC and DEF are homothetic, and O is the **center of homothecy**. Note that line MN connecting midpoints of corresponding sides of the two triangles also passes through the center of homothecy. Furthermore, since one figure is a dilation of the other, we have

$$\frac{OC}{OF} = \frac{OM}{ON} = \frac{OB}{OE} = \frac{OA}{OD} = \frac{CA}{FD} = \frac{BC}{EF} = \frac{AB}{DE}.$$

These are the most important properties of homothecy: that lines through corresponding points in a figure and its image are concurrent, and that the above ratios are all the same.

Using homothetic figures is generally just like using similar figures. Recall from Volume 1 that any two similar figures with the same orientation are homothetic. The advantage of homothecy over simple similarity is the center of homothecy: it is easy to find the ratio of the two figures (for example, just find OC/OF above) and the concurrency of lines through corresponding parts of homothetic figures is often useful.

Always keep an eye open for homothetic figures; they are generally pretty easy to spot. Homothecy is most common in problems involving centroids, equilateral triangles, internally tangent circles, and other problems in which the center of homothecy is some special point.

EXERCISE 22-7 Are two internally tangent circles homothetic? If so, what is the center of homothecy?

EXAMPLE 22-5 An equilateral triangle has sides of length 18. Three 60° arcs of radius 6 and with centers at the vertices are drawn inside the triangle. Find the area of the triangle formed by joining midpoints of these three arcs. (MAΘ 1990)

Solution: The resulting triangle is homothetic to the original triangle, and the centroid of the original triangle is the center of homothecy. (Why?) To find the ratio of the two triangles, we note that the distance from the centroid of the original triangle to a vertex is $(2/3)(\text{altitude}) = (2/3)(9\sqrt{3}) = 6\sqrt{3}$. The vertices of the smaller triangle are 6 units closer to the center, so are $6\sqrt{3} - 6$ away. Hence, the triangles' side lengths have ratio $6\sqrt{3}/(6\sqrt{3} - 6) = (3 + \sqrt{3})/2$, and thus their areas have ratio $[(3 + \sqrt{3})/2]^2 = (6 + 3\sqrt{3})/2$. Finally, the smaller triangle has area

$$\frac{(18)^2 \sqrt{3}/4}{(6 + 3\sqrt{3})/2} = 108\sqrt{3} - 162.$$

Notice the advantage of using homothecy; we don't have to find the ratio of a pair of sides to find the ratio of the triangles' corresponding lengths.

 EXERCISE 22-8 In △*ABC*, *D* is the midpoint of *BC*, *E* is the midpoint of *AC*, and *F* is the midpoint *AB*. Show that △*ABC* and △*DEF* are homothetic. What is the center of homothecy?

22.4 Geometric Continuity

Given a region with area K and a line l, show that we can find a line parallel to l which divides the region into two regions of area K/2.

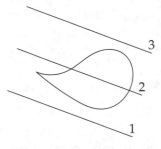

Start from position 1, where the line is entirely below the figure. Consider the area in the region below the line. Initially, this area is 0. As we move the line steadily up from position 1 to position 3, this area ranges continuously from 0 to *K*. Hence, at some point, it must equal *K*/2.

This is all we must do to solve geometric continuity problems: define some continuous function in terms of the given figures (such as the area below the line above), show that this function varies over a range which includes the desired value (the range 0 to *K* above), and finally conclude that the desired value can be attained because the function is continuous.

EXAMPLE 22-6 Given a region of area *A* and a point *P*, show that there is some line through *P* which divides the region into two equal areas.

Proof: Draw a line through *P*. By rotating this line about *P*, we can form any other line through *P*. Now we must find some function in terms of this line which continuously covers some range that includes a case of a line bisecting the area of the region. The only such function which seems plausible is choosing the area on one side of the line. Thus, we choose some point *Q* on the line and consider the region's area to the left of *PQ* (standing at *P* and looking at *Q*). Let the initial configuration be such that this area is *X* as shown. Consider what happens as we rotate the line 180°. The line rotates to itself, but with *Q* on the other side of *P*. Hence, the area to the left of *PQ* is now *Y* = *A* − *X*. In a 180° rotation, the area to the left of *PQ* ranges continuously from *X* to *A* − *X*, so it must at some point be equal to *A*/2 (since *A*/2 always lies in this range).

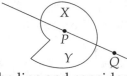

One point we have breezed over in this discussion is proving that the areas really range continuously rather than jumping from one value to the next. While it is intuitively obvious in the first example that by gradually moving the line from below the region to above the region continuously changes the area below the line, we must find a way to mathematically prove this. For this proof, we must show that for a given line which cuts the region into two pieces, we can increase or decrease the area below the line by any small amount, no matter how small, through sliding the line up or down.

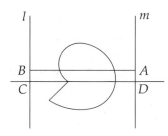

Let ϵ be some very small number. Let the area in the region below the line $\overleftrightarrow{CD}$ shown be X. We wish to show that no matter how small ϵ is, we can find another line parallel to the first which leaves less than $X + \epsilon$ of the region's area below. Since the region is finite, we can draw lines l and m perpendicular to $\overleftrightarrow{CD}$ such that the entire region lies between l and m. Points C and D are the intersections of the original line with these new lines. Let $CD = y$. We choose A and B on lines l and m such that $AD = BC = \epsilon/y$. Hence, the area of the region below line AB is less than $X + [ABCD] = X + \epsilon$, as desired. Hence, for any discrete area difference, no matter how small, we can make a smaller change of area; therefore, the area change as we slide the line across the region is continuous as claimed.

Try to understand the proof, why we need to do it, and why it shows that the area varies continuously from 0 to K as we slide a line from below the region to above it. If you have trouble understanding the details, move on and come back later. While the details aren't trivial, they aren't as important as the other techniques this chapter offers.

It's pretty obvious when these continuity arguments are called for; all these problems require us to find the existence of some line or plane intersecting some continuous region (as opposed to a smattering of points, which we'll look at next section).

EXERCISE 22-9 Given a point P in a finite region Γ, show that we can draw 12 rays from P which divide the region into 12 regions of equal area.

22.5 Given a Finite Number of...

Once again, we introduce this topic with a problem.

> Prove **Sylvester's Theorem**, *which states that given n distinct points in the plane ($n \geq 2$) not all collinear there is some line that goes through exactly two of the points.*

EXERCISE 22-10 Create a few sets of points to see why Sylvester's Theorem seems true, but is not obvious.

For any set of three points which are not collinear, we define a number α as the smallest distance from one of the three points to the line through the other two. There are three such distances for each set of three points (one for each point); α is the smallest of the three. Since there are finitely many points, there are finitely many values for α; consider the three points for which α is smallest. Let the points be A, B, and C, such that the distance from A to BC is this minimum α. We will show that the line containing B and C does not pass through any other of the n points.

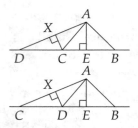

Draw altitude AE of $\triangle ABC$. Since AE is the shortest altitude of $\triangle ABC$, point E must lie between B and C as shown. Note that the length of AE is the aforementioned minimum α value. Suppose for the sake of contradiction that another point D lies on BC. Without loss of generality, let D be to the left of E as in our diagram. We consider two cases: point D outside C and point D between B and C. For the former, we have the first diagram, in which $CX < AE$ since CX is shorter than the altitude from E to AD, which in turn is less than AE. (Prove it.) Thus, points A, C, and D have a smaller α value than the set $\{A, B, C\}$, which contradicts the fact that this latter set has the minimum α value. Hence, D cannot be among the original n points. Similarly, if D is on segment BC we have $DX < AE$, which once again is a contradiction. Hence, no point on line BC besides B and C can be among the original n points and we have found a line through exactly 2 of the n points.

Problems like this are difficult, but if you ever come to a problem involving some finite number of points about which you need to prove the existence of something special, try the showing that the set of three points which form a triangle of maximum or minimum area, perimeter, or even altitude length (as we did with Sylvester's Theorem) is the desired set.

EXERCISE 22-11 In proving Sylvester's Theorem, we assumed the set of points is finite. Why can't we use an infinite set? Find a counterexample to the theorem if infinitely many points are allowed.

Problems to Solve for Chapter 22

Beware, not all of these problems require the concepts taught in this chapter; we've mixed in a few toughies from other geometric subjects. Note that, by the standards of other chapters, many to most of these problems deserve a needle.

351. Consider triangle ABC with medians AD, BE, and CF. If the area of $\triangle ABC$ is 12, what is the area of the triangle $D'E'F'$, where D', E', and F' are the reflections of D, E, and F through A, B, and C respectively? (MAΘ 1991)

352. Given two parallel lines which do not pass through point O, describe the images of the lines upon an inversion with respect to a circle with center O.

353. Show that for any quadrilateral inscribed in a circle of radius 1, the length of the shortest side is less than or equal to $\sqrt{2}$. (Canada 1969)

354. The figure F is such that the projections of F on the non-parallel planes α and β are straight lines. Is it true that F must be a straight line? (M&IQ 1992)

355. Let $\triangle ABC$ be a right triangle of area 1. Let DEF be the points obtained by reflecting A, B, and C respectively in their opposite sides. Find the area of DEF. (Canada 1989)

356. Prove that if the area of a quadrilateral is half the product of its diagonals, then the quadrilateral is orthodiagonal. (M&IQ 1991)

357. Two circles are drawn which intersect at O. Suppose that the tangents to the circles at O are perpendicular. Such circles are called **orthogonal circles**. Describe the images of the circles upon an inversion with respect to a circle centered at O.

358. Suppose that three circles are given in the plane in such a way that they divide the plane into 8 components. Let R be the region in the plane consisting of all points in at least 2 of the three circles. The boundary of R consists of 6 arcs of circles. Prove that the sum of the degree measures of these arcs is a constant, independent of the original three circles. (MOP)

359. Prove that the orthocenter cannot be the midpoint of two of the altitudes of a given triangle. (M&IQ 1991)

360. Let A and B be two simple closed figures in the plane. Prove that there exists a line which simultaneously bisects both the area of both figures. This is called the **Pancake Theorem**.

361. Let quadrilateral $ABCD$ be circumscribed around a circle. Prove that the incircle of $\triangle ABC$ is tangent to the incircle of $\triangle ACD$. (M&IQ 1991)

362. Given $2n$ points in the plane, no three of which are collinear, prove that there exist at least n different lines, each passing through two points in the set and dividing the remaining $2n - 2$ points in half ($n - 1$ points on each side). (Mandelbrot #3)

363. Two circles are internally tangent. A triangle is formed with one vertex on each circle (not at the tangent point) and the third at the tangent point. Find the maximum area of such a triangle if the circles' radii are 1 and 3. (Mandelbrot #1)

364. Let S be a simple closed curve. Prove that there exists some line l which simultaneously bisects the length of curve S and bisects the area of the region enclosed by S. (Mandelbrot #2)

365. Prove that if the altitude of isosceles trapezoid $ABCD$ ($AB \parallel CD$) is equal to $\frac{1}{2}(AB + CD)$, then $ABCD$ is orthodiagonal. (M&IQ 1991)

366. Given any smooth convex figure, prove that it is possible to draw a square which contains the entire figure and has all four sides tangent to the figure. (Mandelbrot #2)

367. A cylindrical hole of radius 1 is drilled along one of the long diagonals of a cube of side length 3. Find the area of one of the six congruent faces of the resulting solid. (Mandelbrot #3)

368. Given two orthogonal circles which intersect at A and B, we draw a third circle with center A and radius AB. Let C and D be the points besides B where this third circle meets the other two. Prove that CD is a diameter of the third circle.

369. Find, with proof, the minimum number of equilateral triangles of side 1 which are needed to cover a square of side 1 entirely. (MOP)

370. The incircle of $\triangle ABC$ touches the sides BC, CA, AB at the points D, E, F respectively. Let X, Y, Z be the midpoints of EF, FD, DE, respectively. Prove that the incenter of ABC, the circumcenter of ABC, and the circumcenter of XYZ are collinear. (IMO 1986)

371. Given points A, B, and C, we draw lines through A, B, and C parallel to BC, AC, and AB respectively. These three lines form a new triangle similar to $\triangle ABC$ but twice as large which has A, B, and C as the midpoints of its sides. We call this new triangle the first outer medial triangle. If we repeat this construction on the vertices of the new triangle we arrive at the second outer medial triangle. (Mandelbrot #3)

    i. Construct the first outer medial triangle of any triangle ABC.

    ii. Given $n \geq 3$ points in the plane, no three of which are collinear, prove that one can find three points whose first outer medial triangle contains all the remaining $n - 3$ points in its interior or sides.

    iii. Given $n \geq 3$ points in the plane, no three of which are collinear, prove that one can find three points whose second outer medial triangle contains none of the other points in its interior.

372. We are given a triangle ABC and three rectangles R_1, R_2, R_3 with sides parallel to two fixed perpendicular directions and such that their union covers the sides AB, BC, and CA. That is, each point on the perimeter of ABC is contained in or on at least one of the rectangles. Prove that all points inside the triangle are also covered by the union of R_1, R_2, R_3. (IMO 1985)

the BIG PICTURE

After Euclid presented his five basic axioms of geometry, many geometers felt uncomfortable with one of them—the **parallel postulate**, which states that given a line *l* and a point *P* not on *l*, there is exactly one line through *P* parallel to *l*. Compared to "through any two points there is exactly one line" or "all right angles are equal," the parallel postulate is ugly, longwinded, complex. Thus many hoped that the parallel postulate might turn out to be provable from the other four axioms.

To attempt to prove the postulate, several mathematicians tried assuming the postulate to be false, seeking a contradiction. Rather than finding a contradiction, though, they found an entire new type of geometry.

In **non-Euclidean geometry**, the parallel postulate does not hold. The simplest type is geometry on the surface of a sphere. Here the equivalent of a straight line is a *great circle*—an equator. Any pair of equators intersects, so there is no such thing as parallel lines on the sphere. Instead of exactly one parallel line through *P*, there are none. In another type of non-Euclidean geometry, there are *infinitely many* parallels. This *hyperbolic geometry* is (obviously) less easy to visualize, but is an equally good geometry in terms of producing interesting results.

As you might expect, strange things happen in non-Euclidean geometry. For example, in spherical geometry the sum of the angles of a triangle is always *greater than* 180°, as you can see if you try drawing a large triangle on a sphere.

Even though prominent mathematicians—Lobachevsky, Riemann, Gauss—studied non-Euclidean geometry in the early 1800's, the subject was kept under wraps for many years, not quite seen as serious. But it later led to many very serious things, not the least of which are Einstein's theory of general relativity, which maintains that our spacetime is curved and non-Euclidean, and many M.C. Escher artworks, which tile the hyperbolic plane with frogs, angels, and devils.

Chapter 23

Number Theory

WARNING: This chapter assumes a full competence with the modular arithmetic discussed in Volume 1. Make sure you are quite comfortable with mods before you continue.

23.1 Divisibility

You may think that we must have exhausted the subject of divisibility in Volume 1. That is nearly true, but there are a number of points which remain to be made. (Don't be discouraged if you find this section sticky, as our discussion is fairly subtle.)

First, though, a quick review. If a number a divides another number b, we write $a|b$; for instance, $6|12$ and $17|1717$. Showing $a|b$ is the same as showing $b = ka$ for some integer k—do you see why? The *greatest common divisor* or *GCD* of two integers a and b is the largest integer which divides both, and is written (a, b). For instance, $(18, 12) = 6$, $(56, 40) = 8$, and $(17, 23) = 1$. Two numbers whose GCD is 1 share no common divisors, and are called *relatively prime*. If you aren't familiar with these concepts, try some more examples until you feel comfortable, or go through the relevant sections of Volume 1.

Consider one number which divides the product of two others: $a|bc$. It should be intuitively clear that a can be split into two parts such that one divides b and the other divides c. That is, we can find two numbers a_1 and a_2 such that $a_1 a_2 = a$, $a_1|b$, and $a_2|c$. For example, for $12|8 \cdot 9$, we have $12 = 4 \cdot 3$, $4|8$, and $3|9$.

If p is a prime, the only way to split it into two parts is as $p \cdot 1$. Thus if $p|bc$, we always have either $p|b$ or $p|c$.

Still another point can be made along these lines. Since $a|bc$, we have $ka = bc$ for some k, and thus $k = bc/a = (b/a_1)(c/a_2)$ for some integers a_1 and a_2 such that $a_1|b$ and $a_2|c$. Hence both b/a_1 and c/a_2 are integers. Thus $b/a_1|bc/a$ since their quotient, c/a_2, is an integer. However, since a_1 divides both a and b, it divides the greatest common divisor (a, b). Thus $b/(a, b)|b/a_1$, so $b/(a, b)|bc/a$ for any a, b, and c.

EXERCISE 23-1 In the last argument, we asserted that since $a_1|(a, b)$, $b/(a, b)|b/a_1$. Why is this so?

Many divisibility-related facts can be understood by referring to the prime factorizations of the numbers in question. For example, a fact we will use occasionally is that if we take two numbers a and b and divide them by their greatest common divisor $g = (a, b)$, the resulting integers a/g and b/g will be relatively prime. Why? We use contradiction. If some prime p divides both a/g and b/g, then a/pg and b/pg are integers, so pg divides both a and b. But g is supposed to be the largest number which divides both a and b, so this is impossible. Hence no prime divides both a/g and b/g, so $(a/g, b/g) = 1$.

EXAMPLE 23-1 Prove that if ab is a perfect square and $(a, b) = 1$, then both a and b must be perfect squares.

Proof: Consider the prime factorization $ab = p_1^{e_1} \cdots p_k^{e_k}$. If ab is a square, all the e_i are even and each term $p_i^{e_i}$ is a square in its own right. (Do you see why?) Each prime in the factorization divides either a or b *but not both*, since we have $(a, b) = 1$. Thus each term $p_i^{e_i}$ in the factorization completely divides either a or b. Hence, a is the product of many terms $p_i^{e_i}$, each of which is a square; since it's a product of squares, a is itself a square. Similarly for b.

The arguments of this section may seem like more trouble than they're worth, but much of both this chapter and Chapter 24 rely on these and similar facts. You may want to go back through some of the proofs again. Focus especially on how we use concepts of the greatest common divisor and relatively prime integers; these simple ideas are at the core of all the number theory you'll study.

23.2 Division in Congruences

In Volume 1, we made the point that division does *not* work in the obvious way with congruences. That is, given a congruence like $ad \equiv bd \pmod{m}$, we can't cancel the d to get $a \equiv b \pmod{m}$. Why not? A simple counterexample: we have $2 \equiv 20 \pmod{6}$, but not $1 \equiv 10 \pmod{6}$. What has happened? [If you don't understand this example, you should go back and review the section on congruences in Volume 1.]

To figure out what has happened, remember what it means for 2 and 20 to be congruent (mod 6). It means that they differ by some multiple of 6, say $6q$. When we halve the two numbers, their difference will also be cut in half, to $3q$. The numbers will still be congruent (mod 6) only if this new difference is a multiple of 6. If q is odd, this won't be the case, and the division will fail. In our specific case, the difference between 2 and 20 is 18; halving gives 9, which is not divisible by 6 anymore.

So can we say anything at all about division? Certainly. The difference $3q$ above may not always be divisible by 6, but it is always divisible by 3. Thus while $2a \equiv 2b \pmod{6}$ does not yield $a \equiv b \pmod{6}$, it does yield $a \equiv b \pmod{3}$.

Let's look back at the general problem. The equation

$$ad \equiv bd \pmod{m} \tag{23.1}$$

means that ad and bd differ by mq for some q. This means that a and b differ by mq/d, which must be an integer since a and b are integers. Thus $d|mq$. By the rules of the previous section, this means that

$m/(m,d)|mq/d$. We thus have that $a - b = mq/d$ is divisible by $m/(m,d)$ (or $a - b \equiv 0 \pmod{m/(m,d)}$), and (23.1) hence becomes

$$a \equiv b \pmod{m/(m,d)}. \tag{23.2}$$

This is the general division rule for congruences. Try a few examples to see how this division works. Notice that $ad \equiv bd \pmod m$ implies $a \equiv b \pmod m$ if and only if $(m,d) = 1$, i.e. if m and d have no common factors.

EXERCISE 23-2 Compare our $2 \equiv 20 \pmod 6$ example to equation (23.2).

EXERCISE 23-3 Divide out the common factors in the following congruences.

    i. $6a \equiv 6b \pmod{20}$

   ii. $23 \equiv 138 \pmod 5$

  iii. $12 \equiv 30 \pmod 9$

EXAMPLE 23-2 A nice thing happens when the base of the congruence is a prime. We then have $ad \equiv bd \pmod p$. We have two cases. First, d can be a multiple of p: $d = kp$. Then $ad = akp \equiv 0$ and $bd = bkp \equiv 0$, and the congruence reduces to $0 \equiv 0$. Not too interesting.

In the other case, d is not a multiple of p so d and p have no common factors besides 1. Since p is prime, this means that $(d,p) = 1$, so we can write

$$ad \equiv bd \pmod p \qquad a \equiv b \pmod{p/(d,p)} \qquad a \equiv b \pmod p.$$

Thus in congruences $\pmod p$, p a prime, division works! Just make sure you don't divide out any multiples of p.

WARNING: It is an extremely common error to forget that division doesn't work in the normal way in congruences. Don't make it. Always remember to divide the modulus m by the greatest common divisor of m and the divided quantity d, as in equation (23.2), which you should study carefully.

23.3 Solving Linear Congruences

The reason division is so important is that it allows us to solve **linear congruences**, expressions of the form $rx + s \equiv t \pmod m$. Let's look at the example

$$1233x + 45 \equiv 9090 \pmod{24}.$$

First of all, we can subtract the 45 from both sides, since we found in Volume 1 that subtraction always works in congruences. We then have

$$1233x \equiv 9045 \pmod{24}.$$

The next step is to mod out both 1233 and 9045 by 24. This is crucial—because working with such large numbers would be messy and confusing, we use the convenient fact that modding everything out will not change the result. Dividing each large number by 24 and taking only the remainder (do this yourself), we find that $1233 \equiv 9 \pmod{24}$ and $9045 \equiv 21 \pmod{24}$. Our equation becomes

$$9x \equiv 21 \pmod{24}.$$

We can immediately divide both sides by 3, the common factor of 9 and 21—but we also need to divide the 24 by $(24, 3) = 3$, as in Section 23.2. The equation is then

$$3x \equiv 7 \pmod{8},$$

and we have only to get rid of the "3" in $3x$ to be finished. To do this, we add 8's to the right hand side, since $8 \equiv 0 \pmod{8}$. We have

$$3x \equiv 7 \equiv 15 \equiv 23 \equiv 31 \equiv \cdots \pmod{8},$$

and we can take our choice of where to stop. In this case, we'll stop at 15, writing $3x \equiv 15 \pmod{8}$, because we can then divide both sides by 3 (the 8 is unchanged because 3 and 8 are relatively prime) to get the final answer of

$$x \equiv 5 \pmod{8}.$$

Thus the solutions to our congruence are $\ldots, -11, -3, 5, 13, 21, \ldots$, or $5 + 8j$ for any integer j.

EXERCISE 23-4 Solve the congruences. (Watch out, some strange things happen!)

    i. $1235x + 45 \equiv 9090 \pmod{24}$

    ii. $1235x + 45 \equiv 9090 \pmod{11}$

    iii. $1235x + 45 \equiv 9087 \pmod{11}$

    iv. $1232x + 45 \equiv 9090 \pmod{24}$

EXAMPLE 23-3 The general solution to a linear congruence looks like $x \equiv a \pmod{m}$. This can also be written as $x = a + mj$ for any integer j. Such a representation allows us to solve more than one congruence simultaneously. Consider two congruences: if one yields $x = 5 + 6j$ ($x \equiv 5 \pmod{6}$) and the other $x = 4 + 7k$ ($x \equiv 4 \pmod{7}$), we write $5 + 6j = 4 + 7k$, or

$$1 + 6j = 7k \qquad \Rightarrow \qquad 7k \equiv 1 \pmod{6},$$

since $7k$ is 1 more than a multiple of 6. Solving the resulting linear congruence yields $k \equiv 1 \pmod{6}$, so $k = 1 + 6l$ for any integer l. Thus $x = 4 + 7k = 4 + 7(1 + 6l) = 11 + 42l$ for any integer l. As usual for simultaneous expressions, simultaneous congruences may have no solution (for example, $x \equiv 2 \pmod{4}$ and $x \equiv 1 \pmod{10}$).

EXERCISE 23-5 Solve simultaneously the three congruences $3x \equiv 4 \pmod{7}$, $4x \equiv 5 \pmod{8}$, and $5x \equiv 6 \pmod{9}$.

WARNING: Although the method of Example 23-3 is a nice, mechanical way to solve systems of linear congruences, don't let it blind you to more clever approaches. For example, the system $x \equiv 4 \pmod{5}$, $x \equiv 5 \pmod{6}$, $x \equiv 6 \pmod{7}$ is most easily solved by noting that it forces $x + 1$ to be divisible by 5, 6, and 7, so that $x + 1 = 5 \cdot 6 \cdot 7 \cdot j = 210j$, and $x = 210j - 1$. Watch for these shortcuts.

23.4 Solving Quadratic Congruences

A **quadratic congruence** is of the form $rx^2 + sx + t \equiv u \pmod{m}$. Unfortunately, this general form is too difficult to do much with, so we'll ignore the sx term. We can then reduce to the form $rx^2 \equiv v \pmod{m}$, with $v = u - t$.

    We can use the division rules just as we used them for linear congruences to get still simpler, to the form $x^2 \equiv v' \pmod{m'}$. Thus the problem is to find the square roots of $v' \pmod{m'}$, or numbers whose squares are congruent to $v' \pmod{m'}$.

EXAMPLE 23-4 Not all numbers even *have* a square root. For example, suppose we are working in $\pmod 6$. The squares of all the numbers are $0^2 = 0$, $1^2 = 1$, $2^2 = 4$, $3^2 = 9 \equiv 3$, $4^2 \equiv (-2)^2 = 4$, and $5^2 \equiv (-1)^2 = 1$. (Note how we have simplified the arithmetic by using the facts that $4 \equiv -2$ and $5 \equiv -1$.) Thus 0 has the square root 0, 1 has the two square roots 1 and 5, 4 has the square roots 2 and 4, and 3 has the square root 3. However, 2 and 5 have no square roots at all, because there are no numbers which, when squared, give 2 or 5 $\pmod 6$.

EXAMPLE 23-5 In the previous example, why did we only consider the squares of the numbers from 0 to 5?

    Solution: Every number after 5 is congruent to some number from 0 to 5 mod 6. Since the squares of congruent numbers are congruent, we need only compute the squares of 0 through 5 to analyze the squares of all integers mod 6. Note also the pattern of the nonzero squares in the example: 1, 4, 3, 4, 1. The sequence is symmetric. This is not an accident. Since $(u)^2 \equiv (-u)^2 \pmod 6$, we have $(u^2) \equiv (-u)^2 \pmod 6$. Noting that $5 \equiv -1 \pmod 6$ and $4 \equiv -2 \pmod 6$ explains the symmetry of our squares.

A number which has a square root $\pmod m$ is called a **quadratic residue** $\pmod m$.

EXERCISE 23-6 Find all quadratic residues in mod 7, 8, and 9.

EXAMPLE 23-6 The *most* quadratic residues there can be $\pmod n$ for an even integer $n = 2m$ is $m + 1$. This is because even if $0^2, 1^2, \ldots m^2$ are all different, the rest of the squares will be copies of these first $m + 1$ numbers: $(m + 1)^2 \equiv (m - 1)^2$, $(m + 2)^2 \equiv (m - 2)^2$, and so on. For example, since $2m \equiv 0 \pmod{2m}$, we can write

$$(m + 1)^2 \equiv m^2 + 2m + 1 \equiv m^2 - 2m + 1 \equiv (m - 1)^2 \pmod{2m}.$$

Write down the squares of 0, 1, 2, 3, 4, 5, and 6 $\pmod 6$ to see this.

EXERCISE 23-7 What is the most quadratic residues there can be $\pmod n$ for $n = 2m + 1$ an odd integer?

EXAMPLE 23-7 Let p be a prime other than 2. If there are two numbers u and v such that $u^2 \equiv v^2 \pmod p$, then $u^2 - v^2 \equiv 0 \pmod p$, so that $u^2 - v^2 = (u - v)(u + v)$ is a multiple of p. Since p is prime, this implies that either $u - v$ is a multiple of p, so $u \equiv v \pmod p$, or $u + v$ is a multiple of p, so $u \equiv -v \pmod p$.

    Thus when we write down the quadratic residues $0^2, 1^2, \ldots, (p - 1)^2$, there can be no duplications, except that the last $(p - 1)/2$ are copies of the first $(p - 1)/2$ nonzero squares, much like described in Example 23-6. In other words, an odd prime p always has the maximum $(p + 1)/2$ residues.

On the other hand, a nonprime like 15 will not achieve the maximum: the squares of 0 through 14 evaluated mod 15 are

$$0, 1, 4, 9, 1, 10, 6, 4, 4, 6, 10, 1, 9, 4, 1.$$

There are only 6 residues—0, 1, 4, 6, 9, 10—rather than the maximum of $(15 + 1)/2 = 8$.

EXERCISE 23-8 Verify the assertions of the previous example for $p = 11$ and $p = 17$.

===

Actually solving the quadratic congruence $x^2 \equiv v \pmod{m}$ (finding the square roots of v) is not at all an easy problem. In number theory, it's very common for simple-seeming equations to contain enormous complexities, and this is one.

The most important use of quadratic residues is in knowing certain special cases of numbers which *aren't* residues. For example, the squares (mod 4) are 0, 1, 0, and 1—the only residues are 0 and 1! This is of paramount importance in many applications.

===

EXERCISE 23-9 Find all quadratic residues (mod 3) and (mod 8).

===

23.5   The Sum of the Divisors

In Volume 1 we derived a formula for the number of divisors of some number

$$n = p_1^{e_1} p_2^{e_2} \cdots p_k^{e_k}, \tag{23.3}$$

namely

$$d(n) = (e_1 + 1)(e_2 + 1) \cdots (e_k + 1).$$

A similar, though more involved, problem is to find the *sum* of all the divisors of n, which we call $s(n)$.

EXAMPLE 23-8   If $n = 12$, the divisors are 1, 2, 3, 4, 6, and 12, so $d(n) = 6$. We write $s(n) = 1 + 2 + 3 + 4 + 6 + 12 = 28$.

A very clever method exists to find $s(n)$. Clearly it is the sum of expressions $p_1^{f_1} \cdots p_k^{f_k}$, where each f_i is nonnegative and less than or equal to the corresponding e_i in (23.3). But rather than write down all such expressions, we can get them in one fell swoop by writing the product

$$s(n) = (1 + p_1 + p_1^2 + \cdots + p_1^{e_1})(1 + p_2 + p_2^2 + \cdots + p_2^{e_2}) \cdots (1 + p_k + p_k^2 + \cdots + p_k^{e_k}). \tag{23.4}$$

EXAMPLE 23-9 The factorization of 12 is $2^2 \cdot 3$, so the product is

$$(1 + 2 + 4)(1 + 3) = 1 + 2 + 4 + 3 + 6 + 12,$$

as desired.

EXERCISE 23-10 Write down and expand the product for $n = 16, 20,$ and 28.

EXERCISE 23-11 Why does this product give the sum of the divisors?

EXERCISE 23-12 Make the product (23.4) simpler using the formula for the sum of a geometric series.

EXERCISE 23-13 Why are

$$d(n) = \sum_{d|n} 1 \quad \text{and} \quad s(n) = \sum_{d|n} d$$

correct expressions for $d(n)$ and $s(n)$? Do you like them?

One ancient fascination in number theory is **perfect numbers**, numbers n for which $s(n) = 2n$. For example, $s(6) = 1 + 2 + 3 + 6 = 12$, so 6 is perfect. Numbers n for which $s(n) > 2n$ are called **abundant**, because they have many large divisors; numbers n for which $s(n) < 2n$ are called **deficient**.

EXERCISE 23-14 Classify 24, 26, and 28 as abundant, deficient, or perfect.

EXERCISE 23-15 Show that any number of the form

$$2^k(2^{k+1} - 1)$$

is perfect if $(2^{k+1} - 1)$ is prime. This form was discovered by Euclid, and *all known perfect numbers* have this form. (In particular, no odd perfect numbers have ever been found.)

EXERCISE 23-16 Show that 6 and 28 have the form of the previous exercise, and find the third smallest perfect number.

23.6   Fermat's Theorem

Consider doing arithmetic (mod p), with p a prime. If we take powers of some number a (where $a \not\equiv 0 \pmod{p}$), the numbers a^2, a^3, etc. cannot all be different (mod p), because they are all in the range from 0 to $p - 1$. Thus some two of them must be the same, say a^r and a^s. Assume $r > s$; if $a^r \equiv a^s \pmod{p}$, we can write $a^{r-s} \equiv 1 \pmod{p}$, since p is prime. Thus the powers of a will hit 1 before they repeat, and will look like

$$a, a^2, a^3, \ldots, a^t \equiv 1, a^{t+1} \equiv a, a^{t+2} \equiv a^2, \ldots, a^{2t} \equiv 1, a^{2t+1} \equiv a, \ldots \tag{23.5}$$

We'll call the smallest integer t such that $a^t \equiv 1$ the **period of a number (mod p)** of a.

EXERCISE 23-17 Find the periods of 1, 2, 3, 4, 5, and 6 (mod 7).

We can say some interesting things about the period of a number a (mod p). Consider the set of numbers $\{1, 2, 3, \ldots, p-1\}$. If we multiply all these numbers by a we get $\{a, 2a, 3a, \ldots, (p-1)a\}$. Since none of the new numbers ka is divisible by p, all are congruent to some number in the set $\{1, 2, \ldots, p-1\}$. (Why do we leave 0 out?) Moreover, no two of $\{a, 2a, 3a, \ldots, (p-1)a\}$ are congruent: if $ka \equiv ja$ (mod p), then $k \equiv j$ (mod p). (Why can we cancel the a?) This means that the set $\{a, 2a, \ldots, (p-1)a\}$ is just a rearrangement of $\{1, 2, \ldots, p-1\}$ when taken (mod p). We thus have

$$a \cdot 2a \cdot 3a \cdots (p-1)a \equiv 1 \cdot 2 \cdot 3 \cdots (p-1) \,(\text{mod}\, p),$$

and cancelling all common factors leaves

$$a^{p-1} \equiv 1 \,(\text{mod}\, p). \tag{23.6}$$

This equation is true for all primes p and for all numbers $a \not\equiv 0 \,(\text{mod}\, p)$, and is called **Fermat's Theorem**. It is an extremely important theorem of number theory, as you will see.

EXERCISE 23-18 Verify Fermat's Theorem for $p = 7$ and $a = 1, 2, 3, \ldots, 6$.

EXAMPLE 23-10 Find 4^{87} (mod 17).

Solution: From Fermat, $4^{16} \equiv 1 \,(\text{mod}\, 17)$. Raising both sides to the fifth power, we have $4^{80} \equiv 1 \,(\text{mod}\, 17)$, so that

$$4^{87} \equiv 4^7 \equiv 4 \cdot (4^2)^3 \equiv 4 \cdot (16)^3 \equiv 4 \cdot (-1)^3 \equiv -4 \equiv \mathbf{13} \,(\text{mod}\, 17).$$

EXERCISE 23-19 Find 6^{1000} (mod 23).

So what does Fermat's Theorem mean for the period of a number a? First of all, the period is at most $p - 1$, since the period is the smallest power which gives 1. Moreover, looking at the list (23.5) we can see that the only powers u which give $a^u \equiv 1$ are multiples of t: $a^t \equiv 1$, $a^{2t} \equiv 1$, etc. Since $a^{p-1} \equiv 1$, $p - 1$ must thus be a multiple of t, meaning that t must be a divisor of $p - 1$ for any a. This puts a strict limit on the possible periods.

EXERCISE 23-20 Find all possible periods a number can have (mod 23), (mod 17), and (mod 7).

EXAMPLE 23-11 We know that every period divides $p - 1$, but especially interesting are elements g whose period is *exactly* $p - 1$. For such an element g, the list

$$g, g^2, g^3, \ldots, g^{p-1}$$

is just a rearrangement of $1, 2, \ldots, p - 1$, since all are different and none is congruent to 0. Thus if we have such a g, called a **primitive root**, every element of $\{1, 2, 3, \ldots, p - 1\}$ is congruent to g^e for some exponent e.

EXERCISE 23-21 Let the divisors of $p - 1$ be d_1, d_2, ... Prove that if we have a primitive root g (mod p), then for each d_i there is an element with period d_i.

23.7   The ϕ Function

Suppose we try to extend Fermat's theorem to systems where the base m is not prime. We will immediately encounter several problems. (Follow along with the proof of Fermat's Theorem from the previous section.) The first comes when we try to show that there are no duplicates in the set $\{a, 2a, 3a, \ldots, (m-1)a\}$ by cancelling the a from the congruence $ka \equiv ja \pmod{m}$. We can only make this cancellation if $(m, a) = 1$, so our entire proof breaks down if a is not relatively prime to m. (Why was this not a problem when m was prime?) The second problem occurs when we try to cancel the common factors from both sides of

$$1 \cdot 2 \cdots (m-1) \equiv a \cdot 2a \cdots (m-1)a. \pmod{m}$$

We can only make this cancellation if all the numbers $1, 2, \ldots, m-1$ are relatively prime to m, which they won't be if m is not prime. This is a more serious problem.

We can get around the problem if we start out listing only those integers which *are* relatively prime to m. For example, for $m = 14$, the list would be $\{1, 3, 5, 9, 11, 13\}$.

EXERCISE 23-22   Write down all numbers relatively prime to $m = 20$, $m = 15$, and $m = 12$.

We are thus forced to use, instead of the list of all positive integers less than m, a new list of integers less than m and relatively prime to it. Using this list, which we'll write as $\{1, r_1, r_2, \ldots, m-1\}$ since 1 and $m-1$ are always relatively prime to m, we can then see that $\{a, r_1a, r_2a \ldots, (m-1)a\}$ is a rearrangement of $\{1, r_1, r_2, \ldots, m-1\}$ if $(a, m) = 1$ by the same argument as before: each r_ia is still relatively prime to m because a and r_i are, and $r_ia \equiv r_ja \pmod{m}$ means that $r_i \equiv r_j \pmod{m}$ (since $(a, m) = 1$). Since the two lists are the same (mod m), we have

$$a \cdot r_1a \cdot r_2a \cdots (m-1)a \equiv 1 \cdot r_1 \cdot r_2 \cdots (m-1) \pmod{m}.$$

Moreover, since all the r_i are relatively prime to m, we can cancel them, getting

$$a \cdot a \cdots a \equiv 1 \pmod{m}.$$

Here's our final problem: how many a's are there? There is an a for each number in our list, or one for every number less than m that is relatively prime to m. We will thus form a new function, $\phi(m)$, to represent the number of integers less than m and relatively prime to m; the statement of our theorem becomes

$$a^{\phi(m)} \equiv 1 \pmod{m}$$

for all m and all a relatively prime to m.

EXAMPLE 23-12   Find $\phi(16)$.

Solution: Since 2 is the only prime which divides 16, the odds are all relatively prime to it, and the evens aren't. Thus we just need to count the odds $1, 3, \ldots, 15$ which are less than 16 to find that $\phi(16) = \mathbf{8}$.

EXERCISE 23-23   Find $\phi(12)$ and $\phi(11)$.

EXAMPLE 23-13 Since $a^{\phi(m)} \equiv 1 \pmod{m}$ for a relatively prime to m, every number relatively prime to m has a period (mod m), and that period must be a divisor of $\phi(m)$.

Any number not relatively prime to m doesn't have a period (mod m). If $(m, a) = g \neq 1$, then $(m, a^k) \geq g$ for any power k. But if $a^k \equiv 1 \pmod{m}$, then $a^k = jm + 1$ for some j, and $(a^k, m) = 1$, a contradiction.

EXERCISE 23-24 Find $\phi(p)$ for p prime. Show why the formula $a^{\phi(m)} \equiv 1 \pmod{m}$ is considered to be a generalization of Fermat's Theorem. (It is called **Euler's generalization**.)

EXERCISE 23-25 Find $\phi(p^k)$ for p prime and k a positive integer.

EXAMPLE 23-14 Prove that the ϕ function is **multiplicative**; that is, $\phi(mn) = \phi(m)\phi(n)$ as long as $(m, n) = 1$.

Solution: This is a difficult proof, but a very worthwhile one, since proving that a function is multiplicative usually tells you an enormous amount about the structure of the function.

List the integers from 1 to mn in a grid, as:

$$
\begin{array}{ccccc}
1 & m+1 & 2m+1 & \cdots & (n-1)m+1 \\
2 & m+2 & 2m+2 & \cdots & (n-1)m+2 \\
\vdots & \vdots & \vdots & \ddots & \vdots \\
m & 2m & 3m & \cdots & mn
\end{array}
$$

Now consider any element r which is not relatively prime to m: $(m, r) = d \neq 1$. Then any element in the row

$$r \quad m+r \quad 2m+r \quad \cdots \quad (n-1)m+r$$

is not relatively prime to mn: since d divides the multiple of m and d divides r, then d divides the whole thing. Thus, when counting elements relatively prime to mn, we only need to consider rows starting with elements relatively prime to m. By definition, there are $\phi(m)$ such rows.

So consider one such row, made up of elements $km + r$ for $k = 0, 1, \ldots, (n-1)$. The row contains n elements, and no two of these elements are congruent (mod n), since $jm + r \equiv km + r \pmod{n}$ would imply $j \equiv k \pmod{n}$. (This is where we use the assumption that $(m, n) = 1$. Make sure you see how.) Since we have n elements and no two are congruent, the elements of the row are a rearrangement of $0, 1, 2, \ldots, n-1 \pmod{n}$. Thus $\phi(n)$ of these elements are relatively prime. All in all, there are $\phi(m)$ rows of elements relatively prime to m, with $\phi(n)$ elements in each row relatively prime to n, so there are $\phi(m)\phi(n)$ total elements relatively prime to mn.

WARNING: A multiplicative function f only necessarily satisfies $f(mn) = f(m)f(n)$ when m and n are *relatively prime*! For example, you can directly calculate that $\phi(4) = 2$, $\phi(2) = 1$, and $\phi(8) = 4 \neq \phi(4)\phi(2)$.

EXAMPLE 23-15 Using Example 23-14 and Exercise 23-25, we can write down a general formula for $\phi(m)$ in terms of the prime factorization $m = p_1^{e_1} p_2^{e_2} \cdots p_k^{e_k}$. We use the multiplicative property of ϕ along with the fact that $(p_i^{e_i}, p_j^{e_j}) = 1$ for $i \neq j$ to write

$$\phi(p_1^{e_1} p_2^{e_2} \cdots p_k^{e_k}) = \phi(p_1^{e_1})\phi(p_2^{e_2}) \cdots \phi(p_k^{e_k}).$$

Since $\phi(p_i^{e_i}) = p_i^{e_i}\left(1 - \dfrac{1}{p_i}\right)$, this becomes

$$
\begin{aligned}
\phi(m) &= p_1^{e_1}\left(1 - \frac{1}{p_1}\right) p_2^{e_2}\left(1 - \frac{1}{p_2}\right) \cdots p_k^{e_k}\left(1 - \frac{1}{p_k}\right) \\
&= m\left(1 - \frac{1}{p_1}\right)\left(1 - \frac{1}{p_2}\right) \cdots \left(1 - \frac{1}{p_k}\right).
\end{aligned}
$$

EXERCISE 23-26   Find $\phi(6876)$.

23.8   Wilson's Theorem

Wilson's Theorem is rarely useful, but is very powerful when it is useful. The theorem states that for any prime p, we have

$$(p - 1)! \equiv -1 \,(\mathrm{mod}\, p).$$

EXAMPLE 23-16   Wilson's Theorem only works for primes. If m is composite, $m = ab$ for some a and b which are less than m. The product $(m - 1)! = (m - 1)(m - 2) \cdots (2)(1)$ contains both a and b, so is divisible by m. Thus $(m - 1)! \equiv 0 \,(\mathrm{mod}\, m)$ if m is not prime.

EXERCISE 23-27   The slick preceding example actually glosses over a major point: what if $a = b$? Then only one of a and b appears in $(m - 1)(m - 2) \cdots (2)(1)$. Does this yield any counterexamples to $(m - 1)! \equiv 0 \,(\mathrm{mod}\, m)$? Find them, and prove that the equation is still true for all other cases.

To prove Wilson's Theorem, we consider some primitive root $g \,(\mathrm{mod}\, p)$. By the definition of a primitive root, the numbers $\{g, g^2, \ldots, g^{p-1}\}$ are the same as the numbers $\{1, 2, \ldots, p - 1\} \,(\mathrm{mod}\, p)$. We then have

$$(p - 1)! = 1 \cdot 2 \cdot 3 \cdots (p - 2) \cdot (p - 1) = g \cdot g^2 \cdot g^3 \cdots g^{p-1} = g^{p(p-1)/2}.$$

But $g^p \equiv g(g^{p-1}) \equiv g$, so $(p - 1)! \equiv g^{p(p-1)/2} \equiv (g^p)^{(p-1)/2} \equiv g^{(p-1)/2}$. Let $t = g^{(p-1)/2}$; then $t^2 \equiv 1 \,(\mathrm{mod}\, p)$, since $t^2 = g^{p-1}$. Thus $t^2 - 1 \equiv 0$, or $(t - 1)(t + 1) \equiv 0$, or $t \equiv \pm 1$. Since the period of g is $p - 1$, we can't have $t \equiv g^{(p-1)/2} \equiv 1$, because $(p - 1)/2 < p - 1$. (Remember, g^{p-1} is the smallest power of g congruent to 1 mod p.) Thus, $(p - 1)! \equiv g^{(p-1)/2} \equiv t \equiv -1$, and we're done.

EXERCISE 23-28   The proof of Wilson's Theorem is an excellent example of the way in which primitive roots and powers can be used to prove statements in number theory. Go through it again, and make sure you understand every step.

Problems to Solve for Chapter 23

373. Show that for all prime numbers p greater than 3, 24 divides $p^2 - 1$ evenly. (AHSME 1973)

374. Given that $n - 4$ is divisible by 5, list which of the following are also divisible by 5:

$$n^2 - 1, \ n^2 - 4, \ n^2 - 16, \ n + 4, \ n^4 - 1.$$

(Mandelbrot #3)

375. If the same number r is the remainder when each of the numbers 1059, 1417, and 2312 is divided by d, where d is an integer greater than one, find $d - r$. (AHSME 1976)

376. Find the sum of all x, $1 \le x \le 100$, such that 7 divides $x^2 + 15x + 1$. (Mandelbrot #3)

377. What is the largest integer which must evenly divide all integers of the form $n^5 - n$? (AHSME 1957)

378. What is the units digit of $7^{(7^7)}$? (MAΘ 1990)

379. What is the size of the largest subset S of $\{1, 2, 3, \ldots, 50\}$ such that no pair of distinct elements of S has a sum divisible by 7? (AHSME 1992)

380. Let $f(x) = x^2 + 3x + 2$ and let S be the set of integers $\{0, 1, 2, \ldots, 25\}$. Find the number of members s of S such that $f(s)$ has remainder zero when divided by six. (AHSME 1964)

381. For any integer n greater than 1, how many prime numbers are there greater than $n! + 1$ and less than $n! + n$? (AHSME 1969)

382. Find the last three digits of 9^{105}. (Mandelbrot #2)

383. What is the smallest possible value of n such that

$$\sqrt{\frac{3}{1} \cdot \frac{4}{2} \cdot \frac{5}{3} \cdots \frac{n+2}{n}}$$

is a rational number? (MATHCOUNTS 1992)

384. Adam and Ben start their new jobs on the same day. Adam's schedule is 3 workdays followed by 1 rest day. Ben's schedule is 7 workdays followed by 3 rest days. On how many of their first 1000 days do both have rest-days on the same day? (AHSME 1993)

385. Find the last two digits of 7^{9999}. (MATHCOUNTS 1986)

386. What is the least number of n consecutive positive integers, $n > 1$, that have a sum of 1000? (MAΘ 1987)

387. Let x and y be integers such that $2x + 3y$ is a multiple of 17. Show that $9x + 5y$ must also be a multiple of 17. (USAMTS 1)

388. Note that 1990 can be "turned into a square" by adding a digit on its right, and some digits on its left; i.e., $419904 = 648^2$. Prove that 1991 cannot be turned into a square by the same procedure; i.e., there are no digits d, x, y, $\ldots$ such that $\ldots yx1991d$ is a perfect square. (USAMTS 3)

389. Prove that for all natural numbers k, $k^5 - k$ is a multiple of 10. (M&IQ 1991)

390. If x and y are positive integers and neither of them are divisible by 5, show that $x^4 + 4y^4$ is divisible by 5. (M&IQ 1991)

391. Prove that if exactly one of the positive integers x and y is a multiple of 5, then $x^4 + 4y^4$ is not a multiple of 5. (M&IQ 1991)

392. Prove that if p and $p + 2$ are both prime integers greater than 3, then 6 is a factor of $p + 1$. (Canada 1973)

393. Let n be an integer. If the tens digit of n^2 is 7, what is the units digit of n^2? (Canada 1978)

394. Prove that none of the numbers $a_n = 1001001 \cdots 1001$ is prime, where $n = 2, 3, 4, \ldots$ denotes the number of occurrences of the digit 1 in a_n. (M&IQ 3)

395. Let p be a prime number. Prove that there exists an integer a such that $p|(a^2 - a + 3)$ if and only if there exists an integer b such that $p|(b^2 - b + 25)$. (This problem originally appeared on a contest used to determine the Chinese national team.) (MOP)

396. Each of the numbers $x_1, x_2, \ldots, x_n$ equals 1 or -1, and

$$x_1 x_2 x_3 x_4 + x_2 x_3 x_4 x_5 + \cdots + x_{n-2} x_{n-1} x_n x_1 + x_{n-1} x_n x_1 x_2 + x_n x_1 x_2 x_3 = 0.$$

Prove that n is divisible by 4. (IMO 1985)

397. Prove that $d(n)$ and $s(n)$, the number of and sum of the divisors of n respectively, are multiplicative functions. (Remember, a multiplicative function f only necessarily satisfies the identity $f(mn) = f(m)f(n)$ when $(m, n) = 1$.)

398. Find the positive integer m such that the polynomial $p^3 + 2p + m$ divides $p^{12} - p^{11} + 3p^{10} + 11p^3 - p^2 + 23p + 30$.

399. Prove that, for all positive integer pairs (a, b) where $b > 2$, $2^b - 1$ does not evenly divide $2^a + 1$.

400. Let d be any positive integer not equal to 2, 5, or 13. Show that one can find distinct (a, b) in the set $\{2, 5, 13, d\}$ such that $ab - 1$ is not a perfect square. (IMO 1986)

401. Let a and b be integers and n a positive integer. Prove that $b^{n-1}a(a + b)(a + 2b) \cdots (a + (n-1)b)/n!$ is an integer. (IMO 1985)

402. Prove that a positive integer is a sum of at least two consecutive positive integers if and only if it is not a power of two. (Canada 1976)

the BIG PICTURE

Number theory has traditionally been viewed as one of the least "applied" branches of mathematics, one distant from ordinary human activities. But with modern approaches to **cryptography**—the study of codes—number theory has come to the forefront of a wide range of present and future applications.

Traditionally in cryptography, if I could send you a code, I could read other codes sent to you. Thus if both Richard and I sent you coded material, I could read his messages and he mine. This was undesirable, but thought to be unavoidable. However, in the late 1970's mathematicians discovered that number-theoretical methods could be used in which I can send you coded messages without being able to decode other coded messages sent to you.

To see the basic idea, let's consider the **Massey-Omura cryptosystem**. We can easily devise a way to convert a message into some (probably large) number, and to convert numbers back into messages. (Come up with a method yourself.) So imagine I have a message/number M to send to you. Everyone interested in sending or receiving coded messages has a secret *encoding number e* and *decoding number d*, such that $de \equiv 1 \pmod{q-1}$, where q is some huge prime (say, 100 digits) used by everyone.

To send me a message M, Richard calculates $M^{e_R} \pmod q$ and sends it to me. This is garble to me, since, not having Richard's encoder e_R or decoder d_R, I can't unscramble the message. I take the message to the power of e_S, and send the result, $M^{e_R e_S} \pmod q$, back to Richard. Even though he knows M and $M^{e_R e_S} \pmod q$, Richard can't extract e_S—at least, no one has yet figured out how to do so in less than 10,000 years or so. Since Richard can't get e_S, my code is still secure. Richard takes the number I gave him to the d_R power now, sending me $M^{d_R e_R e_S} \equiv M^{e_S} \pmod q$. (Since $d_R e_R \equiv 1 \pmod{q-1}$, $M^{d_R e_R} \equiv M \pmod q$ by Fermat's Theorem, which allows this simplification. Make sure you see why.) I then get the message M by taking my number M^{e_S} to the d_S power, again using Fermat's Theorem. Richard's code is secure, since I can't get e_R from $M^{e_R} \pmod q$, which I got initially, and M, which I now have.

So number theory provides a nice way to send codes securely, with neither party learning the other's code. The major caveat is that the whole scheme fails if someone figures out how to get e from $M^e \pmod q$ and M—and mathematicians are, of course, working on that problem.

Chapter 24

Diophantine Equations

A **Diophantine** (die-oh-FAHN-teen) **equation** is any equation with two or more unknowns, with one catch: we are interested only in *integer* solutions. This makes seemingly easy problems much more involved. Since integers are crucial, you might guess that number theory plays a big part in solving Diophantine equations. You'd be right.

24.1 $ax + by = c$

Requiring integer solutions adds a new dimension to the old linear equation. To be specific, the problem is to find integers x and y so that

$$ax + by = c$$

for some integer constants a, b and c.

24.1.1 $c = 0$

Let's first look at the simple case where $c = 0$. We then have $ax = -by$.

EXAMPLE 24-1 The integer solutions of $x = -2y$ are $\ldots, (4, -2), (2, -1), (0, 0), (-2, 1), (-4, 2), \ldots$. In general, the solutions are given by $(-2k, k)$ for any integer k.

EXERCISE 24-1 Find all solutions of $3x = 4y$ in terms of an arbitrary integer k.

The last two problems point the way to the solution of $ax = -by$ if a and b are *relatively prime*. Assume they are. Since a divides the left side of the equation, it must divide the right side as well. But $(a, b) = 1$, so a must divide y! We can thus write $y = ay'$ for an integer y'. By the same argument, $b|x$, and we can write $x = bx'$. Substituting these expressions in, we have

$$a(bx') = -b(ay'),$$

or $x' = -y' = k$ for some common value k. Thus the solutions of the system are given by $(bx', ay') = (bk, -ak)$ for all integers k.

In our previous examinations of the line equation $ax + by = c$ (Volume 1), we relied heavily on graphing. Graphing is less important here, but it still gives us a picture of what's happening. We graph the line equation as always, but now the only solutions we're interested in are those where the line goes through a **lattice point**, a point (m, n) where m and n are both integers.

EXERCISE 24-2 Draw a graph of the equation $2x = -3y$. How do the solutions $(3k, -2k)$ appear geometrically? Does this help you see what's going on?

If a and b are not relatively prime, we only need to make a small change. Let $(a, b) = g$ and write $a = ga'$ and $b = gb'$. Then our equation is $ga'x = -gb'y$, or $a'x = -b'y$ with a' and b' relatively prime. Thus the solutions are $(b'k, -a'k)$, or $(bk/g, -ak/g)$.

EXERCISE 24-3 Write down the solutions of $4x = -6y$ and compare them to the expression $(bk/g, ak/g)$. Do they agree?

EXERCISE 24-4 Graph the equation $4x = -6y$ and find the solutions on the graph. How has the presence of a common divisor changed things from Exercise 24-2?

24.1.2 $c \neq 0$

In the case that $c \neq 0$, we need to take a little more care. Rather than dive into the general formulation, let's consider a set equation, say $20x + 12y = 28$. We're not entirely free in our choice of equation $ax + by = c$, because any common divisor of a and b must divide c. (Make sure you see why.) Thus the equation $20x + 12y = 26$ would have no solutions, because $(20, 12) = 4$ does not divide 26. But 4 does divide 28, so we can divide both sides of the initial equation by 4 to get $5x + 3y = 7$. The key to solving this new equation is to find one solution and build the rest from there.

To solve $5x + 3y = 7$, we write $5x = 7 - 3y$. Considering this equation (mod 3) to eliminate the $3y$, we find $5x \equiv 7 - 3y \pmod 3 \equiv 7 \pmod 3 \equiv 1 \pmod 3$. This congruence has a solution r since 5 and 3 are relatively prime (this is why we divided by the GCD before proceeding). We solve this congruence by adding $3(3) = 9$ to the right, yielding $5x \equiv 10 \pmod 3$, so $x \equiv 2 \pmod 3$. We can let x be any solution of this congruence to find a solution (x, y), so we'll take the simplest, $x_0 = 2$. Hence, $y_0 = (7 - 5x)/3 = -1$ and our specific solution is (x_0, y_0)

EXERCISE 24-5 Verify that $(2, -1)$ is a solution to $5x + 3y = 7$.

EXERCISE 24-6 Show that a specific solution of the equation $ax + by = c$, $(a, b) = 1$, is

$$(x_0, y_0) = \left(r, \frac{c - ar}{b} \right)$$

where r is any solution of $ar \equiv c \pmod b$.

To get the general solution to $5x + 3y = 7$ from the specific solution (x_0, y_0), we find the solutions (x_1, y_1) of $5x = -3y$. The solution of $5x + 3y = 7$ is $(x_0 + x_1, y_0 + y_1)$, because

$$5(x_0 + x_1) + 3(y_0 + y_1) = (5x_0 + 3y_0) + (5x_1 + 3y_1) = 7 + 0 = 7,$$

as required.

Since the solutions of $5x = -3y$ are given by $(3k, -5k)$ for all integers k, the general solution of $5x + 3y = 7$ is $(2 + 3k, -1 - 5k)$.

EXAMPLE 24-2 Find all solutions of $3x + 7y = 12$.

Solution: As before, we write $3x = 12 - 7y$ and consider the equation (mod 7), yielding $3x \equiv 12 \pmod 7$, so $x \equiv 4 \pmod 7$. Hence, we'll take $x = 4$ and find $y = 0$, so $(x, y) = (4, 0)$ is a specific solution. Solving $3x + 7y = 0$, or $3x = -7y$, we get the solutions $(x, y) = (7k, -3k)$. Combining this with our specific solution, we find that our general solution is $(4 + 7k, 0 - 3k)$.

EXERCISE 24-7 Find all solutions of:

i. $6x + 4y = 4$.

ii. $6x + 4y = 5$.

EXERCISE 24-8 Does Example 24-2 have any solutions in strictly positive integers?

EXAMPLE 24-3 The linear equation $ax + by = c$ becomes even more interesting if we require that x and y be nonnegative. Often there is no nonngegative solution at all, for example if the equation is $3x + 7y = 4$.

EXAMPLE 24-4 What is the largest c for which there is no solution in nonnegative integers for $7x + 10y = c$?

Solution: If we start trying small c's, we will be frustrated: there is no solution for $c = 1, 2,$ $\ldots, 6, 8, 9, 11$, and so on. On the other hand, for large enough c there will always be a solution. We can write the c values in a grid, with nonnegative x along the top and y along the side:

	0	1	2	3
0	0	7	14	21
1	10	17	24	31
2	20	27	34	41
3	30	37	44	51

All $c \equiv 0 \pmod 7$ can be obtained from the first row. All $c \equiv 10 \equiv 3 \pmod 7$ such that $c \geq 10$ can be obtained from the second row. All $c \equiv 6 \pmod 7$ such that $c \geq 20$ can be obtained from the third row. We can continue this until the seventh row, where all $c \equiv 60 \equiv 4 \pmod 7$ such that $c \geq 60$ can be obtained.

We can certainly get all $c \geq 60$, since we can get $c \equiv 0, 1, \ldots, 6 \pmod 7$. We can get all $c \geq 50$ except those for which $c \equiv 4 \pmod 7$ (since the smallest $c \equiv 4 \pmod 7$ is in the seventh row), so the largest c we can't get is the largest $c \equiv 4 \pmod 7$ less than 60. This c is **53**.

 EXERCISE 24-9 Prove that the largest c which cannot be obtained by $mx + ny = c$, with nonnegative x and y and $(m, n) = 1$, is $mn - m - n$.

24.2 $x^2 + y^2 = z^2$

Solving the equation $x^2 + y^2 = z^2$ for integers (x, y, z) is the problem of finding **Pythagorean triples**, sets of integers which can be the sides of a right triangle.

If any two of x, y, and z share a common factor d, then that factor must also divide the third. For example, if $x = dx'$ and $z = dz'$, then $y^2 = z^2 - x^2 = d^2(z'^2 - x'^2)$, so $d|y$ as well. Solutions with $d = 1$, so that x, y, and z are relatively prime, are called **primitive**. Once we find all the primitive solutions, the others will follow as constant multiples. (For example, $(3,4,5)$ is a primitive triple, and $(6, 8, 10)$ follows from it as a constant multiple.)

We will thus find the primitive solutions. First let's consider the parity (even or odd) of the solutions. If x and y are both even, then z is also even, so 2 is a common factor, so the solution is not primitive. If x and y are both odd, then each of their squares is congruent to 1 (mod 4), so the sum $x^2 + y^2$ is congruent to 2 mod 4. But every square is congruent to 0 or 1 (mod 4), so this cannot be z^2, and this case is invalid as well. We are left with x and y being one even, one odd, and z thus being odd.

Without loss of generality, let x be the even one of x and y. Then $z - y$ and $z + y$ are both even, but otherwise have no common factors—any common divisor would have to divide the sum, $2z$, and the difference, $2y$, but y and z are relatively prime. Now, consider the equation

$$\frac{x^2}{4} = \frac{z^2 - y^2}{4} = \frac{z - y}{2} \cdot \frac{z + y}{2}. \tag{24.1}$$

All the fractions are actually integers, since x, $z + y$, and $z - y$ are all even.

The product $\frac{z + y}{2} \cdot \frac{z - y}{2}$ is a perfect square by equation (24.1). But $\frac{z + y}{2}$ and $\frac{z - y}{2}$ are relatively prime by our discussion of the previous paragraph, so each must be a square individually. (We proved this in Section 1 of Chapter 23.1; reread the pertinent material if this isn't clear.) Hence there exist integers r and s such that

$$\frac{z - y}{2} = s^2 \quad \text{and} \quad \frac{z + y}{2} = r^2.$$

Solving, we thus have $z = r^2 + s^2$ and $y = r^2 - s^2$.

EXERCISE 24-10 Plug these values into the equation $x^2 + y^2 = z^2$ and show that $x = 2rs$.

EXERCISE 24-11 Prove that r and s must be relatively prime.

Combining our results, we find that the general primitive Pythagorean triple is given by

$$(2rs, r^2 - s^2, r^2 + s^2)$$

for relatively prime r and s with $r > s$. Nonprimitive triples like $(6, 8, 10)$ are obtained as direct multiples of primitive triples and might not have r and s of their own.

EXERCISE 24-12 Find r and s for the triples $(3, 4, 5)$, $(6, 8, 10)$, and $(5, 12, 13)$.

EXERCISE 24-13 Figure out how many primitive Pythagorean triples (x, y, z) there are with $z < 100$.

24.3 $x^4 + y^4 = z^2$

The realm of Diophantine equations is huge, and we have no chance of looking at all the possible equations and techniques in one chapter. Instead, we'll look at a couple more equations which are common, or whose solutions contain especially useful ideas. In this section, we'll look at the Diophantine equation $x^4 + y^4 = z^2$. By proving that this has no solutions, we'll also prove that $x^4 + y^4 = z^4$ has no solutions. (Do you see why?)

To prove that the equation $x^4 + y^4 = z^2$ has no solutions in positive integers, we will assume instead that it does have solutions, and consider the solution whose value of z is the smallest. We'll then show that there is another solution whose value of z is *smaller*—a contradiction. (This common method of proof is called **infinite descent**, because we in effect show that one solution implies another solution with smaller z, which implies another solution with smaller z, and so on.) The proof is long and has far too many letters, but it has lots of important concepts, and taken step by step it's not too bad. Be prepared to read it more than once to understand it completely, though.

Take the solution of $x^4 + y^4 = z^2$ with smallest z to be (x_0, y_0, z_0). If x_0 and y_0 are not relatively prime, their divisor d must divide z_0 twice. (Do you see why?) The solution

$$(x_0/d)^4 + (y_0/d)^4 = (z_0/d^2)^2$$

would then be a solution with $z < z_0$, a contradiction. So we can assume x_0 and y_0 are relatively prime.

The reason we want x_0 and y_0 to be relatively prime is that writing

$$(x_0^2)^2 + (y_0^2)^2 = z_0^2$$

gives a Pythagorean triple (x_0^2, y_0^2, z_0). As long as x_0 and y_0 are relatively prime, this triple is primitive, which means that there are relatively prime integers r and s such that

$$\begin{aligned} x_0^2 &= 2rs \\ y_0^2 &= r^2 - s^2 \\ z_0 &= r^2 + s^2. \end{aligned}$$

EXERCISE 24-14 Prove that s is even. (Hint: First prove that r and s can't be either both even or both odd. Next prove that having r even and s odd won't work by looking at the equation $y_0^2 = r^2 - s^2$ in mod 4.)

Since s is even from Exercise 24-14, we let $s = 2t$. From $x_0^2 = 2rs$, we get

$$\left(\frac{x_0}{2}\right)^2 = rt.$$

EXERCISE 24-15 From Exercise 23-1 of Chapter 23.1 (which you should look back at), $(x_0/2)^2 = rt$ will imply that r and t are both perfect squares if we can prove that r and t are relatively prime. Prove that r and t are relatively prime. (Remember that r and s are relatively prime.)

EXERCISE 24-16 From the previous exercise, r and t are squares. Thus, let $r = r_1^2$ and $t = t_1^2$. Prove that r_1 and t_1 are relatively prime, and that r_1 is odd.

EXERCISE 24-17 Prove that $(2t_1^2)^2 + y_0^2 = (r_1^2)^2$. (Use the definitions.)

EXERCISE 24-18 Show that $2t_1^2$ and y_0^2 are relatively prime, so that $(2t_1^2, y_0, r_1^2)$ is a primitive Pythagorean triple.

From Exercise 24-18, we can (again!) find two relatively prime integers R and S so that

$$\begin{aligned} 2t_1^2 &= 2RS \\ y_0 &= R^2 - S^2 \\ r_1^2 &= R^2 + S^2. \end{aligned}$$

Since $t_1^2 = RS$ and R and S are relatively prime, we can again use Exercise 23-1 to show that R and S are perfect squares: $R = R_1^2, S = S_1^2$.

Using $r_1^2 = R^2 + S^2$, we have

$$r_1^2 = R_1^4 + S_1^4.$$

At long last, here is another solution $(x, y, z) = (R_1, S_1, r_1)$ to our original equation, $z^2 = x^4 + y^4$. And since $r_1 < z_0$, this new solution has a smaller z than the original one. This contradicts our assumption way back when that z_0 was as small as we could get, so there can be no solution in positive integers to the equation $x^4 + y^4 = z^2$.

EXERCISE 24-19 Why is $r_1 < z_0$, as stated above?

24.4 The Pell Equation

The last Diophantine equation we'll look at is the **Pell equation**,

$$x^2 - Dy^2 = \pm 1.$$

EXERCISE 24-20 Play with the Pell equation for $D = 2$. Can you find any solutions?

EXERCISE 24-21 Analyze the Pell equation when D is a square, $D = E^2$.

The solutions to the Pell equation when D is not a square turn out to be closely connected to the continued fraction expansion of $\sqrt{D}$. In fact, if a is the period of the continued fraction and $C_k = P_k/Q_k$ is the kth convergent, then all solutions to the Pell equation $x^2 - Dy^2 = \pm 1$ are given by $(x, y) = (P_{ia}, Q_{ia})$, for all positive integers i.

EXAMPLE 24-5 The continued fraction expansion for $\sqrt{3}$ is

$$1 + \cfrac{1}{1 + \cfrac{1}{2 + \cfrac{1}{1 + \cfrac{1}{2 + \cdots}}}},$$

and the first few convergents can easily be calculated as $\frac{1}{1}, \frac{2}{1}, \frac{5}{3}, \frac{7}{4}$. Since the period is 2 (why?), we expect that the second and fourth convergents will yield solutions to $x^2 - 3y^2 = \pm 1$: $(2, 1)$ and $(7, 4)$ can be verified to work. On the other hand, the first and third convergents will not yield solutions: you can verify that $(1, 1)$ and $(5, 3)$ are not solutions.

EXERCISE 24-22 Find the first few solutions of $x^2 - 2y^2 = \pm 1$, $x^2 - 3y^2 = \pm 1$, $x^2 - 5y^2 = \pm 1$, and $x^2 - 6y^2 = \pm 1$. In each, which solutions correspond to the $+$ and which to the $-$?

EXAMPLE 24-6 Suppose we have two solutions (x, y) and (w, z) to the Pell equation. Prove that if $(x + \sqrt{D}\,y)(w + \sqrt{D}\,z) = u + \sqrt{D}\,v$, then (u, v) is also a solution.

   Solution: If $(x + \sqrt{D}\,y)(w + \sqrt{D}\,z) = u + \sqrt{D}\,v$ then we have $u - \sqrt{D}\,v = (x - \sqrt{D}\,y)(w - \sqrt{D}\,z)$. (Verify this.) Then

$$
\begin{aligned}
u^2 - Dv^2 &= (u + \sqrt{D}\,v)(u - \sqrt{D}\,v) \\
&= (x + \sqrt{D}\,y)(w + \sqrt{D}\,z)(x - \sqrt{D}\,y)(w - \sqrt{D}\,z) \\
&= (x^2 - Dy^2)(w^2 - Dz^2) \\
&= \pm 1,
\end{aligned}
$$

so (u, v) is a solution, as desired. We can even say more: it's clear from this equation that (u, v) corresponds to the $+$ if (x, y) and (w, z) correspond to either both $+$ or both $-$, and (u, v) corresponds to $-$ otherwise.

EXERCISE 24-23 Prove that if (x, y) is a solution, writing $(x_0 + \sqrt{D}\,y_0)^n = a + \sqrt{D}\,b$ will yield a solution (a, b) for any power n.

EXAMPLE 24-7 Suppose we have the smallest solution (x_0, y_0) of a Pell equation. From the previous exercise, writing $(x_0 + \sqrt{D}\,y_0)^n = a + \sqrt{D}\,b$ will yield solutions (a, b). These, it turns out, are all the solutions. Thus we don't have to wade through mountains of convergents to find the solutions to the Pell equation. We find the smallest solution using convergents, and the rest by taking powers. For example, the smallest solution for $D = 3$ is $(2, 1)$. We have $(2 + \sqrt{3})^2 = 7 + 4\sqrt{3}$, and $(7, 4)$ is the next solution. We have $(2 + \sqrt{3})^3 = (2 + \sqrt{3})(7 + 4\sqrt{3}) = 26 + 15\sqrt{3}$, so $(26, 15)$ is the third solution. With this method we can find higher solutions much faster than with the convergent method.

24.5   General Methods

By looking at specific Diophantine equations throughout this chapter, we have failed to put enough emphasis on two of the most generally applicable techniques. Both provide key insights into many Diophantine equations, and should always be kept in mind when a new equation is presented to solve. The first technique is just to look at equations in some modulus. For example, an equation with lots of squares might become clearer in mod 4 or 8, since every square is congruent to either 0 or 1 (mod 4) and to either 0, 1, or 4 (mod 8). The second technique is to make simplifying substitutions.

EXERCISE 24-24 Prove that $x^2 + y^2 = 100000003$ has no solutions in integers.

EXAMPLE 24-8 Solve the equation $x^3 + 117y^3 = 5$.

Solution: The prime factorization of 117 is $9 \cdot 13$, so an idea might be to consider the equation (mod 9). (Of course, your first idea won't always work; sometimes these things take a little experimentation.) The cubes (mod 9) are $1^3 = 1, 2^3 = 8 \equiv -1, 3^3 \equiv 0, 4^3 = 64 \equiv 1, 5^3 \equiv (-4)^3 \equiv -1,$ $6^3 \equiv 0, 7^3 \equiv (-2)^3 \equiv 1, 8^3 \equiv (-1)^3 \equiv -1,$ and $9^3 \equiv 0$: that is, either $-1, 1$, or 0! (Thus *any* equation with cubes may look nicer in mod 9.) Since $117 \equiv 0 \pmod 9$, the equation is $x^3 \equiv 5 \pmod 9$, which has **no solution** since 5 is not a cube (mod 9).

Problems to Solve for Chapter 24

403. Find two nontrivial solutions to $x^2 - 8y^2 = 1$.

404. In how many ways can 1776 identical flags be partitioned into piles of either three or four flags so that every flag is in some pile? (Mandelbrot #2)

405. How many pairs of integers (m, n) satisfy the equation $m + n = mn$? (AHSME 1977)

406. Find the number of pairs (m, n) of integers which satisfy the equation $m^3 + 6m^2 + 5m = 27n^3 + 9n^2 + 9n + 1$.

407. How many distinct pairs of integers (x, y) such that $0 < x < y$ satisfy $\sqrt{1984} = \sqrt{x} + \sqrt{y}$? (AHSME 1984)

408. If q is an integer that can be expressed as the sum of two integer squares, then prove that $3q$ cannot be so expressed. (Mandelbrot #2)

409. List in which of the following two-digit pairs can the square of an integer end: 07, 29, 41, 63, 85. (Mandelbrot #3)

410. How many Pythagorean triangles are there with the property that the area of the triangle is the same as the perimeter? (MAΘ 1991)

411. Prove that no number of the form $3^m + 3^n + 1$, where m and n are positive integers, can be a perfect square. (USAMTS 1)

412. Find the hypotenuse of a right triangle whose legs are 20806 and 408. (Mandelbrot #1)

413. Solve the equation

$$1! + 2! + 3! + \cdots + x! = y^2$$

for all integer pairs (x, y). (M&IQ 1992)

414. Find a primitive Pythagorean triangle one of whose legs is 90 or prove that no such triangle exists.

415. Find all primitive Pythagorean triangles whose area is equal to twice the perimeter.

416. Prove that every Pythagorean triangle has one side whose length is a multiple of 5.

417. Prove that if there exist natural numbers a, b, c, d, e for which $a^4 + b^4 + c^4 + d^4 = e^4$, then at least three of the numbers a, b, c, and d are multiples of 5. (M&IQ 1991)

418. If a, b, c, and n are positive integers with $a < 11$, and $n^a + n^b - n^c = 0$, compute the maximum value of $a^n + b^n - c^n$. (ARML 1988)

419. Show that the equation $14x^2 + 15y^2 = 7^{1990}$ has no solution in nonegative integers x and y. (USAMTS 2)

420. Are there integers m and n such that $5m^2 - 6mn + 7n^2 = 1985$? (IMO 1985)

421. Three relatively prime integers are the sides of a right triangle. If the smallest leg has length 28, find the sum of all the possible values of the hypotenuse. (MAΘ 1990)

422. Prove that there are no integers a and b such that $5a^2 + 6ab + 7b^2 = 1993$. (Bulgaria 1993)

423. Prove that it is impossible for three consecutive squares to sum to another perfect square. (Mandelbrot #2)

424. Suppose D is prime. Prove that $x^2 - Dy^2 = -1$ has no solutions if -1 is not a quadratic residue (mod D).

425. Show that $x^3 + 3y^3 = 9z^3$ has no nontrivial solutions.

426. Prove that the Diophantine equation

$$x^3 + y^3 + z^3 + x^2y + y^2z + z^2x + xyz = 0$$

has no solutions in nonzero integers. (Hint: Consider the parity of the left hand side in various cases.)

Chapter 25

Graph Theory

25.1 Points and Lines

A **graph** is a set of points, some of which are connected together by lines. (The word *graph* is also used to refer to the plot of a function. That's mathematical nomenclature for you.) A graph is shown at left. The points of a graph are called its **vertices**, while the lines are called **edges**.

Graphs can be used to model all sorts of situations. For example, the vertices could represent people, with an edge connecting them if they are friends. The vertices of the same graph could instead represent volleyball teams, with an edge connecting pairs which had played games against each other.

A **complete graph** or **clique** is a graph in which every pair of vertices is connected by an edge. For example, a complete graph with five vertices is shown at right. The complete graph with n vertices is called K_n; thus the graph at right is K_5.

EXERCISE 25-1   Draw K_2, K_3, and K_4.

EXAMPLE 25-1   A graph is determined only by its vertices and their connections, not by the location in space of the vertices. Thus the K_5 above can be drawn in the more symmetric form at right and still be the same graph.

EXERCISE 25-2   How many edges are there in a complete graph with n vertices?

The opposite of a complete graph is a **null graph** or **independent set**, which is a collection of vertices with no connections between them.

EXERCISE 25-3   Find the size of the largest clique and the largest independent set contained in the graph we drew at the start of this section.

A graph is **connected** if any two vertices can be connected by a path. Which of the graphs we have drawn so far are connected? For most problems in graph theory, we will assume the graph under consideration is connected, because otherwise we can look at each connected piece separately.

25.2   Planar Graphs

A graph is said to be **planar** if it can be drawn in a plane with no intersecting edges. For example, K_4 is planar because it can be drawn as at right.

EXERCISE 25-4   Try to draw K_5 such that no edges intersect.

EXERCISE 25-5   Prove that K_5 is not planar.

One interesting thing about a planar graph is that we can define **faces** of the graph. The faces are just the smallest regions bounded by edges; two faces of the planar graph at left have been shaded as examples.

WARNING: There is one face which you may not have thought of. *The entire area outside the graph* is also considered a face, the **unbounded face**.

EXERCISE 25-6   How many faces has K_4 when drawn so as to be planar, as above?

EXAMPLE 25-2   Define the **degree** of a face to be the number of edges which adjoin it. Now think about the sum D of the degrees of all the faces of a graph. Each degree is greater than or equal to three (do you see why?), so that the sum of the degrees is at least 3 per face, so $D \geq 3F$, where F is the number of faces.

EXERCISE 25-7   Let E be the number of edges of the graph. Use the previous example to show that $E \geq \frac{3}{2}F$.

Having defined faces in this way, an interesting relation emerges. Let the number of vertices of a graph be V, the number of edges E, and the number of faces F. Then **Euler's formula** (or one of Euler's formulas, anyway) says that if the graph is connected we always have

$$V - E + F = 2.$$

A proof of Euler's formula follows easily by induction on the number of edges. As a base case, take two vertices connected by one edge. In this case $V = 2$, $E = 1$, and $F = 1$, which clearly obeys the formula. ($F = 1$ because of the unbounded face.) For the inductive step, assume that the formula works for all graphs with $E = k - 1$. To get from a graph with $E = k - 1$ to one with $E = k$, we can add an edge in two ways.

First, we can add an entirely new vertex and connect it by one edge to an existing vertex. In this case, no new face is formed, as at right, but the numbers of vertices and edges each increase by 1. Thus we go from $V - E + F = 2$ to $(V + 1) - (E + 1) + F = 2$—the formula is still satisfied.

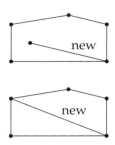

Second, we can add a new edge and connect it by one edge to an existing vertex. In this case, no new vertices are added, but the numbers of faces and edges each increase by 1. Thus we go from $V - E + F = 2$ to $V - (E + 1) + (F + 1) = 2$—the formula is still satisfied.

Since the inductive step covers both possible ways to add an edge, the proof is complete. The technique of this proof, performing induction on the number of edges or vertices of a graph, is a very standard one in proving theorems on graphs.

EXERCISE 25-8 Convince yourself that the two ways we have shown to add an edge are the only two ways.

EXERCISE 25-9 Draw some connected planar graphs and confirm Euler's formula for them.

EXAMPLE 25-3 We can use Euler's formula and Exercise 25-7 to derive an interesting inequality for planar graphs. Starting with $V - E + F = 2$, we write $V + F = E + 2$. Inserting $F \leq \frac{2}{3}E$ from Exercise 25-7, this becomes $V + \frac{2}{3}E \geq E + 2$, or, simplifying,

$$E \leq 3V - 6. \qquad (25.1)$$

Equations like (25.1) are very useful. For example, you proved in Exercise 25-5 that K_5 is not planar; complicated arguments were necessary. But there is a simpler way. For K_5, $E = \binom{5}{2} = 10$ and $V = 5$; these values do not satisfy (25.1), so K_5 can't be planar.

WARNING: While (25.1) holds for every planar graph, it is NOT true that every graph satisfying (25.1) is planar! Be careful that you don't make this mistake.

25.3 Example: The Platonic Solids

In Volume 1 we claimed that there were exactly five regular polyhedra. With graph theory, we have the tools to prove that assertion. The regular polyhedra are often called **Platonic solids**.

First, we observe that any polyhedron can be converted to a graph. Simply punch a hole in one of the faces and open the polyhedron up. (There will be some stretching or squishing involved.) For example, the graph corresponding to a cube is at right. The face we have punched a hole in becomes the unbounded face, so the graph has six faces, just like a cube.

If the polyhedron corresponding to a graph is regular, then all the vertices must have the same degree, say d. Similarly, all faces must be bounded by the same number of edges, say f.

EXERCISE 25-10 Show that E, the total number of edges, is equal to $\frac{1}{2}dV$, where V is the number of vertices.

EXERCISE 25-11 Show that F, the total number of faces, is equal to dV/f.

Using the results of the two exercises, we can write Euler's formula, $V - E + F = 2$, as $V - \frac{1}{2}dV + dV/f = 2$. This simplifies into $V(2f - df + 2d) = 4f$. Since V and $4f$ are both positive, we thus conclude that $2f - df + 2d$ is positive, so that

$$df - 2f - 2d < 0.$$

Adding 4 to both sides, we can then factor, to get

$$(d - 2)(f - 2) < 4.$$

Since d and f are positive integers greater than or equal to 3, there are only a few solutions to this inequality.

EXERCISE 25-12 Find all solution pairs (d, f).

Each pair (d, f) you found in Exercise 25-12 corresponds to one of the Platonic solids. You should have found 5 pairs (d, f), thus proving that there are only 5 regular polyhedra! For example, you can confirm that the octahedron has $f = 3$ (faces are triangles) and $d = 4$. The corresponding graph is at right.

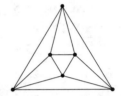

EXERCISE 25-13 Verify that every vertex in the graph above is of degree 4, and that every face (including the unbounded face!) is surrounded by exactly 3 edges.

EXERCISE 25-14 Pair up the remaining four (d, f) pairs to the corresponding Platonic solids.

25.4 Walking Around on Graphs

Imagine that a graph is a network of roads. Two roads intersect when they meet at a vertex. We can imagine walking around on this network, going from one intersection to another which is connected by a road. A general **walk** is just any way to do this. On the other hand, there are many interesting types of restricted walks. For example, a **path** is not allowed to go through any vertex more than once, while a **trail** is not allowed to go along any *edge* more than once. (You'll have to forgive these names.)

EXERCISE 25-15 On K_5, draw a path, a trail which is not a path, and a walk which is neither.

A **cycle** is a path which ends at its starting point. A cycle can be a graph all its own, as at left, or can be part of another graph.

EXERCISE 25-16 In a cycle n vertices long, how many edges are there?

EXAMPLE 25-4 A **tree** is a graph with no cycles. We can draw a tree by placing one vertex at the top, all vertices connected to that vertex one level down, all vertices connected to *those* vertices another level down, and so on. Clearly no edge can jump over a level, because that would create a cycle. (Do you see why?) The picture looks like that drawn at right.

EXERCISE 25-17 How many edges are there in a tree with n vertices?

25.5 Euler Trails

The simplest question related to graph walking is, when is it possible to form a trail which uses all the edges? This question was actually the first graph-related question ever addressed, by Leonhard Euler in the 1730's. A trail of the type we're looking for is thus called an **Euler trail**.

EXERCISE 25-18 Draw some graphs and see if you can draw Euler trails. When you can't, why can't you? When you can, why can you?

The key insight is that except for the starting and ending vertices, the trail you are following must go *into* a vertex along one edge and then *out of* the same vertex along a different edge. Such a process always uses up two of the edges which emanate from the vertex. We may go through the same vertex again any number of times, but each time we are eliminating exactly two edges. Thus each vertex which is not the starting or the ending point has an even number of edges coming out of it!

The number of edges which come out of a vertex is called the **degree** of the vertex. We have just shown that a graph which possesses an Euler trail has at most 2 vertices of odd degree—only the starting and ending points of the trail are exempted.

We can actually qualify this a little bit more, however, using a method similar to that we used in looking at the degree of a face. Consider the sum of the degrees of all the vertices of a graph. Since this sum counts all the edges coming out of each vertex, it counts each edge twice: once for each of the vertices it connects. Thus the sum of the degrees of all the vertices equals $2E$.

Since $2E$ is obviously even, the sum of the degrees of the vertices must be even! Thus there must be an even number of vertices with odd degree in any graph. (Do you see why?) We have stated that a graph with an Euler trail must have at most two vertices of odd degree; but since exactly one vertex of odd degree is forbidden (since that would be an odd number), our graph must have either zero or two. The question is, do all graphs with zero or two odd-degree vertices have an Euler trail?

Let's look at the case of zero vertices of odd degree. When we leave the starting vertex (which has even degree), there will be an odd number of edges left there to use. Each time we go through that vertex after that, we will use up two edges, leaving the number odd, until there is only one edge left. When we follow that edge in, there will be no edge to take back out, so we had better be finished with the trail. We must end up where we started. What if we get back to the starting point before we use all the edges? In this case, there must be some vertex Q on the trail which has edges left over, as at right. We form a new walk by backtracking our original trail to Q, then forming a new trail from Q using all unused vertices and ending back up at Q, then continuing the old trail to the end. We can keep doing this as long as there are any leftover edges, and so form an Euler trail of the entire graph.

EXERCISE 25-19 The one hole in the proof above is that we need to be sure we can always form a trail on *only unused edges* which starts and ends at Q. Prove that we can do so.

EXERCISE 25-20 Examine the case of graphs wil two odd vertices. Do they always have Euler trails? Where must such trails start and end?

Similar to the Euler trail problem is that of **Hamiltonian paths**, paths which cross every *vertex* exactly once and end up at the start. **Hamiltonian cycles**, which end up where they started, are of particular interest. However, this problem turns out to be much harder than the Euler trail problem; there is no known way to characterize graphs with Hamiltonian cycles easily.

25.6   Colorings

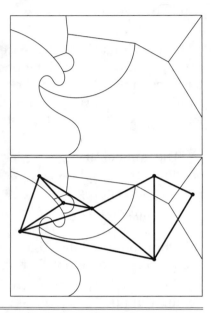

Imagine you work at a mapmaking company. The drawing person brings in the latest black-and-white print, and you, the colorist, must color the map for final publication. The map might look something like the picture at right. In coloring a map it's essential that no two adjacent countries be the same color, or it's hard to tell them apart. So the basic problem of the colorist is to assign a color to each country in such a way that no two countries which share a boundary are the same color.

So what does this have to do with graph theory? The key step is realizing that we can replace the map with a graph. (Indeed, many problems can be converted into graph theory problems in this way. The advantage? As soon as you have graphs, you have a great deal of ready-made machinery to bring to bear on your problem.) Instead of countries, we have vertices; instead of sharing a boundary, two countries/vertices share a common edge. For example, the original map would be replaced with the graph above.

EXERCISE 25-21 Determine which vertices of the graph correspond to which countries on the map.

Since colored ink is relatively expensive, it's the colorist's job to color a map with as few colors as possible. Similarly, it is the mathematician's job to color a graph with as few colors as possible— coloring every vertex with a different color would be legitimate, but not very interesting! In math, we thus define the **chromatic number** χ of a graph to be *the smallest number of colors needed to color the vertices so that no two vertices which are connected together share the same color.*

EXAMPLE 25-5 It's easy to make graphs with a high chromatic number: just connect everything together. For example, suppose we are trying to color K_7. We give the first vertex color 1. Then no other vertex can be color 1, since they are all connected to the first vertex. We thus color the second vertex color 2. Again, no other vertex can be this color. Proceeding likewise for all the vertices, we need 7 colors to color the graph. Similarly, we need n colors to color K_n for any n.

EXERCISE 25-22 Describe all graphs with $\chi = 1$.

A particularly interesting class of graphs is those with $\chi = 2$. We can draw such a graph with the vertices of each color in a line; since there may be no connections between vertices of the same color, all connections must be from one line to the other, as at right. Graphs of this type are called **bipartite**.

A bipartite graph with s vertices of one color and t of the other which contains *all possible edges* is denoted by $K_{s,t}$. For example, $K_{3,4}$ is shown at left.

EXERCISE 25-23 Draw $K_{2,3}$ in the same way as $K_{3,4}$ is drawn above, then draw it with no edges crossing.

EXERCISE 25-24 Draw $K_{3,3}$ in the normal way, then draw it with no edges crossing.

EXERCISE 25-25 How many edges does $K_{3,3}$ have? How many vertices? Do these values satisfy (25.1)? What does this say about whether or not it is planar?

EXAMPLE 25-6 If you tried to draw $K_{3,3}$ so as to be planar in Exercise 25-24 and failed, don't worry too much. It isn't. How do we prove this? Our first thought is to mimic the simple proof that K_5 is not planar, based on the inequality (25.1). However, you saw in the previous exercise that $K_{3,3}$ *does* satisfy the inequality (25.1), so this won't work.

A slight refinement will do the trick. Remember that we proved in Exercise 25-7 that $E \geq \frac{3}{2}F$ by noting that every face of a graph has at least three edges around it. On the other hand, for bipartite graphs every face has at least *four* edges around it! (Prove this to yourself.) Thus we can write $E \geq 2F$. Substituting this into Euler's formula, we now have $E \leq 2V - 4$. Compare this to equation (25.1). We have improved that inequality for bipartite graphs: if a *bipartite* graph is to be planar, its number of edges must be less than $2V - 4$ rather than the larger $3V - 6$.

The punchline, which you probably saw coming, is that for $K_{3,3}$ we have $E = 9$ and $V = 6$, values which do not satisfy $E \leq 2V - 4$ (just barely!). Thus $K_{3,3}$ is not planar.

EXERCISE 25-26 Prove that $K_{s,t}$ is not planar if $s \geq 3$ and $t \geq 3$.

EXERCISE 25-27 Prove that $K_{2,t}$ is planar for all t. (Remember: just satisfying the inequality is NOT enough!)

EXERCISE 25-28 The **girth** of a graph is the length of the shortest cycle in the graph. (For example, the girth of a bipartite graph is at least 4.) Find an analogous inequality to $E \leq 2V - 4$ (which we found for bipartite planar graphs) for planar graphs with girth g.

Problems to Solve for Chapter 25

427. Prove that the sum of the degrees of all the vertices of a graph is equal to twice the total number of edges.

428. What possible numbers of vertices can a graph have if the graph has 20 edges and all vertices of the same degree?

429. N players form seven teams, with each pair of teams having one common member and each player on two teams. How many players are there?

430. What is the smallest number of vertices a graph can have if it has 50 edges?

431. What is the smallest number of vertices a *planar* graph can have if it has 50 edges?

432. Draw a planar graph with six vertices, all of degree 3, or prove it is not possible.

433. Show that any planar graph has some vertex whose degree is less than or equal to 5.

434. If a planar graph has V vertices, each with degree 4, and 10 faces, find V.

435. Two pyramids with common base $A_1A_2A_3A_4A_5A_6A_7$ and vertices B and C are given. The edges BA_i, CA_i ($i = 1, \ldots, 7$), the diagonals of the common base and the segment BC are colored in either red or in blue. Prove that there exists a triangle whose sides are colored in one and the same color. (Bulgaria 1993)

436. 500 Basketball players are divided up into 250 two-person teams for a tournament. On each day of the tournament, the teams are rearranged such that no two people ever play together twice. What is the longest possible such tournament?

—*the BIG PICTURE*—

One of the most famous problems in mathematics arose in connection with graph coloring. Experimenting with coloring a map of England, a student of Augustus De Morgan, a nineteenth century mathematician, noticed that it required only four colors to make sure no two adjacent regions were the same color. The problem became known as the **four-color problem**: does any map in the plane require more than four colors? (Try coming up with a map which requires more!)

Around 1890 a proof was proposed which gained wide acceptance, showing that four colors always suffice. Ten years later, however, a fatal flaw was found. The proof would still show that *five* colors are always enough, but the four-color problem was intact.

As it grew older, the four-color problem attracted the attention of more and more prominent mathematicians; Hermann Minkowski asserted that he could find a proof if he tried, then later had to recant. As more people thought about the four-color problem, graph theory matured from an unserious branch of math to a subject of wide interest. (Today graph theory has applications from computer science to physics.)

In 1976 Appel and Haken showed that it would suffice to look at a certain class of subproblems, then used a computer to analyze them all. After some hours of computer time, they declared the problem solved. And while they later had to go back and add a few more cases, it is now widely accepted that their proof is correct. Such a computer-driven proof leaves a bad taste in many people's mouths, though, for two reasons. First, it can't be checked by a human. Second, and more important, it is aesthetically not too satisfying. Such a simple, elegant fact; such a complex, brute-force proof.

Chapter 26

Parting Shots

Problems to Solve for Chapter 26

437. If $\ln x^4 = (\ln x)^3$, find x. (MAΘ 1991)

438. Given A, a set of 13 (distinct) elements, what fraction of the functions from A to A have a well-defined inverse function? (MAΘ 1992)

439. With $1000 a rancher is to buy steers at $25 each and cows at $26 each. If he has no money left over, and he bought at least one of each animal, how many cows did he buy? (AHSME 1958)

440. If the terms $\ln a$, $\ln b$, $\ln c$, $\ln d$ form an arithmetic sequence with common difference 1, then what type of sequence is a, b, c, d? (MAΘ 1992)

441. If x is real, compute the maximum integral value of $\dfrac{3x^2 + 9x + 17}{3x^2 + 9x + 7}$. (ARML 1986)

442. Find the volume of the solid generated by revolving $\triangle ABC$ about line l if $AB = 13$, $BC = 15$, and $AC = 14$. (MAΘ 1990)

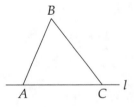

443. A circular disk is divided by $2n$ equally spaced radii ($n > 0$) and one secant line. What is the maximum number of non-overlapping areas into which the disk can be divided? (AHSME 1971)

444. Let
$$f(n) = \frac{5 + 3\sqrt{5}}{10}\left(\frac{1 + \sqrt{5}}{2}\right)^n + \frac{5 - 3\sqrt{5}}{10}\left(\frac{1 - \sqrt{5}}{2}\right)^n.$$

Find $f(n + 1) - f(n - 1)$ in terms of $f(n)$. (AHSME 1964)

445. Let r be the distance from the origin to a point P with coordinates x and y. Designate the ratio y/r by s and the ratio x/r by c. What values can $s^2 - c^2$ have? (AHSME 1958)

446. Find two factors greater than 1 whose product is $6^6 + 8^4 + 27^4$. (MAΘ 1987)

447. If $\dfrac{x^2}{y^2} = \dfrac{8y}{x} = z$, find all possible z. (Mandelbrot #3)

448. Given $xyz = 1$, find the sum

$$\frac{1}{1 + x + xy} + \frac{1}{1 + y + yz} + \frac{1}{1 + z + zx}.$$

(M&IQ 1992)

449. If P is the product of n quantities in geometric progression, S their sum, and S' the sum of their reciprocals, then find P in terms of S, S', and n. (AHSME 1971)

450. If $i^2 = -1$, find the sum

$$\cos 45° + i \cos 135° + \cdots + i^n \cos(45 + 90n)° + \cdots + i^{40} \cos 3645°.$$

(AHSME 1977)

451. Find the minimum value of $\sqrt{x^2 + y^2}$ if $5x + 12y = 60$. (AHSME 1961)

452. Find the radius of the smallest circle containing the shown symmetric figure composed of three unit squares. (AHSME 1972)

453. A man lists the integers from 1 to n, inclusive. He omits one of the numbers. The average of the remaining numbers is 18.8. What number did he omit? (MAΘ 1992)

454. How many triples (a, b, c) of positive integers satisfy the simultaneous euqations

$$\begin{aligned} ab + bc &= 44 \\ ac + bc &= 23? \end{aligned}$$

(AHSME 1984)

455. The population of Nosuch Junction at one time was a perfect square. Later, with an increase of 100, the population was one more than a perfect square. Now, with an additional increase of 100, the population is again a perfect square. What was the original population of the town? (AHSME 1962)

456. In the diagram, $AB < AC$, $AC = BC$, and $60° < \angle B < 90°$. Isosceles triangles ABC and $AB'C'$ are congruent. (Mandelbrot #1)

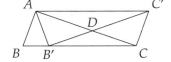

i. Show that $\triangle B'DC$ is an isosceles triangle.

ii. Show that $ABCC'$ is a parallelogram.

iii. Prove that $AD/AC = DB'/CB'$.

iv. Show that a single circle passes through A, B', C, and C'.

v. Show that AB is tangent to this circle.

457. Two perpendicular chords intersect in a circle. The segments of one chord are 3 and 4; the segments of the other are 6 and 2. What is the diameter of the circle? (AHSME 1957)

458. Prove that given $n \geq 4$ points in a plane, no three forming a right triangle and no three of which are collinear, at least one-fourth of the triangles with vertices among the n points are obtuse. (Mandelbrot #3)

459. Through the interiors of how many lattice squares does the line segment connecting $(0,0)$ and $(119,153)$ pass? (A lattice square is a unit square with lattice points as its vertices.) (Mandelbrot #1)

460. Find a polynomial $P(x)$ such that $xP(x-1) \equiv (x-3)P(x)$.

461. Find the least positive integer n for which $\dfrac{n-13}{5n+6}$ is a non-zero reducible fraction. (AHSME 1985)

462. For each positive number x, let

$$f(x) = \frac{\left(x + \frac{1}{x}\right)^6 - \left(x^6 + \frac{1}{x^6}\right) - 2}{\left(x + \frac{1}{x}\right)^3 + \left(x^3 + \frac{1}{x^3}\right)}.$$

What is the minimum value of $f(x)$? (AHSME 1979)

463. Let F_i represent the ith Fibonacci number. Let F_a, F_b, F_c, and F_d be the sides of a convex (nondegenerate) quadrilateral, with $a < b < c < d$. Find the greatest possible value for $d - b$. (ARML 1983)

464. If A and B are both in $[0, 2\pi)$ and A and B satisfy the equations

$$
\begin{aligned}
\sin A + \sin B &= \frac{1}{3} \\
\cos A + \cos B &= \frac{4}{3},
\end{aligned}
$$

find $\cos(A - B)$. (MAΘ 1992)

465. In parallelogram $ABCD$ let E be the midpoint of AB and F on CD be such that $CF = 2(FD)$. If G is the intersection of EC and BF and $[ABCD] = 252$, find the area of pentagon $AEGFD$.

466. In the diagram, let $\angle ADM = \angle ACD$ and $\angle ABM = \angle ACB$. Prove that BC, AC, and AD form the sides of a right triangle. (Mandelbrot #2)

467. Prove that if n is an integer greater than 11, then $n^2 - 19n + 89$ is not a perfect square. (USAMTS 1)

468. If a set of one or more integers $\{a_1, a_2, \ldots, a_n\}$, not necessarily distinct, has the property that $\sum_{i \neq j} a_i a_j$ (the sum of the products of all pairs of integers in the set) is a perfect square, then we will call such a set a square set. We also associate a number b with a square set, where

$$b = a_1 + a_2 + \cdots + a_n + 2\sqrt{\sum_{i \neq j} a_i a_j}.$$

(Mandelbrot #2)

   i. Suppose that $\{a_1, a_2, \ldots, a_n\}$ is a square set, and b is defined as above. Show that the set $\{a_1, a_2, \ldots, a_n, b\}$ is also a square set.

   ii. Let $\{a_1, a_2, \ldots, a_n\}$ and b be as in the above problem. Prove that $\{a_1, \ldots, a_{i-1}, b, a_{i+1}, \ldots, a_n\}$ is also a square set. Thus, show that if any element of the original set is replaced by b, the new set is also a square set.

469. Find a polynomial $F(x)$ with leading coefficient 1 such that $F(\cos a) = \cos 7a$ for any angle a. What is the coefficient of the x^2 term of F? (MAΘ 1992)

470. Three different integers are chosen between 1 and 13 inclusive. What is the probability that the sum of the three integers is divisible by 4? (MAΘ 1992)

471. Prove that there is no set of rational numbers (x, y, z, t) such that

$$(x + y\sqrt{2})^2 + (z + t\sqrt{2})^2 = 5 + 4\sqrt{2}.$$

(M&IQ 1992)

472. In base R_1 the expanded fraction F_1 becomes $.373737\ldots$, and the expanded fraction F_2 becomes $.737373\ldots$. In base R_2 fraction F_1, when expanded, becomes $.252525\ldots$, while the fraction F_2 becomes $.525252\ldots$. What is the sum of R_1 and R_2 in base 10? (AHSME 1966)

473. One of the sides of a triangle is divided into segments of 6 and 8 units by the point of tangency of the inscribed circle. If the radius of the incircle is 4, then what is the length of the shortest side of the triangle? (AHSME 1953)

474. In $\triangle ABC$, $AB = 3$, $AC = 6$, and $BC = 7$. Let AX be the bisector of $\angle BAC$ and Y be the foot of the perpedicular from X to AC. Determine XY. (Mandelbrot #2)

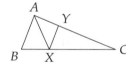

475. What is the smallest integer multiple of 49 whose digits are all the same? (USAMTS 1)

476. A subset of the integers $1, 2, \ldots, 100$ has the property that none of its members is 3 times another. What is the largest number of members such a subset can have? (AHSME 1990)

477. Show that $x^{1992} - x^{1990} + (2n - 1)x^3 - x = y^2$ has no solutions in positive integers (x, y) when $n = 1$ or $n = 2$. (M&IQ 1992)

478. A line segment is divided so that the lesser part is to the greater part as the greater part is to the whole. If R is the ratio of the lesser part to the greater part, then find

$$R^{\left[R^{(R^2 + R^{-1})} + R^{-1}\right]} + R^{-1}.$$

(AHSME 1974)

479. Points A_1, B_1, and C_1 are respectively the feet of the bisectors of angles $\angle CAB$, $\angle ABC$, and $\angle BCA$ of $\triangle ABC$. Prove that if $\angle ABC = 120°$, then $\angle A_1B_1C_1 = 90°$. (M&IQ 1991)

480. How many integers from 1 to 1992 inclusive have base three representations that do not contain the digit 2? (Mandelbrot #2)

481. Evaluate $\cos\frac{\pi}{7} \cos\frac{2\pi}{7} \cos\frac{3\pi}{7} \cos\frac{4\pi}{7} \cos\frac{5\pi}{7} \cos\frac{6\pi}{7}$. (MAΘ 1992)

482. The numbers from 1 to 50 are printed on cards. The cards are shuffled and then laid out face up in 5 rows of 10 cards each. The cards in each row are rearranged to make them increase from left to right. The cards in each column are then rearranged to make them increase from top to bottom. In the final arrangement, do the cards in the rows still increase from left to right? (Canada 1980)

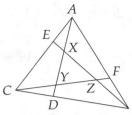

483. In the figure, CD, AE, and BF are one-third of their respective sides. It follows that $AX : XY : YD = 3 : 3 : 1$, and similarly for lines BE and CF. Find the area of XYZ in terms of the area of $\triangle ABC$. (AHSME 1952)

484. In triangle ABC, BD is a median. CF intersects BD at E so that $BE = ED$. Point F is on AB. If $BF = 5$, find BA. (AHSME 1959)

485. Triangle ABC has a right angle at C, $AC = 3$ and $BC = 4$. Triangle ABD has a right angle at A and $AD = 12$. The line through D parallel to AC meets CB extended at E. Find DE/DB. (AHSME 1991)

486. Let a, b, and c be the sides of triangle ABC. If a^2, b^2, and c^2 are the roots of the equation $x^3 - Px^2 + Qx - R = 0$ (where P, Q, and R are constants), express

$$\frac{\cos A}{a} + \frac{\cos B}{b} + \frac{\cos C}{c}$$

in terms of one or more of the coefficients P, Q, and R. (ARML 1983)

487. Prove that for any positive integers m and n the equality

$$(5 + 3\sqrt{2})^m = (3 + 5\sqrt{2})^n$$

is impossible. (M&IQ 1992)

488. Find all ordered pairs of non-negative integers (b, c) such that

$$\lim_{n \to \infty} \left(\frac{u_n}{u_{n-1}} \right) = 3,$$

if $u_0 = u_1 = 1$ and $u_n = bu_{n-1} + cu_{n-2}$. (Mandelbrot #1)

489. Show that every positive even integer n has a base three representation $n = a_k 3^k + \cdots + a_1 3^1 + a_0 3^0$ where each a_i is 0, 2, or 4. (Mandelbrot #2)

490. How many polynomial functions f of degree ≥ 1 satisfy

$$f(x^2) = \left[f(x) \right]^2 = f\big(f(x)\big)?$$

(AHSME 1987)

491. Show that every integer n has base three representation $n = a_k 3^k + \cdots + a_1 3^1 + a_0 3^0$ where each a_i is -1, 1, or 3. (Mandelbrot #2)

492. $ABCDE$ is a regular pentagon. AP, AQ, and AR are the perpendiculars dropped from A onto CD, CB extended, and DE extended, respectively. Let O be the center of the pentagon. If $OP = 1$, then find $AO + AQ + AR$. (AHSME 1986)

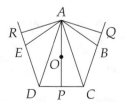

493. If $x^2 - x + a$ evenly divides the polynomial $x^8 + 5x^6 + 13x^4 + 20x^2 + 36$, determine the positive integer a. (Mandelbrot #1)

494. On a large, flat field, n people ($n > 1$) are positioned so that for each person the distances to all the other people are different. Each person holds a water pistol and at a given signal fires and hits the person who is closest. When n is odd show that there is at least one person left dry. (Canada 1987)

495. Find the greatest integer less than $(\sqrt{7} + \sqrt{5})^6$. (Mandelbrot #2)

496. In triangle ABC, $AB = 5$, $AC = 6$, and $BC = 7$. If point X is chosen on BC so that the sum of the areas of the circumcircles of triangles AXB and AXC is minimized, then determine BX. (Mandelbrot #2)

497. Find the largest value of y/x for pairs of real numbers (x, y) which satisfy $(x - 3)^2 + (y - 3)^2 = 6$. (AHSME 1984)

498. In the figure, $\triangle ABC$ has $\angle A = 45°$ and $\angle B = 30°$. A line DE, with D on AB and $\angle ADE = 60°$, divides $\triangle ABC$ into two pieces of equal area. (Note: the figure may not be accurate; perhaps E is on CB instead of AC.) Find the ratio AD/AB. (AHSME 1987)

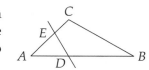

499. ABC is a triangle and X, Y, Z are points on the sides BC, CA, AB (respectively) such that the lines AX, BY, CZ are concurrent at D, an interior point of ABC. Prove that if two of the quadrilaterals $DYAZ$, $DZBX$, $DXCY$ are circumscriptible, then so is the third one. (IMO 1986)

500. In an isosceles triangle, the altitudes intersect on the inscribed circle. Compute the cosine of the vertex angle. (ARML 1983)

501. Find the number of real solutions (x, y, z, w) of the simultaneous equations

$$2y = x + \frac{17}{x}, \quad 2z = y + \frac{17}{y}, \quad 2w = z + \frac{17}{z}, \quad 2x = w + \frac{17}{w}.$$

(AHSME 1986)

502. Given $0 \le x_0 < 1$, let

$$x_n = \begin{cases} 2x_{n-1} & \text{if } 2x_{n-1} < 1 \\ 2x_{n-1} - 1 & \text{if } 2x_{n-1} \ge 1 \end{cases}$$

for all integers $n > 0$. For how many x_0 is it true that $x_0 = x_5$? (AHSME 1993)

503. A *magical set* is a group of three or more positive integers, not necessarily distinct, such that each number in the set exactly divides the sum of the remaining numbers. We also require that these numbers have no common divisor except 1. (Mandelbrot #1)

    i. Prove that a set is magical if and only if each element in the set divides the sum of all the elements.

    ii. Show that the set $\{1, 1, 2, 2^2, 2^3, \ldots, 2^n\}$ is magical for all $n \ge 1$.

    iii. A proper divisor of a number n is a positive integer less than n which divides n. A perfect number is a number which equals the sum of all its proper divisors. Show that all the proper divisors of a perfect number form a magical set.

    iv. Find all magical sets with exactly three numbers.

    v. Find all magical sets with four numbers whose smallest elements are 1 and 3, i.e. of the form $\{1, 3, m, n\}$ with $m, n \ge 3$.

    vi. Prove that given any magical set, one can include an additional number in the set so that this new set is magical.

504. A particle moves from $(0, 0)$ to (n, n) directed by a fair coin. For each head it moves one step east and for each tail it moves one step north. At (n, y), $y < n$, it stays there if heads comes up and at (x, n), $x < n$, it stays there if tails comes up. Let k be a fixed positive integer. Find the probability that the particle needs exactly $2n + k$ tosses to reach (n, n). (IMO 1986)

 505. Given any 7 real numbers, prove that there are two of them, say x and y, such that

$$0 \le \frac{x - y}{1 + xy} \le \frac{1}{\sqrt{3}}.$$

(Canada 1984)

 506. In acute triangle ABC, we are given $AD \perp BC$, $DF \perp AB$, and $DE \perp AC$. The circumradius of a triangle is the radius of the circle circumscribed about the triangle. Find $\angle A$ if the product of the circumradii of $\triangle ABC$ and $\triangle AEF$ is the area of $\triangle ABC$. (Mandelbrot #1)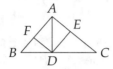

 507. An "unfair" coin has a 2/3 probability of turning up heads. If this coin is tossed 50 times, what is the probability that the total number of heads is even? (AHSME 1992)

508. The points A, B, C are in this order on the line l, and $AB = 4(BC)$. M is a variable point on the perpendicular to l through C. Let MX and MY be tangents to the circle with center A and radius AB. Determine the locus of the orthocenter of the triangle MXY. (IMO 1985)

509. A set of regular polygons of side 1 is chosen such that the polygons can be made to fill the 360 degree angle about a point, as the hexagon, two squares, and triangle do at right. In how many ways can the polygons be chosen? The order of placement is irrelevant.
(Mandelbrot #3)

Index

www.artofproblemsolving.com

The Art of Problem Solving (AoPS) is:

▷ **Books**

For over 14 years, *the Art of Problem Solving* books have been used by students as a resource for the American Mathematics Competitions and other national and local math events.

Every school should have this in their math library.
– Paul Zeitz, past coach of the U.S. International Mathematical Olympiad team

▷ **Classes**

The Art of Problem Solving offers online classes on topics such as number theory, counting, geometry, algebra, and more at beginning, intermediate, and Olympiad levels.

All the children were very engaged. It's the best use of technology I have ever seen.
– Mary Fay-Zenk, coach of National Champion California MATHCOUNTS teams

▷ **Forum**

As of February 2008, the Art of Problem Solving Forum has over 38,000 members who have posted over 1,000,000 messages on our discussion board. Members can also join any of our free "Math Jams".

I'd just like to thank the coordinators of this site for taking the time to set it up... I think this is a great site, and I bet just about anyone else here would say the same...
– AoPS Community Member

▷ **Resources**

We have links to summer programs, book resources, problem sources, national and local competitions, and a LaTeX tutorial.

I'd like to commend you on your wonderful site. It's informative, welcoming, and supportive of the math community. I wish it had been around when I was growing up.
– AoPS Community Member

▷ **... and more!**

Membership is **FREE**! Come join the Art of Problem Solving community today!

www.artofproblemsolving.com